> Lois,
> Search the Scriptures to see if what is said herein is the truth. I believe it's God's testimony for the last days.
> Jeff

The Corruption and Death of Christendom

Book #3 of the Son of Man Series

J. L. Reintgen

WESTBOW PRESS
A DIVISION OF THOMAS NELSON
& ZONDERVAN

Copyright © 2014 J. L. Reintgen.

All rights reserved. No part of this book may be used or reproduced by any means, graphic, electronic, or mechanical, including photocopying, recording, taping or by any information storage retrieval system without the written permission of the publisher except in the case of brief quotations embodied in critical articles and reviews.

Scripture taken from the New King James Version®. Copyright © 1982 by Thomas Nelson, Inc. Used by permission. All rights reserved.

WestBow Press books may be ordered through booksellers or by contacting:

WestBow Press
A Division of Thomas Nelson & Zondervan
1663 Liberty Drive
Bloomington, IN 47403
www.westbowpress.com
1 (866) 928-1240

Because of the dynamic nature of the Internet, any web addresses or links contained in this book may have changed since publication and may no longer be valid. The views expressed in this work are solely those of the author and do not necessarily reflect the views of the publisher, and the publisher hereby disclaims any responsibility for them.

Any people depicted in stock imagery provided by Thinkstock are models, and such images are being used for illustrative purposes only. Certain stock imagery © Thinkstock.

ISBN: 978-1-4908-4010-9 (sc)
ISBN: 978-1-4908-4011-6 (hc)
ISBN: 978-1-4908-4009-3 (e)

Library of Congress Control Number: 2014910656

Printed in the United States of America.

WestBow Press rev. date: 07/11/2014

Contents

	Preface	*ix*
1.)	The Kingdom of Heaven	1
2.)	The Parable of the Wheat and Tares	25
3.)	The Outward Professing Body	67
4.)	The Candlesticks: the Responsibility of Christendom	80
5.)	The Seven Churches	114
6.)	Ephesus: the Beginning of Decline and Decay	148
7.)	Smyrna: the Time of Persecution	164
8.)	Pergamos: The World comes in	190
9.)	Thyatira: Christendom's Internal Corruption	204
10.)	Sardis: Protestantism is Dead	221
11.)	Philadelphia: God Preserves a Remnant	235
12.)	Laodicea: Christendom's Candlestick Removed	262
13.)	The Babylonian Harlot: Christianity or Islam?	271
14.)	The Babylonian Harlot: the Angelic Interpretation	291
15.)	The Scarlet Beast; the Angelic Interpretation	303
16.)	The Last Caesar and the Antichrist	321
17.)	The Olive Tree	346
18.)	The Ruin of Professing Christianity	373
19.)	What in the World are we to do?	408
20.)	The True Calling of the Church	432
21.)	The Mystery of the Kingdom of Heaven	445
	One Final Thought	*475*

Cover photo thought:

Matthew 13:31-32

"Another parable He put forth to them, saying: "The kingdom of heaven is like a mustard seed, which a man took and sowed in his field, which indeed is the least of all the seeds; but when it is grown it is greater than the herbs and becomes a tree, so that the birds of the air come and nest in its branches."

Preface

This book is written to tell the story of the times of the church on earth. It is a history from beginning to end of the public witness and testimony of the body of professing Christianity. It is a story told from God's perspective, directly from the testimony of His infallible and incorruptible Word. It is a spiritual analysis of what has gone before and of what has already been done, but then to make the story complete, also what its end will be. It is really God's account from His Word of the moral history of Christendom, as opposed to man's record of it.

The professing church's responsibility was to be a public witness in the earth to the present glory of Christ. She was to be a testimony to the same world that rejected Christ in the flesh and cast Him out. The church's responsibility while in the world is to show to the world the Christ that was in her. The professing church was to be the epistle of Christ, known and read by all men. She has the candlestick representing her work in responsibility, the light that God intended for her to shine into the darkness of the unbelieving world.

This book deals with the history of the church's testimony and witness for Christ while it remains on the earth. It deals with the moral quality of that testimony through time, but with this one stipulation – it is as God sees and testifies of it, not man. Jesus is walking among the candlesticks of the churches, and He is there as a Judge (Rev. 1, 2, 3). He sees the works of Christendom. In Revelation 2, 3, His dealings with the church world are not in the character of giving inward grace through the Holy Spirit. These messages are not His affections for His beloved saints, His body, His bride. There is no promise or supply of strength as is commonly found in the epistles. He speaks of works and motives, future promises of Christian hopes in glory, encouragements, warnings, threatenings, and judgments. But it is never, *"My grace is sufficient for you..."* He is dealing with the responsibility of Christendom and its testimony to the world, and judging whether its position can and is being maintained.

The object being judged is not the true church, although the body of Christ is certainly hidden in this object of His attention. We will discover that the seven churches represent all of Christendom – all that has a profession of the name of Christ – as one public corporate body. Its responsibility was to maintain the light of its candlestick. In the end we will find the utter rejection by God of Christendom as a public witness on the earth. In the last of the seven messages to the churches, the character of Christ presented is as the Faithful and True Witness. This is because the public body of Christendom couldn't maintain a suitable witness for God and preserve this role in its time of responsibility.

Jesus, the Son of God, is judging and speaking to the church world. In every message it is, *"He who has an ear, let him hear what the Spirit says to the churches."* These messages should be treated with the greatest importance. They speak of Christendom's history. They reveal Christianity's responsibilities, as these existed before God in that history. But the professing church isn't listening and isn't learning. Its interests are found elsewhere. Christendom has been occupied with the world and has been corrupted. She is no longer guided and empowered by the Holy Spirit, but embraces the wisdom of the world (I Cor. 1:17-28). Her testimony has been a failure. Her candlestick is to be removed.

Many will object saying, "Christ will build His church, and the gates of hell will not prevail against it. What you are saying cannot be right!" But professing Christianity is not His body, the church. It is a mistake if you think it is. And Christendom on the earth can fail and has failed; the testimony of the Holy Spirit in Scripture proves this. It is another mistake if you think it cannot. In the beginning of the book of Revelation (Rev. 2, 3) we see the public testimony of the church world judged as a failure. Toward the end of the book we see the public manifestation of His bride, the true church (Rev. 19). This is not failure. There she is the sovereign grace, power, and work of God. There God displays her, as His workmanship, in His glory. There she is what Christ is saying, *"I will build My church…"* And the gates of hell will not prevail against her because she is the sovereign work of God.

This book will be difficult for many Christians to read. There is no reason to sugar-coat the truth and authority of the testimony of God's Word. There is no doubt that God has a different opinion of the church world from the exaggerated ones of ministers and men. We are always guilty of thinking more highly of ourselves and our own work than we ought to think. We do not think soberly. We are hesitant to call evil as evil, and become content to live and function as believers in the midst of it. We attach the label of God's work and the name of Christ to many things. And we become comfortable in and with the present state and conditions.

We will not allow ourselves to admit that Christendom will never return to Pentecost. We think and teach that this is her right and privilege to do so. We think that God will pour out His power and His Spirit on the mess we've created, while all along we are failing to recognize it as the mess it is. I speak of the external body of Christendom as a corporate entity. We will discover just how much Scripture directly refers to this corporate structure. I am not speaking of individual believers, however spiritual or faithful they may be, and God's willingness to give grace and bless them. I am not referring to local assemblies, and whether they may or may not receive blessings from the Lord, however more difficult this may be than individual blessing. But I speak of how God views Christendom as one single body before Him in testimony, and how every professing Christian is connected to the corporate responsibility of that public entity. Individually we are all part of its testimony and its light.

We plead with God in prayer to bless it. But we can't even define what the 'it' is we want God to bless. "It is the church, the body of Christ!" But how and where do you really see the true body of Christ? If we are honest with ourselves we will admit that we can't know this. The body of Christ is scattered everywhere and today there remains no discernible bond of unity. When a minister calls out to the body of Christ to rise up and do anything, how is this actually done? Who are they speaking of? Who are they including? Who are they excluding? How do you see the body of Christ today, to be able to actually speak to it? Isn't it the Baptists, the Church of God, the Independents, maybe Presbyterians or Pentecostals that you are asking for? What do you think of the Roman Catholics? I know one thing we must admit about all the groups – they all name the name of Christ and every last individual is part and member of the professing church. And this is the same corporate body you and I are part of, for good or bad, better or worse. This is Christendom, and man has made a mess of it.

God is a holy God and He will not bless the unholy mess. He will not compromise His own nature and character. God looks at Christendom and He sees what man has done. Nothing can be hidden from Him. If God knows the thoughts and intentions of the human heart, and He knows us more intimately than we know ourselves, then I believe He sees and fully understands what man has done in the corporate history of Christianity. Our thoughts and reasoning rarely turn out to be the thoughts and reasoning of God. Today man charges ahead to do his thing, having received a feeling in prayer, a confirmation from somewhere, without ever seriously consulting the one authority we have been left with – the Word of God.

This book is filled with passages from the Scriptures that are intended to serve to impress upon the reader the validity of the points being made. This book is my attempt to allow God's Word to bring in its own testimony concerning the state and condition of the professing church. It is my effort to pull out from God's Word His account of the times of the church on earth. My source is not the history books of men, but the testimony of the Son of God walking among the candlesticks. I pray that the eyes of your understanding will be opened by the teaching of the Spirit of God. I pray that you will understand and know the truth of God, as it can only be found in His Word. I sincerely pray that when the Lord comes for His church, that you and I will be found in the character of Philadelphia. May you learn how to keep the patience of Christ (Rev. 3:10). May God bless you in your reading and efforts.

<u>Personal note:</u> Paul said in Romans 8:11, *"But if the Spirit of Him who raised Jesus from the dead dwells in you..."* As I said in the previous book, the seal of the Spirit in the individual believer is not something Paul could see or we can see, being in this physical world (Eph. 1:13). I do believe, and the Scriptures teach this, that every individual sealed with the Spirit knows he is a son of God because the Spirit of sonship given to him cries out in his heart, "Abba, Father." The presence of the Holy Spirit in the individual believer is witnessed to

that individual and made apparent by the Spirit. *"The Spirit Himself bears witness with our spirit that we are children of God."* (Rom. 8:15-16) The individual believer may not fully understand his redemption and justification in Jesus Christ, but he will know if he belongs to God. God sees the seal and knows those who are His (II Tim. 2:19). But again, the seal of the Spirit in others is not obvious to us.

There is a similar thought that involves the teaching of the Scriptures and Christian doctrine. God's ways are simply not man's ways or the world's ways. His ways of teaching His truth do not involve human wisdom or worldly wisdom. God's wisdom is foolishness to man and the world. Man's wisdom and the world's wisdom is foolishness to God. There is a portion of Scripture in first Corinthians that attempts to make these differences clear (I Cor. 1:17 - 2:16). God's wisdom and God's ways in teaching His truth are expressed here:

1 Corinthians 2:9-12

"Eye has not seen, nor ear heard,
Nor have entered into the heart of man
The things which God has prepared for those who love Him."

(10) But God has revealed them to us through His Spirit. For the Spirit searches all things, yes, the deep things of God. (11) For what man knows the things of a man except the spirit of the man which is in him? Even so no one knows the things of God except the Spirit of God. (12) Now we have received, not the spirit of the world, but the Spirit who is from God, that we might know the things that have been freely given to us by God."

What does it mean to be taught the things of God only as they can be taught, that is, by the Spirit of God? Do we even know what this is, what it looks like? The underlying nagging problem is that we can't really put our physical fingers on this. We can't measure it and bottle it up, and so, we often have a dullness of ability to recognize it if ever we do experience it. What does the teaching of the things of God by the Spirit look like or sound like? Just as we cannot see the seal of the Spirit in other believers, the teaching of the Word by the

Spirit becomes difficult to see and recognize. Yet it is essential that we have this. We must have this and this alone, for teaching Christian doctrine and knowing God's truth.

For the most part the masses of Christendom sit back and assume that this is automatically accomplished by God on their behalf in the ministers that are set before them. Then by association, the same assumptions are made of the institutions and seminaries that teach and prepare the ministers. And the assumptions go on and on. The theologians and professors in the schools of higher learning in Christendom assume that their brand of theology represents the truth of God ascertained by their great efforts in Biblical scholarship.

Is that what God intended in the above passage? I am convinced that man's ideas about Biblical scholarship are not God's thoughts or ways, or anywhere close to being so. Man loves his intelligence and he loves his efforts and accomplishments. So we emphasize these things in the learning of the Hebrew and Greek languages, to examine sentence constructs and derivations of words, breaking it down so we can discover our hidden meanings and interpretations of passages. How is this not the use of worldly wisdom, which God says is foolishness to Him? If an unbeliever can and does accomplish the same type of scholarship, given the opportunity, how is this unique to the believer as stated in the above passage? *"Now we have received, not the spirit of the world, but the Spirit who is from God, that we might know the things that have been freely given to us by God"* Many unbelieving Jews have far more understanding of the use of the Hebrew and Greek languages, even in a Biblical setting, than we do. How can this be Christian scholarship if the world can accomplish the very same thing?

We speak of orthodoxy of Christology, soteriology, ecclesiology, and eschatology and bring in hermeneutical systems of exegesis – literal, classical, prophetic, apocalyptic, or spiritualized – in order to form our sense of theological order. We have covenant structure theologians arguing and debating with the supposedly less than scholarly dispensationalists about abstract logic, historical progress, retrospective interpretation, and the process of differentiation. How is this not human wisdom? Is this really the Spirit of God teaching the things of God? Does this sound like Paul? He says in the broader passage referred to above, *"And I brethren, when I came to you, did not come with excellence of speech or of wisdom declaring to you the testimony of God...I was with you in weakness, in fear, and in much trembling. And my speech and my preaching were not with persuasive words of human wisdom..."*

I know the world cannot receive the Spirit of God (John 14:17). Therefore the world cannot know the things of God, and cannot possibly have the ability to teach those things by the Spirit (I Cor. 2:12-14). But I also know the world can easily do many of the things mentioned above; things that Christendom has become dependent on; things its leaders put forth as Christian or Biblical scholarship. How does that make sense? Why do we depend, as it appears we do, on worldly wisdom or the means and ways of the world? We must have the truth of the Word taught by the Spirit; that which is not available or possible for the world to experience or accomplish for the reason they do not have the Spirit of God. Why do we depend so much in mimicking worldly scholarship and assume this is what God has provided for us?

There is always a sense of infiniteness about God's Word. It has a living source from which it flows – it is from God Himself. There is a living power at work that permeates its connections and composition. All its principles and truths, so instrumental in understanding the details of passages, center on Christ and refer to Him. The purpose and plan of God, who works all things by the counsel of His will, will have in the dispensation of the fullness of times all the glory of God – both heavenly and earthly – centered on Christ as its Head (Eph. 1:9-11). It is the workings of the Spirit of God alone, through the Word, which serve to reveal these things and give us understanding of them. Even that which we learn, and learn well, is only knowing in part and seeing through a glass dimly, demonstrating our human feebleness in apprehension. That is why in this day we desperately need divine teaching – only God's Word – taught through a divine agent – the Spirit of truth (John 15:26, 16:13-15).

"For the time will come when they will not endure sound doctrine..." This time is today in the church world (II Tim. 4:3). Either we are taught the things of God by God's Spirit, or we may as well not learn

at all. We should always go to Scripture not to explain Scripture, but to receive from it only what God is saying. In teaching and doctrine we should only say what is in the Scriptures without adding human thoughts. This may seem much to do about nothing, but without this discipline we soon have the creation of systems of doctrine and hermeneutical schemes instead of actually benefiting from divine teaching. This is what is desperately needed today. It only comes out of the Word by the Holy Spirit. It is my hope that this book will motivate you to study God's Word on your own, for your own benefit.

This is the third book in a series of seven. I use the NKJV translation for all quoted scriptures in the book. There are many more passages listed in the text of the chapters and endnotes. These books are written is such a way that in reading them you have to continually refer to your own bible. It is how you determine for yourself that the things I'm saying are not just made up, the makings of a cynical mind. Your prayerful efforts to do this are part of the Spirit of God teaching you the things of God for yourself. It is your efforts to be in a position to have 'ears to hear what the Spirit is saying to the churches'. It is work. But you are becoming a workman, approved unto God, rightly dividing the word of truth (II Tim. 2:15). I hope that in all I write, I am always pointing you to the only source of truth, the Word of God.

I am not trying to sound arrogant. I do not think I have great knowledge. I apologize if that is the impression you have of me already from this preface. I simply believe that God has taught me these things by His Spirit. I am confident that He has. I have a desire to share these things as a teacher with any believer who 'has an ear to hear'. I believe these things are so important and that the time is short.

Jezebel in Thyatira is corruption

Sardis is spiritually dead

God gathers His faithful remnant – Philadelphia

The corporate body is spewed out of His mouth. The candlestick is removed.

Chapter 1:
The Kingdom of Heaven

As a nation and people, Israel is seen in Scripture as a vineyard of God's own planting. They are God's chosen people, separated by Him from the Gentiles. As a nation they were delivered out of Egypt, wandered in the wilderness for forty years, and were brought into the land of God's promise. God did many things for this people, privileged them in many ways above all others, even blessing them with His own presence dwelling in their midst. He was expecting to see fruit pleasing to Himself, suitable to His own nature. He was looking for obedience, justice, and righteousness. However, God's vineyard failed to produce fruit unto God.

Isaiah 5:1-7

"Now let me sing to my Well-beloved
A song of my Beloved regarding His vineyard:
My Well-beloved has a vineyard
On a very fruitful hill.
(2) He dug it up and cleared out its stones,
And planted it with the choicest vine.
He built a tower in its midst,
And also made a winepress in it;

*So He expected it to bring forth good grapes,
But it brought forth wild grapes.*

*(3) "And now, O inhabitants of Jerusalem and men of Judah,
Judge, please, between Me and My vineyard.
(4) What more could have been done to My vineyard
That I have not done in it?
Why then, when I expected it to bring forth good grapes,
Did it bring forth wild grapes?
(5) And now, please let Me tell you what I will do to My vineyard:
I will take away its hedge, and it shall be burned;
And break down its wall, and it shall be trampled down.
(6) I will lay it waste;
It shall not be pruned or dug,
But there shall come up briers and thorns.
I will also command the clouds
That they rain no rain on it."
(7) For the vineyard of the Lord of hosts is the house of Israel,
And the men of Judah are His pleasant plant.
He looked for justice, but behold, oppression;
For righteousness, but behold, a cry for help."*

God's Ways and Dealings with Israel

Jehovah had given the law to Israel at Mt. Sinai, looking for obedience, specifically for the fruit of righteousness. When they strayed in disobedience He would send His prophets to them to call them back to the law (II Kings 17:13, Neh. 9:26, Zech. 7:12). When they took up idolatry in the son of David, God divided them into two kingdoms. He sent more of His servants to them with little results. Israel's abominations grew and festered to the limits of God's patience and longsuffering. He scattered the ten tribes of the northern kingdom of Israel into the nations by the hand of the Assyrian, while a remnant of the southern kingdom of Judah He delivered into captivity (Jer. 2:8, Lam. 2:9, Zeph. 3:4). At this time Israel's and Judah's apostasy was so great that God could not tolerate dwelling in their midst any longer. He removed His presence and glory out of Jerusalem and from the earth, and He allowed Nebuchadnezzar to destroy Jerusalem and the temple. Years later, when Judah was delivered from its spirit of idolatry, God made provision for the return of this remnant to the land from Babylon. The ways of God toward this people had one final purpose in their testing.

Matthew 21:33-44

(33) "Hear another parable: There was a certain landowner who planted a vineyard and set a hedge around it, dug a winepress in it and built a tower. And he leased it to vinedressers and went into a far country. (34) Now when vintage-time drew near, he sent his servants to the vinedressers, that they might receive its fruit. (35) And the vinedressers took his servants, beat one, killed one, and stoned another. (36) Again he sent other servants, more than the first, and they did likewise to them. (37) Then last of all he sent his son to them, saying, 'They will respect my son.' (38) But when the vinedressers saw the son, they said among themselves, 'This is the heir. Come, let us kill him and seize his inheritance.' (39) So they took him and cast him out of the vineyard and killed him.

(40) "Therefore, when the owner of the vineyard comes, what will he do to those vinedressers?"

(41) They said to Him, "He will destroy those wicked men miserably, and lease his vineyard to other vinedressers who will render to him the fruits in their seasons."

(42) Jesus said to them, "Have you never read in the Scriptures:

*'The stone which the builders rejected
Has become the chief cornerstone.
This was the Lord's doing,
And it is marvelous in our eyes'?*

(43) "Therefore I say to you, the kingdom of God will be taken from you and given to a nation bearing the fruits of it. (44) And whoever falls on this stone will be broken; but on whomever it falls, it will grind him to powder."

When God sent the Messiah of prophecy to Israel, that nation rejected Him as their King. They would not have Jesus but rather said that Caesar was their king. He came unto His own to fulfill promises and prophecy, but they would not receive Him. God came looking for fruit from the vineyard He had planted long ago, but this privileged nation had produced none (Matt. 21:18-19). *"Then last of all the owner of the vineyard sent His Son to them, saying, 'They will respect my son.'"* But they caught Him, and cast Him out of the vineyard, and killed him (Matt. 21:37-39).

Israel Set Aside by God

The passage from Isaiah and this parable from the Lord tell of the history of Israel as the vineyard planted by God. Also both show the outcome for Israel when no fruit was harvested or, as we saw in Isaiah, only wild grapes were produced. Israel, as the very privileged people of God, has been set aside by Him. As God remarks in Isaiah, *"What more could have been done to My vineyard, that I have not done in it?"* (Isaiah 5:4) The kingdom of God was taken from them[45]; at least there would be no Messianic kingdom at that time (Matt. 21:43). Again in the passage in Isaiah God tells us what He will do to His vineyard. The hedge of protection would be brought down; the vineyard would be trampled underfoot; it would be laid to waste and burnt; He would not allow it to be watered by the rain (Isaiah 5:5-6).

The vineyard of God's own making would be made desolate by God Himself. The house of God that is Israel, as a nation, would be set in desolation. Isaiah declares the judgment eight hundred years before the coming of the Messiah to Israel. The setting aside of the vineyard is the same as the house of Israel being made desolate. It is Jesus Christ, their Messiah that speaks of this desolation. Further, He tells them their house will remain desolate until He comes to them a second time as their Messiah, and they say, *'Blessed is He who comes in the name of the Lord.'* They have been in this state for nearly two thousand years (Matt 23:37-39, Luke 13:34-35).

The Jews, as the people of God, were given the prophecies and promises. They had the oracles of God as well as the covenants (Rom. 3:1-2, 9:3-5). The Messiah was to be presented to them. God remained patient and faithful with His people until they rejected Him. In His faithfulness God would not set Israel aside to establish anything else that denied their privileges, prophesies, and promises. He would not do this until Israel rejected the Son, and thereby rejected the promises themselves.

It is important to realize the Biblical principles involved in God's dealings with the Jews. It is more than just prophesies and promises and the detail of words, but the principles and character of Judaism itself. God could not deny the distinction He had set up between Jew and Gentile through the law. The religion God gave Israel is what built up the wall of separation around them. God had divided them from the nations by choosing Israel and giving them His law. There couldn't have been a greater distinction between Jew and Gentile than what Judaism established. The Jews religiously maintained this separation.[46]

God came to the Jews in the flesh and they rejected Him. Now everything changes. With Israel set aside as the people of God, their house pronounced desolate, and their city and temple marked for destruction (Luke 19:41-44, Matt. 24:2), the counsels of God turn to something different. This turning in God's plan is seen in the distinct and new revelation of the kingdom of heaven.

The Dispensation of the Kingdom of Heaven

With John the Baptist and Jesus Christ Himself, the preaching was always that the kingdom of heaven was at hand (Matt. 3:1-2, 4:17). It was not set up and existing as yet, but was soon in coming. The reasoning for this is simple – the kingdom of heaven would not exist until Jesus Christ, the Son of Man, had gone away, that is, back to heaven. Until then the kingdom of heaven was proclaimed as not yet, but 'at hand.' If we are spiritually perceptive in our study of the scriptures on this important topic, we will see certain distinct features associated with the kingdom that are valuable to point out:

1. When Jesus first came to Israel there was a heightened expectation among the Jews that the Messiah would soon appear and establish a Messianic kingdom in Israel that would throw off the shackles of Gentile bondage. The Lord's disciples had this expectation (Luke 19:11). They maintained these same thoughts even after His resurrection (Acts 1:6). But we have shown already from Scripture that the Messianic form of the 'kingdom of God' was taken from Israel. That specific form, which was according to the detail of prophecies and promises to Israel, would be held off or set aside at this time (Matt. 21:43).

2. In the time of Jesus in the flesh on earth the kingdom of heaven was only at hand. It does not come into actual existence until the Son of Man goes away, back to heaven.

3. The revelation of the kingdom of heaven is connected to the title of Jesus as the Son of Man, and is consequent to the completion of His perfect and efficacious work of redemption (Matt. 13:37, Luke 9:22, John 12:23-24). In the specific teachings concerning the kingdom this is seen as the Son of Man going away to the right hand of God in heaven. He went away as the Son of Man resurrected and glorified, which becomes a central point of understanding. The main component of the kingdom of heaven at the present time is the body of Christ being gathered on the earth. This forming of the church by the Holy Spirit come down from heaven could not happen before Jesus Christ was glorified to the right hand of the throne of God (John 7:37-39).[47] He did not go away to heaven in the title or character of a Jewish Messiah coming to Israel according to the flesh.[48]

4. All the specific references to the kingdom of heaven are only found in Matthew's gospel, mentioned there thirty-two times. All the specific teaching concerning the kingdom of heaven is found here, revealing what the kingdom is

in mystery (Matt. 13:11). It shows the kingdom's general progression on the earth through time, the judgments at the end of the age, and its outcomes and results in open manifestation in the age to come.

The gospel of Matthew presents us with some great biblical insights. If the kingdom of heaven is at hand, and not existing until the Son of Man was glorified, then there is a transition presented in this gospel. It is a dispensational transition – between Judaism and Christianity; between a Jewish dispensation and the dispensation of the kingdom of heaven; between the corporate entities of Israel and professing Christianity.

The Jewish dispensation encompasses the time from Israel being delivered out of Egypt to the presentation of Messiah.[49] It would include the giving of the law at Sinai with the priesthood, Israel being brought into the land, the judges, prophets, and kings, and their scattering into the nations or captivity in Babylon. This dispensation is physically ended by the destruction of Jerusalem and the temple by the Romans in 70 AD. This was after the presentation of Messiah to Israel and their refusal of Him as their King.

The Closing of the Jewish Dispensation

With the destruction of the temple for the second time during the same dispensation, the practice of Judaism is brought to a halt by God. Why? Because *"the hour is coming and now was at hand when the true worshipers will worship the Father in spirit and truth; for the Father presently seeks such to worship Him."* (John 4:23) Jesus prefaces this by saying, *"Woman, believe Me, the hour is coming when you will neither on this mountain, nor in Jerusalem, worship the Father."* Judaism is a partial revelation of God's truth and a limited worship of the true God from a distance and through a veil. Yet these partial truths and the Jewish system give way with the coming of God's Son to Israel (John 1:17). The name of Father is strictly a Christian possession and represents a revelation of God in truth far beyond that of the name of Jehovah with the Jews (Ex. 6:2-3). The worship of the Father in spirit and truth is strictly a Christian position and privilege (John 4:19-24).[50]

The practice of Judaism requires their temple, the Samaritans required Jacob's mountain – both of which are fixed physical locations involving religion that was earthly, sensual, and outwardly in the flesh.[51] This explains the desire of the returning remnant from Babylon to rebuild the temple in Nehemiah's day. Without the physical location of the temple in Jerusalem, there is no practice of Judaism, notwithstanding they do so without God's presence and throne. However, God destroys the temple in 70 AD, effectively putting aside Judaism in dramatic fashion.

In Matthew's gospel we have the distinct understanding of the closing of the Jewish dispensation and the declaration that the dispensation of the kingdom of heaven is 'at hand.' (Matt. 3:2, 4:17, 10:7) The two corporate entities involved in this transition are Israel and professing Christianity. The house of Israel was to be made desolate, and would remain that way throughout the time between the two comings of Messiah to that nation (Matt. 23:38-39). Israel had to be set aside, the Jewish dispensation closed, and the practice of Judaism ended in order for God to bring forth the beginnings and development of the kingdom of heaven.[52] Christendom is the corporate object in the world that becomes the subject of the revelation and teachings of the kingdom of heaven. This is all of professing Christianity.

The Mystery Hidden from the Prophets

Associated with the revelation of the kingdom of heaven is a similar biblical understanding related to the true church. The body of Christ is the mystery of God kept hidden from the prophets, but now revealed by the Holy Spirit sent down consequent to the Son of Man glorified to the right hand of God (Eph. 3:1-11). What also is mystery is the revelation of the kingdom of heaven; this likewise was hidden from prophecy and the prophets. You will not find one Old Testament passage pointing to it as a kingdom or revealing the existence of professing Christianity in the world. This character of mystery concerning the kingdom is obviously directly related to the fact that the body of Christ, the true mystery of God, is a prominent component in the corporate body of professing Christianity. There is mystery, previously hidden and now revealed, associated with the kingdom of heaven. The label associated with the present dispensation would better be called 'the kingdom of heaven in mystery'. To understand more we must look into the nature and character of the kingdom, and its teachings.

Matthew 13:11

"He answered and said to them, "Because it has been given to you to know the mysteries of the kingdom of heaven, but to them it has not been given."

Chapter 1: Endnotes

[45] The kingdom of God is a term in Scripture used in a broad and general way. In a sense it depicts the idea of God being present and working, or the general rule of God. When Jesus came in the flesh to Israel the kingdom of God was present among them, because Emanuel was there and working (John 5:16-19). When He cast out demons, He would say the kingdom of God has come upon you, for that particular person had experienced God's power and authority used on their behalf (Luke 11:20, Matt. 12:28). When the sick were healed in Israel, whether by Jesus or disciples given power and authority to do so (Luke 9:1), it was generally said that the kingdom of God had come near to you (Luke 10:9). When pressed by the Pharisees as to when the kingdom of God would come, Jesus answered and said, *"The kingdom of God does not come with observation; nor will they say, 'See here!' or 'See there!' For indeed, the kingdom of God is within you."* (Luke 17:20-21) So in John, Jesus says you must be born again to see or enter the kingdom of God. This is the new nature you must have to have a relationship with God. It is an inward work of the Holy Spirit (John 3:5-7). And it is without observation because the work of God in the believer is only in spirit and soul at this present time, and does not yet reach to our bodies of flesh (John 3:8).

But there is a more detailed description of kingdoms in name and associated workings found in Scripture when we consider the term 'the kingdom of God' as the general rule and sovereignty of God. What we find is what we may consider as the kingdom of God in its different forms and developments.

1. The kingdom of God is first offered to Israel in its Messianic form and according to promises and prophecy. Messiah is for the Jews and a Messianic kingdom would be for Israel. The covenants and the promises pertain to the Israelites. Therefore the Messiah and His kingdom needed to be presented to them (Rom. 9:4-5). Jesus came to His own, announced He was their long waited for Messiah (Luke 4:17-21), went about their towns and villages preaching the kingdom of God (Luke 4:43, 8:1, Mark 1:14-15), and did the work that the Messiah was promised to do – healing the sick, raising the dead, casting out devils, and feeding the poor with loaves and fishes (Psalm 132, Matt. 11:2-6). The kingdom could have been Israel's if the Jews would have received Him as King. But they

rejected Him, fell on the stumbling stone set by God in Zion, and had the kingdom of God withdrawn from them (Matt. 21: 33-44).

2. Upon the glorifying of the Son of Man to the right hand of God and the sending down of the Holy Spirit, the kingdom of God develops as the kingdom of heaven in mystery. God had set Israel aside, took the kingdom from them, and turned His attention to the Gentiles. The kingdom develops on earth as a spoiled crop in the field of the world (Matt. 13:24-29). This is all the while the King is away and hidden from the world in heaven (Col. 3:1-3). The kingdom of heaven is what is present now, and is in mystery. The kingdom of heaven, I believe, speaks of the rule, power, and dominion of the heavens over the earth (Dan. 4:26). The end of the age brings judgments from God and the crop in the field is separated out (Matt. 13:30).

3. After the end of the age the kingdom of God in general is seen as the kingdom of the Father in the heavens (Matt. 13:43), and the kingdom of the Son of Man on the earth (Matt. 16:28, 25:31). The Messianic kingdom and the throne of David will be established in Israel by sovereign grace, and as a subset of the kingdom of the Son of Man.

All this shows the specific development through time and in Scripture of the kingdom of God. We see there are distinct kingdoms with definite understandings and revelations that come under the broad heading of the kingdom of God.

[46] The cross and crucifixion of Christ put an end to the middle wall of separation between Jew and Gentile (Eph. 2:14-15) – but of greatest importance to understand is that this is only true in the body of Christ. In Christ there is neither Jew nor Gentile (Gal. 3:26-28, Col. 3:10-11). In the body of Christ there are no nations. In contrast to this, in the world and on the earth Israel remains a nation and maintains a separation from the Gentile nations as before. Israel is not in Christ. Israel has always been in the world and very much part of the world (John 8:23). On the earth their religion was a wall of separation from the Gentiles; however, it was never a separation from the world. The body of Christ *is* separated from the world, which is an opposite standing and position from Israel (John 17:14, 16). This is the reason there are no nations in Christ, the body of Christ. It is also why Israel is always viewed by God as a nation on the earth, because 'nations' belong to the earth and are connected to the earth. The body

of Christ, the true church, is the heavenly calling of God – you see, not connected to the earth. Israel is the earthly calling of God, and as such, is connected to this earth, and is part of this world.

I simply could go on and on speaking of these insights that find their source in the general biblical principles that relate to how God distinguishes Israel from the church. The understanding of them is truly spiritually profound. When you see these principles by the Spirit and divine teaching, then all of Scripture makes sense and falls into place and is easily understood. All of it! However, the pairing and distinction of Israel and the body of Christ is not the beginning of these insights. Rather, it is the two Adams, the first being a type of the second, who is Christ (Rom. 5:14). *"The first man was of the earth, made of dust; the second Man is from heaven."* (I Cor. 15:47) The first man is of the world; the second Man is not (John 17:14, 16, 8:23). The first man is of the first creation; the second Man is the new creation of God, and the firstborn of it (Rev. 3:14, Col. 1:15). Which of the two Adams is Israel related to? Which of the two Adams is the church connected with? Having said all I have, the answer to these two questions is fairly easy. Yet do you realize that the answers and their associated consequences will never change throughout the entire millennium? Also, I really see no indication in Scripture that these biblical principles will ever be completely undone, even in the eternal state. Please note – all of God's eternal counsels and plans have as a foundation the suffering and death of the Son of Man, come down from heaven (John 3:13). All God's counsels are based on the second Adam, even the eternal state, that is, the new heavens and new earth. [The comprehension of these and other biblical principles, and the spiritual insights issuing forth from them as divine teaching and understandings, are the things so missing in theological discussions today.]

As long as Judaism was fully practiced, the wall of separation between Jew and Gentile was firmly in place. This ended in 70 AD when the temple and city was destroyed by the Roman army. God used the Romans to stop the practice of Judaism, the Law of Moses. When this event happened, God scattered the remainder of the Jews into the nations, to live there as the Gentiles and in appearance not separated from the Gentiles. Israel's identity as 'God's people' is strongly dependent on three things:

1. The nation living in the extent of the Promised Land, without strangers in the land sharing it with them. The original promises to Abraham on behalf of Israel, his physical descendants, did not include sharing the land with strangers or Gentiles.

2. The nation being able to practice their religion, Judaism. This is the wall of separation for them from the Gentiles. This is what makes them a people and a nation chosen and separated by God. They cannot properly practice their religion being scattered into the nations and out of the land. Without the temple, animal sacrifices, and their priesthood, and these things necessarily in Jerusalem, there is no separation from the Gentiles.

3. A temple for worship in the city of Jerusalem. This is crucial to the practice of Judaism and is central to their identity as a separated people and nation.

The failure of Israel in the above three points, only serves to blaspheme the name of Jehovah in the earth (Ez. 36:16-23). Israel's failure was based on God's testing of the principle of human responsibility.

There are Jews and Gentiles still on the earth, but there are no Jews or Gentiles distinguished in the body of Christ (Gal. 3:26-28). The true church is a heavenly body with no purposed connections to the earth, the world, or the original creation. If it had these earthly connections it would have nationalities in it. But such things do not exist in Christ.

The believer has been privileged by God to know what He will do for Israel in the future (John 15:15). At the time of the coming millennium God will be faithful to fulfill every promise to Israel in the form of a chosen Jewish remnant. All three points above will be meticulously fulfilled through God's faithfulness by sovereign power and grace, and according to the literal details of prophecy. They will be restored in the land with a new and glorious temple, and they will practice Judaism by God writing His law in their minds and on their hearts (Ez. 36:24-38, Jer. 31:31-34, Heb. 8:7-13).

God cannot be unfaithful to His promises, any of them. He cannot be unfaithful in His gifts, which are His grace. He cannot be unfaithful to any of His callings. These are all without repentance (Rom. 11:28-29). He cannot go back on one jot or title of His Word. He simply cannot (Is. 55:11), for He is the Lord God. He must remain faithful. Regardless of the unfaithfulness of man, and of Israel in their history, He still will be found faithful (Rom. 3:3-4).

[47] The Biblical doctrine of the church, the body of Christ, is this: *The church exists by the fact that there is a glorified Man exalted to the right hand of God, in heavenly glory, where He became the Head of the church as the glorified Man, and now the church as His body joined to Him.* That is the

Spirit revealed doctrine of the church – a doctrine and revelation that was hidden by God as His very own mystery, hidden from prophecy and the prophets, and even hidden before time began and the world was created (Eph. 3:3-5, 8-10, Rom. 16:25, Col. 1:24-27). This is the doctrine. Everything associated with the body of Christ in God's counsels revolves around this doctrine.

This body has a heavenly calling and a heavenly position. It has a glorious inheritance, always to be found in Him and with Him sharing His glory, His inheritance, His rule and dominion. Until His exaltation, the Holy Spirit could not be sent down to the earth to gather in the church (John 7:37-39). Those who are asleep in Christ have gone on to be with the Lord in soul and spirit, while their bodies remain on earth corrupting in the grave. We that are alive and remain on the earth, where the Comforter abides, always are the redeemed that form the church. The rapture is the event that joins these two groups together, the assembling of all that are His, the body of Christ as one, by resurrection and change, in glorified bodies, to go to the Father's house in the heavens (John 14:1-3, I Thess. 4:13-18). This event is also part of the mystery of God that is the true body of Christ (I Cor. 15:51-52). The church in the heavens is the tabernacle of the Father and the Lamb throughout the ages to come.

[48] The title of Messiah to Israel according to prophecy and promises is set aside as long as the house of Israel remains desolate. There cannot be a Messianic kingdom over a united Israel (twelve tribes and all, that is, the two kingdoms, Israel and Judah, brought back together and united again after being split apart after the time of Solomon), throwing off all Gentile power and rule, if the house of Israel remains desolate. Israel's calling, as the people of God, is set aside. Now this doesn't mean they are forsaken forever. The gifts and callings of God are without repentance. At a future point in time God will again take up Israel as His people and deal with them as a people, as a nation – the prophecies that point to the future millennium declare Israel's restoration in the land as again recognized as 'the people of God'. But their desolation, which has continued for nearly two thousand years, is clearly taught by Jesus in the gospels – Matt. 23:37-39 and Luke 13:34-35.

Matthew 23:37-39

"O Jerusalem, Jerusalem, the one who kills the prophets and stones those who are sent to her! How often I wanted to gather your children together, as a hen gathers her chicks under her wings, but

you were not willing! See! Your house is left to you desolate; for I say to you, you shall see Me no more till you say, 'Blessed is He who comes in the name of the Lord!' "

We should note that Israel's desolation is said by Jesus to be the entire time between His first coming to Israel and His second coming to them – you shall see me no more until... When Jesus came at first it was in love, goodness, and mercy. *However this first coming was based on the principle of human responsibility in Israel. They were tested in this same principle for fifteen hundred years by the giving of the law at Mt. Sinai. God was looking for obedience and righteousness, but never found any fruit. The presentation of Messiah to Israel was the last testing of responsibility in man.* This final testing was God Himself coming to Israel, not by law, but in goodness and grace (John 1:17). It was met with failure. Israel did not receive Him, although He had come unto His own (John 1:11). When He appears to this nation a second time, they will look on Him whom they have pierced and say to Him, 'Blessed is He who comes in the name of the Lord!' But this will be a Jewish remnant of God's choosing, sealed and preserved by God through a future time of great trouble, delivered out of it (Rev. 7:1-8, Jer. 30:7-11, and Jer. 31:7-14).

This second coming of Messiah is all sovereign choice, grace, and power, according to the faithfulness of God to fulfill all and every promise He made to Israel. This second coming has nothing to do with Israel being responsible. What God does in the end for the Jewish remnant, exalting them as the greatest nation on the face of the earth during the millennium, is not conditional – it is not dependent on Israel meeting certain conditions of obedience in human responsibility. In this way, God alone receives the credit and man will have absolutely no reason to boast. It is simply all for the glory of God and for His glory alone.

Messiah coming to Israel two thousand years ago proved to be an utter failure for that nation. God judged their responsibility as a failure according to these words by the Lord:

Luke 19:41-44

(41) "Now as He drew near, He saw the city and wept over it, (42) saying, "If you had known, even you, especially in this your day, the things that make for your peace! But now they are hidden from your eyes. (43) For days will come upon you when your enemies will build an embankment around you, surround you and close you in

on every side, (44) and level you, and your children within you, to the ground; and they will not leave in you one stone upon another, because you did not know the time of your visitation."

Luke 21:20-24

(20) "But when you see Jerusalem surrounded by armies, then know that its desolation is near. (21) Then let those who are in Judea flee to the mountains, let those who are in the midst of her depart, and let not those who are in the country enter her. (22) For these are the days of vengeance, that all things which are written may be fulfilled. (23) But woe to those who are pregnant and to those who are nursing babies in those days! For there will be great distress in the land and wrath upon this people. (24) And they will fall by the edge of the sword, and be led away captive into all nations. And Jerusalem will be trampled by Gentiles until the times of the Gentiles are fulfilled."

In the first passage it is Israel as a nation that *did not recognize the time of their visitation.* It is this nation that *specially failed in their day,* when they could have seen the fulfillment of prophecy and promises in their Messiah. In the second passage it is the pronounced judgment of God through the Roman army bringing *great wrath upon this people Israel.* This all came to pass in 70 AD. It was Israel's capital city that would have no stone left upon another. It would be the people of Israel that would either fall by the edge of the sword or be scattered into the nations. It is Israel, as the house of God, that was made desolate. God Himself tore down the hedge of protection around His own vineyard (Isaiah 5:5-6).

Israel, as the people of God and a nation, has been set aside by God Himself. At this present time God does not recognize them as His people, saying to them, *"For you are not My people, and I will not be your God."* (Hosea 1:9) If we are taught by the Spirit in these biblical principles we will realize that biblical prophecy is set aside at this present time and the counting of time on the earth has stopped. Both the subject of prophecy and the counting of time on the earth are directly related to Israel and their earthly calling from God (Dan. 9:24-27). This earthly calling is set aside presently. It becomes an easy spiritual insight to understand that the prophetic promises in and through Messiah to Israel are all set aside as well. These are all scriptural principles related to each other, centering on Israel.

One more important point needs to be made as relating to these very principles – it was not the church that was made desolate. It was not the church in the above passage that did not recognize the time of its visitation by Messiah, not knowing 'its day.' The body of Christ (the church) did not exist at the time the Lord was speaking. He had said, *"I will build My church..."* Unless we are willing to accuse the Lord of misspeaking, the church was not wandering around in the wilderness for forty years as the nation of Israel. If Israel is the church in the wilderness, then Israel is still the church at the time of His speaking on which desolation has been pronounced, and has continued in desolation for some two thousand years between the two comings of Messiah. Why would Jesus say 'I will build My church' if it was already built and wandering around? When God says, *"For you are not My people..."* is He speaking to the church? (Hosea 1:9) Is He setting aside the church before He ever builds it? He is speaking to somebody and they were His people, but not anymore? It is Israel, as a people and a nation, which is set aside.

The point of great importance is this – Israel and the body of Christ (the church) are always completely separate and distinct corporate entities. God sees them as such and the Scriptures treat them as such, as I have shown you with just a few passages above, a few among many readily available to press this scriptural truth. The two entities have completely different callings, completely distinct destinies. One was made desolate so the other could be revealed, come into existence, and be built by God. One is the common subject of biblical prophecy, while the other is the mystery of God hidden from prophecy and the prophets.

The body of Christ has a heavenly calling (Heb. 3:1), and this is, in part, the reason it is hidden from prophecy. The proper subject of biblical prophecy is the earth and God's government of it. This government will be centered in Israel during the millennium. Prophecy concerns earthly things. The church has a heavenly character, a heavenly citizenship, and heavenly calling. The one, according to prophecy, will be restored in the Promised Land and become the greatest nation on the earth during the coming millennium, the Gentiles gathered to them for blessing. The other, hidden from prophecy, will be removed from the earth to the heavens, and will become the tabernacle of the Father over the earth during the coming millennium. The church will sit in heavenly places in Christ, the seat of God's government over the millennial earth, showing forth how the heavens will rule the kingdoms of men (Dan. 4:25-26), and there as kings and priests to His God and Father (Eph. 2:6, Rev. 1:6). The church in the heavens will be the means and vessel by which God will bless the millennial earth. The differences between the two entities are as different as night and day, as separate as the earth from the heavens.

What is the big deal and why is this so important? The mixing of the two corporate entities, with their callings and all associated principles and teachings, is the means by which Satan corrupts professing Christianity. The Judaizing of the Christian faith, by all its multifaceted forms and ways, is the ruin of Christendom on the earth. By Judaism, Israel exalted itself in pride and self-righteousness. Paul describes it as the confidences of man in the flesh – all that man can glory in by birth and natural descent, and an erroneous thought of working out, by human endeavor and accomplishment, one's own righteousness from the law (Phil. 3:2-9). The Judaizing of the Christian faith is an insidious leaven of false teaching and understanding that has already saturated the three measures of meal representing the Christian world (Matt. 13:33). The Judaizing continues on in all Arminian thoughts which are now firmly entrenched in the teachings of Christianity today. It is not sound doctrine (II Tim. 4:3-4). At its root and source is the pride of human accomplishment and boasting. It is humanism. I do not doubt there is no means or power to stop its spread and influence. It will penetrate the whole unto the end, until it is all leavened. This is the clear teaching of Scripture and the testimony of God. But, at the same time, what is also the clear teaching of Scripture is that the true believer has the responsibility to recognize corruption and evil, and to turn from it (II Tim. 2:19-22, 3:5).

To finish this endnote allow me to return to the original thought that lead to the above teaching. The title of Jesus as Messiah is associated with Israel, and Israel now is desolate and set aside. Therefore the title of Messiah and all associated prophetic promises are set aside. In like manner there is an association of the title of the Son of Man with all the revelation and workings of the kingdom of heaven. But it remains an association with a Son of Man who has *gone away – He is the Son of Man resurrected and glorified to the right hand of God.* This is not a Christ in the flesh, nor is it knowing Him in that way any longer (Rom. 9:5, II Cor. 5:16). All the principles concerning the kingdom of heaven, as it is known presently, do not relate to a Jesus in the flesh, but rather to a Jesus in a glorified state and position. The kingdom relates to Him in heaven, as the Son of Man exalted and glorified there (Luke 22:69, Mark 14:62, Matt. 26:64, John 6:62), and as sitting down on His Father's throne, hidden from the world (Col. 3:1-3).

This is not a Messiah in the flesh come to Israel, the physical descendant of David as such, nor is it the Davidic throne He presently sits on. He sits at the right hand of God, as the Son of Man on God's throne. The throne of David is not God's throne (Jer. 33:14-17). The throne of David is for the son of David, a human descendant of David's according to the flesh. Yes, it will be the Son of God, the One in whom all the fullness of the Godhead dwells bodily. But this is the key point – the fullness dwells bodily, in human form. By physical descent and physical birth and according to the flesh, He is associated with David, the tribe of Judah, and the nation of Israel. This is His connection to the Davidic throne, as in the flesh and not as God. He will sit eternally on the Davidic throne as the Messiah of Israel and the son of David after the flesh. But presently He sits on His Father's throne (Rev. 3:21). When He said that He ascends to His Father and our Father, to His God and our God, He was not ascending to David, nor to David's throne(John 20:17). David is a human being, he is not God.

To complete the original thought, the kingdom of heaven is not a Messianic kingdom over Israel according to prophecy. The Messianic kingdom in Israel is yet to come – during the coming millennium. Presently what we see on the earth is the kingdom of heaven as it exists and is being developed in the world. This is the present form and state of the general subject known as 'the kingdom of God'.

[49] The Jewish dispensation involved many different things in the ways of God toward Israel. It ranged from deliverance through judgments out of Egypt to prophets and kings. Yet the common element that defines this dispensation, running the entire time from beginning to end, is God testing man in Adam in the principle of responsibility. It is God testing man in the flesh, looking for obedience and righteousness. Israel was tested by God in two specific ways: one by the giving of the law, the other by the presentation of Messiah (John 1:17). The testing by the law basically ends with the Babylonian captivity. Israel's apostasy and idolatry brought on these consequences – the presence and glory of God is removed from Israel and the earth, the throne of Jehovah is lost, and what remains of the people are under Gentile captivity and rule. God's purpose for bringing a remnant out of captivity and back to Judah is for Israel's final testing – the presentation of Messiah. *"Then last of all he sent his son to them, saying, 'They will respect my son.'"* (Matt. 21:37)

However, Israel produced no fruit. There was nothing but failure. The *testing* of man in Adam ended when the Jewish dispensation ended, soon after the rejection of Messiah. The following two scripture passages confirm this biblical understanding – Gal. 4:4-5 and Heb. 9:26. Israel was the test case for God's testing of man in the flesh. Israel represented all mankind. They were the most privileged people by God on the face of the earth. But man in the flesh could never please God (Rom. 8:8). The testing proved that man in Adam was lost and utterly depraved and could not produce fruit unto God (Matt. 21:19). The testing of Israel by God proved that man always fails in responsibility. This is the testimony of God concerning man in Adam and this is man's story played out in the Scriptures.

The realization and comprehension of this principle of responsibility is important. God's distinct testing of mankind by His privileging of Israel, using them as the test case, is the understanding that is paramount to the sound doctrine of theological systems. Above all, these systems should be skillful and masterful at rightly dividing the word of truth (II Tim. 2:15). However, if you cannot see and understand the principle of responsibility being tested by God, if you don't understand what God was doing, what God was proving, then you cannot possibly understand the Old Testament or even the New. Can you explain why God only gave the law to Israel, and kept it there for fifteen hundred years? Can you explain why the Spirit of God calls that which was written and engraved on stones a ministry of death and condemnation? (II Cor. 3:7-9) When God was testing and the testing was over, what did He prove? How did He test man and when did the testing end? Has man been convinced of the results? If you can't answer these questions properly, then you shouldn't be devising theological systems and presenting them as divine teaching. The ending of the testing by God is the hinging point of human history and the Scriptures.

Man's responsibility is his works. When any man is judged by God, he is judged concerning his works, which were to be done in obedience to God. Man in Adam was required to manifest a perfect human righteousness before Him. What was demanded was a righteous of the law that would be particular to the individual (Phil. 3:9). However, all men are sinners in Adam. Man in the flesh could not obey. Israel produces no fruit. The parable in Matthew 21:33-40 depicts God's testing of Israel when they represented all mankind in the first Adam. The coming of Messiah to Israel was the last and final testing of man in the flesh, as this parable points out. Finding no fruit on the fig tree represents the results of the testing (Matt. 21:19). Man in the flesh could not produce fruit; Israel could not produce fruit. Then the judgment comes. God sets Israel aside and He condemns the entire world (John 12:31, Rom. 3:19). It is man in Adam, man in the flesh, that is condemned, and this is what the world is (Rom. 8:3).

[50] Even though the true believer worships the Father in spirit and truth according to the revelation of God to us as our Father in His Word, we are still hindered by sin in the flesh and our physical separation from Him. The ultimate realization of our Christian position and privilege will be after the rapture of the church and in the presence of the Father. We will have been conformed by God into the image of His Son, our bodies being glorified (Rom. 8:29-30, Heb. 6:18-20, Eph. 1:3-4). It will be without the presence of sin in us (for sin in the presence of God is an impossibility), away from this world, and out of the reach of Satan. It will be all the sons of God with the Father, in the Father's house. This is our proper biblical standing. This is our privileged position. This is our calling. The revelation of the Father is only to the sons by Christ Himself (please read Matt. 11:25-27). The house of the Father is only for the sons, to be brought there by Christ Himself (Gal. 3:26, John 14:1-3). The name of God as Father is the name by which God has been revealed to the church. The relationship with the Father is solely and distinctly for the Christian believer (please see I John 2:23, II John 1:9). In order to have the Father you have to have the Son. Israel never had the Son. The revelation of God as the Father is strictly a Christian privilege and relationship.

Please bear with me here as I emphasize again the understanding of one of the above statements. God has promised that all true believers will eventually enter into His rest (Heb. 4:1, 3, 6, 9-11). The rest of God is the glory of God, and how believers, and the church for that matter, no longer fall short of that glory (Rom. 3:23). The rest of God is the Father's house, to which Jesus went away to prepare a place there for us. When we are there, we are apart from sin in the flesh, apart from the world, and apart from Satan. These three things encompass all the present struggles and conflicts of the believer in his walk of faith. What an eternal difference the rapture will make! Oh, blessed day that will be!

[51] The Samaritan woman at the well says this to Jesus, *"Our fathers worshiped on this mountain, and you Jews say that in Jerusalem is the place where one ought to worship."* (John 4:20). This statement and the Lord's response afford us an insightful understanding of human nature, involving the progressive revelation of truth from God. The Samaritans stubbornly held on to an ancient yet revealed truth from God concerning their father Jacob. This turns out to be to their detriment. The Samaritans held so tightly to what truth they knew they had, that they couldn't and

wouldn't progress spiritually when God provided greater revelation – the tabernacle with the nation of Israel that becomes distinct to Israel as the fixed location of the temple in Jerusalem. This is how worship of the true God progressed in its level of revealed truth. By Jesus responding to her by saying what He did (John 4:21), He was announcing how the revealed truth concerning worship of the true God is now progressing beyond the truth that the Jews embraced. The obvious question is whether the Jews would stubbornly and blindly hold on to their ancient truth, and refuse to spiritually progress when God provides greater revelation? And we easily see it is greater revelation of the truth in that Jesus speaks of God as the Father, and not of the Jewish 'Jehovah'.

This holding on to previous truths, allowing them to blind you to greater and further revelations, is seen in many situations.

- Israel belittles and holds blasphemous the Christian truth of the trinity of the Godhead. Israel's ancient truth is, *"Hear, Oh Israel: The Lord our God, the Lord is one."* (Deut. 6:4) This is why Jesus is accused of blasphemy at His trial and why the high priest tore his clothes. Jesus doesn't really ever respond to the question of whether He is the Messiah, but when directly asked if He is the Son of God, He never remains silent. Son of God is who He is intrinsically, and never can be denied. But even though the Messiah title is His alone to possess, He knows it is presently set aside in the counsels of God.

- Paul was given great revelations and consequently, great responsibility for them. He was the minister for the body of Christ, the church, and the steward of the mystery of it. He was also given to complete the revelation of the word of God (Col. 1:24-26). Yet the early history of the church in the first few centuries is a disappointment to all this revealed truth which was given to her by God to possess (I Tim. 3:15). The so-called 'church fathers' were often seen as regressive concerning the Christian truth they taught. By the sixth century, Romanism can be seen as the great Judaizing of the Christian faith – the holding to the ancient Jewish system in forms, carnal ordinances, and such. This was systematically done in the face of the revealed truth of God in true Christianity – that which Paul delivered to us.

- Many ministers today, in an unhealthy way, point to the so-called 'fathers' or the Reformers in what they taught, as the basis and determining factor of God's truth. Judgments are made as to which 'fathers' they can find that first taught this particular doctrine and mark the amount of elapsed time between then and now. The greater amount of time elapsed, the greater the validity of truth assigned to the doctrine. The different theological camps beat each other up with these silly searches and claims.

The Reformation was not greater truth revealed by God, progressing past what previously had been given. Rather it was a re-discovery of certain truths that were long lost by Christendom. And the Reformers did not rediscover all the truth of God, which had been lost by man's failures in the history of the church. If we want the whole revealed truth of God, what should we do? Go to the fathers or the Reformers? No! We go to Paul, Peter, and John – the Spirit inspired writers of New Testament Scripture. And ask God to teach you the things of God by the Spirit He sealed you with (I Cor. 2:7-16).

[52] God raising Jesus from the dead was the accomplishment of the redemption of the believer/church (Eph. 1:18-23, Rom. 4:25). At the same time it also was the placing of Jesus in a personal position by which He establishes 'the sure mercies of David' (Acts 13:34). He establishes in His Person, by His resurrection, all the promises and future blessings to Israel, who are the earthly calling.

But in resurrection only, He had yet to take the heavenlies, so that the kingdom of heaven might begin and be established. Being raised, He had as yet to fill all things, and to associate the church in this new and heavenly glory (Eph. 4:8-10). The church in heavenly glory is the counsel of God, determined and prepared before the foundations of the world (Eph. 1:3-11). Yet she is hidden from preceding ages and generations as the mystery of God, now revealed by the Holy Spirit sent down (Eph. 3:1-11). The rejection of Jesus by His people as the Jewish Messiah, in the wisdom of God's plan, brings an end to the Jewish dispensation, and makes the way for the bringing forth of the kingdom of heaven. The kingdom of heaven is based on the glorified Son of Man, not a rejected Jewish Messiah who came according to the flesh and natural descent.

Also we should note that this transition between the two dispensations – the Jewish dispensation to that of the kingdom of heaven in mystery – is particularly seen in Matthew's gospel. The reason for this has to do with the specific character of Matthew's gospel given to it by the Spirit of God. If the term 'the kingdom of heaven' is exclusive to this gospel, then it certainly forms part of its specific character. Matthew's gospel is said to be the gospel of Messiah – it has the character of Jesus coming to Israel to fulfill promises and prophecy according to what was written in the law and prophets (Matt. 1:22, 2:5, 15, etc.). The Messianic theme of Matthew's gospel is also established in its very first verse – *"The book of the genealogy of Jesus Christ, the Son of David, the Son of Abraham."* (Matt. 1:1) So then, the term 'the kingdom of heaven' is distinctly used by the Spirit to show this transition of dispensation, and the spiritual reality of the setting aside of all things related and connected to Israel.

Chapter 2:
The Parable of the Wheat and Tares

The vineyard of God – the house of Israel – did not produce any fruit that God was pleased with. As His vineyard they only produced wild grapes. This was not what God was expecting or looking for. The judgment of the vineyard by God was predicted by the prophet Isaiah eight hundred some years before it was carried out (Isaiah 5:1-7). Jesus quotes Isaiah and says that his prophecies are fulfilled in the multitudes of Israel He was speaking to (Matt. 13:13-15).[53] The Jews, in general, are proven to be the ones who do not have, and even what they have will be taken away from them (Matt. 13:12). This would be the Messianic kingdom, the promises and prophecies, the practice of their religion, and their beautiful temple and city. Israel set aside is blinded and hardened by God (Rom. 11:7-10). God's vineyard would be laid waste and burned (Psalm 80:8-16).

The Old Vineyard made Desolate; The New Planting of God

In the time period of Israel's hardening, and after the completion of the foundational work of the cross, there is the opportunity for God to bring forth the fruit of His eternal counsels. As a consequence to

Israel being set aside, there would need to be an entirely new and distinct planting from God – the sower went out to sow (Matt. 13:3-9). The dispensation of the kingdom of heaven replaces the Jewish dispensation now set aside by God. With the going away of the Son of Man to the right hand of God, the kingdom of heaven is no longer at hand, but presently exists, in whatever form it may take in the world. The kingdom would contain the new planting of God after He had made the house of Israel desolate.

The parable of the sower reveals to us the divine agent used by God in establishing the kingdom of heaven. The sower is Jesus, the Son of Man; the divine agent used is the Word of God. The parable graphically depicts the general expected results of the seed falling into good or bad soil – the hearts of men (Matt. 13:18-23). Only he who receives the seed on good ground is the Christian example; it is he who produces fruit, some a hundredfold, some sixty, some thirty. The three examples of bad ground show different means and agents Satan uses to occupy the hearts of men. In them the Word is eventually rejected, and there is no fruit produced at all.

I would caution the reader to take the interpretation that Jesus gives of the parable in its simplistic literal form without adding human thoughts to it. For example, the sovereignty of God surrounds the entire chapter beginning with the Lord's answer to the disciples' question, *"Why do you speak to them in parables?"*

Matthew 13:11

"He answered and said to them, "Because it has been given to you to know the mysteries of the kingdom of heaven, but to them it has not been given."

The giving that Jesus is speaking of that takes place is from God. It is God doing the giving. Understanding of the mysteries of the kingdom of heaven is given by God. It is grace. It was not earned or merited by the disciples in any way so that God was obligated to respond to them in debt – this would not be grace. The verse describes the sovereign choice of God – to some it was given, to others it was denied. When we look at the interpretation of the parable of the wheat and tares Jesus declares, *"He who sows the good seed is the Son of Man."* (Matt. 13:37) He is solely responsible for the planting and bringing forth of all the wheat in the crop in His field. It is the work of God and His work cannot fail – this is sovereignty.[54] The wheat is planted, and the wheat comes up. It is a simple thought and understanding. All the choices, all the work – they are God's choices and only God's work. Therefore, in the parable of the sower, if we find good soil, we know it has to be the work of God beforehand. If there is good soil for the Word to enter into, it has to be God who prepared it. In man, that is, in the flesh, there is no good thing (Rom. 7:18). There is no good soil. Man in Adam is lost, utterly depraved, and by nature a child of wrath and disobedience. There is no such thing as good soil all on its own, or by chance or circumstances.

The Corrupting Leaven in Christendom

It is such a temptation in contemporary Christian teaching to add in Arminian and Judaizing thoughts – the corrupting leaven of human achievement and accomplishment.[55] When we see good soil in the parable we are tempted to say man has accomplished this or man is responsible for it. We slip and fall into the conclusion that man is basically good at his core, and the only difference between those producing fruit and others is better decisions, better circumstances, and more human effort.

Let us entertain an example of how the leaven penetrates the teaching in Christianity, and does so in a hidden and very subtle way. If the subject is Christian financial planning, we have a church program or class you can take to get you free of debt and start you on the road to saving for your 'Christian retirement'. We have nationally known names who have designed these very programs. This is all done in the name of Jesus Christ and according to so called Christian principles. Lay up treasure in heaven? – Well, let's just hold on to that thought, after all, we do not want to be so heavenly minded that we are no earthly good! We dare not lay up treasure in heaven until we've laid up enough treasure on earth for that comfortable future, or family properties and trusts, or inheritances we want to provide (Luke 12:15-21). *"After all, I'm sure these are*

Christian things as well and we should be able to find some Scripture to support it. It is family we're talking about, and there isn't anything more important to God than family." Can we not see that this is the cares of this world or, at the very least it is laying up treasures on the earth and in the world where we can readily see them and get at them? By our Christian teachings are we not compromising our Lord's own teachings concerning the kingdom of heaven?

Luke 12:33-34

"Sell what you have and give alms; provide yourselves money bags which do not grow old, a treasure in the heavens that does not fail, where no thief approaches nor moth destroys. For where your treasure is, there your heart will be also."

Luke 14:33

"So likewise, whoever of you does not forsake all that he has cannot be My disciple."

Matthew 6:19-20

"Do not lay up for yourselves treasures on earth, where moth and rust destroy and where thieves break in and steal; but lay up for yourselves treasures in heaven, where neither moth nor rust destroys and where thieves do not break in and steal."

Matthew 19:21

"Jesus said to him, "If you want to be perfect, go, sell what you have and give to the poor, and you will have treasure in heaven; and come, follow Me."

The above four passages represent the Lord's teaching in the area of money and finances concerning those who are part of the kingdom of heaven. For that matter, all His teaching in Matthew 5-7 is teaching concerning the kingdom of heaven that was 'at hand' (Matt. 4:17), and emphasizes the contrasts and differences from the Jewish teachings 'of old' in the Jewish dispensation. When we examine what He says concerning money and earthly things we should easily recognize that He is not teaching the old Jewish tithe from the law as a new Christian principle. He isn't teaching the Jewish tithe at all. His teaching goes far beyond any thought of a tithe. It is to sell all you possess; it is to forsake all that you have; it is to lay up treasures in the heavens *only*, where robbery and rust do not exist and cannot touch.

Another issue we have with this specific subject is how we trick ourselves into thinking that we can lay up treasures on the earth with certain purposes and under certain circumstances that will gain the Lord's approval. In our thinking we are laying up treasures on the earth that actually count for us as treasures laid up in the heavens. This is a strange way of thinking. The bottom line of the truth is whether thieves can break in to steal, or rust and moth can degrade? This is true concerning any treasure on the earth and in this world. Such things do not qualify as what Jesus is speaking about – treasures in the heavens.

This is not the teachings contained in our popular Christian retirement seminars, nor is it the tithe funding the building of church structures on earth. I say all this on the subject of money to show how contemporary church teachings actually circumvent and contradict the very words of Christ. How easily we attach the name of Christ to what the church world does, and then ask God to pour blessings on it. The leaven corrupts Christian teaching: in the area of finances it robs it from the heavens and brings it back down to the earth, and very much a part of the cares of this world and the pride of human accomplishment (Luke 12:15-21). And in doing so it is connected to the earth, and becomes a very Jewish teaching.

The New Teachings of the Kingdom of Heaven

The three chapters found in Matthew 5-7 are the teachings of the kingdom of heaven. Many times He uses the phrase, 'it was said to those of old', or something very similar to this. He is referencing the teachings of the Jewish dispensation and how the Jews properly understood and practiced the law (Matt. 5:20-21, 27, 31, 33, 38, 43).

Immediately after these sayings He starts His contrasting teachings with the phrase, "But I say to you..." (Matt. 5:22, 28, 32, 34, 39, 44). It is the difference between the Jewish dispensation and the kingdom of heaven. These are some of the distinctions between Judaism and Christianity.[56]

If we are to understand the existence of the kingdom of heaven, its progression through time as well as what it is at the end of the age, then we must consider the seven parables in Matthew thirteen (13). Seven is the number symbolizing perfection or completeness, and the parables give us a complete picture of the times of the kingdom of heaven in mystery, from its beginnings to the end of the age. They also give us a prophetic completeness in allegory form of the kingdom, which at the time of the Lord speaking, was only a kingdom at hand.

The Prophetic Story of the Kingdom of Heaven – Matthew 13

We have already discussed in part the parable of the sower. This first parable shows the divine agent of the kingdom of heaven and who it is that sows the new planting of God. The divine agent is the Word of God, and the sower is Jesus, the Son of Man.[57] All seven parables concern the kingdom of heaven, yet this first is apart from the remaining six in that it is not a similitude depicting the prophetic progression of the kingdom over time.

The first four parables of the chapter were spoken to the multitudes, in the presence of the disciples. These were spoken to the world in general, and in a certain sense take on a worldly viewpoint. However, the interpretation of the parable of the tares and the three remaining parables were spoken to the disciples alone, after He had sent the multitudes away. We must remember Jesus saying of the disciples, *"Because it has been given to you to know the mysteries of the kingdom of heaven, but to them it has not been given."* (Matt. 13:11) This is the sovereign difference God makes between the disciples and the multitudes of the Jews.[58] In this sense the last three parables, which were spoken in private to the disciples, take on a divine perspective and viewpoint of the kingdom.

The Wheat and Tares

The importance of the second parable – the wheat and tares – should soon become obvious to us. It is the one of the seven that is comprehensive of the kingdom of heaven in mystery. In it we see the kingdom from its beginning, then as it progresses to the end of the age.

Matthew 13:24-30,

(24) "Another parable He put forth to them, saying: "The kingdom of heaven is like a man who sowed good seed in his field; (25) but while men slept, his enemy came and sowed tares among the wheat and went his way. (26) But when the grain had sprouted and produced a crop, then the tares also appeared. (27) So the servants of the owner came and said to him, 'Sir, did you not sow good seed in your field? How then does it have tares?' (28) He said to them, 'An enemy has done this.' The servants said to him, 'Do you want us then to go and gather them up?' (29) But he said, 'No, lest while you gather up the tares you also uproot the wheat with them. (30) Let both grow together until the harvest, and at the time of harvest I will say to the reapers, "First gather together the tares and bind them in bundles to burn them, but gather the wheat into my barn."""

The parable contains allegories that need proper and accurate interpretation. These symbols and events all have their own literal meanings. It may be worthwhile to list what we are looking at;

- There is the man and his field.
- There is the assurance that good seed was planted in the field.
- There is the enemy and his work.
- There are men sleeping and at fault, allowing the enemy to work.

- There is a crop in the field – wheat and tares mixed together – which exists 'as is' for a period of time. What are the wheat? What are the tares?

- There is a time of harvest at the end, and different events associated with this general time. There is the bundling of tares and there is the intention to burn the tares. Separate from this, there is the wheat removed out of the field and into the barn.

- The reapers are different from the men that slept.

All this and more has its appropriate literal meaning, and prophetically tells the story of the kingdom of heaven. The fortunate thing for believers is that the Lord gave to His disciples and gives to us the literal interpretation.

Matthew 13:36-43

(36) "Then Jesus sent the multitude away and went into the house. And His disciples came to Him, saying, "Explain to us the parable of the tares of the field."

(37) "He answered and said to them: "He who sows the good seed is the Son of Man. (38) The field is the world, the good seeds are the sons of the kingdom, but the tares are the sons of the wicked one. (39) The enemy who sowed them is the devil, the harvest is the end of the age, and the reapers are the angels. (40) Therefore as the tares are gathered and burned in the fire, so it will be at the end of this age. (41) The Son of Man will send out His angels, and they will gather out of His kingdom all things that offend, and those who practice lawlessness, (42) and will cast them into the furnace of fire. There will be wailing and gnashing of teeth. (43) Then the righteous will shine forth as the sun in the kingdom of their Father. He who has ears to hear, let him hear!"

The existence of the kingdom of heaven is dependent on Jesus, the Son of Man. He is the owner of the field and He is responsible for planting the wheat. There are certain themes and meanings that are carried on throughout the parables depicting the kingdom of heaven. One example of this is that the field always means the unbelieving world and is the purchased possession of the Son of Man. The field is the world (v.38), but it is His field (v.24). This theme is repeated in the parable of the treasure hidden in the field (Matt. 13:44). The Son of Man ends up buying the field because of the value of the treasure hidden in it.

The Son of Man Gone Away

Another theme that is expressed in other parables of the kingdom of heaven is that the kingdom presently exists in the world and carries out its business there, while the Son of Man has gone away, back to heaven. He is the Bridegroom that will return for whom the ten virgins are waiting (Matt. 25:1-12). He is the man traveling to a far country (Matt. 25:14) or the certain nobleman who went into a far country to receive for himself a kingdom and to return (Luke 19:12-27). Jesus does not say this last parable in Luke is of the kingdom of heaven. It is not in Matthew's gospel where all the kingdom parables and teachings are found. Yet it does depict the same general events of the kingdom on earth, particularly those that occur while the Son of Man is away.[59]

During the time of the kingdom of heaven on earth the King remains 'hidden' in heaven at the right hand of God (Col. 3:1-3). The kingdom progresses on earth without His presence. It takes certain forms and characteristics over time, which testifies of the King's absence. It appears to the world that the absent King is not much concerned about His kingdom. But known to the believer's faith is the reality of His work and action – in sovereign grace He plants the wheat, He calls His own, and He makes them grow (Mark 4:26-29).

It bears repeating that the Son of Man goes away after His rejection as a Jewish Messiah in the flesh, and it encompasses His resurrection and glorification to the right hand of God. This is the foundation for God's work in bringing forth the wheat in the kingdom of heaven. It is how the Son of Man relates to the wheat and how they relate to the Son of Man in glory. He is their Head in glory, and the wheat united to Him is His body, the church (Eph. 1:20-23). The wheat are the sons of the Father in heaven (Matt. 5:45), and the true sons of the kingdom (v.38). They are the ones who will be taken by the Son of Man to His Father's house, a place specifically referenced by His promise, *"...that where I am, there you may be also."* (John 14:1-4) The wheat, at the time of harvest, will be taken from the field of the world and placed in His barn (v.30).[60]

The Crop in the Field

If we, as believers, are to get very far in our understandings of the mysteries of the kingdom of heaven, we must understand the dynamics of the crop in the field. Allow me to list some of the salient points describing the character of the crop (the following verses are from Matthew 13).

- The composition of the crop is wheat and tares together. The wheat is the work of the Son of Man, the tares the work of Satan (vs. 37-38). The individual wheat are true Christians – sons of the kingdom (v. 38), and sons of the Father. The individual wheat together is the body of Christ, the true church. The seed planted by the Son of Man comes up as individual wheat (this is seen as God's sovereign work). The wheat does not and will not come up as tares. As the crop existing in the world over time the wheat does not change into tares, and the tares do not change into wheat – everything will follow after its own kind, its own nature, and its own seed.[61]

- The tares are the sons of the wicked one, and they are his work to hinder and corrupt the plan and work of God during all the time the crop is in the field of the world (vs. 25-30). The tares are truly a special work, for they are distinct from the field, that is, distinct from the unbelieving world. They acknowledge their profession of Christ in order to be part of the crop, but nevertheless are the work of Satan.

- The crop is not a part of the field (world), but is growing in the field (world). The world sees the crop as one big corporate entity united together.

- Satan sowed the tares among real Christians to spoil the crop on the earth (in the field). The spiritual mind will see that the crop has become spoiled and corrupted in this world. On the earth it is always a spoiled crop. The world does not see this, and neither does the carnal mind. The crop is a mixture of good and evil – the work of God and the work of Satan. It remains this way, growing in its corruption and evil until the time of harvest at the end (vs. 26-30). This is the kingdom of heaven at this present time.

- The state and condition of the crop in the world refers to Christianity. The crop in the field of the world is all of Christendom (v. 26). The world sees it all as one. God sees it for what it really is – a corporate entity that *contains* His work, the body of Christ, yet as a corporate entity it is a spoiled crop, corrupt, and growing in evil.

- All the time of the crop in the field, that is, when it is a mixture of wheat and tares together, is when you see professing Christianity on the earth and in the world. This is the time while the body of Christ (the true church) is still contained within it. It is the time when evil and corruption grows and ripens in the outward body of Christendom.

- All the time of the crop in the field, His servants are not to be occupied with trying to separate and purify the spoiled crop (vs. 27-30).

- The time of harvest requires special reapers (angels – vs. 39-41) and involves bundling and then burning tares (vs. 40-42) and removing the wheat from the field (v. 30). The time of harvest in the end is when the crop stops existing. It is the time when God will work to separate out the mixture.

The Work of Satan Enters into the Kingdom of Heaven

The wheat and tares are mixed together as a crop in the field – *professing Christianity in the world.* The entire crop professes Jesus Christ, confessing Him as Lord. The enemy came in and planted tares while men slept. This is failure in human responsibility in the church world, and the failure of safeguarding can mostly be assigned to its ministers. Responsibility is a biblical principle involving human beings on the earth, corporate or individual, and whether they will be found obedient to the will of God. The outward society of Christendom has a corporate responsibility to God. All individuals in professing Christianity have individual responsibility to account for before God. On the earth responsibility is always placed in the hands of man and therefore becomes the subject of the judgment of God. The history of man in the Scriptures tells the story of man's continual failure in responsibility, and this is usually immediately when given to him. This particular failure of men sleeping, which is said to be from the beginning sprouting of the crop (vs. 25-26), permitted the enemy to do his work.

As believers we are mostly naïve concerning the work of Satan. When Jesus appears again to this world, He will destroy the instruments of evil that the devil will have brought forth on the earth to oppose Him. He will throw them into the lake of fire, destroy their armies, and bind Satan in chains in the bottomless pit (Rev. 19:17-20:3). It has to be this way for the government of God to spread out over the entire earth under the authority and kingdom of the Son of Man (Dan. 2:34-35). Satan can no longer be the god of this world, nor can he be allowed to remain in the world to continue his rebellions against God. Before Christ's return there is a period of great tribulation, during which time Satan is removed from the heavens (Rev. 12:7-12). Again, it has to be this way because the body of Christ is brought into the heavens prior to this, by the rapture of the church.[62]

In considering the low state and condition of the church world, we cannot forget about the influence of the power of darkness, and the active instruments of the devil who rules the darkness of this world. Without considering this, our estimate of the condition of Christendom in the world will be false. From the beginning of time, there has been no greater source of evil and alienation from God than the power of the adversary. We should have a serious consideration of what Satan's intentions are at this present time. He planted tares in the crop in the field. His work is to falsify the overall profession and testimony of the corporate entity. He does this for the corruption and ruin of professing Christianity. He cannot touch or harm the wheat, for this is the work of God.[63] However, the crop is a corporate entity that bears responsibility to God on earth, and it is the devil's intention to bring evil and corruption in. Satan is in the heavens now (Rev. 12:3, 12:7, Eph. 6:12). He is there for the purpose of ruining the church world.

How does he accomplish this task? While he is still in the heavens it is not the time for murder, rebellion, idolatry, and outright blasphemy – this will be the character of his final evils in civil power *after he is removed from the heavens and cast down to the earth* (Rev. 13). While in the heavens he acts as a serpent, beguiling and deceiving, lying with false teachings of unsound doctrine, spreading leaven in the professing church.[64] The point is this – from the beginning of the kingdom of heaven and the crop existing in the field, while Satan is still in the heavens, he is concentrating his efforts towards the internal corruption of Christendom.

Satan holds a specific enmity against Christ and those things associated with Christ. He knows that the true church – those sealed by the Holy Spirit individually and then baptized by the Holy Spirit into the one body – is Christ in the world (Eph. 1:13, I Cor. 12:12-13, I John 4:17). Although he cannot touch the divine purpose of God concerning the true church, he can corrupt the vessel that contains the body of Christ on the earth. This he does by corrupting professing Christianity. Satan has the following two evil effects while in the heavens:

- He is the god of the unbelieving world, the spirit who works in the sons of disobedience (Eph. 2:2). Satan in the heavenlies is his place of authority and power as ruling the world, and all things that are part of the world – the rulers of the darkness of this world. At this time the world is under his sway and does his bidding, while God restricts and restrains the fullest development of evil (II Thess. 2:6-7). Yet evil is progressing and ripening to the end. The world is not under the sway of God or the gospel. God has condemned the world that Satan is god over (John 12:31). In saving anyone and giving them eternal life, it is God choosing them out of the world that He has already condemned (John 15:19, 17:1-3).

- He is the antipriest in the heavens as the accuser of the true church (Rev. 12:10). Although all his accusations hold no substance before God, yet his presence in the heavens allows for the true church to suffer persecution, tribulation, and hatred while still on the earth. This would be considered suffering with Christ, because He suffered the same while He was in the world. Also while the devil is still in the heavens he works by the mystery of lawlessness in the professing church – secret subtle hidden corruption in doctrine and works (II Thess. 2:7). The ripening of this principle has provided the opportunity for God to characterize professing Christianity as mystery Babylon (Rev. 17:5). We also cannot forget that the devil sowed tares in Christendom early in its history.

Satan in the heavens is for the work of corrupting the heavenly calling. You see, Satan knows that the earthly calling in Israel has been presently set aside. When he is cast out of the heavens and he is on the earth, he must turn all his attention to destroying the earthly calling of Israel.[65] Why? It is because at that time the heavenly calling of the true church will have been fulfilled in God's sovereign power – physically fulfilled through the rapture and glorifying of the body of Christ to the heavens. The true church brought to the heavens is the reason he is removed and cast down to the earth. The body of Christ will replace the devil and his angels in heavenly authority with Christ over the millennial earth (Heb. 2:5).

Satan in the heavens, as the accuser of the brethren, brings certain consequences on the earth for the true church. His accusations and power in heavenly places result in trials and persecutions. Satan in the heavens presently means the body of Christ suffers on the earth. The church's struggle and warfare is carried out on the earth, while she remains here and as believers in these bodies of flesh. However, the weapons of our warfare are not in the flesh. We overcome the accuser by the word of our testimony and the blood of the Lamb, even unto death if necessary (Rev. 12:11). Yet the struggle for the true church is carried on in suffering because Satan remains in the heavens (Rom. 8:18, 5:3-4, II Cor. 4:7-11, 17, and 12:9-10).

The Spoiled Crop in the Field

It is the Lord's will that the mixture of wheat and tares remains 'as is' until His separation and judgments that come at the end of the age. His instructions are, *"Let both grow together until the harvest."* Man cannot be trusted to separate things. He forbids any attempts by His servants at separating the evil, saying, *"No, lest while you gather up the tares you also uproot the wheat with them"* (vs. 28-30). This is the Lord's will, and it is revealed by His words in the parable and the interpretation He gives.[66] Unfortunately, throughout the history of the church world, there have been many instances where the Lord's words were not obeyed, and men have taken authority unrighteously into their own hands and evil ensued.

To the spiritually minded believer, the presence of tares means the presence of evil and corruption. The crop in the field is a spoiled crop. Tares are weeds that multiply, easily grow, and dominate. They are in fact Satan's work and Satan's representatives. The crop is overrun by its corruption. All the time before the harvest the kingdom of heaven on the earth exists as an unholy mixture of good and bad in the world. The crop is all of professing Christianity, all that professes Christ. The crop is not the body of Christ – this would be the wheat only. The crop in the field is a much larger corporate body that contains and encompasses the smaller body of Christ. The profession of the name of Christ by the entire crop is reason why this corporate entity bears responsibility before God.

The Will of God Concerning the Spoiled Crop

For all Christians what is of importance is to have an accurate spiritual and moral assessment of the crop in the field. Every true believer is a grain of wheat in this crop growing in the field. The only assessment of value is God's. Only what God says, only what God judges, only what His Word already declares, is of any substance in the matter. You do not have to seek God in prayer to know His thoughts about the crop – He has already declared His opinion. You do not need to seek God in prayer to know what He wants to do about it – this He has already declared as well.[67]

- *"Let both grow together until the harvest..."* (Matt. 13:30) This is the mind of God for the present time. God planted the wheat and His work cannot fail. The wheat does just fine through the entire time of the parable. But the work of the enemy in bringing in tares has spoiled and corrupted the overall crop. In considering the crop there are other understandings and dynamics in play, other than the sovereign work of God in the wheat that cannot fail. There is responsibility and failure by the overall crop, and then separation and judgment of the corporate entity by God. Also, men are forbidden to separate the crop (Matt. 13:28-29). It is not man's work to do. The mind of God is that the crop stays as a mixture of good and bad until the end of the age, and men cannot be trusted to separate in responsibility.

- If the crop remains 'as is' until the end of the age, then its witness before the world is falsified by the evil that is present. The light that Christendom is to be to the world, a lighted city on a hill, is also compromised by the present evil and corruption. The crop is not in good shape and we should never presume that it is. It is spoiled by the evil and corruption that has come in, and it will remain spoiled until the end of the age.

- At the time of harvest there will be a separation of the mixed crop. *'...I will say to the reapers, "First gather together the tares and bind them in bundles to burn them..."* (Matt. 13:30) The tares are gathered and bundled and left in the world. They are to be burnt – this is their judgment from God. Seeing that the reapers are angels, we know this work of separation is not man's work, but the work of God.

- *"...but gather the wheat into my barn."* (Matt. 13:30) The detail added in the interpretation that goes beyond the substance of the parable is, *"Then the righteous will shine forth as the sun in the kingdom of their Father..."* (Matt. 13:43) The wheat are removed from the world, but notice, they shine forth in the kingdom of their Father, not in the kingdom of the Son of Man on earth. The parable speaks distinctly of the kingdom of the Son of Man when He says, *"The Son of Man will send out His angels, and they will gather out of His Kingdom all things that offend..."* This is on the earth. However the wheat is taken to the house of the Father in the heavens. This is where the kingdom of their Father is. It is in the heavens that the sons will shine as the Sun – the Son of the Father, the Son of God (John 20:17).

The four bullet points above answer the question, 'what will God want to do about the crop?' This is His mind and intention. It is His work, and notice, man is not involved in any of it. It is all that God does to fulfill His purpose and plans.

There simply is no reason for man to boast when we consider the kingdom of heaven in the parable of the wheat and tares. The only thing that man did was *'while men slept the enemy came and sowed tares among the wheat.'* The only thing that resulted from what man did is the evil and corruption present in the external body of Christendom. Are there any words in the parable relating to the improvement of the crop over time before the time of harvest? Is there found in the parable the promise of revival of the state of the spoiled crop?

The Public Effect in the World of the established Kingdom

Then Jesus tells the multitudes two more parables of the kingdom of heaven before He sends them away and retired to the house to speak with His disciples privately.

Matthew 13:31-33

(31) "Another parable He put forth to them, saying: "The kingdom of heaven is like a mustard seed, which a man took and sowed in his field, (32) which indeed is the least of all the seeds; but when it is grown it is greater than the herbs and

becomes a tree, so that the birds of the air come and nest in its branches."

(33) Another parable He spoke to them: "The kingdom of heaven is like leaven, which a woman took and hid in three measures of meal till it was all leavened."

In this setting these two parables finish off what He tells to the multitudes, that is, what He speaks to the world. After the parable of the Sower, the three parables that follow carry a decidedly worldly perspective – they unfold the outward apparent effects, the external appearance of the kingdom of heaven in the world, consequent to the sowing of the seed. In a similar way that the world views Christendom as a large unified crop growing in the field, it also sees it from small and insignificant beginnings growing up into a great world power. This is the great tree in the field rising up from such a small seed. In the book of Daniel the use of a large tree in its prophetic language was indicative of the great earthly power of Babylon (Dan. 4:10-12, 20-22). In the allegory of the tree, professing Christianity grows up to be a great worldly power. All kinds of things, both good and bad, will find their sustenance and habitation there.

Christendom: the Great Tree in the Field

The viewpoint of the great tree is what Christendom becomes on the earth and in the world through the work of man. This is not the work of God. Long before the kingdom of heaven was taught, God had separated the 'principle of calling' from the 'principle of civil government.' He did this in Israel when Jehovah removed His presence from Solomon's temple and gave world government to the Gentiles. The two principles will only be united again in Israel in the millennium, under the authority and throne of the Son of Man, but not until then.

When Christendom, through the irresponsible works of men, aspired to world power and wealth, it did so by prostituting itself with the kings and nations of the earth (Rev. 17:1-2). This hardly constituted the mind and will of God, nor did it garner approval from Him. In prophetic language this is known as adultery and fornication (Rev. 2:20-22, 17:4). Christendom had a professed relationship with the Father and the Son. Yet in its history, Christendom showed closer ties with the world, and with the world's intoxicating power and deceitful riches. In the parable of the Sower, the birds eating the seed on the wayside were interpreted by Jesus as the wicked one coming and snatching away. The great tree housing all kinds of birds cannot be interpreted any differently. Satan and his agents come to professing Christianity and have their habitation there.

False Doctrine Spreads in Christendom

The last of these first four parables is the church world infiltrated by false doctrine, and by its end all three lumps are saturated. Leaven, in scripture, usually is reference to false teachings (Matt. 16:5-12, Gal. 5:7-9). Paul told Timothy *'the time will come when they will not endure sound doctrine...'* (II Tim. 4:3) That time has come already. The church world does not endure the truth of God, but has developed its own teachings by which it is comfortable. All three lumps are saturated, and this is not with good, but with evil.

What follows this is what Jesus shares in private with His disciples. The teaching takes on a divine perspective of the kingdom of heaven – the thoughts of God and the mind of Christ (which believers are taught by the Holy Spirit they possess - I Cor. 2:10-16). Also remember the interpretation of the parable of the tares of the field was given to the disciples privately (Matt. 13:36). Any interpretation reveals the true meaning of the allegories used in the particular parable or prophecy. God reveals the mysteries of the kingdom of heaven to the disciples, those who were chosen by God (Matt. 13:11).

The True Church – the Eternal Purpose and Counsel of God

Matthew 13:44-46

(44) "Again, the kingdom of heaven is like treasure hidden in a field, which a man found and hid; and for joy over it he goes and sells all that he has and buys that field."

(45) "Again, the kingdom of heaven is like a merchant seeking beautiful pearls, (46) who, when he had found one pearl of great price, went and sold all that he had and bought it."

The treasure hidden in the field is the body of Christ. It is no longer an allegory depicting all of Christendom on the earth, but instead, depicting only the true church. This is what is important to God. This is what is of value to the Son of Man, for He sells all that He has in order to buy the field where it is hidden. The Son of Man pays the greatest of prices to purchase the field, but it is the church, the hidden treasure, that He desires to possess. The Son of Man's affections are for the church, for Christ loves the church and gave Himself for it (Eph. 5:25).

God sees the church as a treasure, for His thoughts concerning her is a view of the church in His eternal purposes and counsels. Christ will present it to Himself a glorious church, not having spot or wrinkle or any such thing, but that it should be holy and without blemish in the presence of God (Eph. 1:4, 5:27). The treasure is Christ's body and is His bride, and it is destined for the glory of God (Col. 1:26-27, Rom. 5:1-2, Eph. 1:12-14).

The parable of the pearl of great price follows similar reasoning. The pearl is the true church and the Son of Man sells all to buy it. Its value to Him is beyond question or comparison. He gives up all that is His to have it.[68]

An important point of understanding is that both the treasure in the field and the pearl of great price are 'hidden'. The body of Christ, the true church, is hidden in the world. For that matter, the body is hidden in the spoiled crop of Christendom in the world. By the eye of faith the believer knows that it is there, that it exists, but he cannot really see it as it is hidden. We cannot see the body of Christ as God does, for He knows those who are His and all those He has sealed (II Tim. 2:19, Eph. 1:13, Rom. 8:9). The contrast of great value to see and understand is that the treasure and pearl are unseen in the world, while the crop, the great tree, and the three measures of meal are readily apparent to anyone's eyesight.

The Parable of the Dragnet – the Separation and Judgment

Matthew 13:47-50

(47) "Again, the kingdom of heaven is like a dragnet that was cast into the sea and gathered some of every kind, (48) which, when it was full, they drew to shore; and they sat down and gathered the good into vessels, but threw the bad away. (49) So it will be at the end of the age. The angels will come forth, separate the wicked from among the just, (50) and cast them into the furnace of fire. There will be wailing and gnashing of teeth."

The last of the seven parables is the dragnet thrown into the sea that gathers some of every kind, both good and bad. Again, this is professing Christianity that is gathered in the net that is thrown into the sea (world). It only gathers until the net is full. Our understanding has to be that there are plenty more left behind in the sea. Drawing the net to the shore when it is full is the time of harvest at the end of the age (Matt. 13:39). This is the time when the tares will be separated from the wheat. Here the separation is portrayed as the good being gathered into vessels, but the bad is thrown away (v. 48). The parallels between the parable of the tares and this parable are fairly obvious.

- Both parables picture the world – in the one it is a field, in the other it is the sea.

- Both parables picture Christendom as a corporate entity in the world – in one it is the spoiled crop, in the other it is the net that is dragged to the shore when full.

- Both parables picture Christendom as a mixture of both good and bad in the world.

- Both parables depict the same exact separation and judgment of professing Christianity. The bad is discarded and burnt. In both cases the good is placed in a special place.

The parable of the dragnet is told in the first two verses (vs. 47, 48). Jesus gives us the interpretation in the following two verses (vs. 49-50). This parable doesn't deal much with the time the net is still in the sea,[69] but rather focuses on the time of separation and judgment by the angels at the end of the age. The exact same phrasing concerning the final results for the bad is used in both interpretations of the two parables – *cast them into the furnace of fire where there will be wailing and gnashing of teeth* (Matt. 13:42, 50). The parable of the dragnet particularly focuses on the judgment and condemnation of the bad of professing Christianity.

Matthew 13:51-52

Jesus said to them, "Have you understood all these things?"

They said to Him, "Yes, Lord."

Then He said to them, "Therefore every scribe instructed concerning the kingdom of heaven is like a householder who brings out of his treasure things new and old."

If you are taught by the Spirit and understand these things, then you'll be a scribe instructed in the mysteries of the kingdom of heaven. Every true believer has been given to know... (Matt. 13:11).[70]

Chapter 2: Endnotes

[53] Not only does Jesus say that Isaiah's prophecies are fulfilled in Israel, but Paul in speaking to the Jews in Rome at the end of the book of Acts (Acts 28:23-29) essentially says the same thing – *"The Holy Spirit spoke rightly through Isaiah the prophet..."* This was after Jesus on the cross interceded for Israel, saying, *"Father, forgive them, for they do not know what they do."* (Luke 23:34). The book of Acts, particularly the first eight chapters, represents Israel's last chance for a Messianic kingdom under the principle of responsibility. With the stoning of Stephen there is a definite turning by God to the Gentiles in the book of Acts, and you can see the transition between dispensations for yourself in the Scriptures. Israel committed sin against the Holy Spirit, refusing and rejecting His testimony of Jesus, and it would not be forgiven them (Acts 7:51). The kingdom of God is taken from Israel (Matt. 21:43). But with Paul in Rome this turning of God to the Gentiles and the setting aside of Israel is obvious in his words (Acts 28:28). The destruction of Jerusalem and the temple by the Romans in 70 AD is the obvious bringing in of physical judgment by God to end the Jewish dispensation, to end the practice of Judaism, and to set aside the Jews in a very physical way – death by the sword or scattering into the nations (Luke 21:20-24, Matt. 22:7).

If we are spiritually perceptive we will see the transition between the two dispensations in many biblical passages. Examples may be seen in the Lord's use of the two titles – Messiah for the Jewish dispensation and Son of Man for the kingdom of heaven in mystery. You see this in both the general use and specific use of the titles. Generally speaking Jesus rarely uses the Messiah title; only once with the Samaritan woman at the well, and away from Judea and Jerusalem (John 4:25-26). Otherwise, the few times it does come up it is always someone else speaking it. He never really embraces it for He knows it must be set aside. In specific instances when the title is forced into the conversation around Him, He quickly puts the title behind Him and immediately references the Son of Man title in its place. This you can see in all the following passages (John 1:48-51, Matt. 16:20-28, 26:59-64, Luke 9:20-22, 22:66-70). The proper Jewish understanding of the Messiah was when He came to Israel He would stay forever (John 12:34). But the Son of Man would be lifted up and He would go away, that is, back to heaven. This they did not understand at all. Neither did the disciples understand, even though they were closest to Him (Luke 18:31-34).

There are many examples and passages in Matthews' gospel related to the transitioning between the two dispensations – Matt. 12:43-50, 13:1-3, 13:11-17, 13:24-53, 17:1-13, 21:18-19, 21:33-44, 22:2-9, 23:13, 23:37-39, 24:1-2 are just a few. The passage in Matt. 11:7-15 is a particularly interesting one concerning the two dispensations. *"For all the prophets and the law prophesied until John."* This is when the Jewish dispensation ends, with the coming of the Baptist. From the days of John the Baptist it has been the kingdom of heaven at hand. Then Jesus says that John is greater than all the prophets and all those born of women; yet the least one in the kingdom of heaven is greater than him. How is this? The least one in the kingdom of heaven is born of God. This will always be greater than the greatest born of women. The last point of the passage is figurative, dealing with the two kingdoms – the future Messianic kingdom for Israel and the kingdom of heaven – and how Elijah, in figure, will precede both kingdoms in time (Mal. 4:5-6, Rev. 11:3-12, Matt. 11:14, Luke 1:17). John the Baptist is Elijah in figure, for the kingdom of heaven at hand (Matt. 3:1-2). This does not negate the one in the spirit of Elijah that is yet to come during the coming tribulation, associated with the future Messianic kingdom in Israel.

[54] The entire Jewish dispensation was based on the responsibility of man to be obedient to God. Therefore it was based on what man could do and his obedience; *it had nothing to do with the sovereign work of God.* The entire dispensation was the testing of man in the flesh by God. He was looking for fruit. God never found the fruit He was looking for. This Jewish dispensation represents the testing of man in Adam, and whether by human effort and accomplishment man could please God and produce human righteousness by the law as a fruit unto God. He gave Israel every advantage possible. However, God's testing in the Jewish dispensation proved that the idea of good still residing in man was totally false. The testing proved that it was impossible for man to produce any fruit pleasing to God.

Also then, by specifically testing Israel in responsibility and showing their failure in it, Israel could not have the kingdom of God through human responsibility. They could not have the kingdom through their disobedience to the law. They could not have the kingdom by rejecting the Son who was sent to them by the God they claimed to worship and serve (John 8:42-47). Jesus was sent unto His own as the Jewish Messiah, according to promises and prophecy. They rejected Him and would not have Him as King (Messiah). The Jewish dispensation had failed, not because of sovereign grace or God's workmanship failing – this would be impossible. The dispensation fails because the basis of the law and the Messianic kingdom, at that time, was settled on and propped up upon the principle of human responsibility.

Are we not able to see that these two things – the law with Israel and the Messianic kingdom with Israel – will be made good by God in the millennium to come? At that time they will be based on an entirely different principle with Israel – sovereign power and grace of God.

This was the testing of the principle of responsibility that, in my opinion, the doctrinal systems devised by men fail to address with much understanding. I referred to the doctrinal systems of men in the first chapter-endnotes #'s 46 and 49. Also, the thought of good still to be found in man after the fall is a foundational tenant of the Judaizing and Arminian leaven that has spread throughout Christian doctrine today. This thinking prevailed in Judaism and lead to the Jews thinking they were justified by the doing of the law. It leads to the Judaizing of the Christian faith, in the days of Paul as well as today. The leaven also is the reason why the doctrinal systems do not properly see God testing man in responsibility, and that He did so from the fall of man to the rejection of Messiah. Before the cross, God's testing was completed, and so it ended as to its purpose. He then sets Israel aside and condemns the world and Satan (John 12:31).

The ways of God in His dealings with man at this point, at the cross, take on a dramatic change. God brings in sovereign grace through the blood of Christ and His one eternal sacrifice. This is not human responsibility, nor is it any longer the testing of human responsibility. However, the Arminian and Judaizing leaven of human accomplishment will not stand for this. It perverts the principle of sovereign grace and the true work of God by mixing human responsibility with it. This exalts man and robs glory from God, and changes grace into an unholy mixture, something very different and unrecognizable from sound biblical teaching (Rom. 11:5-6, 4:2-5). The leaven creates a vicious circle where it falsely pictures God attempting the same failures over and over again, only now with the Gentiles. That is why the cross must be seen as a complete change in the ways of God dealing with man. It is a complete change from what God did before.

Those who preach that God is always the same and never changes simply display their spiritual ignorance of the verses they quote (Mal. 3:6, Heb. 13:8). When evil filled the earth and every thought of man's heart was evil continually, God destroyed the habitable earth with a flood. He then makes a covenant with creation to never do this again. Do we not acknowledge this as a change in God's ways? When God's presence was removed from Israel and the earth, and Nebuchadnezzar destroyed the temple and Jerusalem, God gave the principle of government to the Gentiles and their prophetic statue (Dan. 2:31-33). This was a change of God's ways in His government of the earth. We have to acknowledge this as a change!

The cross of Christ represents the greatest change in God's ways ever! We cannot view God's dealings with man before the cross as the same as after the cross. If we do then the leaven has blinded us. The leaven will have us believing that God is using the same principle — human responsibility — and the only difference now is God turning to the Gentiles in order to give them their fair shake and opportunity. The evil leaven will have us explaining the success of the gospel among the Gentiles in some strange thoughts and in some strange ways — by human responsibility, which is the Gentiles doing better than the Jews in some type of human difference that resulted in the better success. How else can the leaven explain the difference, except by some form of human performance? And man gets his glory and reason to boast, and it is all evil reasoning of the human mind.

Now here are the questions of great importance: Why would God set up a new dispensation just to test the same old stuff? Why would the principles of the new dispensation be the same as the old? If human effort, human accomplishment, and human responsibility miserably failed in Israel and the Jewish dispensation, why would God base His new planting and subsequent dispensation on the same principles that are obviously doomed for failure? Why would God repeat exactly the same thing? Well, the answer is that He doesn't. The dispensation of the kingdom of heaven begins with the sovereign work of God — the Son of Man plants the wheat (Matt. 13:37). It is not based on the work and effort of man as the Jewish dispensation was in its entirety. Works are not grace, and the law is not of faith (Rom. 4:1-5, 11:5-6, Gal. 3:11-12). The only way to define grace is as the sovereign work of God, the sovereign choice of God. Grace does whatever it pleases in goodness and this according to the nature and character of Him who acts in grace. Matthew 13 makes this fairly clear.

The principles of the dispensation of the kingdom of heaven are the sovereign choice of God, the sovereign grace of God, and this is the sovereign work of God in planting and bringing forth the wheat. He preserves the wheat as wheat in the spoiled crop of the field, and then He gathers the wheat at the end of the age. *This is the principle in the kingdom of heaven as regards God's work only.* Even faith is not something we do. If it is something we do then it is a work of man, and only wages from God can be coupled with it. Faith is not of ourselves; it is the gift of God (Eph. 2:8), so there is no human boasting by human effort and working (Eph. 2:9). God gives the measure of faith (Rom. 12:3) so we do not think of ourselves more highly than we ought to think.

The kingdom of heaven is seen by man as a large crop in the field – Christendom. The crop is a mixture of different works – God's work, man's work, and the devil's. Only God's work involves the new principle of sovereign grace through faith, based on an already accomplished eternal sacrifice and redemption. Only God's work has eternal results. Man's failures are still seen associated with the kingdom in general, as long as the crop is still sitting in the field and the time is still prior to the harvest. The tares planted by Satan are associated with the kingdom as well (Matt. 13:25). As we know, these last two things are not the work of God and are not based on the new principle of sovereign grace. When man looks at the kingdom of heaven these things are all mixed together in what he sees, and so he associates all as part of the kingdom. But God can easily distinguish His work from that of man and the devil (Matt. 7:21-23, 8:10-12, 11:11, 13:11, 13:37-38, 13:44-46, 25:11-12).

It is a Biblical understanding then, that the two dispensations are based on principles that are opposite in definition. It is not that the principle of human responsibility does not still have its effects during the new dispensation – it certainly does. *This entire book you are reading is documenting from Scripture God's accounting of the effect of man's responsibility on the progress and failure of the present dispensation.* Yet responsibility is simply not the basis of the new dispensation, and has no effect on the work of God, nor does it ever change the final results. Also of importance to understand is that even though human responsibility still exists and even has its deleterious effects, it isn't being tested by God as the basis of receiving promises and eternal blessings (Rom. 4:13-25, Gal. 3:7, 9, 16-18, 22, Heb. 6:12). God plants the wheat. The wheat stays as wheat all the time it is in the field. During the time of harvest the wheat is removed from the field. All three are the sovereign work of God alone – the planting, the preserving, and the removal of the wheat.

There is another important distinction between the two dispensations that needs to be noted. It will serve to clear up a lot of things that are improperly emphasized. During the Jewish dispensation the measure of God's favor towards the Jews was always *present physical blessings* seen both nationally and individually. Nationally this is seen in privileges such as dwelling in the land, the presence of God in their midst, freedom from Gentile rule, the population growing and multiplying as well as their vineyards and storehouses. Prosperity and health were always seen as the measure of God's favor for the individual Jew. Israel is the earthly calling of God. Their promises, covenants, and desired blessings reflect this. All their teachings, the law and the prophets, reflect this calling and emphasis.

The church is the heavenly calling of God, and so, God has provided every spiritual blessing in heavenly places for her. Although the olive tree provides favor from God presently for the Gentiles in a general and dispensational way, and Israel's fall means riches for the world (Rom. 11:12-17), the church's promises from God are in glory and beyond this present dispensation. Believers have been justified by faith and have no guilt, but rather peace with God. Through faith we have access to grace to stand in this present dispensation. But where we rejoice is in the hope of the glory of God (Rom. 5:1-2). Jesus Christ is in us as our present life, but also our hope of glory and immortality (Col. 1:27, II Cor. 5:4). Paul tells believers that the sufferings of this present time are not worthy to be compared with the glory which shall be revealed in us (Rom. 8:18). This is what a walk of faith is, where we do not see, in this present dispensation, the things God has promised to us, the things hoped for. Yet we still believe the promises, for God is not a man that He should lie. And besides this, He has given us His Spirit as the present deposit, guaranteeing that He will be faithful to fulfill all the future promises to us (Eph. 1:13-14, Rom. 8:11, 23, II Cor. 1:20-22, 5:1-5).

[55] **Arminian doctrine – its true source.** Arminian teaching and philosophy is not Scriptural truth, and is simply another form of Judaizing the Christian faith. It is interesting how widespread its acceptance is in professing Christianity today. By their religion and law the Jews were convinced that they had accomplished righteousness before God, and therefore would receive life. God has proven this idea wrong, although He showed much patience and forbearance with man in the process. Israel practiced the law for over fifteen hundred years, yet when God came to the fig tree He couldn't find any fruit (Matt. 21:18-19). Then He cursed the tree. This was the end of Judaism, the end of the religion of the Jews. There was no profit in it. God only found faults with the first covenant – transgressions, unrighteousness, and a multiplying of sins (Heb. 8:7-8, Rom. 5:20). Why? The first covenant was based entirely on human responsibility!

The Judaizing of Christianity is by making additions to the simplicity of the work of Christ, whatever these additions may be. They mostly take the form of something man can do, something man can accomplish – human responsibilities. These are the confidences of the flesh the Scriptures speak of (Phil. 3:2-7). Sometimes it is a philosophy or way of thinking that in a general way, encourages man to do things in order to feel better about himself and his status. The religions that man accepts and embraces are the religions he can do, that is, those based on his own initiative and performance. This is what Judaism is. Christianity is the opposite of this.

Judaism is the religion of the Jews. It is God's religion given to man in the flesh. Man in the flesh is a sinner. In the flesh there is no good thing (Rom. 7:18). Man in the flesh cannot please God (Rom. 8:7-8). Man in the flesh is man in the first Adam. Judaism is God's religion given to man in the first Adam. Christianity is for man in the Second Adam. There is a world of difference between the first Adam and the Second Adam.

Arminian teaching is the doctrine of human accomplishment and self-exaltation, and by it man dishonors God and robs Him of His glory. It is 'the leaven' that penetrates, saturates, and dominates Christendom in the time of the kingdom of heaven in mystery (Matt. 13:33). It is a form of humanism. When man was in the garden in innocence, his unholy desire was to exalt himself to be like God, his Creator. He came to this by listening to and believing the lies of the devil, *"...you will be like God..."* This lusting to exalt himself has been in fallen man's heart ever since.

Satan is the source of the Arminian teaching. These are the reasonings and philosophies of the carnal mind of man in the flesh, resulting from believing the lies of the devil. Satan is the one who plants the thoughts and ideas that man is not as utterly depraved as God actually states in His Scriptures. We see him doing this in the beginning, *"You will not surely die."* And so he is always casting doubt concerning what God has actually said and declared. *Surely it is not so bad; surely man's will is still free; surely you are not totally lost; surely your righteousness is not all filthy rags; surely God will not judge you, after all He is love; surely this is not what God is saying about you; did God really say that?* Satan has been a liar from the beginning (John 8:44). We think these things are actually sound Scriptural teachings, yet their source is the lies of the enemy.

[56] The teachings of the kingdom of heaven are for the sons of the kingdom – the wheat planted by the Son of Man in the field of the world (Matt. 13:24, 37-38). These sons are all the workmanship of God created in Christ Jesus for good works, which God prepared beforehand that we should walk in them (Eph. 2:10). The teachings are all the good works we are

to walk in as sons of the kingdom of heaven (Matt. 7:21). They are not teachings on how one becomes a son of God – this is by faith in Christ and the workmanship of God (Gal 3:26, John 6:37, 44). By faith we are the new creation of God in Christ Jesus, the second Adam. The teachings from Jesus concerning the kingdom of heaven represent the responsibility of those who are made sons in the kingdom, sons of the Father (Matt. 5:45). It is the responsibility of sonship. This is where the believer's responsibility is found, in the relationship we have with the Father. But the Lord's teachings concerning the kingdom of heaven do not touch upon how we are made sons and born of God. Rather they speak of our responsibility after becoming sons.

The teachings of the kingdom of heaven will only be accomplished by those who are new creations of God in the second Adam. God proved by testing Israel that man in the first Adam is totally lost and utterly depraved. The old teachings of Judaism were given to him and he could not obey them. That is why, in part, the Jewish dispensation came to an end, and we see this in the gospel of Matthew. God had finished His testing of man by the principle of responsibility through the law`. God had finished His testing of man in the flesh, and this is all Israel ever was, that is, man in Adam, man in the flesh. This is all that Judaism was – the teachings of old designed for man in the flesh, man in the first Adam, and the religion given to Israel. Judaism is given by God to man as part of the world. It is God's religion for the world, for man as part of the world. If you will closely read Galatians 4:1-5 you will see exactly this point – the law is the elements of the world, the weak and beggarly elements (Gal. 4:9), and only brings bondage.

[57] Another popular teaching that carries an Arminian flavor of human exaltation is replacing Jesus, the Son of Man, with us as the sowers of the Word. We make the same mistake when we see ourselves as the shepherd seeking the one lost sheep while the ninety-nine are left behind (Luke 15:3-7). The simple truth is that we are always the sheep and nothing different from this! The shepherd never sends the ninety-nine out to find the one that is lost. That would be madness if you would consider the ability of sheep to actually go and find another that is lost. God is the Shepherd and the Son of Man is the sower who plants. The work is of God and in His sovereignty.

We are only instruments used in His work of grace (I Cor. 15:10). We are only earthen vessels, so that the excellency of the power is of Him and not of us (II Cor. 4:7). We are given to preach the gospel, but all the work is of God and His sovereign grace. He prepares the soil of men's hearts, and does so before the Word enters in. Unless the Father draws the man, how can they come to Christ? (John 6:44) Unless the Father gives them to Christ, how can they come to Him? But all that are given by the Father to Christ will, in fact, come to Him (John 6:37). Christ gives them eternal life (John 17:2). Anything true and good that results from the preaching of the gospel is the sovereign work and grace of God through it. The excellency of any good result is of the power of God and not of us.

What is the other side of this coin? When we honestly look in Scripture as to the negative results of the gospel, it is he who does not believe that will be condemned (Mark 16:16, John 3:18-20). And look at what the apostle says – *"But even if our gospel is veiled, it is veiled to those who are perishing, whose minds the god of this age has blinded, who do not believe..."* (II Cor. 4:3-4) Why was the apostle content with this? Why didn't he use his authority in the name of Jesus and bind the devil and stop him from doing this? Why didn't he try harder, use different words, or pray more in preparation? These are the common thoughts of Evangelical Christianity inundated with the leaven. We do not even realize the biblical truths associated with the preaching of the gospel.

One final truth presented here – there is no possibility the wheat will ever be cast out. This is the work of God, and it will not fail. But when we see ourselves as the sower, then we entertain the idea that the eternal welfare and destiny of another individual is dependent on us, what we do, how we speak, what our presentation is, etc. These are arrogant thoughts of human boasting – that someone could be lost for all eternity based on what you do or do not do. This wasn't the case with Saul on the road to Damascus. God was there and God was working. He knows how to get along quite well even without the help of man.

[58] It is a remarkable thing to see how the sovereign choice of God is emphasized by the Lord's words in this chapter. In speaking of the multitudes of the Jews He says, *"Therefore I speak to them in parables, because seeing they do not see, and hearing they do not hear, nor do they understand. And in them the prophecy of Isaiah is fulfilled..."* There are no ifs, ands, or buts about His condemnation of their low state and condition. He isn't thinking if He tries a different method or uses different words that maybe some of the multitude will see, hear, and have a chance at perceiving (Matt. 13:11-16). He knows that these are not His sheep and have no chance at comprehending (John 10:14, 10:26-28). The words spoken to them become a testimony against them in judgment (John 12:47-48).

Farther on in the chapter the sovereign choice of God is emphasized again. This time it is a contrast between the Old Testament prophets and the privilege of the disciples (Matt. 13:16-17). Many prophets and righteous men of old were not blessed by the choice of God, as were these privileged disciples. God gave these blessed disciples eyes to see with, ears to hear with, and understanding of the mysteries of the kingdom of heaven (Matt. 13:11, 51-52).

[59] The parable found in Luke 19:12-27 was told by the Lord to counter the rising expectations of the disciples for a Messianic kingdom in Israel (Luke 19:11). The Jewish dispensation, which will eventually culminate in a Messianic kingdom in Israel and from Jerusalem, had to be set aside by God in order to bring forth the dispensation of the kingdom of heaven. Most of the parable contains the typical teachings and events related to the kingdom of heaven, except for an additional judgment found at its end. This added part is particularly the judgment of unbelieving Israel – those enemies of mine, who did not want me to reign over them (v.27). This added part is not properly the subject of the dispensation of the kingdom of heaven in mystery, but rather belongs to the Jewish one. That is probably why it is not prefaced by the words 'then the kingdom of heaven is likened to…' and not placed in Matthew's gospel by the Holy Spirit.

[60] The removal of the wheat from the field of the world and taking it to the barn, the Father's house, is the specific subject of the doctrinal teachings of the second book of this series. Its title is 'The Blessed Hope of the Church'.

[61] Nothing in God's creation had the ability to change its nature, and could only produce after itself. Every creature, including man, was bound to keep its first estate. Only God could change His nature – the Son of God, being in the form of God, but then taking on human flesh and the form of a servant, He came in the likeness of men for the reason of death (Phil. 2:6-8). The Son, who was high and sovereign, not of this creation, but rather the Creator of it, could come down in grace, humbling Himself, and take on another nature. By this work of redemption the believer now has a changed nature, and this is the work of God. Our nature is changed from the first Adam to the nature of the second Adam, Jesus Christ. We are born of God (John 1:13) and are the new creation of God (II Cor. 5:17), and made partakers of the divine nature morally (II Pet. 1:4).

Arminian thought is that we can change the tares into wheat. Further, it is also Arminian thought that the wheat can become a tare over time. Although these represent quite opposite results, they are both examples of pretentious and foolish thinking that has no Scriptural support. What is born of God is the work of God, and it will stay that way. What is the work of Satan as tares in professing Christianity will stay that way as well. I don't believe the parable can read any other way, nor do the Scriptures teach anything different from this.

The teaching of Evolution is also similar to the leaven. It maintains that all living things evolve and change their natures with the passage of time and under the right circumstances. By this type of philosophy man exalts himself in his own mind, and this, against God and the Word of God.

God knows if a tree is good or bad without waiting to see its fruit. The good trees are His children, the bad trees are not, and this is in His sovereignty. The waiting for the fruit is for our benefit and safety – you will know them by their fruits (Matt. 7:15-23). It does not say that God only knows them by their fruit, and therefore God has to wait and see what is produced. That thought would deny and diminish God, His attributes and character. We are the ones who have to judge by their fruits, and therefore must wait to see the fruits in order to determine whether the tree is good or bad. However, the last two verses in the passage help to explain God's position through Jesus, the Son of Man (Matt. 7:22-23). When certain Christian works are presented as fruit by some, He says, *"I never knew you..."* From the beginning He knows whether the tree is good or bad, whether it is His or not. How does He know this? It is more than just that He is God and He knows. It is because He is the one who planted the wheat. He did not plant the tares. He knows those that are His, as His own work and planting. He knows who planted the tares. He knows that all things produce after their own kind. If there was going to be wheat, He had to plant it, and if there are tares He knows exactly from whom and from where these came (Matt. 13:28). He doesn't think, "I must have had some bad seed to begin with." (Matt. 13:26-27) So He says to these, "I *never* knew you," because we find that He knows those that are His.

The fruit doesn't determine the tree. This is the Arminian leaven of human works and accomplishment, and is humanism. It is the tree, good or bad, in its original state as planted, which determines the fruit (Matt. 7:17-18). Things produce after their own kind. A bad tree only produces bad fruit. But our danger is how we do not know as God knows. Often the real fruit is covered over or our judgment of it is misled – sheep's clothing covering over wolves (Matt. 7:15) or the many things done in Christ's name as Christendom is prone to boast of (Matt. 7:22). So the Lord tells us this. We should judge by the fruits. We cannot know as He knows from the planting of the tree. It is for our good and our protection, and so that we may not be so easily deceived. The biblical principle running through the entire passage (Matt. 7:15-23) is that things produce after their own kind. The principle in the background of the passage is the sovereignty of God, and this mostly by a comparison in its contrast with human judgment and responsibility.

[62] The body of Christ seated in heavenly places in Christ is its proper place and position in the Father's house and in the government of God over the millennial earth (Eph. 2:6-7). We are the habitation of the Father in the heavens, the New Jerusalem, the city of His God, and the bride of the Lamb. In Revelation 4 the church is seen as twenty-four elders sitting on endowed thrones around the governmental throne of God in the heavens. This is where we function as kings and priests to His God and Father (Rev. 1:6). The habitation and scene of the glory of the church is the heavens, being blessed there with every spiritual blessing (Eph. 1:3). The church is the tabernacle God has set in the heavens for the Sun, and during the millennium the saved nations will walk in the light of it. This glory of the church will be manifested over the earth, and the earth will enjoy its blessings.

In the heavens all things will be subordinate to Christ and the church: the angels, principalities, powers, etc. The heavenly calling of the church in Christ, as well as our union with Him is seen in Ephesians 1:3-5 and 1:18-23. It is a calling and position far above all principality and power and might and dominion. The Father's purpose and intentions for the church in its calling is described in Ephesians 2:6-7 as well as in Ephesians 3:9-11. His intention is to make known through the church His manifold wisdom to all things in the heavens throughout the ages to come. All this is consequent to the church being raised and ascended, as physically united to Christ in the heavens. God's power towards us to accomplish this event has already been demonstrated by God raising Christ from the dead and exalting Him to His right hand in the heavenly places (Eph. 1:19-20). Jesus is the forerunner, who has entered in ahead of us (Heb. 6:19-20). Jesus is the firstborn among many brethren (Rom. 8:29). When these things begin to happen, Satan will know his time in the heavens is soon coming to an end.

[63] I make the statement that the devil cannot touch or harm the wheat, and I realize I must explain what I mean by this. Satan has no ability to destroy

the wheat or to foil God's intended purpose for the wheat. It is the work of the Son of Man and all that was planted comes up wheat. In the end all the wheat will be removed from the field as one, with no individual grains left behind. In this sense, Satan cannot harm or touch the wheat as to God's intended plan and purpose for it. However, in our walk on this earth it is the believer's responsibility to be strong in the Lord and in the power of His might, taking up the full armor of God, by which he is able to stand against all the deceptions of the devil. All believers are responsible to be able to wrestle against the powers of darkness that may come against them. All individual Christians are responsible for resisting the devil, so that he must flee from them. By the shield of faith the believer quenches all the fiery darts of the evil one (Eph. 6:16). Faith simply believes the words God has spoken and is confidence in God Himself. The fiery darts would be the words, lies, and deceptions of the enemy. If the individual believer fails in the above mentioned responsibilities, Satan can touch and harm him. But this is different from God's overall purpose and calling of the individual grains of wheat – God's purpose and calling cannot fail and is without repentance.

[64] While Satan is in the heavens he seduces and corrupts professing Christianity by his character as a beguiling serpent in lies and subtle deceptions. The forms of his wiles are not so much graven images of wood and stone, although these things still exist and persist in Christendom. Rather the forms of idolatry have been the love of money and the love of power. The church world has a colorful history of many sustained periods of time lusting after political and civil power, and with this the gain of worldly luxury and earthly riches. This is without mentioning the many unholy pretentions of ecclesiastical authority in its history and their accompanying abuses. Man has done these things in Christendom, and he has built an unholy mess that is beyond recovery.

The subject of political and civil power relating to professing Christianity is one of great interest. There were two great biblical principles found in Israel as a nation from its time at Mt. Sinai through the existence of Solomon's temple:

1. The government of God over the earth
2. The calling of God.

These two existed simultaneously in Israel as long as Jehovah was living on the earth and in their midst. Judah's captivity to Babylon marked the presence of Jehovah leaving the earth and the loss of His throne, the Ark of the Covenant. Civil world power was given by God to the Gentiles, and with Nebuchadnezzar and Babylon the times of the Gentiles begin (Luke 21:24). This marked the separation of these two principles by God. Israel would retain its calling for some time after this. However without the presence of Jehovah in their midst they would no longer be the center of the government of God over the earth. Their city and temple were destroyed. This serves as a symbolic consequence of the time of this separation.

God's intention and will is for these two principles to remain separated for the duration of 'the times of the Gentiles.' His purpose is to unite again these principles in Israel at the start of the millennium, when His presence and glory returns to the earth, and He again acknowledges Israel as His people (in their earthly calling). At that time Israel will again be the center of God's government of the earth.

The principle of God's calling of Israel is presently set aside by God. Their city and temple were destroyed by the Romans in 70 AD, and this serves as a symbolic consequence of the setting aside by God of this principle in this people. The calling of God is now with the believer/church and is heavenly. The government of God over the earth remains with the Gentiles until the 'times of the Gentiles' are over. God never intended the church world to seek and desire after governmental power on the earth. This is not the mind of God, nor His will. It is a violation of the principles that explain the counsels of God.

It is noticeable how men, in human responsibility in Christendom, have perverted the proper biblical understanding of both of these principles. The principle of calling is with the church presently, and not with Israel who has been set aside. God did not simply take Israel's calling and hand it to the church. Yet this is exactly what many theologians and teachers think and teach, in the character and leanings of all their doctrines. The church has a heavenly calling (Heb. 3:1, Eph. 1:3-5). To bring her calling down to the earth and make her earthly, like Israel, is the perversion of biblical truth. To have the church involved in civil power on the earth in the present evil age is also a perversion of biblical principles. Yet that is what you find the professing church has done in its history in this present age (Rev. 17:1-2).

[65] Rev. 12:12-13 explains this thought very well. In the heavens Satan is attempting to corrupt the heavenly calling of the true church. This he can't

do, so he corrupts professing Christianity on the earth. When he is cast out of the heavens and down to the earth, he must turn his attention to what is of the earth. This is the reviving of the Roman civil power in the Gentile earth, and the persecuting of the earthly calling that is Israel. Revelation 13 describes what he does in earthly civil power – the two beasts. Rev. 12:13 describes his immediate turning to persecute the Jewish remnant when he finds himself cast down to the earth: *"Now when the dragon saw he had been cast to the earth, he persecuted the woman..."* He has been cast out of the heavens and no longer has any influence over that which is heavenly. Down on the earth he desperately attempts to hold on to what he previously was the god over. This is specifically the world – unbelieving Jews and Gentiles. On the earth he must turn to that which is earthly.

When Satan is removed from the heavens he loses his anti-priestly character. He no longer can accuse the brethren. What is left for him, as cast down to the earth, are his anti-king and anti-prophet characters. This is what he brings forth in the two beasts (Rev. 13), especially when the second beast merges into the false prophet role. His three anti-characters mimic the three characters of Jesus Christ – prophet, priest, and king. Christ's role as prophet has been completed. He was the great prophet to Israel that Moses spoke of (Deut. 18:15, 18). If you think about it, these three roles present another interesting truth. He was Prophet to Israel; He is High Priest now for the church; He will be King of kings to the world.

When you know biblical principles and are taught by the Spirit, you can trace the above thoughts to their proper biblical conclusions. The character of prophet relates to prophecy, which in turn relates to the earth and Israel. That is why His role as prophet was for Israel and has been completed at His first coming. He was sent as the great Prophet to Israel. This has no application to the church. The church is the mystery of God hidden from prophecy and the prophets, and the church has a heavenly calling and is not of the earth or this world. Prophecy is of the earth and of the world, and therefore of Israel, which will be the central nation on the earth in the government of God. The prophet's role is only related to the earth and earthly things. The church is not made to be 'prophets' unto His God and Father (Rev. 1:6).

Jesus Christ is the King of Israel and will be so to the saved Jewish remnant upon His return. He is also the Messiah of prophecy to Israel, the Anointed One promised in covenant from God to sit on the throne of David, descending according to the flesh from David. He is the Prince of Israel in the millennial temple in Jerusalem of Ezekiel's prophecies. He is the Melchizedek priest for Israel: an eternal priest, a royal priest on a throne, whose blessings bring righteousness and peace to Israel. All His characters in some way do relate directly to Israel – the Prophet promised by Moses, the Melchizedek Priest who blesses Israel after the defeat of their enemies, and the Messianic King of the Jews. All are fulfilled on the earth and according to the prophecies.

All true believers are made kings and priests. But please notice we are not made kings and priest unto Christ, but unto His God and Father. We are priests unto the Father, because we are 'in Christ' and are privileged with the nearest place to the Father in His presence. We are nearest as priests because 'in Christ' we have unlimited access to the Father. We are kings unto the Father, because we have been given 'in Christ' conferred thrones of authority in the government of God our Father over all creation (Rev. 4). Our God and Father has raised us up together from the earth, and made us sit together in heavenly places in Christ Jesus (Eph. 2:6). This is not Israel and it is not on the earth. It is for the heavenly calling and is in the kingdom of our Father in the heavens (Matt. 13:43). This is all a result of the redemptive work of Jesus Christ. After His resurrection all believers were placed in the same position and relationship that He has with His God and Father (John 20:17).

Also, it should be known that once God fulfills the heavenly calling by taking the church into the heavens, He will once again recognize Israel as His people and acknowledge their earthly calling in the Jewish remnant. God will do so to be faithful to fulfill all His ancient promises to Israel. Satan knows this, and when cast down to the earth his intention will be to stop the earthly plan and prophecies concerning Israel.

[66] "It is the Lord's will..." becomes the easiest words for ministers to insert into their teachings to imply the authority of God and His seal of approval on what they are teaching. Often what is taught is based on assumptions made of the will of God, and these originating from man's thoughts instead of revealed from His Word. This parable depicting the kingdom of heaven, the wheat and tares in the field, is a case in point. The Lord's will concerning the crop is revealed in His own words, *"Let both grow together until the harvest..."* In all the words of the parable and its interpretation there is no evidence of some great work of man. The actual work that man was responsible for was the sleeping, which allowed the enemy to sow corruption and evil. There is no great work of man, by the gospel or otherwise, that rectifies the situation and condition of the spoiled crop

in the field, that is, of professing Christianity in the world. Only God's judgment of it in the time of harvest will set things correct.

Men will preach saying, "We have to do this or we have to do that, because it is the Lord's will. We will win America, and we will win the world for Christ." Really? Is that what the parable of the wheat and tares is teaching? Is that the prophetic progression of the kingdom of heaven on the earth depicted by the parable? From the parable do we understand there is a difference between the field itself and the spoiled crop in the field? Do we recognize the difference between the spoiled crop and the wheat contained in the crop? America is the world, it is the field. Why are we talking about saving the field when God's estimate of the crop in the field is one of growing corruption and evil? It is foolish talk.

Ephesians 1:9-14

(9) "...having made known to us the mystery of His will, according to His good pleasure which He purposed in Himself, (10) that in the dispensation of the fullness of the times He might gather together in one all things in Christ, both which are in heaven and which are on earth—in Him. (11) In Him also we have obtained an inheritance, being predestined according to the purpose of Him who works all things according to the counsel of His will, (12) that we who first trusted in Christ should be to the praise of His glory.

(13) In Him you also trusted, after you heard the word of truth, the gospel of your salvation; in whom also, having believed, you were sealed with the Holy Spirit of promise, (14) who is the guarantee of our inheritance until the redemption of the purchased possession, to the praise of His glory."

God has already revealed His will to us, and it was His good pleasure to do so. His counsels are His will. He had His counsels before the foundation of the world but they could not be revealed until Jesus Christ had come and finished His work and returned to heaven. His work on the cross was the foundational work on which all God's counsels depend. The counsels of God now come out, after redemption is accomplished, and righteousness fully established. Jesus returned to heaven and the Holy Spirit was sent and revealed everything. We have been given the Holy Spirit. If you want to know the will of God, His counsels are found in His Word, taught by the Holy Spirit. One more thought. God has ended His revelation, it is complete. It ended with the book of Revelation. He has already made known His will.

[67] I believe it might be a bit strange for some Christians to read that you actually go to God's word instead of prayer or other sources to find out the 'will of God' concerning the spoiled crop in the field. God's opinion of Christendom is already declared in His word, and this in view of its entire history on the earth. It is only a question of whether you have ears to hear what the Spirit is saying concerning Christendom.

The only reason anyone would argue with the above statements would be if you think it is possible to change the low state of Christendom, its failures in responsibility, and its eventual outcomes from what God has already declared in His word. Christendom has failed in its corporate responsibility, and no amount of human effort will be able to rescue it. It was human effort and human responsibility that quickly brought it to failure. You will never be able to change God's opinion of it, however well your intentions may be. You are hoping for something that is truly beyond the revelation of God's word, beyond His thoughts, and beyond the mind of Christ. There is no wisdom in that!

[68] The Son of God gave up all that was rightfully His in order to possess the church. *"...Christ Jesus, who, being in the form of God, did not consider it robbery to be equal with God, but made Himself of no reputation, taking the form of a servant, and coming in the likeness of men. And being found in appearance as a man, He humbled Himself and became obedient to the point of death, even the death of the cross."* (Phil. 2:5-8) Not only changing His state, lowering Himself for a time below the angels and coming in the form of man, but He submits Himself to death, which was the power of the enemy.

John 12:24

"Most assuredly, I say to you, unless a grain of wheat falls into the ground and dies, it remains alone; but if it dies, it produces much grain."

If He did not go to the cross He still would have been the Messiah and King of Israel. These were rightfully His after the flesh and according to prophecy. But in ruling over Israel, and even over the Gentile nations, He would have remained alone. His desire was not to be alone. It was a mystery, hidden from prophecy, but His greatest desire was to have the church, His body, His bride. He sets aside for a time all the things that were rightfully His – His title as Messiah, His earthly Messianic kingdom, and His earthly glory, and goes on to His death in order that He would not be alone. He would have and possess the church, and He would sell all to do so.

[69] The dragnet thrown into the sea can easily be viewed as the gospel in the hands of men (fishermen). Unfortunately, by the gospel, men gather out of the world both good and bad (see also Matt. 22:8-10). Man does this in his responsibility while on the earth and in the world. The preaching of the gospel has these results – it gathers, as a dragnet, both good and bad as a mixture. The separation on shore is the work of God and done by His angels, not by man. This is done in God's timing, when He views the net as full, which is at the end of the age and in the time of harvest.

Then again, the net, including all in it, can be viewed as simply the corporate entity of profession. It is the outward society of Christendom, and equal to the spoiled crop in the field. However, in the parable the net is cast into the sea by fishermen (an assumption), bringing thoughts of the gospel being preached in the world by men, and gathering its common results – a mixture of good and bad.

[70] There is an interesting sequence of events that leads up to Jesus' telling of the seven parables of the kingdom of heaven in Matthew 13, and even what He chooses to tell the multitudes in comparison to what He shares privately with His disciples. The Jewish dispensation is ending. In Matthew 12, Jesus condemns the Jewish leadership, calling them a brood of vipers (v. 34), and accusing them of blasphemy against the Holy Spirit (vs. 31). He condemns the nation of Israel by what He says in verse 32 – Israel sins against the Son of Man by hanging Him on a cross. For this, the Son of Man would pray and ask forgiveness – 'Father, forgive them, they know not what they do.' (Luke 23:34) Their sin against the Son of Man is forgiven by the intercession of Jesus on the cross. At Pentecost the Holy Spirit is sent to Israel to testify to that nation of a risen Messiah that they were guilty of putting to death (Acts 2:22-36). The nation, as a whole, rejects the testimony of the Holy Spirit. Here the nation is guilty of sinning against the Holy Spirit, and Israel would not be forgiven this (Acts 7:51).

He calls Israel an evil and adulterous generation (Matt. 12:39). When He teaches about the unclean spirit, Israel is the man the spirit goes out of (Matt. 12:43-45). The final state of the nation, during the coming tribulation, will be seven times worse than it was in the time of Jeremiah. When Israel was taken captive to Babylon they were delivered from their idolatry. They have been empty and swept clean of idols for a long time. However, in the end, the evil spirit, with others, returns to the nation and their final state is far worse.

While talking to the multitudes, His mother and brothers approach (Matt. 12:46-50). This passage shows how He breaks all natural relationships with Israel according to the flesh. To the end of this chapter He was Jehovah - Messiah, come in the flesh and according to prophecy, the descendant of David after the flesh, preaching the kingdom of God in Israel – to those who were Abraham's descendants in the flesh. He then quits the house of Israel and the dispensation of the Jews (Matt. 13:1), no longer looking for fruit from the fig tree. When He goes into the boat by the sea He is now the Sower going forth to sow in the dispensation of the kingdom of heaven (Matt. 13:2-3). This is the transition between dispensations, and a definite change in the ways of God. Finally, the multitudes of Israel are part of the dispensation of the Jews that now stands judged, but the disciples are chosen to know all the mysteries of the coming kingdom of heaven (Matt. 13:10-17).

Chapter 3:
The Outward Professing Body

The unbeliever's entrance into the kingdom of God is by <u>being born again,</u> being born of the Spirit. This is the sovereign work of God because it is said of the Spirit that it is like the wind that blows where it wishes (John 3:8). By this work the unbeliever is made alive, having been dead in trespasses and sins (Eph. 2:1). His conscience is now awakened to the spiritual truth that he is a sinner, desperately lost in his sins, and in need of a Savior (Luke 15:17). His conscience makes him aware of his present state and condition before a holy and righteous God. His conscience is now enlightened to the reality that the wrath of God's judgment rests upon him. This makes him nervous and uncomfortable. He must know and find out all that God has to say to him, and how he is to stand in the presence of God. He is drawn by God to Jesus Christ, usually by the preaching of the gospel message. He is drawn to Christ as the only possible solution to his present sinful condition. This is the sovereign work of God (John 6:44).

The sinner, being quickened in conscience and now drawn to Christ by the Word, will believe in Jesus Christ as his Lord and Savior, believing in His death and shed blood (Rom. 3:23-26, John 3:16). His faith in Jesus Christ is not from himself, but rather a gift from God.

Ephesians 2:8-9

"For by grace you have been saved through faith, and that not of yourselves; it is the gift of God, not of works, lest anyone should boast."

The assumption made in Ephesians should never be that of grace being from man himself – 'that not of yourselves'—but instead the error is made in presuming that at least the faith is of man's doing.[71] No, all is from God and the work of God. God gives to each the measure of faith. Believing in Christ, he is no longer an unbeliever, but now a believer. He is then sealed by the Holy Spirit.

The Seal of the Spirit – the One Baptism

Ephesians 1:13

"In Him you also trusted, after you heard the word of truth, the gospel of your salvation; in whom also, having believed, you were sealed with the Holy Spirit of promise."

Unbelievers are born again and drawn to faith in Jesus Christ. Believers are sealed by God with the Holy Spirit.[72] By this seal we are marked as sons of God, we have His Spirit dwelling in us, by which we cry, Abba, Father. Individually we are sons, and all of the above is the sovereign work of God on behalf of the individual. But having received the Holy Spirit individually, we are now members of the one corporate body, the body of Christ.

1 Corinthians 12:12-13

"For as the body is one and has many members, but all the members of that one body, being many, are one body, so also is Christ. For by one Spirit we were all baptized into one body— whether Jews or Greeks, whether slaves or free—and have all been made to drink into one Spirit."

There is one baptism (Eph. 4:4-5). The baptism of the Spirit is the seal of the Spirit by which the Holy Spirit dwells in us individually (I Cor.

6:19), and in the church body corporately (I Cor. 3:9, 16-17). These two blessed truths define the reality of Christianity. It is the promise of the Comforter and is unique to Christianity. By one Spirit we are baptized into one body, and this is Christ. This explains our entrance into Christ, both individually and corporately.[73] *He who is joined to the Lord is one spirit with Him, and both He who sanctifies and those who are being sanctified are all of one, for which reason He is not ashamed to call them brethren* (I Cor. 6:17, Heb. 2:11).

The True Church vs. the Spoiled Crop in the Field

Our entrance into the visible outward assembly on earth (Christendom) is by a human work and outward sign – water baptism. The person who professes faith in Christ will be baptized in water by man and therefore outwardly manifested in this way to the world. It was always as being baptized into the one outward body on the earth – the crop in the field – as a member of the professing church and introduced into Christ's assembly, as it is on earth. The Ethiopian eunuch's baptism by Timothy was his admission into the outward general assembly (Acts 8:35-38). (No one in the Scriptures was ever baptized as a member of a local church)

We must learn the biblical importance of the distinction I make above. There is a difference between what Christ builds and what man builds on the earth. What Christ builds is what God does on His own, without any help from man. It is done by sovereign grace. Jesus said, *"I will build my church..."* This is the body of Christ. This is the true church. In reference to my argument above, only the Holy Spirit baptizes individual believers into the true church that Christ builds (I Cor. 12:12-13). Man's work of water baptism is not this work at all. Man's work cannot be the sovereign work of God. Man is not building the true church. Men water baptizing others is a human work by which the crop in the field is increased.

The true church that Christ builds is the wheat in the field planted by the Son of Man (Matt. 13:37-38). It is presently in the field (world), but that is not the calling or destiny of the wheat. The calling and purpose of the body of Christ is for the heavens, and eventually the wheat is removed from the field and taken there (Matt. 13:30). What Christ builds is for the heavens, although the church is presently gathered by the Holy Spirit on the earth. Yet it has only one calling and it is a heavenly calling. It has only one citizenship and this is in heaven. It is blessed with every spiritual blessing in the heavenlies, and it is seated in heavenly places in Christ Jesus. Christ builds this, and Hades cannot prevail against it. It is the work of God which cannot fail.

What Christ builds is not the work of man. What man builds on the earth is always in his responsibility. Therefore what man builds is always subject to the judgment of God (I Cor. 3:12-15). Whereas, God's sovereign work is never subjected to judgment (John 5:24). What man builds on the earth is God's building. Paul was commissioned by God to lay the foundation for this building, and he did so through sovereign grace (I Cor. 3:10-11). However, we must never confuse what Paul did by the grace of God with what man builds in human responsibility. You must never confuse the foundation with the building. This is clearly taught in the passage in I Corinthians 3, yet this is a reality few Christians take time to fully understand. There the Spirit declares, *"...you are God's field, you are God's building,"* and *"...another builds on it (the foundation). But let each one take heed how he builds on it (the foundation)."* (parentheses by author)

To Timothy Paul describes the building as a great house (II Tim. 2:20). In the teaching of the kingdom of heaven, Jesus describes this same thing as the spoiled crop or the great expansive tree, both growing in the field (Matt. 13:26, 31-32). Also, in the same chapter, He describes the same thing as the dragnet (Matt. 13:47).

The work of man	**The work of God**
The spoiled crop (Christendom) in the field (world) – Matt. 13:26	The wheat (the body of Christ) planted by the Son of Man, in the spoiled crop.
The great tree (Christendom growing in the field (world) – Matt. 13:31-32	The treasure (the body of Christ) hidden in the field (world) – Matt. 13:44

The three measures of meal (Christendom) – Matt. 13:33	The pearl of great price (the body of Christ) kept by the merchant – Matt. 13:45-46
The dragnet (Christendom) cast into the sea (world) gathers both good and bad	The good (the body of Christ) gathered into vessels – Matt. 13:48

The Mixing of Good and Bad

In all these particular descriptions of man's work it is easy to see the mixture of good and bad that results. True ministers of Christ build on the foundation of God's building with gold, silver, precious stones, wood, hay, and straw (I Cor. 3:10-12). False ministers of Christ only bring defilement to the building (I Cor. 3:17). There is true and false in the ministry of man and both have the potential to bring forth that which is bad for the building.

In the great house there are both vessels for honor and dishonor (II Tim. 2:20). In the spoiled crop there are both wheat and tares mixed together (Matt. 13:38). The great tree in the field is the indiscriminate place of shelter for all kinds of things, both good and bad. There is good soil that produces fruit. The bad soils – the waysides, the stony places, and the soil with thorns – do not produce fruit. The dragnet thrown into the sea gathers some of every kind, both good and bad (Matt. 13:47-48). The unfruitful branches are cast out and burned, while the fruitful branches are pruned so to produce more fruit (John 15:2, 6). When the Jews made light of the invitation of grace and were found unworthy of it, the King sent His servants out into the highways to find as many as they could, both good and bad (Matt. 22:1-10). It is the gospel that does this. The ten virgins were five wise and five foolish (Matt. 25:1-2). The kingdom has both faithful and evil servants. (Luke 12:42-46). In every example given, the good is the work of God in sovereign grace, while the bad is the direct working of Satan complicit with the failure of man in responsibility.

The church world is this mixture of good and bad, the work of the Son of Man mixed in with the work of the evil one. Look at the ten virgins, five wise and five foolish – we easily see what the world sees of Christendom, that the ten virgins look the same and are associated together (Matt. 25:1-12). They are one group. They go out together, they sleep together, and they go back out again together when awakened. The bad are associated with the people of God in profession and outwardly appear to belong with them. Many Christians do not distinguish the reality of the corporate body, believing it is all the work of God and it is all basically good.

In these examples it is easy to see man's responsibility and failure. All ministers must take heed how they build on the foundation of God's house on earth (I Cor. 3:10). While men slept the devil came in to do his work (Matt. 13:25). When the bridegroom was delayed, all the virgins slumbered and slept. The candlesticks for the churches were to burn bright in testimony toward a dark and unbelieving world (Rev. 1:12-13).

The Judgment of the Bad

We also see the judgment of God. The minister's work *'will become manifest...because it will be revealed by fire; and the fire will test each one's work, of what sort it is.'* (I Cor. 3:13) Then there is judgment of individuals. Those which are bad are easily seen as being judged by God on the earth. The tares are bundled together, left in the field, to be burned (Matt. 13:30). The foolish virgins are shut out from the wedding feast, and are told, *"...I do not know you."* The unfruitful branches are cut off and burned (John 15:6). The man without the wedding garment is bound hand and foot and cast into outer darkness (Matt. 22:11-13). The evil servant is appointed his portion with the unbelievers (Luke 12:46). The Son of Man appears to judge the candlestick of Christendom on the earth as it progresses through time, and he makes the prophet turn around to see it (Rev. 1:10-16). His appearance is saturated with the character of judgment and His messages to professing Christianity, found in Revelation 2, 3, are certainly the atmosphere of judgment. The vision of the Son of Man walking among the candlesticks takes place on the earth, and not in the heavens, because the church world's responsibility is viewed and judged as what man has done on the earth and in the world.[74]

Man's failures bring in corruption to Christendom

This brings us back to the subject of water baptism. This is a work of man on the earth and another area of responsibility in the church world. Through baptism the individual is received into the outward society of professing Christianity. No sincere believer, taught in the Scriptures by the Spirit, would consider water baptism as one's entrance into the body of Christ or that which communicates to the individual eternal life. Both are direct operations of the Holy Spirit and are the sovereign work of God. However, all individuals who profess Christ will be water baptized. It is the demonstrated sign to the world that you are a member of this external society of Christendom according to your profession of faith.

Seeing it is done by the hands of men, what safeguards are in place and have they been kept up to ensure the purity of God's house? Early on in the church there was evident power of the Holy Spirit in strength and discipline. There was apostolic authority as well. But those days are long gone. There are no more apostles. The church world has consistently grieved the presence of the Holy Spirit dwelling in the building of God (Eph. 2:22). The safeguards were compromised or have disappeared. Evil corrupt men were allowed to creep in unawares (Jude 4). The mystery of iniquity was already working in the church (II Thess. 2:7). Savage wolves devouring the flock and perverse men rising up from among them drawing away disciples would be the result of the end of apostolic ministry (Acts. 20:28-31). By the fourth message to the churches in Revelations, the Son of Man no longer acknowledges the external corporate entity of Christendom as vital.

The church was to be the salt of the earth, the light of the world. She should have belonged entirely to Christ in the midst of the world, thus glorifying Him on earth. The church was to let her light shine before men. She was to be closely united together in love for one another and as members one of another in one body. She was to be a corporate entity outside the world, glorifying our Lord while in the world. The church is the house of God on the earth, and should have kept herself pure because of the holiness of the Spirit that dwells in her (Eph. 2:22, I Cor. 3:16). She was to be the pillar and ground of the truth where the winds of doctrine and the trickery of men would not prevail (I Tim. 3:15, Eph. 4:13-16). She was to endure nothing but the truth of God.

Yet Christendom was corrupted and no longer answers to God's purpose and intention for its establishment on the earth. It has lost all its early discipline and power. It has steadily declined and decayed from its first estate (Rev. 2:4-5). It has been guilty of permitting unholy doctrines taught for power and wealth, to control the masses and gain earthly riches (Rev. 2:14-15). Over time it became the seat and throne of Satan's influence and power, openly prostituting itself to the world (Rev. 2:13-14, 20-24).

What cannot be denied is the existence of this external entity – distinct from the body of Christ, yet containing the body – set under the principle of responsibility in the kingdom of heaven. What also cannot be denied is the failure of the corporate entity to obey God in its responsibility, and as a consequence the entrance of evil, corruption, and apostasy.

God will judge the failure. Why? The spoiled crop in the field was to be the habitation of God in the Spirit, representing to the world the name and glory of God on the earth. It was to be His witness, His lighted city on a hill. However, morally, the corporate entity does a better job at representing the power and work of Satan than that of God. The evil and corruption that entered early on into the external body of professing Christianity is continuing on today, just worsening and ripening to its end.

How can God bless Christendom? How can God pour out His power on the corporate body of professing Christianity? God would have to compromise His own holiness and character in an unscriptural way in order to do so. This He will not do. God will not sanction evil with blessing. The evil only ripens for judgment, while the remnant, in the midst of this evil, is encouraged to keep His word and not deny His name (Rev. 3:8). *"Behold, I come quickly! Hold fast what you have..."* (Rev. 3:11)

Chapter 3: Endnotes

[71] This is the last foothold or stronghold for sincere believers to deal with in ridding themselves of the Arminian leaven – that by free will at the very least man accomplishes his own faith, that he is responsible for choosing God or Jesus Christ, and that the 'exercise of faith' is something that he does. If man does it, then it is a work by man. But our faith in God is really a gift from God. He gives the measure of faith to every unbeliever that He chooses. Jesus said, *"You did not choose Me, but I chose you..."* and *"... but I chose you out of the world..."* (John 15:16, 19) We cannot be thinking that man's free will can deny the choice of God. And it is an odd thought that some of those chosen by God out of the world are brought into the kingdom against their will, kicking and screaming.

God quickens the conscience of the unbeliever. God changes the unbeliever's will. God makes the unbeliever's conscience alive, in contrast to being dead in sins (Eph. 2:1). I believe these three thoughts are the essence of the meaning of the biblical term 'born again'. As such he will see the kingdom of God and be drawn to it as a sinner (John 3:3). But seeing the kingdom of God does not mean that you are in it or have already entered. So then, Jesus uses the term 'born of water and the Spirit' for *entrance* into the kingdom (John 3:5). Now water being added in this term is not a reference to physical water or water baptism. It refers to God's use of His word to 'reveal' the sinners true condition and to draw the 'enlightened' unbeliever to faith in Jesus Christ. Water is a figure used in Scripture signifying the application of God's word by the power of the Holy Spirit. The unbeliever, now quickened, comes to an understanding of what his situation is, standing before a holy God. The preaching of the Word becomes effective as used by the Spirit of God. The unbeliever is drawn by God through the word and the power of the Spirit to believe in Christ's death and blood as his only hope of salvation (John 3:14). By faith the unbeliever becomes a believer, and is, in fact, now in the kingdom of God (John 3:15). Once a believer, he then can be sealed with the Spirit of God. But John 3 does not deal with this final step. The seal of the Spirit is after believing in Jesus Christ (Eph. 1:13), and is the seal of sonship with God, that is, he is now a son of God (Gal. 3:26, 4:5-7, Rom. 8:14-17).

When praying to the Father Jesus says, *"...as You have given Him authority over all flesh, that He should give eternal life to as many as you have given Him."* (John 17:1-2) By the Arminian leaven we negate the choice of God in sovereign grace and make it a human accomplishment, a choice of man's supposed 'free will.' This may seem like a minor thing to many, but it does sow confusion concerning the ministry of the gospel and its results. It does rob glory from God and His work, and it does give man a foothold for boasting.

The parable of the prodigal follows the above paragraphs and explanation (Luke 15:11-32). Evangelical Christianity, being saturated by Judaizing and Arminian leaven, loves to use this story in an improper way and meaning – teaching the possibility of the believer losing his salvation and having the need, perhaps frequently, to come back to God from the precipice of destruction, being restored and renewed. They use it incorrectly as an example of a believer back-sliding. However, the prodigal parable follows the same theme of teaching that is found in the two parables immediately preceding it in the chapter – the lost sheep and the lost coin (Luke 15:4-10). These two are definitely about God seeking the 'lost' and doing so in His sovereignty – that is, both the lost sheep and the lost coin do absolutely nothing that would indicate human effort, human decisions, or human will in the stories. The entire work is done by God, who is represented by the shepherd and the searching woman.

In the prodigal story the elder son represents the Jews and the younger son represents the Gentiles. The Jews are closer and nearer to God by their privileges and history. The Gentiles are far off from God, not having the privileges that Israel enjoyed (Rom. 9:4-5, Eph. 2:11-18). In the parable the two take these distinctive positions. The elder son is always acting like a servant, not knowing his relative position, yet staying near or close to the house and God. The younger son's position we see as in the world and with the pigs, dirty and destitute, far away and without help or hope (Luke 15:13-16). By their position in the parable both sons are unbelievers – the prodigal is said by the father to have been dead, but now alive, lost, but now found (Luke 15:24). The prodigal coming to his senses is the same as a Gentile unbeliever being quickened in his conscience and born again (Luke 15:17). Then you see him being drawn to God. What is emphasized in the parable is the seal of sonship – the robe, shoes, ring, and fatted calf; how he is shown to be a son in the household by the Father in front of all the servants. Notice the elder son's disrespect and jealously – this is typical of the Jews (Matt. 18:28-30, 23:13, Gal. 4:29-31).

Another foothold of Arminian leaven to be liberated from is dealt with by the Lord farther on in His prayer to the Father. The foothold is discredited in these words, *"Those whom You gave Me I have kept; and none of them is lost..."* (John 17:9-12) Also in John 6 He said, *"This is the will of the*

Father who sent Me, that of all He has given Me I should lose nothing, and should raise it up at the last day." (John 6:37-44) Arminian thinking, based on the faulty idea of man's 'free will,' simply cannot reason or accept the Scriptural truth of eternal security, and that this security as well is solely the work of God. And here their thinking must fall back to the first stronghold that salvation and justification is the choice of man, and therefore, man also has to be responsible for keeping it. If it is the choice of man, it is the work of man. If it is the work of man, I readily admit, there is no eternal character or security associated with it. Only the work of God has eternity associated with it. Only the work of God cannot fail, and will last eternally. The believer's justification is solely the work of God. We are His workmanship created in Christ Jesus (Eph. 2:10). The only one that can create is God! God secures the believer eternally as His workmanship. Jesus says, *"And I give them eternal life, and they shall never perish; neither shall anyone snatch them out of My hand."* (John 10:27-29)

[72] God does not seal an unbeliever or unbelief with His Spirit. He only seals that which is the accomplishment of His work – the believer as a son of God. The seal of the Spirit is the seal of sonship and the stamp of authenticity on all His sons. Faith in Christ comes first (Gal. 3:26-27). Then the 'believer' is sealed with the Spirit because he is now a son (Gal. 4:5-7). When it comes to God's seal of the future Jewish remnant, it is not an internal seal of the Holy Spirit. Rather it is an earthly seal and physical, and matches their earthly calling (Rev. 7).

[73] There are two very important understandings unique to Christianity that separates the believer and the body of Christ from being mistaken as Israel – our relationship as sons of God to the Father and the sending of the Comforter to the earth. The Spirit, having been sent by the Father (John 14:16), is the seal of our sonship *individually*. The Spirit, having been sent by Jesus Christ (John 15:26, 16:13-15), is our baptism into the body of Christ *corporately*. This is our union with Christ. In this He is Head of the body, the church (Eph. 1:22-23).

Individually we stand with Christ as His brethren, heirs of God and co-heirs with Him. Individually we are sons of God with Him, and eventually we will individually be conformed into the image of God's Son. Corporately, we have union with Christ as His body – the true assembly, the church. We are baptized into the body by the Spirit, and we are members one of another (I Cor. 12:12-13). This is the baptism of the Spirit, and there is only one baptism (Eph. 4:3-5).

These two understandings are exclusively Christian. They cannot be spiritualized back to Israel. The revelation of the Father is only for the believer because it is solely determined and given by Jesus Christ, the Son (Matt. 11:27). Israel does not possess them in any way possible. These understandings are part of the uniqueness of the Christian position (please see John 8:34-36).

[74] In Revelation chapter one, John is standing in the role and character of an Old Testament prophet. The Revelation of Jesus Christ is given by God to Jesus Christ, who in turn gives it to John by an angel (Rev. 1:1). It is a book of prophecy and prophetic visions (Rev. 1:3). To understand the book of Revelation it is important to see its inherent character and unique position. It is a book of prophecy. It is not an epistle written from the Father and Son through the Holy Spirit to the church body, communicating and fellowshipping with His body and instructing it. Rather, it is about things that must shortly take place (prophecy – Rev. 1:1). And the proper subjects of prophecy are threefold, yet interconnected:

1. Prophecy is about the earth
2. Prophecy is about God's government of the earth
3. Prophecy is about the nation of Israel, the earthly calling, and God's dealings with them, and how, in the end, Israel is on the earth and is the center of God's government of the earth

The body of Christ, the church, is never the proper subject of prophecy. It is the mystery of God hidden from prophecy and the prophets (Eph. 3:1-11). That is why the subject of the book of Revelation is not the church. The church is only personalized in the beginning greeting and ending salutation (Rev. 1:4-6, 22:16-21). However, even though prophecy isn't about the body of Christ, the outward society of the spoiled crop is on the earth and viewed by God in responsibility, and subject to His judgments.

Therefore, before God deals with the judgment of Israel and the world, which is found starting in chapter four, He first must judge professing Christianity. This He does in chapter two and three. But because the body of Christ, which is part of Christendom, is not the proper subject of prophecy, the prophet is looking out to view the world that God will judge. The Son of Man appears and makes the prophet turn around so he could view the judgment of professing Christianity on the earth – the Son of Man walking among the candlesticks. Judgment begins at the house of God – this is a biblical principle, and another reason for judging on earth the candlesticks first, and why chapter two and three precede the remainder of the book. The judging by God of Christendom had to precede the judgment of the world, as it does in the book.

This is, I believe, the only place in all of Scripture where a prophet receiving the word of the Lord and prophetic visions had to turn around in the vision itself. It is because of the unique character of the book and the unique character of professing Christianity on the earth in the view of the candlesticks. It all comes together and makes for a very unique event – the prophet being made to turn around – in the first chapter of the book (Rev. 1:12).

The book of Revelation is a book given to the church, written for the church. It is not a book written about the church to instruct the church concerning its relationship with the Father and its proper conduct in that relationship. It is given to the church for the church to know the things which will take place after the church is removed from the earth. The Revelation is about the judgment of the world and all things on the earth that belong to the world. This is why professing Christianity is brought in for judgment first in the book. It is the spoiled crop progressing along in time on the earth. The true believer and the true church have been given these things to know and understand, even though they are things that do not directly concern the believer/church (John 15:15).

Chapter 4:
The Candlesticks: the Responsibility of Christendom

God looks at and judges man's works on the earth. This is man's responsibility before God. God is looking for fruit which is pleasing to Him. It can only be produced when man is obedient to God. Adam, in the garden and in innocence, had one command to obey. He was deceived, believed the devil, and disobeyed God. Man was no longer in innocence, he was fallen, and this because of his failure in responsibility to God. The tree of the knowledge of good and evil now represents man's responsibility and his failure when tested. Graciously, man was cut off from the tree of life and evicted from the garden. Having an immortal sinner would have been intolerable to God and would have no place in His plans.

The Principle of Responsibility

All mankind individually is responsible to God. He has revealed Himself to all men by His creation, so that all are without excuse.

Romans 1:19-20

"...because what may be known of God is manifest in them, for God has shown it to them. For since the creation of the world His invisible attributes are clearly seen, being understood by the things that are made, even His eternal power and Godhead, so that they are without excuse."

He has given this revelation to every man without exception. All are responsible to God, and are held accountable without excuse.

This is why all mankind, individually, will be judged by their works. And from the garden on, all men are fallen and sinners, and under the mastery of the principle of sin (Rom. 5:12, John 8:34). All man's works, all his righteousness, is filthy rags before God (Is. 64:6). His works are his failures in responsibility. His works are his sins, and he will be judged for them. And the failure of man in responsibility before God is universal. *"...we have previously charged both Jews and Greeks that they are all under sin...that every mouth may be stopped, and all the world may become guilty before God...for all have sinned and fall short of the glory of God..."* (Rom. 3:9, 19, 23) The blame for this universal failure of man in responsibility before God goes no further than the simple fact that the principle of sin is universally passed from Adam to all mankind – *"Therefore, just as through one man sin entered the world..."* (Rom. 5:12) *"For we have previously charged both Jews and Greeks that they are all under sin."* (Rom. 3:9)

God's testing of Man in Responsibility

The history of mankind in the Scriptures, from his removal from paradise to the coming of Messiah to Israel, is the history of God's *testing* of man in the principle of responsibility. What is paramount to understand concerning this entire period of *testing* is that man is fallen and a lost sinner. The entire time he is utterly depraved, a man in the flesh, and a man in the first Adam. Regardless of what God did or how He privileged some, the man being *tested* was under the mastery of sin (John 8:34). The outcome of the *testing* was predictable to God. When He looked for fruit in man, even from His privileged people Israel, He found absolutely nothing (Matt. 21:19). It was proven that man in the flesh cannot please God (Rom. 8:8). In the flesh there is no good thing (Rom. 7:18). Without exception, man in Adam was a universal failure.

- Adam failed in what God had entrusted him with – obedience to the one command.

- Israel failed immediately with the law, building a golden calf as the tablets of stone were brought down the mountain.

- Aaron's sons failed on their first day of service, offering strange fire and falling dead under the judgment of God. Aaron never again is free to enter the holy place as he wills, and never again wears the holy garments of his consecrated priesthood.

- Saul fails as Israel's first king, a man chosen after the appearance of the flesh.

- Although given glory and riches by God, Solomon's heart turns from God by foreign wives and their idols. Israel's kingdom is divided in two from that point on.

- Nebuchadnezzar is the head of gold in the great image of the Gentile powers. He fails by joining religious idolatry with civil power in the kingdom of Babylon.

- Israel's final failure in responsibility was crucifying their own Messiah and King when God came and visited them.

During much of the time of God's *testing* of man, Israel served as the *test case*. God had chosen them and privileged them above all other peoples. They were given the covenants, the tabernacle, the glory of God in their midst, the calling, the oracles of God, the law, the priesthood, etc. In Israel's *last testing*, representing mankind in Adam, God sent His Son to them. They took the Son, threw Him out of the vineyard, and killed Him (Matt. 21:33-41).[75]

At this time God had finished the *testing* of man in responsibility. The result was fully brought out. When man had no law, he produced intolerable sin and lawlessness (Rom. 1, 2). Under the law, he produced offences and transgressions. When he was visited by grace and goodness, he rejected God and cast Him out. The testing proved that man naturally produced sin and could not be subject to the law of God (Rom. 8:7). It proved that the mind of the flesh was nothing but enmity against God – not only when God gave the law and was their Judge, but also when God came to them Himself, showing grace and mercy. They would not have it. Such was man proven to be when tested.

Sin and guilt were complete as to human responsibility. Israel had killed the servants sent, and then they killed the Son. When Messiah came to Israel and was rejected, the time of *testing* was over. God had proven man in Adam was dead in sin (Eph. 2:1), a comprehensive failure, and without recourse. Man's history was complete.[76] God universally condemns all mankind. At this time God condemns the world (John 12:31).

It is not that the principle of responsibility just disappears. Rather, it is that the *testing* by God was finished. It had proved that man in Adam could not be saved, could not be changed, could not be fixed, and literally could not be remedied.[77] Why else would God condemn man in Adam? Why else would God, at that time, condemn the world? After God did all He could for man in Adam, and this was played out by all the ways God had privileged the Jews, He simply found no fruit (Matt. 21:18-19).

Responsibility in Adam and the Believer's Redemption

However, this failure of man also served to open the way for a dispensation far more excellent and glorious in the wisdom of God. With the *testing* of responsibility complete and the entire world condemned, Israel and their promises set aside, God turns to the establishment of sovereign grace through the redemptive work of Jesus Christ, the Son of Man.

An in-depth discussion of the redemptive work of the Son of Man is not my purpose here, and will have to wait for another time. However, the principle of responsibility in man is deeply connected to Christ's work. Apart from His redemptive work all men will be required to stand on their own, by themselves, before God. God will judge the unbeliever's responsibility, and by his works he is guaranteed condemnation.

It is the believer who has an entirely different situation in relation to this principle of responsibility. The true Christian is *'justified freely by His grace through the redemption that is in Christ Jesus.'* (Rom. 3:24) The believer, by virtue of his new position 'in Christ', has had his responsibility in Adam already judged by God. That is why Christ was made to be sin for the believer (II Cor. 5:23). He was condemned by God. God did what the law could not do by condemning sin in the flesh. In order for God to accomplish this, and for Him to be glorified by it, Jesus had to come in the likeness of sinful flesh. Jesus was made to be 'sin' and God condemned 'sin' in the flesh, that is, God condemned Jesus on the cross (Rom. 8:3).

Jesus bore the believer's sins away – that is the scapegoat sent out into the wilderness with the sins of the people on its head. Jesus *also* put away 'sin' by the sacrifice of Himself – this is the other goat that was sacrificed, its blood sprinkled in the holiest, and its body burnt on the Day of Atonement.[78] *"For the wages of 'sin' is death..."* (Rom. 6:23) He had to be a sacrifice and die for the principle of 'sin'. There are great redemptive truths associated with these thoughts. The believer's responsibility in the first Adam was our sins, and these He bore away forever. The believer's responsibility has been met by Christ in the cross. Jesus then becomes 'life' for the believer in righteousness.

In Christ and in the cross, God again takes up the question of the two trees (of the garden), but no longer requiring or forbidding, but by acting on behalf of man in grace. God gives life – life in Christ; then Christ takes all the consequences of our responsibility on Himself. In Christ it is all put away – our sins, our judgment, and our condemnation. God having been perfectly glorified in His work, places redeemed men, according to His sovereign grace, in His own glory. Only here can man find the reconciliation of responsibility and the possession of life – the two trees. It was only through sovereign grace. It was the act and work of God. He has given His only begotten

Son that we might live through Him, and that He would be the propitiation for our sins through His blood and death. This is the two trees of paradise united in one, responsibility and life, in Christ Jesus for us.

God solves in sovereign grace what could never be solved in any other way. Certainly the law could not do this. It could not solve the dilemma. The law only pointed out the problem, requiring and demanding man's perfect responsibility toward God and his neighbor (Matt. 22:36-40). The law made these demands after man became a sinner, now without strength and resources. The law never gave man any power or strength to do other than what he was doing as a sinner. God does, by the cross, what the law absolutely could not accomplish (Rom. 8:3).[79] Grace reigns through righteousness unto eternal life, through Jesus Christ our Lord (Rom. 5:21). The believer's responsibility is met, He is our life.

Life First, then Responsibility

Our failure in all our responsibility as unbelievers is met by the cross. The true Christian enters into responsibility on a new ground, and in a new position. We are 'in Christ' and we are in this position as a 'new creation.' (II Cor. 5:17). This is something that did not previously exist. That is the simple reason why man in Adam, man in the flesh, could not be brought there. This is not man in the first Adam, but it is the new creation in the second Adam. This position is entirely new. In Christ, we are sons of God. The believer has a place at the right hand of God. The Son of Man is in the glory of God, and God has given us a place and standing in Him. This is where the believer's responsibility issues from – his new position as a son of God in the house of his Father.[80]

The Son of God was manifested in this world to reveal the Father (Matt. 11:27). This is the revelation of the name of God as Father, and it is uniquely Christian. The saints are taken into a relationship with the Almighty and Eternal God as children to a father, in the satisfaction of eternal life given to them. *"I will be a Father unto you..."* (II Cor. 6:18) Only those who possess the Spirit of adoption and who actually are His children born of Him can answer to this relationship with God as Father. The sons of the Father possess the nature and Spirit of the Father. We know God as our Father, and it is eternal life to know Him as such (John 17:2-3).

The two trees — the tree of responsibility and the tree of life — are now together in grace. To reiterate, under the law and with the Jews the principle was that responsibility is first, and then life (Rom. 10:5, Gal. 3:10-12, 5:3). What was by the law mimics what we found in the garden — responsibility first in Adam being given a command, then life to follow. However under grace the principle is life given first, and then the believer walks in responsibility. We find that the responsibility of the Christian flows from the position and relationship he is now in. Previously our responsibility was in Adam, because our position was in Adam. Now it is in Christ. Our responsibility is not as a child of Adam, but as a child of God. We are seated with Christ in heavenly places, we are sons of God (Eph. 2:6, Gal. 3:26). We are heirs of God and joint heirs with Christ (Rom. 8:17). We are the epistle of Christ (II Cor. 3:2-3), known and read by all men.

The Believer's Responsibility from his New Position

If the believer is in Christ, then Christ is in the believer (John 14:20). We being in Christ, He represents us in the presence of God. He is our righteousness, or better, the righteousness of God for us. But Christ living in the believer is for the purpose of showing forth Jesus Christ in us to the world. Are we doing this? This is our responsibility in testimony before the world. Christ is before God, where He fully and perfectly represents the believer (John 16:10). We are in Him as He is in the presence of God on our behalf (Heb. 9:24). But Christ is also in us, and we represent Him in testimony before the world. We are to bear witness to Him while He is away in heaven, hidden in God (Col. 3:1-3). We do this on His behalf, in the presence of the world. The believer is not in the flesh, but in the Spirit, and the life of Jesus is to be manifested in our mortal bodies (Rom. 8:9, Gal. 2:20, II Cor. 4:11). This is our responsibility as individual Christians.

God is light. In Him there is no darkness (I John 1:5). As long as Jesus was in the world, He was the light of the world (John 8:12, 9:5). The believer's responsibility is to walk in the light as He is in the light (I John 1:7).

Ephesians 5:8

"For you were once darkness, but now you are light in the Lord. Walk as children of light."

Our walk is always by faith and our walk is only the time we spend on this earth. Actually, what the Scriptures teach about following Jesus is that He was on a road heading out of this world. *"Foxes have holes and birds of the air have nests, but the Son of Man has nowhere to lay His head."* (Matt. 8:20, Luke 9:58) We are to walk as children of light while we are in the wilderness, because God is light and He is our Father. We do not simply walk in the light, but walk as light in this sinful world. There is a level of difference between these two thoughts. It is one thing to walk in the light, it is another thing to be the light. While Christ was in the world He was the light, and the disciples walked in it. After He left, the Comforter was given, the Spirit of sonship, by which they were sealed as sons, as children of light. In Christ we are the light of God in this world. This is our new position, this is the relationship we have from which flows our individual responsibility as believers – we are children of God, we are children of light.

Ephesians 5:1-2

"Therefore be imitators of God as dear children. And walk in love, as Christ also has loved us and given Himself for us, an offering and a sacrifice to God for a sweet-smelling aroma."

Imitators of God

In our walk on this earth we are to imitate God. We can do this, as believers, because we have been made partakers of His divine nature (II Peter 1:4). We cannot imitate God's power and strength, His wisdom and knowledge, or His sovereign rights. These are divine attributes in which He is transcendent above all created things. But we are to imitate God morally, having been made partakers of the divine nature, morally. We walk in the light and walk in love, because God is light and God is love. We are to walk in this world as Christ walked in this world (I John 1:6). Individually, we are responsible to walk in love for the brethren, with Jesus as our example. And this was His commandment to His followers, who are to walk as He walked; *"...that you love one another as I have loved you."* (John 15:12, II John 1:5-6)[81]

Ephesians 4:30

"And do not grieve the Holy Spirit of God, by whom you were sealed for the day of redemption."

The Holy Spirit is God dwelling in you as an individual believer, and this is eternally. He is not a guest that is going to leave someday. He dwells in the true Christian forever. As believers, our bodies are the temple of the Holy Spirit, and there is no indication in the Scriptures that the Holy Spirit will ever leave you, even when you are glorified. *"And I will pray the Father, and He will give you another Helper, that He may abide with you forever...for He dwells with you and will be in you."* (John 14:16-17) This makes it the believer's responsibility to not grieve the Holy Spirit of God who dwells in him (I Cor. 6:17-20).

Is the Christian beyond responsibility? Do we have none because Jesus bore our responsibility and satisfied the penalty for it on the cross? What He bore was our responsibility as a product of our life in Adam. The believer has died with Christ and no longer exists in his old position and relationships. The believer's responsibility is according to a new place, not according to the one he failed in and was saved out of. Our responsibility is now as a son of God.

The Principle of Responsibility in a Corporate Body

The nation of Israel was the chosen people of God. As a nation and as a people they had responsibility based on the profession of the name of their God Jehovah. As a nation they had a corporate responsibility. This principle is easily seen in the following passage:

Ezekiel 36:16-38

(16) "Moreover the word of the Lord came to me, saying: (17) "Son of man, when the house of Israel dwelt in their own land, they defiled it by their own ways and deeds; to Me their way was like the uncleanness of a woman in her customary impurity. (18) Therefore I poured out My fury on them for the blood they had shed on the land, and for their idols with which they had defiled it. (19) So I scattered them among the nations, and they were dispersed throughout the countries; I judged them according to their ways and their deeds. (20) When they came to the nations, wherever they went, they profaned My holy name—when they said of them, 'These are the people of the Lord, and yet they have gone out of His land.'(21) But I had concern for My holy name, which the house of Israel had profaned among the nations wherever they went.

(22) "Therefore say to the house of Israel, 'Thus says the Lord God: "I do not do this for your sake, O house of Israel, but for My holy name's sake, which you have profaned among the nations wherever you went. (23) And I will sanctify My great name, which has been profaned among the nations, which you have profaned in their midst; and the nations shall know that I am the Lord," says the Lord God, "when I am hallowed in you before their eyes. (24) For I will take you from among the nations, gather you out of all countries, and bring you into your own land. (25) Then I will sprinkle clean water on you, and you shall be clean; I will cleanse you from all your filthiness and from all your idols. (26) I will give you a new heart and put a new spirit within you; I will take the heart of stone out of your flesh and give you a heart of flesh. (27) I will put My Spirit within you and cause you to walk in My statutes, and you will keep My judgments and do them. (28) Then you shall dwell in the land that I gave to your fathers; you shall be My people, and I will be your God. (29) I will deliver you from

all your uncleannesses. I will call for the grain and multiply it, and bring no famine upon you.(30) And I will multiply the fruit of your trees and the increase of your fields, so that you need never again bear the reproach of famine among the nations. (31) Then you will remember your evil ways and your deeds that were not good; and you will loathe yourselves in your own sight, for your iniquities and your abominations. (32) Not for your sake do I do this," says the Lord God, "let it be known to you. Be ashamed and confounded for your own ways, O house of Israel!"

(33) 'Thus says the Lord God: "On the day that I cleanse you from all your iniquities, I will also enable you to dwell in the cities, and the ruins shall be rebuilt. (34) The desolate land shall be tilled instead of lying desolate in the sight of all who pass by. (35) So they will say, 'This land that was desolate has become like the garden of Eden; and the wasted, desolate, and ruined cities are now fortified and inhabited.' (36) Then the nations which are left all around you shall know that I, the Lord, have rebuilt the ruined places and planted what was desolate. I, the Lord, have spoken it, and I will do it."

(37) 'Thus says the Lord God: "I will also let the house of Israel inquire of Me to do this for them: I will increase their men like a flock. (38) Like a flock offered as holy sacrifices, like the flock at Jerusalem on its feast days, so shall the ruined cities be filled with flocks of men. Then they shall know that I am the Lord."'"

This passage may be lengthy for one to read, but it contains numerous Scriptural principles worth pointing out. The last one in the listing below is the responsibility of a corporate body, like Israel, in its profession and representation of the name of God. For the Jews, God had made Himself known to them by the name Jehovah (Ex. 6:2-4).[82]

- We see that the future restoration spoken of by Jehovah in the passage is of the nation of Israel, and hasn't taken place yet. This passage alone should be sufficient enough to settle in all doctrine the distinction between Israel and the church. Jehovah speaks of the time when the house of Israel dwelt in their own land and defiled it. He speaks of how He scattered Israel among the nations, dispersing them throughout the countries. How can this ever be thought of as the church? The body of Christ was formed by the Holy Spirit gathering out of the nations! When the above passage speaks of restoration, Jehovah says, *"Then you shall dwell in the land that I gave to your fathers."* (v. 28) The church doesn't have fathers! The church doesn't have a promised piece of land! It is Israel restored according to prophecy in the end, not the church. It is impossible to spiritualize this prophecy to the church.

- The future restoration of Israel is not because of Israel, for anything they had done, or for anything they were or become, in and of themselves. Their restoration is for the glory of Jehovah and the hallowing of His name. Israel, when initially in the land, had only profaned the name of Jehovah (v. 17). The sins and evils were done by the people of the Lord. This associated sin and evil with the name of Jehovah. Their presence now scattered among the nations only continues the profaning of the name of Jehovah (v. 20, 21). Why? Again, it is because Jehovah could not keep this nation in the land He originally gave them, and the Gentiles remark, *"These are the people of the Lord, and yet they have gone out of His land."* (v. 20)

- The reason why the future restoration of Israel glorifies God is because it is His sovereign work alone (v. 23). I will take you, I will gather you, and I will bring you (v. 24). Then I will sprinkle you and I will cleanse you (v. 25). What He does as His sovereign work just continues on in the passage (v. 26, 27). Then Israel will dwell in the land that God gave to their fathers (v. 28). *"...you shall be My people, and I will be your God."* This prophetic phrase, regardless of where and which prophecy it is found in, always is speaking of Israel being restored at the beginning of the millennium. It is a phrase by which God acknowledges them again, as His people, consequent to setting aside their calling for thousands of years. Presently, they are not His people, and He is not their God (Hos. 1:9). The end for Israel is dependent on Jehovah being faithful to His promises to the patriarchs.

- Israel's restoration in the end is all physical blessings on the earth and in their promised land (vs. 29, 30, 33-38). Israel has an earthly calling, which is very different from the believer's heavenly calling. All God's promises to their fathers were earthly blessings to be fulfilled in a land that was promised to the descendants of the patriarchs. Certainly all their sins are forgiven (v. 25, 29, 33) and Jehovah places His Spirit in them (26, 27), but it is for the reason that by sovereign grace they will do the law that He writes on their minds and hearts (v. 27, Jer. 31:33). By Israel finally being obedient in doing the law, and this is not until their restoration at the beginning of the millennium, they receive all the physical blessings associated with doing the law listed in Deuteronomy 28.[83]

- Israel's responsibility as the people of Jehovah, as a corporate entity, is easily seen in the passage. It is an association with the profession of His name. It was the house of Israel that profaned the name of Jehovah, both in the land and scattered among the nations. This was their failure in responsibility. Also we can see how judgment is connected to failure in the principle. (Also compare Rom. 2:23-25)

The Responsibility of Christendom

The church world has an association with the profession of the name of God the Father and His Son, the Lord Jesus Christ (I John 2:22-23, 4:14-15, 5:10-13). Professing Christianity on the earth has a corporate responsibility before God. The entire crop of wheat and tares in the field has only one candlestick that burns before this dark and depraved world. The candlestick is the totality of the light of Christendom's testimony in representing God and Jesus Christ, in words and actions, in the world and on the earth.[84]

The church doesn't exist until after the Son of Man was glorified to the right hand of God, and the Holy Spirit was sent down (Eph. 1:19-23, John 7:39, I Cor. 12:12-13). The body of Christ exists in relation to its glorified Head in heaven. The union of the body to the Head is by the work of the Spirit. *The body now has this formed relationship, existing through grace, from which her responsibility flows.* The responsibility of the church was to manifest on earth the glory of Him who placed her in the relationship and position she has in heaven. On the earth she is the house of God, the habitation of God by the Spirit (Eph. 2:22). The church, as united to Christ, is always one body. Her responsibility on earth was always to keep the bond of unity of this one body by the Spirit (Eph. 4:2-4).

There is another aspect of the relationship the church has with Christ – she is the bride, or at this time, the betrothed. What sort of responsibility naturally issues from this relationship? How should a bride act? What should her affections be, where should her attention be? If she is betrothed, should she not be looking for His arrival? How should she be preparing for Him? This is the relationship and the responsibilities come from it.

Responsibility can never change the grace of God that placed the church in such a position in His eternal counsels, but she should reflect and testify to that position. While the church remains on the earth, she is responsible for the glory of her absent Head down here. She is responsible to represent the glory of the One who redeemed her. She is to be a light in the midst of darkness, *in the midst of a crooked and perverse generation, among whom ye shine as lights to the world.* (Phil. 2:15) She was to show forth the praises of Him (I Pet. 2:9). She was to be the epistle of Christ, known and read by all men (II Cor. 3:2-4).[85]

We should pay particular attention not to confuse the body of Christ with the kingdom of heaven as a dispensation. God always begins a dispensation by a sovereign work. This dispensation of the kingdom of heaven begins with the Son of Man sowing wheat (Matt. 13:37-38). But with all things on the earth God must place the care of His sovereign work in the hands of men. This is responsibility. In a short amount of time man had failed, allowing the enemy to come in and corrupt the crop by planting tares. Now there was a mixture – good and bad together – remaining in the field undisturbed and irreconcilable. At the end of the age there will be another sovereign work of God in judgment that will rectify the problem (Matt. 13:24-30, 37-43).

All the time the crop is in the field is all the time professing Christianity is on the face of the earth and in the world. All this time it is a corrupted crop with evil mixed in. All this time it also has a candlestick of responsibility before the world. I believe you can see the problem. The corporate society of Christendom would not have a proper witness and testimony of Jesus Christ. It was to be God's lighted city set on a hill, shining its light into the dark world. Paul had the responsibility to lay the foundation for the house of God on earth, which no other man could lay. By the grace of God this was done well, in apostolic power and authority, and demonstration of the Spirit (I Cor. 2:1-5). But soon after he was gone, men did not heed how they built on the foundation, and failed in their responsibility (I Cor. 3:10-11).

The testimony of God's Word is that professing Christianity is corrupted as it sits in the field of the world, regardless of whether we are willing to acknowledge this reality. It has a candlestick in which the entire whole is responsible for what light is given off to the world. This light, in testimony and witness, was bright at its beginning, when God did a sovereign work to establish it. This was Pentecost, and the time of apostolic authority and power early on. Paul's testimony of his work being:

I Corinthians 3:10

"According to the grace of God which was given to me, as a wise master builder I have laid the foundation..."

It was God's sovereign grace and work to ensure the establishment of the building of God on the earth in purity (I Cor. 3:6-11). But could it and did it continue on in this way?

The One Candlestick

Allow me to address the importance of the thought of one candlestick in contrast to many. God sees professing Christianity as one crop in the field, and He sees it as having a unified responsibility before Him. All believers and the entire body of Christ, from Pentecost to today, are part of this professing body. As a believer, you may say you do not feel your connection to the spoiled crop, and you may say you aren't responsible for what has gone before and others have done. You may feel there is no such thing as corporate responsibility. However, I believe biblical principles would oppose your objections.

> *The only way corporate responsibility doesn't exist is if there is no corporate structure existing in relationship with God.*

Yet you see the crop in the field – it is Christendom. And you can see that it must answer to God. He sees it as one external corporate entity having the profession of His name. Besides, should you not be thinking of yourself as contributing to the overall shining of the one candlestick as part of a corporate body? Individual responsibility should never deny the existence of corporate responsibility, of being members one of another, and the existence of the building of God on the earth.

Let us take the first Adam as an example of this principle. His one act of disobedience brought the corporate ruin and condemnation of all mankind (Rom. 5:16-19). From the time of Adam being chased from the garden, all men were born in sin and as sinners (Rom. 5:19), children of wrath and sons of disobedience (Eph. 2:1-3). Now that is quite a connection. Will you say that you were not responsible in Adam and not connected to him, but entirely independent from him? I know this is the mantra of the unbelieving world, but I have not met many true believers that would make this boast. Why? When God calls an unbeliever, He first makes him aware of the utter depravity and lostness of his position in Adam and sin (Luke 15:14-17). God makes him aware of his failure in responsibility connected to Adam – his sins and guilt. Then the Father draws the unbeliever to the Son (John 6:44).

Also let us consider another case where we find Jesus speaking to Israel. Before He declares the house of Israel made desolate (Matt. 23:37-39), He speaks of that generation being held responsible and guilty of all the blood of the prophets and righteous men from the time of Abel on (Matt. 23:30-36). They protest they are innocent of the evils committed by their fathers, saying, *"If we had lived in the days of our fathers, we would not have been partakers with them in the blood of the prophets."* But Jesus identifies them as associated and says, *"Fill up, then, the measure of your fathers' guilt."* That generation, in a sense, held a connection with all the responsibility of all the blood that was shed (v. 36).

We are connected to professing Christianity. There is a corporate responsibility of all of Christendom. In Mystery, Babylon the Great, the Mother of Harlots, there is found the guilt of the blood of the saints and martyrs of Jesus (Rev. 17:6). This is professing Christianity, and at the close is connected with all the responsibility. Is not the entire body of Christ contained within the spoiled crop in the field? Is not the wheat mixed in with the tares?

The Son of Man, the Stars and the Candlesticks

The candlesticks found in the first chapter of the book of Revelation represent the responsibility of the external society of Christendom. John's vision and the candlesticks have a location on the earth where God looks at and judges the responsibility of man. The Son of Man is seen walking among the seven candlesticks and His character and appearance is that of judgment.[86] He is not presented here as the Head of the body, the church. It is not grace flowing down from Him to the members of the body. He is not presented here in His present role as High Priest to the church – His waist is not girded in the role of a servant, washing the believer's feet. It is not a vision of Jesus Christ on high or Christ in heaven or of any of the roles He presently fulfills in the heavens. Rather the presentation is of the risen and glorified Son of Man on the earth, appearing in the judicial majesty of the Ancient of Days. He is present to judge Christendom – that which professes His name, and how it progresses through time on the earth.[87]

The stars found in chapter one of the book do not represent the responsibility of Christendom. They represent something entirely different from the candlesticks, although still related and connected to the church. Actually, the seven stars are placed in contrast to the seven candlesticks (Rev. 1:12-13, 16). They are the mystical representation of the body of Christ in the heavens (seven stars), seated in Christ in heavenly places. They represent the true church as the sovereign work of God according to His eternal counsels.

Revelation 1:20

"The mystery of the seven stars which you saw in My right hand, and the seven golden lampstands: The seven stars are the angels of the seven churches, and the seven lampstands which you saw are the seven churches."

The stars are in the right hand of His sovereign power and He will not allow them to fail. This is what Christ builds in saying, *"I will build my church, and the gates of Hades will not prevail against it."* The true church, as represented by the seven stars in the Son of Man's right hand, is truly the sovereign work of God. The idea of the stars is how Christ keeps and preserves the church corporately as His body, holy and blameless in the heavens. The stars as symbols have a heavenly association, for they are heavenly bodies (Matt. 13:43). They have a heavenly authority subordinate to that of the sun. The raised and glorified Son of Man is the Head of the body, the true church (Eph. 1:22-23). He is the One who appears in the full countenance of the Sun (Rev. 1:16). But the church is His body joined to Him in heavenly places (Eph. 2:6-7). This is how God views the true church – His workmanship created in Christ Jesus, a work that cannot fail, and blessed with every spiritual blessing in the heavens according to His eternal purpose and plan (Eph. 1:3-11).

The stars are kept in the right hand of His power. This represents a sovereign work and security. The candlesticks are in contrast to this character. They are the work of men on the earth in responsibility. The stars are the work of God for the heavens. The work of men always results in failure. The work of God never fails. The candlesticks are judged by God, while the stars are secure, and free from judgment. There is quite a difference between the two. The stars represent the true church in spiritual perfection (Eph. 4:12-16), according to the counsels of God (Eph. 1:4), and according to the sovereign work He has done and will do on her behalf (Eph. 5:27). The candlesticks represent Christendom in actual present imperfection, under responsibility on the earth and in the world.

The Crucial Understanding:
Christendom and the Body of Christ

For the believer this is a point of the greatest importance to see and understand. What the stars represent and what the candlesticks represent are two entirely different things. They are in contrast to each other. The stars represent the body of Christ, the true church, seated in heavenly places by God in Christ Jesus (Eph. 2:6). The candlesticks represent professing Christianity, the spoiled crop in the field. One is the sovereign work of God, the other is not – it is the work of man. One is for the heavens in the eternal purposes of God's counsels. The other is on the earth and will be judged, and will come to an end. The one cannot fail and is in the right hand of His sovereign power, while the other has already failed and is in ruin, the work of Satan having corrupted it. For the spoiled crop, the work of the enemy has already prevailed.

The problem we have is seeing correctly and comprehending these Biblical realities. When Jesus said, *"I will build my church..."* we assume it is what man builds on the earth. This assumption is a big mistake. When He said, *"...the gates of Hades will not prevail against it"* we incorrectly think this is a guarantee of success and blessing for what man does on the earth. But this thinking is all wrong – it is extremely wrong! It is always true that the power of the evil one cannot touch the sovereign grace and work of God. But the subtlety and deception of Satan has already prevailed against the work of man. It is my hope that you do not think that the kingdom of heaven is the body of Christ. It is my hope also that you do not think that wheat and tares mixed together is the true church. None of these things are the body of Christ. If we cannot see the differences, our doctrine and teachings will be nothing but confusion in the pretenses and assumptions we make.

The stars are of the heavens. The candlesticks are on the earth. The stars He keeps secure in the right hand of His power. The candlesticks are not in His hand and are not secure, but He is walking among them to judge them (Rev. 2:1). The stars in His possession signify the body of Christ in eternal purpose and sovereign power. The candlesticks represent the responsibility of professing Christianity – the works of men that God judges – and are growing dimmer in their light by the passing days. Through the failure of men in the professing church, the candlesticks are destined to be removed from their place (Rev. 2:5).

The Prophetic Number Seven

There are seven stars and seven candlesticks. There are seven churches. For that matter there are seven Spirits before God's throne, seven seals on the scroll, seven heads on the great, fiery red dragon, seven trumpets, seven bowls, seven heads on the Roman beast, and seven horns and eyes on the Lamb that had been slain. The number seven is a prophetic number signifying completeness and perfection.[88] For the seven churches the number refers to the *whole* of professing Christianity as a corporate body, the *entire* spoiled crop in the field. The seven candlesticks represent a picture of the singular responsibility of the crop during its *complete* time as a crop on the earth. Seven often represents the forming of the 'whole' from differing parts or states. The number portrays the complete circle of God's thoughts about Christendom.

This is where the issues are confounded for those struggling to understand the meaning of the vision and messages. It is confusion with the recognition of these three symbols: stars, candlesticks, and the number seven. The number seven is attached to both the stars and the candlesticks. If you are simply counting from one to seven when thinking of the stars and candlesticks, you are losing most of the intended meaning. If you do not realize that the stars and candlesticks stand in contrast to each other, both in principle and source, you are losing the rest of their true meaning. It is not just what the stars represent and what the candlesticks represent. It is also what the number seven represents when it is used as an adjective for those particular symbols? The number seven is itself an allegory.

We truly are not looking at individual churches in the seven messages. We are not really looking just at the church located in Smyrna or Pergamos. We are looking at the complete corporate 'whole' of professing Christianity as it progresses through these seven specific conditions or states. Yes, we admit, individual Christians could benefit from the moral instruction found in each of the messages. And we admit there were these particular seven churches in Asia in these conditions at the time John was banished to Patmos. But this would not be their properly intended use as given by Christ and spoken by the Spirit. So we have the seven stars representing the complete or entire body of Christ as she is seen in the eternal counsels and purpose of God, and kept in Christ's sovereign grace and power. We also have the seven candlesticks as actually one candlestick progressing through seven divisions or characters of the outward professing body in time on the earth. Therefore the vision concerns the entire church world during its time of existence, from the time after John to its end. And because it is the responsibility of man in Christendom, God must judge the works of man and how much light, if any, is being given by the candlestick.

Chapter 4: Endnotes

[75] What is the deal with Israel? Have you ever asked this question? All the Arminian leaven inundating Christianity would crumble to dust if all Christians would critically look at this question and endeavor to answer it from a Biblical perspective. What is their deal? What explains Israel's history? The Arminian thinking and doctrine of human effort, human achievement, human intelligence, and general human goodness certainly doesn't explain their history. Arminianism would properly predict the opposite from what their actual historical results were. Let us look at the facts: Israel had the covenants, the oracles of God, the patriarchs, the tabernacle, the throne of God and the glory of God in their midst, the giving of the law, the priesthood, the calling. Israel was chosen by God and special to Him above all other peoples on the face of the earth (Deut. 7:6). They were the people closest to God and the most privileged nation of any. God Himself said, *"What more could have been done to my vineyard that I have not done to it?"* (Isaiah 5:4) Well, God did do more. God came and visited them – in the flesh! God came, taking on human flesh, and walked among His own chosen people.

If there ever was any sliver of God's truth in Arminianism, then Israel would have welcomed God with open arms. Their set up for this event was impeccable. There weren't any more preparations that could have possibly been done. God was there, God was with them! And what did they do in this last testing? They cast God out. They cast God out of the very world He created. We think man can reason and be saved by his will. Israel's history proves this to be utter nonsense.

The cursing of the fig tree shows that Israel could not produce fruit unto God when tested in human responsibility (Matt. 21:19). Then Jesus tells the parable of the vineyard, which is the story of Israel's history of failure when tested in responsibility (Matt. 21:33-41). But there is a double judgment and conviction of the Jews. They were tested in responsibility and produced no fruit. Sin was complete. Then in Matthew 22:1-14 the invitation of pure grace in the marriage of the King's Son is offered to them, but they refuse and reject it. Even though the fig tree was cursed and sin was complete, God shows this nation great patience in the intercession of Christ on the cross – *"Father forgive them, for they know not what they do."* What followed for Israel was the time of the invitation to the marriage. In the first seven chapters of Acts you see Israel's rejection of the marriage invitation.

76 The history of man was complete – *"but now, once at the end of the world, hath He appeared to put away sin by the sacrifice of Himself."* Sin was complete. It was not historically the end of the world, but morally its end (Heb. 9:26). Man had not only sinned by his will, but he was irrecoverable, if it depended on his own nature or will. This was proven true even after all God had done to reclaim man. We must remember that the new creation of God in Christ Jesus is not a reclaiming of the old man in Adam. Also Galatians 4:4 says, *"But when the fullness of the time had come, God sent forth His Son..."* The fullness of time is the end of God testing the principle of responsibility in man. It was the time of the end of the world.

77 The testing of man in Adam was completed when Israel rejected their Messiah. The testing proved that man in the flesh could not produce fruit unto God. Yet the principle of responsibility in Adam had to be addressed, and this by God in a just and holy manner. God's judgment was condemnation and death, and so, Christ died on the cross. This was the end of the history of man in the flesh. He was condemned, the world was judged (John 12:31).

Here are the two great Biblical realities found in all of Scripture concerning man's standing before God: Every individual is either in Adam under responsibility and condemned, or he is in the second Adam under sovereign grace and saved. While it was the rejection of Messiah that completed man's testing, it was the cross by which God dealt with the principle of responsibility, and this, by honoring and glorifying His holiness and righteousness by judging sin.

78 I keep referring to the Day of Atonement and the understanding of the great redemptive truths. They were accomplished on behalf of the believer by the death and shed blood of the Son of Man. After Israel made the golden calf and the tablets of the law were broken at the foot of the mountain, Moses returned up the mountain to Jehovah with the thought of making atonement for the people. What we should understand is that this wasn't possible. Moses could not make atonement. His standing before God would not allow this. He simply was 'man in the flesh' like all of Israel and the rest of the human race. He was in no position to make atonement. Also his position would not allow him to see the glory of the face of Jehovah. He was told that no man can look on His face and remain alive. This is another reference to man in Adam, man in the flesh. He was only permitted to see Jehovah's goodness pass by. And all Moses could do was make intercession on behalf of the people.

There is only one who could ever make atonement for fallen man – Jesus Christ, the Son of Man come down from heaven. This atonement was accomplished by the cross. When we look at the events and rituals of the Day of Atonement, it stands to reason they all directly point, by types and shadows, to the redemptive work of Christ. There is more there, hidden in the shadows, than just our redemption. It is clear from the Scriptures that Christ's redemptive work is the foundation on which all the counsels of God depend. If the Day of Atonement points to Christ's foundational work, which is more easily seen in its figures, then we may also see how the eternal counsels of God are hinted at in its shadows. These important redemptive truths and insights will be the subject of the next book in this series, 'The Redemptive Work of the Son of Man'.

[79] The law only demanded and had no power to give to man to enable him to accomplish what it required. Man with the law was still a hopeless sinner, the law only enabled the principle of sin to abound more and more (Rom. 5:20). These truths concerning the law are portrayed in the story of the man who had an infirmity for thirty-eight years (John 5:1-10). He was waiting at the pool of Bethesda for the troubling of the waters by an angel, if perchance he could enter in first and be healed. Notice 'he had been in that condition a long time' (v. 6). When asked by Jesus if he wanted to be made well, he says he has no one to help him, nor does he have the strength to accomplish the requirement of being first in after the troubling (v. 7). The law had infirmed the Jews and for a long time they were found in this condition. The law could not help them. It could not give them power or strength. They had no ability in themselves to accomplish the requirements, just like this infirmed man. He remained a long time in that condition until Jesus came, and all was changed. What the law could not do, God did by condemning His own Son on the cross. Not until Jesus came (Gal. 4:4-5).

[80] All responsibility corresponds to the position and relationship the individual is in. If I am a husband, then my responsibility is to speak and act as the husband of my wife. If I am a father, my responsibility is as a father to my children. If I am a child, my responsibility is in obedience to my parents. Responsibility is always based on the position you are in – as believer's we are sons of God (Gal. 3:26).

[81] *"And this is His commandment: that we should believe on the name of His Son Jesus Christ and love one another, as He gave us commandment."* (I John 3:23)

His commandment is twofold: to believe on Jesus Christ and love the brethren. We are not instructed to love the world, but rather the contrary, *"Do not love the world or the things in the world. If anyone loves the world, the love of the Father is not in him."* (I John 2:15) But you say God so loved the world that He gave His Son. Yes, I know this is true and God sent His Son, and I thank God that He did. But it is a general statement based on the intrinsic nature of God – 'God is love'. It is not a statement of detail concerning the eternal purpose and plans of God. There is no specific detail except the word 'whosoever' and that only serves to add to the generalness of the passage. Later in the gospel of John, God condemns the world (John 12:31). He condemns the very world that He so loves! Then He chooses certain ones out of the world He condemned (John 15:19, 17:2). Farther still the same Holy Spirit inspiring the same Scripture writer instructs us saying, "Do not love the world..." Also saying, "...or the things in the world." Then He says that the love of the world is incompatible with the love of the Father. As believers and teachers we need to be able to reconcile these statements of Scripture. Being taught of the Spirit we find that all contradictions and paradoxes are eliminated – if they are not, then you are not being taught of God by the Spirit.

We are instructed, we are commanded to love the brethren (John 15:12). This is the individual believer's responsibility.

1 John 3:14-19

(14)"We know that we have passed from death to life, because we love the brethren. He who does not love his brother abides in death. (15) Whoever hates his brother is a murderer, and you know that no murderer has eternal life abiding in him.

(16) By this we know love, because He laid down His life for us. And we also ought to lay down our lives for the brethren. (17) But whoever has this world's goods, and sees his brother in need, and shuts up his heart from him, how does the love of God abide in him?

(18) My little children, let us not love in word or in tongue, but in deed and in truth. (19) And by this we know that we are of the truth, and shall assure our hearts before Him."

We know we are of God because we love the 'brethren'. The same commandment and responsibility is repeated numerous times in John's writings – I John 3:10-12, 23, 4:7-12, 4:19-21, 5:1-3, II John 1:5-6. It is, without a doubt, our individual responsibility. We are held accountable for this as members of the body of Christ.

[82] The revelation of God to the patriarchs was through the name of God Almighty – El Shaddai. The revelation of God to Israel was through the name of Jehovah (Lord). This is seen in Exodus 6:3:

"I appeared to Abraham, to Isaac, and to Jacob, as God Almighty, but by My name Lord I was not known to them."

Jehovah is the ever existing One who would be faithful to keep covenant and promises to Israel (Ex. 6:4). In the millennium, this is exactly what you see Jehovah doing for Israel. Even though the Jews had miserably failed in responsibility to Jehovah, He will still be faithful to keep His promises to them. This is the revelation of His name and this is how He exalts His own name in the earth among the Gentiles in the end (Ez. 36:23). When Israel leaves the land because of their iniquities and idols, and is scattered into the nations, this automatically profanes Jehovah's name because He is their God, He is the One who promised them the land. He is the One who brought them into the land initially. But He is the One who could not keep them there. The nations say, *"These are the people of the Lord, and yet they have gone out of His land." (Ez. 36:20)*

The revelation of God to the believer/church is through the name Father. Our relationship and position with God affords us an intimacy, fellowship, and communion that is far higher and greater than that of Israel and their earthly blessings. We are the ones who are the new creation of God 'in' the resurrected Son of God (Rom. 1:4, II Cor. 5:17). We are the ones who God will conform into the image of His Son by glorification (Rom. 8:29-30). This will never be Israel's position. Their position is always connected with the first creation and of the earth (John 8:23), and servants in the house (John 8:34-36).

[83] During the coming millennium Israel will have a new covenant with Jehovah, by which God's law, statutes, and judgments are written by the finger of God in their minds and on their hearts (Jer. 31:31-34). Jehovah will place His Spirit within them, which enables and causes them to obey and keep His law (Ez. 36:26-27). When this happens, the blessings of finally 'doing' the law will be theirs.

Deuteronomy 28:1

"Now it shall come to pass, if you diligently obey the voice of the Lord your God, to observe carefully all His commandments which I command you today, that the Lord your God will set you high above all nations of the earth."

It is remarkable how physical and earthly these promised blessings are for Israel; these millennial blessings match their calling:

Deuteronomy 28:2-13

(2) "And all these blessings shall come upon you and overtake you, because you obey the voice of the Lord your God:

(3) "Blessed shall you be in the city, and blessed shall you be in the country.

(4) "Blessed shall be the fruit of your body, the produce of your ground and the increase of your herds, the increase of your cattle and the offspring of your flocks.

(5) "Blessed shall be your basket and your kneading bowl.

(6) "Blessed shall you be when you come in, and blessed shall you be when you go out.

(7) "The Lord will cause your enemies who rise against you to be defeated before your face; they shall come out against you one way and flee before you seven ways.

(8) "The Lord will command the blessing on you in your storehouses and in all to which you set your hand, and He will bless you in the land which the Lord your God is giving you.

(9) "The Lord will establish you as a holy people to Himself, just as He has sworn to you, if you keep the commandments of the Lord your God and walk in His ways. (10) Then all peoples of the earth shall see that you are called by the name of the Lord, and they shall be afraid of you. (11) And the Lord will grant you plenty of goods, in the fruit of your body, in the increase of your livestock, and in the produce of your ground, in the land of which the Lord swore to

your fathers to give you. (12) The Lord will open to you His good treasure, the heavens, to give the rain to your land in its season, and to bless all the work of your hand. You shall lend to many nations, but you shall not borrow. (13) And the Lord will make you the head and not the tail; you shall be above only, and not be beneath, if you heed the commandments of the Lord your God, which I command you today, and are careful to observe them."

In a similar but different way this principle bears true for the believer – the blessings match the calling. The believer has a heavenly calling (Heb. 3:1). The blessings are heavenly and spiritual, as contrasted with physical blessings with Israel, the earthly calling they have:

Ephesians 1:3

"Blessed be the God and Father of our Lord Jesus Christ, who has blessed us with every spiritual blessing in the heavenly places in Christ."

[84] There is only one candlestick representing the responsibility for professing Christianity. It is seen as one crop in the field of the world. There are not numerous candlesticks for all the local churches, as if there was a competition with the church down the street to see who has the greatest light. You can think of multiple candlesticks assigned to multiple local churches only if you force a literal meaning on an obvious allegory. As I said previously, when you do this you lose the majority of the Spirit's intended meaning and teaching. God sees the crop and treats it as one corporate entity of profession, and with one corporate candlestick. The seven candlesticks are actually one. Seven is the smallest indivisible number and in prophetic language often carries the meaning of 'complete' or 'whole' or 'perfection'. An example is the seven Spirits before the throne are only one Holy Spirit in the 'perfection' of God's governmental power in the earth (Rev. 1:4).

When we consider the subject of unity as part of man's overall responsibility in professing Christianity, we see that man is responsible for the schisms, the divisions, and the denominations found today. Man has divided up Christ (I Cor. 1:13). And all of it perverts the Word of God, as well as violating the true doctrine of the church, the one body of Christ. Man has done exactly what Paul pleaded with them not to do. By his work on the earth, man has willingly divided up Christ. And then we ask God to bless our work and efforts, praying He pour out His Spirit and power on it. Are we kidding ourselves? Christ stands divided. This is an irrevocable reality regardless of our human emotional thoughts about a unity we desperately want to create out of thin air. Are we so blind and deceived by our own will and arrogance? Are we not willing to see the pretense in this? If it is not in agreement with God's Word, how do we not see this as sin and evil? This is the point of all departure from God – will we hold to and be faithful to the truth of God's word? Or will it be compromise and concessions?

1 Corinthians 1:10

"Now I plead with you, brethren, by the name of our Lord Jesus Christ, that you all speak the same thing, and that there be no divisions among you, but that you be perfectly joined together in the same mind and in the same judgment."

Ephesians 4:3-6

"...endeavoring to keep the unity of the Spirit in the bond of peace. There is one body and one Spirit, just as you were called in one hope of your calling; one Lord, one faith, one baptism; one God and Father of all, who is above all, and through all, and in you all."

1 Corinthians 12:12-13

"For as the body is one and has many members, but all the members of that one body, being many, are one body, so also is Christ. For by one Spirit we were all baptized into one body—whether Jews or Greeks, whether slaves or free—and have all been made to drink into one Spirit."

There is only one body of Christ. This is Christ. This is the doctrine of the church (at least this particular part of the doctrine, but not its entirety). When God began this work on the day of Pentecost by sending the Comforter, it had pure beginnings. Yet when man was placed in charge of caring for God's building on the earth, he soon failed in his responsibility. We now have a mixed crop of good and bad in the world. But it is seen as only one crop. And there is only one candlestick for the whole. Just because man has brought in divisions and denominations into Christendom doesn't mean that God acquiesced by providing multiple candlesticks.

The body of Christ is one body — "For as the body is one and has many members, but all the members of that one body, being many, are one body, so also is Christ. For by one Spirit we were all baptized into one body. (I Cor. 12:12-13). The Scriptural fact of one body is mentioned four times in the two verses quoted. That being established, it is the reality today that the members of the body of Christ are scattered into many different places and organizations.

[85] While believers are on the earth we have responsibility to be one in unity and testimony before the world:

John 17:20-21

"I do not pray for these alone, but also for those who will believe in Me through their word; that they all may be one, as You, Father, are in Me, and I in You; that they also may be one in Us, that the world may believe that You sent Me."

This speaks of the world seeing believers united as one, as one family, not many. Here it refers to the responsibility of individual sons to be united as one family under the Father, with Christ as firstborn among many brethren. In a separate and distinct unity from what is spoken here, there is the unity of the body of Christ. In this body individual believers are members one of another, while all the members are united by the Holy Spirit to Christ (I Cor. 12:12-13). We were to keep the bond of our unity as one body united to Christ by the Spirit (Eph. 4:3-4). This was so that the world might believe that the Father sent the Son. These two unities have not been kept in our responsibility, nor is it possible today to do so.

Man fails in his responsibilities. This will always be the case corporately, while we are still in the flesh. Individually when we fail we are restored by the Advocacy of Christ at the right hand of the Father (I John 2:1-2). This is to restore individual communion and fellowship with the Father and the Son in our walk on this earth. It is the washing of our feet with water by Jesus in John 13. But individual communion is different from unity of the family under the Father and unity of the body of Christ. And obviously an individual cannot, by himself, act in unity.

The two verses that follow the above passage take the unity of the Father's family on to perfection when we appear with Christ in glory to the world (Col. 3:4). It is the Father presenting and manifesting all His sons to the world (Rom. 8:18-19). This is done completely by the Father without human responsibility. The Father shows the world that He loves all His sons as He does His one Son. Both the unity of the family in human responsibility and the perfection of it accomplished in glory are in the same prayer of Jesus to the Father.

John 17:22-23

"And the glory which You gave Me I have given them, that they may be one just as We are one: I in them, and You in Me; that they may be made perfect in one, and that the world may know that You have sent Me, and have loved them as You have loved Me."

This does not say the world would believe, but the world would know because they now see with their eyes. When the world sees all the sons in glory with Christ, it will know beyond any doubt that we have been loved by the Father in the same way as He loves His Son. In the glory, the sons will be made perfect in one with Christ. But this is not responsibility on the earth as the first passage above is.

[86] It is the Son of God as the glorified Son of Man in the midst of the candlesticks. He is looking for what kind of light is given off in witness and testimony to the world. The amount of light represents the value of the responsibility of man's works in Christendom. Christ is there to judge the brightness of the light being given off. He presents a character of judgment that is obvious (Rev. 1:12-18). His garment is girded about the chest instead of the loins. His eyes are a flame of fire, His feet like brass refined in a furnace, the use of His right hand of power and authority, and out of His mouth a sharp two-edged sword – all point to the exercise of judgment. The use of the word 'sun' to describe His countenance refers to His supreme authority, as in, *'all authority has been given unto Me in heaven and on earth."* (Matt. 28:18) He is in the appearance and similitude of the Ancient of Days as seen in Daniel (Dan. 7:9-10), who gives an earthly kingdom and throne to the Son of Man. Yet in Revelation chapter one, He is both the Son of Man and the Ancient of Days.

John 5:26-27

"For as the Father has life in Himself, so He has granted the Son to have life in Himself, and has given Him authority to execute judgment also, because He is the Son of Man."

All judgment is in the hands of the Son of God, as the Son of Man. This is by virtue of His title as the Son of Man and how that title is intimately connected to His redemptive work (Luke 18:31-34). We can easily see how the above verse is rightly applied to the vision of the Son of Man in Revelation 1. This title becomes even more prominent in the words of the chapter:

Revelation 1:5-7

(5) "...and from Jesus Christ, the faithful witness, the firstborn from the dead, and the ruler over the kings of the earth.

To Him who loved us and washed us from our sins in His own blood, (6) and has made us kings and priests to His God and Father, to Him be glory and dominion forever and ever. Amen.

(7) Behold, He is coming with clouds, and every eye will see Him, even they who pierced Him. And all the tribes of the earth will mourn because of Him. Even so, Amen."

- The faithful witness on the earth was Jesus Christ, the Son of Man, for He only did the works and only spoke the words that the Father had given Him.

- The Son of Man is the first Man born from the dead. He conquered death and all the power of the enemy. And again, this was accomplished on the earth.

- The Son of Man is the King of kings and Lord of lords over all the earth. And He will reign, sitting on the throne of the Son of Man (Matt. 25:31).

- The Son of Man title is particularly connected to His death and the shedding of His blood, by which the believer was redeemed and washed in His own blood.

- It is the Son of Man risen from the dead that identifies His God as our God, and His Father as our Father, the believer's position now the same as His position before God (John 20:17). In this position we will be like Him during the coming millennium – kings and priests to His God and Father.

- It is the Son of Man that is ever spoken of as 'coming with clouds.' (Compare with Dan. 7:13, Matt. 24:30, Mark 13:26) This is the Son of Man's return to this earth for judgment. That is why all the nations will mourn, even Israel who pierced Him.

You may notice that the three direct descriptions of Jesus Christ as the Son of Man portray His connection to the earth. In the previous verse the description of the Holy Spirit is not one of Comforter to the church, but rather the direct agent of God's providential workings on the earth, issued from His throne of government in heaven (Rev. 1:4). The key phrase is *'before the throne,'* which always references that which has a firm moral relationship with God and the throne, yet is on the earth or in the earth in its action or presence. This is true concerning this phrase throughout the entire book. It stands in a bit of contrast to the other two phrases used in association with the throne – *'around the throne'* and *'in the midst of the throne'*. These last two have a definite reference to physical location near God and the throne. The twenty four elders are never described by the phrase 'before the throne', because the church is the heavenly calling and no longer on the earth after chapter three.

A gentle reminder: Revelation is a book of prophecy. Prophecy is about the earth and God's government of the earth. In the introduction we see this connection being made with the earth.

[87] This is an interesting observation that speaks to the character of the book and certain Biblical principles. In all the varied character descriptions of Jesus Christ in the first chapter of Revelation, the two roles distinctly omitted are those of Head of the body, and High Priest for the church. The Biblical principle maintained is that the body of Christ, the church (not the person of Jesus Christ), is the mystery of God hidden from prophecy and the prophets. The term, the body of Christ, is never used in the entire book. Even when the Spirit speaks to the churches it is Christendom being addressed. Later on the reference to the Bride of the Lamb is an allegory. The twenty-four elders are the church, but again, not a direct reference but an allegory. The dwellers in the heavens are as well, all terms carefully avoiding directly identifying the body of Christ. When the male Child is caught up to God and to His throne (Rev. 12:5), His body goes with Him (Eph. 1:18-23). Jesus Christ is hidden there now from the world, and we are hidden there as well (Col. 3:1-3).

The book doesn't reference God in His relationship with the church, never using the term 'our Father.' When Father is used it is always connected to Jesus Christ Himself, as My Father (Rev. 3:21), His Father (Rev. 1:6), or Father of the Lamb (Rev. 14:1). The book never references the Holy Spirit in His relationship to the body of Christ as Comforter. The closest we get to this relationship is the Spirit's use of the word 'us' in the opening greeting (Rev. 1:5-6), and the ending salutation of 'the Spirit and the bride say, "Come!"' (Rev. 22:17) We get this vague inferring of relationship in the opening and closing of the book because it is not part of the main body, which is prophetic. The book is not an epistle written to the church, but is a book of prophecy (Rev. 22:19). The body of Christ will be hidden from its content, as well as the relationships the body enjoys. So Jesus is not depicted here in His heavenly roles of Head of the church at the right hand of God or the High Priest for the church presently. The heavens and the heavenly calling, or His heavenly roles and character are not the proper subject of prophecy and have no earthly connections.

[88] The number seven is often used in the book of Revelation. It has a prophetic character for perfection and completeness. Thus in Revelation 1:4, "...the seven Spirits who are before His throne..." is not the Holy Spirit as the Comforter to the church, but the perfection of the providential wisdom and power of the Spirit of God in the earth as related to God's throne of government in heaven. Also in Matthew 13 we are given seven parables that provide a 'complete' prophetic picture of the progression of the dispensation of the kingdom of heaven. In Matthew 12 when the unclean spirit that came out of Israel returns and finds the house swept and clean, he goes and takes with him seven other spirits more wicked than himself to occupy the empty house. This is the perfection and completeness of evil and idolatry of Israel's last state under the future Antichrist (Matt. 12:43-45).

Chapter 5:
The Seven Churches

The seven messages from the Son of God to the churches found in Revelation 2 and 3 form a historical picture of the progression of Christendom during the time of the dispensation of the kingdom of heaven. The chapters contain moral judgments depicting the state and condition of the church world at different periods of time during the dispensation. The messages involve the use of allegories which is common to prophetic language. It is far more than seven messages to seven different churches in Asia in the first century. Those specific churches no longer exist, their time has passed.

There is no reason to doubt that the seven messages were literally true, and that these conditions existed in these specific locations at the close of the first century. At face value there are two things that are simple to see and understand concerning the seven churches:

- It is a historical fact that these churches existed in these described conditions at the time of John's writing.

- The moral instruction provided by the seven messages is available for every believer who has an ear to hear, by which he may profit. This is true regardless of living in the first century or the twenty-first century.

To take the messages literally would be to deny any use of the allegories in them, to deny any prophetic character in their language, and to do so in a book that is overwhelmingly prophetic. God's intention in giving the messages was to provide a successional impression of the general history of the professing church in the two chapters. This goes well beyond a simple literal reading. In the introduction of the book its character is established. *"Blessed is he who reads and those who hear the words of this prophecy..."* (Rev. 1:3)

The Book of Revelation is a Book of Prophecy

Revelation 1:1

"The Revelation of Jesus Christ, which God gave Him to show His servants—things which must shortly take place. And He sent and signified it by His angel to His servant John."

Things that must shortly take place are things that are prophetic. Everything in the book will take place after John is gone. He is the last living apostle in the ministry of the church.[89] For God's purpose for the book he stands in the role of an Old Testament prophet, receiving visions and prophecies. And further there is a biblical characteristic descriptive of a prophet and his prophecies – that which is communicated to him is never about him or for his time and contemporaries. The prophecy is always for others in a future time.

1 Peter 1:10-12

(10) "Of this salvation the prophets have inquired and searched carefully, who prophesied of the grace that would come to you, (11) searching what, or what manner of time, the Spirit of Christ who was in them was indicating when He testified beforehand the sufferings of Christ and the glories that would follow. (12) To them it was revealed that, not to themselves, but to us they were ministering the things which now have been reported to you through those who have preached the

gospel to you by the Holy Spirit sent from heaven—things which angels desire to look into."

This is the proper character of prophecy. The things revealed to the prophet were not for the prophet. The prophet's contemporaries, even if they may have had ears to hear, were not the recipients of these things. Prophecy is addressed to one, but intended for another. It is not a present blessing for the prophet or the ones actually hearing the prophecy. The passages in II Peter 1:19-21 and Matthew 13:16-17 imply a similar thought about prophetic scriptures.

The messages to the seven churches are, in this sense, prophetic – they are the announcement of outcomes and consequences for those to whom the particular message applies in the future. This is why a literal view is a short-sighted view and with limited benefit. The messages are 'not to themselves' – they are not directly intended for the people or the churches in Asia that existed in the time of the prophet. They are purposed by God to explain the progression of Christendom on the earth after John was gone.

Although prophecy has a character that is far more than just what is future in time, it is, nevertheless, about those things that will take place in the future. Except for the beginning greeting and the ending salutation, both of which have portions where the church responds to Jesus Christ, the subject of the entire Revelation is biblical prophecy. That is why, apart from the church speaking at the beginning and at the end (Rev. 1:5-6, 22:16-20), the book has a decidedly Jewish character and flavor.[90]

The Divisions of the Book of Revelation

Revelation 1:19

"Write the things which you have seen, and the things which are, and the things which will take place after this."

This verse from chapter one shows us there are three divisions of the book.

1. The vision of the Son of Man in the midst of the candlesticks is the first division. It is what John *'had seen.'*

2. *'The things which are'* involve Christendom on the earth. This second division is the seven messages for the seven churches found in Revelation 2, 3. Although this division tells a successional history of the professing body as it progresses through the age, it is not properly part of the prophecy of the book. The churches are the present things – the things that are – and this cannot be prophecy. Prophecy is about the things that will be – the things which will take place after this. Again I remind the reader that the true church is the mystery of God hidden from prophecy. This is the reason why the professing church is found and judged in the second division of the book, and not in the third.

3. *'The things which will take place after this'* involve God's throne of government and His dealings and judgments of the world. This includes Israel as part of the world (John 8:23-24). This excludes the true church as being apart from the world (John 15:19, 17:14, 16). This final division begins in chapter 4 and continues on to the ending salutation (Rev. 4:1-21:8). It forms the main part of the book. This is properly the prophetic part. It involves 'the things which will take place after this', or will be after 'the things which are'. The third division is the prophecy. It contains the prophetic details (Rev. 4:1).

The Importance of Understanding Biblical Principles

Responsibility attaches itself to every creature that is placed in a conscious and intelligent relationship with God. Where there is consciousness of this, there is obligation to God. Whether it is the judgment of the world or professing Christianity, it is still the responsibility of man on the earth being judged by God. He will always do this, because it is man's works accomplished while he is in the flesh.

In this sense the judgment of the professing church is indirectly related to the principle and character of prophecy. Prophecy is about the earth and God's government of the earth, and judgment is an essential characteristic of that government (Rom. 1:18, 2:5, 3:5-6, 9:22, Eph. 5:6, Col. 3:6, Matt. 13:40-42). But I also remind the reader in speaking of these things, that the professing church and the body of Christ are not the same thing (Matt. 13:37-38). The body of Christ, the true church, is the sovereign workmanship of God (Matt. 13:37, 16:18, Eph. 2:4-10). As His own work it will not and cannot be judged by Him (John 5:24). However, the professing church is a spoiled crop in the world and corporately represents the workmanship of man and the devil mixed up with the wheat of God. This corporate entity has its own responsibility, and while it is on the earth it can and will be judged by God.

Men upon the earth are responsible for that which is committed to their trust. The entire book of Revelation is a book of judgment. God is revealed in the introduction and the early chapters as the One about to execute judgment. But let us remember that God has given all judgment into the hands of His Son, as the Son of Man (John 5:22, 27). Regardless of what we see in the book – the slain Lamb opening seals, the King of kings and Lord of lords with the white horse and sword out of His mouth, or even the One who sits upon the great white throne to judge the wicked dead – it is always Jesus, the Son, as the Son of Man (see also Matt. 25:31-46).[91]

The only exception to this judicial character of the book is the viewing of the true church as the heavenly Jerusalem at the end (Rev. 21:9). Here it is the tabernacle of God in high places over the millennial earth, and her character is in grace and blessing. Before this the church appears on white horses in a judicial role towards the earth in chapter 19. For the greatest part the Revelation is God's dealings with the responsibility of man on the earth and what those outcomes in judgment will be. Until we are clear in our minds regarding this understanding, the intent of the book will never be appreciated. Comprehending these principles in relation to the book keeps one from many errors and false conclusions. Therefore, if Jesus is walking in the midst of the candlesticks, He is God's Son as the Son of Man, and He is beginning to judge Christendom (Rev. 2:1).

When we look at the detail of the seven messages to the churches we must remember the above mentioned biblical principle. It will give us a certain understanding concerning the messages. God never judges His own sovereign work. When God created the heavens and earth, He said 'it was very good.' He is not a workman that has to judge and criticize Himself. You might be thinking, why is He judging the church in chapter two and three if the church is the sovereign work of God? He really isn't judging the body of Christ. He judges professing Christianity – the spoiled crop in the field. It contains the true church, but it is so much more than this. What He judges is the corporate entity, the outward body of Christendom. It is on the earth and under responsibility for its communal testimony and witness. This is what Jesus, the glorified Son of Man, judges.

The House of God on the Earth

2 Timothy 2:19-20

"Nevertheless the solid foundation of God stands, having this seal: "The Lord knows those who are His," and, "Let everyone who names the name of Christ depart from iniquity."

But in a great house there are not only vessels of gold and silver, but also of wood and clay, some for honor and some for dishonor."

The house of God on the earth was started by the sovereign work of God. In this great house of professing Christendom, God knows all that are His – the wheat planted in the field by the Son of Man (Matt. 13:24, 37-38). But the tares in the field did come in and they are not His work. They are the work of the enemy (Matt. 13:25, 28, 38-39). It remains that God knows His own work and He will not judge the wheat. There will be a final separation of the mixture. God will separate His work from that of the enemy, and then judgment will come on the tares (Matt. 13:40-42). At this present time the great house of God is on the earth. It is the same thought as the great tree grown up in the field (Matt. 13:31-32). Both symbols show a mixture of good and evil being contained within.

Ephesians 2:22

"...in whom you also are being built together for a dwelling place of God in the Spirit."

1 Corinthians 3:9

"For we are God's fellow workers; you are God's field, you are God's building."

At first, the house of God on the earth was the pure work of God, the habitation of God corporately, and this by His Spirit (I Cor. 3:16, Eph. 2:22). After the laying of the foundation through the grace of God in the apostle Paul (I Cor. 3:10), the responsibility and care for the constructing of the building was given to men (I Cor. 3:12-13). This is when the enemy was allowed to come in and do his work of corruption. The great house of God on the earth is this:

- God's sovereign work in grace
- Man's failed work in responsibility
- The enemy's work of evil and corruption

It is a mixture of God's work, the devil's work, and man's work. The first of these is never the object of God's judgment, while the last two are always the subject of it. What the house of God has become on the earth is of importance. Judgment must begin there, before God judges the world (I Pet. 4:17). Hence, chapter two and three in the book of Revelation precede chapter four — the start of the judgment of the world.

Certain events occurred in the history of the church on earth which can only be described as the sovereign work of God. We know that Pentecost and the Reformation were examples of the power and energy of the Holy Spirit. Because God does not judge His own work you do not see evidence of these two events included in the messages to the churches. What you see is the judgment of

Christendom after man was given responsibility to care for these particular works of God.

Ephesus represents the state of the church world after Pentecost and after the end of apostolic authority and power. Sardis represents Protestantism after the sovereign energy of the Spirit in the Reformation. God is looking to see how far Christendom had fallen from its original state of blessing in the sovereign grace of God.

The Divisions of the Seven Churches

1. **The first three churches** – God's judgment of these is with His consideration of Pentecost and the original state of blessing in which the church was established. God deals with how far they had morally strayed from the original position. In these three we are always looking back to Pentecost with the possibility of returning to the original state of blessing. It is in these that the Son of Man acknowledges the outward corporate body of Christendom, and encourages it to repent and return to the place from where it had fallen. The saints are looked at as part of and in this external society at large.

2. **The final four churches** – God's judgment of these is with His consideration of the ending state of blessing of the true church, after its rapture and glorification. God deals with how far their moral state is from compatibility with this future glory. There is no longer any thought of return to the original position. There are no thoughts of returning back to Pentecost and apostolic order and power. In these final four there is only a looking forward to the hope of the true church and future glory. The coming of the Lord for the body of Christ is held out by the Son of Man as the earnest expectation of the distinctive remnant. Although the remnant is contained in the external body of professing Christianity, in these last churches it is distinguished by Him. In the final four churches the remnant is properly acknowledged by the Son of Man (Rev. 2:24, 3:4).

3. **The first four churches** – These four as a group represent a straight-line prophetic progression of the state of Christendom. What this means is the first is replaced by the second, the second by the third, and the third by the fourth. The progression continues until Christendom is utterly corrupt and set aside in its Jezebel state. This final state continues on unaltered and unrepentant to the end. Even today it still represents the overwhelming majority of the corporate body of Christendom.

4. **The last three churches** – These represent a divergent path resulting from a new sovereign work of God's grace in the time of the Reformation. These may be seen as distinctly separated and subsisting away from the general Jezebel state.

The seven churches and seven messages represent the complete circle of God's thoughts concerning the progression of Christendom from after the time of John on Patmos. There were many other churches that existed at the time: Corinth, Rome, Antioch, Philippi, etc. These, as well as many others, were left out of the addresses. The wisdom of God is shown by the Holy Spirit's use of these particular seven churches. They provided the moral elements needed in order to present the complete successional picture.

The Two Prophetic Elements Involved

The seven messages present the real and varied state of the church world. All the messages together cannot apply to the whole at the same point in time because the messages themselves are very different from each other. As we mentioned above, one of the elements we see is that of prophetic progression. This raises the question: Do the messages represent a simple successional picture of one through seven? Does the new one that comes forth end the existence of the one that preceded it?

Besides the use of progression, there is another element found in the messages for us to be aware of. This element involves the particular and differing parts existing at the same time, being brought together to form the complete whole. We will find that both prophetic elements are involved in the 'complete' picture of the seven churches given to us by the Son of Man.

The first three churches are a fluid progression through time – church one is succeeded by the second, which is then succeeded by the third. The fourth church does, in fact, succeed the third and is a part of this original progression. This is where the element in use is changed from simple succession to that of parts subsisting at the same time making up the whole of the professing church. The fifth church eventually emerges out of and away from the fourth, but does not end the existence of the fourth. Thyatira continues on, and Jezebel is cast into the tribulation (Rev. 2:22). The last two churches emerge out of the fifth at relatively the same time, but again, do not necessarily replace the fifth. What is presented in the last four church characters is a co-existence of four until the end. The four parts together form the whole of professing Christianity which presently exists in the world. In summation, the prophetic picture presented by the seven churches is one of succession in the first four. This is followed by four distinct and final parts emerging and co-existing at the end. Together the final four churches make up the whole of Christendom.

"...so it will be at the end of this age."

The end of Christendom on the earth has already been revealed in the parable of the tares and wheat (Matt. 13:24-30). Close to the end the tares are bundled together and left in the world. The wheat is removed from the world. The tares are judged and destroyed in the world, and the impression is that their judgment takes place before or with the judgment of the world.[92] When we consider the seven messages and the seven churches, we do not have to look for a different outcome. There isn't going to be a different ending for Christendom than this. The surety of this ending is repeated for us in the parable of the dragnet (Matt. 13:47-50).

How then does this relate to the seven messages? The conclusion of the messages cannot give us a different ending. Revelation 2 and

3 are speaking of the same subject matter as Matthew 13 and both are found in God's Word. The two parables mentioned above are given literal interpretations by the Lord Himself (Matt. 13:37-43, 49-50). I believe we can have confidence in knowing how things occur, and this according to God's mind and thoughts. The wheat will be removed. Of this we are certain. But the vessel God is using to bear His name before the world, having failed and in ruin, must be judged and broken. Of the existing churches at the end, three of the four are left in the world for judgment.

God had previously cast off Israel as the visible witness to bear His name before the world. When their failure was complete, their dispensation was ended and their house made desolate (Matt.13:10-15, 23:37-39). In the same way He will cast off the church world, which has failed in its responsibility on the earth.

Romans 11:21-22

"For if God did not spare the natural branches, He may not spare you either. Therefore consider the goodness and severity of God: on those who fell, severity; but toward you, goodness, if you continue in His goodness. Otherwise you also will be cut off."

Israel as a people and a nation were set aside by God (Rom. 11:7-10). Now the Gentiles enjoyed the blessing and goodness of God (Rom. 11:11-13). But Christendom, as a Gentile dispensation, will not continue in the goodness of God. The Gentiles will be cut off. This is in agreement with what the Lord says in the two parables in Matthew 13, *"...so it will be at the end of this age."* We also find it agrees with Revelation 2 and 3 as well.

I mentioned above that the wisdom of God is displayed in the Holy Spirit's selection of the seven churches.[93] The Spirit uses their literal condition to paint a specific and accurate overall picture of the church world progressing through time in the dispensation. It is a prophetic view but we must remember it is the infallible Word of God. *If we are taught by the Spirit and understand the messages properly, we have God's history of the times of the church on the earth.*

The wisdom of God is also shown in all seven messages having a certain arrangement in their structure to indicate certain truths concerning the corporate entity.[94] The configuration of the first three messages indicates that God still acknowledges Christendom as vital, with a chance of repenting and returning. In the first three the corporate entity is recognized, addressed, and even encouraged by Christ. In the last four the arrangement of the messages indicates that God no longer acknowledges the corporate entity. By this time God views the corporate body as entirely corrupt, and a decidedly individual message is given. As the professing church world grows in size and earthly power, the true church is seen, more so, as a small remnant in it.

Is it possible that God would stop acknowledging the corporate entity of Christendom? Allow me to answer this with another question. Did God ever see fit to set His chosen people Israel aside? Did He ever say to Israel, *"...you are not my people, and I am not your God?"* (Hos. 1:9) In their history God twice destroyed Jerusalem and the temple, each time signifying a setting aside and disregarding of this privileged people (Heb. 8:9). The first destruction by Babylon concerned the separating of Israel from the principle of God's government of the earth.[95] The second destruction by the Romans served to separate the Jews from the principle of God's calling.[96] If you can see these biblical principles in relation to Israel, then it isn't hard to understand that at this time God is not pleased with the public testimony of the crop of wheat and tares in the world. He judges the crop as corrupt.

God's Ways of Judgment of a Corporate Body

In the messages to the seven churches we see God's two ways of judging a corporate body under responsibility to Him.

1. The first is in relation to the original blessing given in grace and how far the corporate society has departed from that first condition of blessing. God wants to see if the church world is benefiting by the blessings previously given. There is a return in grace expected by God according to the privileges bestowed. In Israel's case, they were the vineyard planted

by Jehovah when Joshua first brought them into the land (Is. 5:1-7). Yet God says concerning them, *"What more could have been done to My vineyard that I have not done in it?"* When first planted by God they enjoyed tremendous privileges. Yet Israel produced no fruit to God's liking, and so judgment is pronounced (Is. 5:5-7). So also the church was planted in original blessings. She enjoyed sovereign grace at Pentecost and a time of apostolic order and power. This was her first position. We will see that Christ will not accept anything but this original position that God Himself had established.

2. The second way that God will judge is by seeing how unfit we presently are in light of the blessing to which He is calling us. Is the corporate entity suitable for future blessings that are promised? For Israel this was the glory of Jehovah's throne in their midst and a Messianic kingdom in Israel. This future glory for Israel was seen by Isaiah (Is. 6:1-5). It is one chapter after God's discussion about the vineyard, Israel's first position of blessing. When Isaiah sees the glory his immediate thought is, *"woe is me, for I am undone! Because I am a man of unclean lips, and I dwell in the midst of a people of unclean lips."* Israel is judged unfit for this future glory, even though God had patience with them for some eight hundred years beyond this declaration. The church also has future blessings. She is called to heavenly glory. Is she walking in a manner suitable to this promised glory? Does her heart answer to the glory God is calling her to? (I John 3:1-3)

It is by our past blessing and future blessing that God judges our responsibility. This is the main difference between the two divisions of the seven churches – in the messages to the first three churches there is no mention of the Lord's future coming in any fashion or form. The first three are looking back to Pentecost, being asked to repent, turn around, and return to the original position. The possibility of this is held out to the church world and Christ is still acknowledging the outward public body of Christendom. The entire professing body would have to repent for it to return. They are being judged in reference to the original blessing.

In the second division (the final four churches) the outward society is found utterly corrupt, with no corporate pureness. The professing body of Christendom is not acknowledged by the Lord. He knows that a return to Pentecost would require repentance of the entire corporate entity, and cannot be accomplished on an individual basis. In the final four churches the Lord's return is mentioned in each message. When failure of the corporate body had completely set in, it is the blessed hope of the church that is held out to the faithful remnant for their strengthening (Rev. 2:24-25). This is the thought presented specifically for this time of ruin. His coming for us is our joy and our hope to sustain us when all else fails (Rev. 3:11). In these final four messages, individual faithfulness is encouraged, and instruction is given to look for the Lord's return and glory. The character of the final four churches is judged as to whether they are fit for this calling and future blessing.

The Character of Jesus, the Glorified Son of Man

Another interesting feature we find at the beginning of each of the seven messages is how the character of Jesus Christ is adapted to the state of the church world during that period of time. For Ephesus, Christ is revealed in the general character of judgment, walking among the candlesticks (Rev. 2:1). This period begins the decay and decline of Christendom. For Smyrna, the eternal One is also the Son of Man who suffered and died, and is alive (Rev. 2:8). This period saw much persecution and martyrdom.

The ecclesiastical character of Christ, as applied to the churches, comes directly from John's vision of Christ in the midst of the candlesticks (the churches – Rev. 1:12-18). This church character is applied to the first three states of the professing church because they are acknowledged by Christ as the church in general (Rev. 2:1, 2:8, and 2:12). The fourth and fifth churches involve a transition. We find that the fourth church is no longer acknowledged. The fifth church is the result of a new work of God. Therefore these two have one ecclesiastical character paired with a character of Christ that is more revealing of His person (Rev. 2:18, 3:1). The last two churches have only the personal character of Christ applied and no general church recognition (Rev. 3:7, 3:14).

The Seven Divided into three and four

There are four separate clues found in the messages that point to the dividing of the seven churches into the two groups.

1. The structural arrangement of the language in the messages is what mostly creates the division into three and four. This will be explained shortly.

2. There is a slight difference in the descriptions of the character of Christ as applied to the first three churches that is in contrast to what is applied to the final four. As we said above, the first three have strictly ecclesiastical characteristics applied. The last two have no ecclesiastical character at all.

3. In the message to Thyatira it is implied that the fourth church will continue on in its character until the end, being thrown into great tribulation (Rev. 2:22). We could assume that the three churches that follow after Thyatira – Sardis, Philadelphia, and Laodicea – would continue on in their existence to the end as well. In this view the last four parts make up the whole of Christendom.

4. The first three churches are instructed to return to the original state established by God, with the possibility of return. This possibility doesn't exist for the fourth church, nor does it for the three that follow it. To these the return of the Lord is presented, either in hope for the faithful in the rapture, or in threat of judgment for the tares. This threat shows a similarity to the judgment of the world.

The Seven Divided into four and three

The seven churches are divided by use of the two different prophetic elements. The straight progression of the professing church reaches its end with Thyatira and the Jezebel state. The last three are the divergent path of Protestantism, separate from Romanism.

The Structuring of the Seven Messages

Let us look at the general structural arrangement of the individual messages and see the differences I referred to above. The first three messages have this form:

1. The message begins with a description of an aspect of the character of Christ, as it would have special application to that particular church in its described condition. This is true except for the first church addressed. For Ephesus Christ is seen in a general character as a judge, walking in the midst of all seven candlesticks. He is the Judge of Christendom during its entire time on the earth.

2. The main body of the messages continues with the Son of Man's observations, judgments, warnings, and encouragements to the 'corporate body' of Christendom. When He uses the words 'you' and 'your', He is speaking to the corporate entity of professing Christianity. This is His general testimony to the church world, the corporate assembly. One thing is noticeable in every message – they all begin with, *"I know your works..."* God takes notice of all that is done in the professing body.

3. The phrase *"He who has an ear, let him hear..."* is spoken to the individual believer and not the corporate assembly. It always comes at some point following the message spoken to the corporate entity of Christendom. However, that does not mean all of Christendom has the ability to hear. The placement of this phrase immediately following the general address is only found in the first three churches. Its positioning shows Christ's acknowledgment of the corporate body as still remaining vital in these three. Remember that Christendom is the great house of God on the earth, built by men under responsibility. In its early times it was the habitation of God in the Spirit (Eph. 2:22, I Cor. 3:9, 16), being set on the earth for the manifestation of God's glory. This is the thought process concerning whether the corporate body is acknowledged by God or not. In the first three churches

the corporate structure is still being recognized by Christ as such.

It is important to realize the significance of the use of this last phrase mentioned above. It comes from the prophecies of Isaiah to Israel concerning the future judgment of that nation. In the midst of Isaiah's condemning words you see God distinctly separating a believing remnant (Isa. 6:12-13). Isaiah receives the cleansing coal but he dwells in the midst of a people with unclean lips (Isa. 6). So Jehovah says of them, *"Keep on hearing, but do not understand; keep on seeing, but do not perceive."* It was similar with Elijah when he felt he was left all alone against an apostate nation. God had preserved for Himself a remnant of seven thousand (I Kings 19:10, 18, Rom. 11:2-4). Yet this remnant is small in size in the midst of the unbelieving nation.

When Jesus came to the Jews He told them the prophecies of Isaiah were fulfilled in them at that time (Matt. 13:13-15). By the Spirit John confirms in his gospel the same prophecies as spoken against Israel (John 12:35-41). Jesus speaks of the multitudes of Israel in this way, *"Therefore I speak to them in parables, because seeing they do not see, and hearing they do not hear, nor do they understand."* In John's gospel Jesus says to Israel, *"But you do not believe, because you are not My sheep, as I said to you. My sheep hear my voice and I know them..."* (John 10:26-27) The multitudes are not acknowledged by Him as His sheep, and He says of them they have no ability to spiritually see and hear from God. *"He who is of God hears God's words; therefore you do not hear, because you are not of God."* (John 8:47)

"He who has ears to hear, let him hear..."

Who does have ears to hear, eyes to see? Or as it is said by Isaiah, *"Lord, who has believed our report? And to whom has the arm of the Lord been revealed?"* If the masses cannot hear the word of God, who is it that has the ability to hear? Well, you know the answer to this – it is the remnant. God always chooses and preserves a remnant in the midst of the mass of unbelief. In the days Jesus walk on this earth His disciples were this small chosen group (Matt. 13:11). He says, *"...it has been given to you to know the mysteries of the kingdom of heaven, but to them it has not been given."* Yet the realization is more than just the mere discovery of the existence of this small believing group. Any remnant that comes into existence does not result from an accidental occurrence or some fortunate human endeavor. No! It is God, in His sovereignty, who does this work. It is God, by His choice, who gives the remnant the ability to see and hear (Matt. 11:25-27). It is always God.

"He who has ears to hear, let him hear!" is a phrase that is only spoken by Jesus (Matt. 11:15, 13:9, 43, Luke 14:35). We know that God alone gives the remnant the potential to hear. He speaks this phrase always to the believing remnant in order to distinguish them from the unbelieving nation. To the nation His words are a testimony to their state of unbelief and only serve to advance their condition (John 12:39-40, Matt. 13:12). To the remnant however, it is His grace in giving understanding that only has God as its source (Matt. 13:51-52, 11:25-26).

Therefore, when Jesus says, *"He who has an ear, let him hear what the Spirit says to the churches,"* it is a similar phrase used in a similar manner (Rev. 2:7, 11, etc.). There is again a small remnant chosen and preserved by God in the midst of a much larger corporate entity. His words are testimony and judgment for the external body while they are wisdom and instruction for the true believer. God allows only certain ones to have the ability to hear what the Spirit is saying. The major difference is that now He is speaking to the corporate entity of Christendom instead of national Israel. It is the spoiled crop in the field, mixed together as wheat and tares.

In the first three of the seven messages this phrase shows that the corporate body of Christendom is still recognized by the Lord. He gives it the opportunity to repent and return to its original position. Yet His continued acknowledgment of the corporate body through the first three states of Christendom does not mean that the entire body is made up of wheat. The work of Satan was allowed to be mixed in early in the history of the church. It took time before the evil grew and the tares dominated the works and corporate responsibility of the crop. It is one thing to say that Christ acknowledges the corporate structure and encourages Christendom to repent. This is different from Christ knowing all those that are given to Him by the Father and that none of them will be lost (John 6:36-39, 17:2, 6, 9-12).

In the messages to the last four church states, the corporate body is no longer acknowledged by Christ. In these the 'hearing ear' phrase is moved by the Lord to the absolute end of the entire message. From that point on God sees Christendom as either corrupt or spiritually dead, with no chance of returning to Pentecostal and apostolic blessings. Jesus never gives the last four churches the opportunity to look back and return. There is only looking ahead. This is equally true even for Philadelphia.

The phrase, *"He who has ears..."* is found in all seven messages. It is an appeal to the individual believer to hear and act accordingly, when the corporate body is judged as failing and fallen. When the corporate responsibility has been corrupted, God's principle is to point the individual back to the Word of God for himself. This is why it is said each time, *"He who has an ear, let him hear what the Spirit says to the churches."* Individually it is our solemn responsibility to hear and understand the judgment of Christendom. Then we must act in accordance to the wisdom of the Word for the given circumstances.

4. The phrase *"To him who overcomes..."* is also spoken to the individual believer and never to the corporate body. This phrase is also found in all seven messages. All true believers will overcome and are overcomers by the grace of God and the measure of faith given to them. All believers are the branches that abide in the vine (Christ) and produce fruit (John 15:1-6). It is the life of the vine flowing into the branches by which the fruit is produced. The branches are simply the location where the fruit appears. His grace is sufficient for the true believer to overcome in every trial. The overcoming phrase in the seven messages identifies the wheat among the tares. It distinguishes branches bearing fruit from those that are cut off and burnt.[97]

The failure of man in responsibility, even what we see in Christendom, does not affect the source of divine grace. From Adam on down, everything placed in the care of man has failed. Yet this failure and evil of man has led to the occasion of God showing us greater riches in grace (Rom. 5:20-21). He judges the failure, and then presents an object of hope. When Adam sinned there was the 'seed of the woman' promised (Gen. 3:15). When the law was broken and Israel had failed in many ways, God brought out the prophetic testimony of Messiah as Jehovah's Anointed One, and all associated promises to Israel through Him. '*Promise*' is that on which faith can rest and be sustained, when everything else has failed.

The things said directly to the 'overcomers' in the seven messages are all in the form of promises made to true believers. The promises are the Christian's true hope. All these promises remain beyond the rapture of the church, and can only be ascertained in glory with Christ.[98] The believer's promises are in hope, and serve to sustain the individual believer in his present walk of faith.

Every true believer is an overcomer, because we have already overcome Satan by the blood of the Lamb and the word of our testimony (Rev. 12:10-11). In chapter twelve of the Revelation, the true church is celebrating in the heavens because she is physically present there. This celebration is after the rapture and physical removal of the church from this world. The glorifying of the true church and taking her to the heavens is the reason why Satan will be removed from there. He is cast down to the earth (Rev. 12:7-9). Any further accusations by Satan are meaningless after the church has been removed from the earth. We will be glorified to the heavens and will be there with Christ as perfectly holy and blameless before our God and Father in love (Eph. 1:3-4).[99] We will have overcome the devil and the world through the sovereign work of God, in a very physical and final way.

The seven messages are for the church world while the true church is still on the earth. The overcoming spoken of in the messages is less of the world and Satan outside, and more of overcoming the evil discovered within Christendom. Each one of the messages contains a section of promises in hope spoken to 'him who overcomes'. The promises all refer to when the individual believer is in glory, and after Christ has taken the true church to Himself in the heavens. Nevertheless, the true believer is addressed as an 'overcomer' of the world and Satan while he is still on the earth. Revelation 12 shows it as a physical reality after the rapture, while Revelation 2, 3 shows it more so as associated with positional truth in Christ before the rapture. The true believer is the 'overcomer' spoken to in the messages (I John 5:5).

The Difference in the Final Four Messages

In the messages to the final four churches the *'hearing ear'* phrase is placed at the end, instead of being after the general testimony addressed to the corporate body. *This modification in the pattern indicates a change in how Christ now views the professing church.*

- The corporate body of Christendom has grown utterly corrupt and is no longer acknowledged by Christ. Starting with Thyatira, the church world as a whole is proved hopeless as to its testimony as a visible body in the world.

- The true church is viewed as a remnant in the external body and something that only God can see, as in *'The Lord knows those that are His.'* In the last four churches any encouragement given is individual. The 'hearing ear' phrase is now after the phrase that signifies the individual believer/true church – the 'overcomer' phrase. In the first three churches the 'hearing ear' phrase was directed to the corporate body. The change of position of this phrase in the last four churches directs it to the individual believer. The Lord's positive emphasis now is no longer with the professing church but on the individual believer or small remnant.

- Revelation 2:24 identifies the true church as a remnant in the greater body that is Thyatira. Revelation 3:4 identifies the remnant in Sardis. Philadelphia is a remnant church in the midst of the other three, yet truly distinct from them. Christ knocks on the door at Laodicea to see if any of the remnant still remains within (Rev. 3:20). In the final four messages the remnant is more distinctively seen as the true church and those that are His.[100]

- Instead of entertaining the thought of repentance and return to the original Pentecostal position, for the last four churches Revelation 2:25 starts their looking forward in time to the return of Christ. There will be no recovery of apostolic power in the professing church. Here the true believer/remnant is addressed with the blessed hope of the church held out before them. In the final four churches the end is in view, whether it is His coming for the body of Christ (I Cor. 15:23, II Thess. 2:1, Rev. 3:11), or His appearing to the world (Col. 3:4, I Thess. 5:2-5, Rev. 3:3). His return for us is now the remnant's hope to strengthen and sustain them in the midst of the evil.

There are other features we should be able to see in the messages:

- In each church we see the special nature and character of the trials of the faithful.

- A special promise is given to sustain the faith of those under trial.

- Each message has rewards given to those that overcome. This will be after Christ has taken the saints unto Himself (John 14:1-3). The overcomers are the wheat.

God's Account of the History of Christianity on Earth

If these chapters paint a prophetic picture of the spoiled crop of Christianity in the world from the first century on, then we realize that most of what is said in the messages is history already. There are few true Christians today that do not believe we are in the last days. The simple passage of time brings us closer to the end. If we look at the prophetic character in each of the seven churches, we can see that the first three had come and gone by the latter part of the fifth century. The last four churches seem to exist in their distinct characters all the way to the end of the age, although each of the four emerged at different times. Already all seven have either been present or are present and accounted for in the history of professing Christianity. We are very near the end of the age when the separation and judgments of Christendom will occur (Matt. 13:40-42, 49-50).

If we want to know the history of professing Christianity we could consult the books and accounts written by men. Or we could study and understand that which is written by the Holy Spirit. This is what Revelation 2 and 3 is – God's account of the spoiled crop in the field of the world and man's responsibility concerning it. I prefer to understand these things by the teaching of the Spirit of God. As a believer you should also. It is odd to me that men prefer to understand these things by consulting their own works, and the works of other men. I would think we would recognize a bias exists. Men are prone to think of themselves more highly than they ought to think (Rom. 12:3). In the history of Christendom, men have always done this. They do not think soberly, especially of their own work. They do this rather than consulting the work and Word of God.

Chapter 5: Endnotes

[89] Even though John is the last living apostle to the church, he does not stand and function in that capacity for the purpose of the book. The book is given to the church to know, but it does not have the form and framework of an epistle written to the church. The word 'church' and the phrase 'body of Christ' are nowhere to be found in the entire writing of the book. Neither are there any subtle references made concerning the church in the body of the book. If the book was an epistle then we should find these observations an oddity. Any reference to the church we find is never direct, but in the form of an allegory, suitable for the prophetic language of the book. The term 'the bride of the Lamb' is an example of this symbolism. When the first three chapters use the term 'to the churches' or 'to the seven churches,' it is an allegory referring to all of Christendom (Rev. 1:4, 2:7, 17, etc.). When the term 'church of Ephesus' or 'church of Smyrna' is used, this again is referring to the entire outward society of professing Christianity in that particular period of time. If the church as the mystery of God is hidden from the book, and all Christ's present relationships with the church are hidden (Head of the body and High Priest), then John's apostleship relating to the church will be hidden as well.

The book is about biblical prophecy (Rev. 1:3). It has a definite Jewish character that is common to all prophecy. John stands in the role of an Old Testament prophet. The book parallels the prophecies of Daniel. In the first chapter John has a vision that is strikingly similar to the one Daniel has in Dan. 10:4-7 (Rev. 1:13-16). The physical effect of the visions was the same for both (compare Dan. 10:8-9 and Rev. 1:17).

Standing in the character of an Old Testament prophet, John would be looking at the world and the things that involve God's government of the world. That is why at the beginning of his vision he is looking in the wrong direction, and is made to turn around to see the judgment of Christendom (Rev. 1:12). It is interesting how the verse emphasizes his turning by mentioning it two different times. The church is the mystery of God hidden from the Old Testament prophets and prophecy. In the book John is not functioning in his role as an apostle to the church.

All the above does not negate the fact that this prophetic book was given to the church. The reason for this is because of her position and relationship with the Father and Son. The church is privileged of God to know all that

God is doing (John 15:15). God will not hide anything from His friends. This was the same privilege afforded to Abraham as a friend of God (Gen. 18:17). He observed how God judged Sodom and Gomorrah from a high and distant position. In this example Abraham prefigures the privilege of the church. We will observe the judgment of the world from a high and distant place. In the same way the judgments never touched Abraham and he was not in the midst of them, so also God's coming judgments of the world will not touch the true church.

[90] The book of Revelation is about biblical prophecy (Rev. 1:3), and this alone gives the book a decidedly Jewish flavor. The subject of prophecy is about the earth, the nation of Israel, and God's government of the earth through Israel. Prophecy is about earthly things and Israel is the earthly calling of God. Knowing the principle and character of prophecy explains the Jewish flavor of the book. We should be able to see these characteristics of prophetic writings in many examples in the book.

From the outset of the book God is viewed as Jehovah (Rev. 1:4). When Jesus is not viewed as the glorified Son of Man (Rev. 1:12-16), He also is viewed as Jehovah (Rev. 1:8, 11, 17). This is the name by which God made Himself known to Israel (Ex. 6:2-3). The prophet Isaiah saw Jehovah on His throne (Is. 6:1), and the Spirit of God through John identifies Isaiah's vision as that of Jesus (John 12:41). This is definitely Jewish in character.

The revelation of God to the believer/church is that of Father. All the epistles preceding this book were written to the church or individual believers. The character of the epistles is communication from the Father and Son, through the Comforter, the Holy Spirit. Most all the epistles have a greeting of grace from God our Father. Also in the epistles you find the Holy Spirit using the word 'us'. It is how the Holy Spirit is united with the church as one in all communications to the church. *"He hath loved us and washed us..." "...to the glory of God by us." "...who has blessed us with every spiritual blessing..." "...just as He chose us in Him..." "...having predestined us..." "...He has made us accepted in the Beloved." "In Him we have redemption through His blood..." "He made to abound toward us..." "He delivered us..." "...and raised us up together, and made us sit together in the heavenly places in Christ Jesus..." "...His kindness toward us in Christ Jesus."* The Holy Spirit includes all the saints in all the blessings. All the Father has given us 'in Christ' is appropriated to all saints through the Holy Spirit's use of the words 'us' and 'we' in the epistles. This use is not found in the Old Testament writings, or in the Revelation.

However this is the proper character of the Holy Spirit to the church. He joins in with the believer in the 'us' and 'we' because He is our seal, our earnest, our deposit and guarantee, the assurance of the blessings and the glory in Christ that is to come. *"But if the Spirit of Him who raised Jesus from the dead dwells in you, He who raised Christ from the dead will also give life to your mortal bodies through His Spirit who dwells in you."* (Rom. 8:11). The Spirit will dwell in us forever (John 14:16-17). We see then that prophecy – that which will happen on the earth and concerns others, judgment, etc. – is not the proper character of the Spirit to the church. Prophecy does not involve the church. The church, of which believers are all individual members of the one body, is the mystery of God hidden from the prophets and prophecy. If the book of Revelation is prophecy then I would expect the body of Christ to be hidden from its content. Guess what? It is hidden throughout. Not one mention of 'the church' or 'the body of Christ'. That is why the communication and character of the book of Revelation is so different from the communication and character of the epistles.

The book of Revelation does not fit the mold of the epistles, but is similar to the Old Testament writings. The introduction of the book is not an address of personal relationship. Rather it shows God as Jehovah and El Shaddi – a character of supremacy over all things, over all creation. The introduction shows the Holy Spirit as the providential power and working of Jehovah's throne of government in the earth, not as the Comforter to the church (Rev. 1:4). In the book, whenever the name of Father is used in reference to God, it is only attached to the name of Jesus Christ (Rev. 1:6) or the Lamb that was slain (Rev. 14:1). It is never directly attached to the believer/church as in the epistles (Rom. 1:7, I Cor. 1:3, II Cor. 1:2, etc.). The relationship of the wife with the Lamb isn't even mentioned until the marriage of the Lamb in chapter 19. The system and relationships found in the book of Revelation are those commonly found in prophetic writings. They do not adhere to the character or relationship in which the epistles were written.

The book of Revelation is a Jewish book of prophecy. It is a book given to the church for the knowledge of the church. It is not given because these things will directly involve the church, but given because of our position and relationship in Christ and with Christ. *"No longer do I call you servants, for a servant does not know what his master is doing; but I have called you friends, for all things that I heard from My Father I have made known to you."* (John 15:15) Israelites are always servants in the house of God, but the believer is a son (John 8:34-36). It is the church's privilege to know and understand all that the Father has given to the Son (John 16:13-15), to know the very counsels of God (Eph. 1:11).

Abraham and Lot serve as a figure in depicting this relationship. God said, *"Shall I hide from Abraham what I am doing…"* What God showed Abraham did not directly involve him. He watched the destruction of Sodom and Gomorrah from a distant height. The same is true with the book of Revelation given to the church. This book of God's dealings in judgment with the world does not directly involve the church. Nevertheless it is given to the church to know. The true church is like Abraham – far removed from the judgments. The Jewish remnant in the end is like Lot – in the midst of all the trouble.

The book has an emphasis relating to the throne and the One who sits on the throne (Rev. 1:4, 4:1-3). But this is not a throne of grace for the church age. It is a throne of government of the earth, and what proceeds forth from it are judgments (Rev. 4:5). A throne of grace is related to the church. A throne of God's government is related to the earth, and to Israel as the earthly calling and as the center of God's government of the world. This is not depicting the loving relationship the church enjoys with the Father, as His children and sons.

The last point of Jewish character associated with the book is the use of the administration of angels. The book is given to John from Jesus Christ through His angel (Rev. 1:1). Many things in the book are delivered to John by and through angels, and they play a prominent role throughout. This should bring to mind the use of angels in the giving of the law to Israel at Mt. Sinai (Gal. 3:19), or the administration of angels with the prophet Daniel. This only adds to the Jewish flavor of the book.

[91] All the characters in which Jesus is viewed in the book of Revelation are related to judgments in the book. All judgment has been given by the Father to the Son, and this in the title of the Son of Man (John 5:22, 27). All the characters for Jesus in the book are related to the title, Son of Man. The Son of God took up this title when God prepared a body for Him and He came from heaven to die as a sacrifice for man's sins (Heb. 10:1-14). He was the Son of Man in heaven, who came down from heaven, and having been lifted up on the cross and gone down under death, is the Son of Man that God raised from the dead to go back to heaven from whence He came (John 3:13-14, Matt. 17:9, John 6:62). It is the Son of Man who sits now at the right hand of God (Luke 22:69), waiting until His enemies will be made

His footstool. For the understanding of the believer's redemption it is of great importance that we comprehend that there is a Man who has gone into the glory of God. It is the Son of Man who returns with clouds, with power and great glory, to sit on His throne of glory and set up His kingdom (Matt. 16:28, 24:30, 26:64, Mark 13:26, Luke 21:27). When we see the Lamb as though it had been slain (Rev. 5:6), it is Jesus in the title of the Son of Man and how the redemptive work is always associated with that title (Mark 8:31, 9:31, 10:33, Matt. 12:39-40, 20:18, Luke 9:44, 11:29-30). When we see the King of kings coming in warring judgment we know it is the Son of Man coming with clouds and great glory (Rev. 1:7, 19:11-16, Matt. 24:30). It is Jesus, the Son, as the Son of Man, sitting on the great white throne.

Messiah is a title as well, but as to its own character and as a subject of prophecy, it is a title set aside. As long as Israel is set aside and not acknowledged by God, the Messiah title and all associated promises and prophecies are set aside as well. Messiah is a Jewish promise. This title involves the throne of David, the Promised Land, the houses of Judah and Israel joined back together as one people and one nation, twelve tribes restored and prospering in the land, and Jerusalem as the earthly capital of the government of God in the millennium – all Jewish and earthly blessings. This title has little to do with the true church.

It should be easy to see the Son of Man title associated with the redemptive work. And it should be easy to see all judgment associated with this title as well. It is the Son of God as the Son of Man who is Head of the body, the church. After all she is His body, bone of His bone, flesh of His flesh (Eph. 5:29-30). And it can only be seen as the Son of Man raised up out of the grave by the power of God, and His body with Him exalted (Eph. 1:17-23). We remember that it was Jesus as the Son of Man and not Jesus as the Messiah to Israel who planted the wheat, the true sons of the kingdom (Matt. 13:37-38). The church only exists because the Son of Man is now at the right hand of God, glorified. Until He was glorified, the Spirit couldn't be sent down to gather the church (John 7:39, I Cor. 12:12-13).

All the promises and blessings to Israel related to the Messiah title (those promises and covenants made to both David and Abraham on behalf of Israel) were promises secured by the resurrection of Christ from the dead (Acts 13:30-34, Rom. 15:8). All Israel's promises and their having their Messiah, although they rejected these when He came to them in the flesh, are secured in a Christ in resurrection power and glory. The redemptive work of Christ is the foundation of all that God will bring to pass in the ages to come.

[92] The tares are different than the unbelieving world. In the parable the field is the world. It is made up of unbelieving Jews and Gentiles. The tares have a profession of Jesus Christ and are part of the crop. This is different from the field. I believe the scriptures make a basic difference relating to the tares. If the 'unworthy servant' did not do his master's will, he was judged and punished still as a servant. He was judged as a hypocrite, according to the position in which he was responsible. It is not said to him, 'you are not a servant' or 'you were never my servant'. All of Christendom has this position on the earth, as servants to the Master. We all have this position by profession. What is said of the unworthy servant is, *"the master of that servant will come…and will cut him in two and appoint him his portion with the hypocrites. There will be weeping and gnashing of teeth."* (Matt. 24:50-51) It is hypocrisy. The tares have a profession of faith in Christ without having any genuine faith or actual relationship. The tares are judged and condemned on the basis of their profession. We are all servants by our simple profession of faith in Christ. Everyone in Christendom is a servant of the Master, whether they are wheat or tares. Therefore the evil servant is judged as a servant. He is never viewed as a son. Only true faith in Christ, and this as the gift of God, makes one a son of God and a true believer (Gal. 3:26, Eph. 2:8-10).

The great error of doctrine is in thinking and teaching that the evil servant is a believer and a Christian. It is the evil leaven we have spoken of that creates this dangerous assumption. In the parable we see that the evil servant is judged as a hypocrite and the wrath of God comes on him. The leaven would then have us assume this poor believer has lost the salvation that he once possessed as a Christian. The leaven creates the understanding that eternal life is not really that eternal. We are forced to make the false assumption that a true believer can forfeit his salvation and that this is dependent on some measure or level of human behavior. So much for Jesus saying, *"And I give them eternal life, and they shall never perish."* (John 10:27-30) The leaven will always lead us to circumvent the truth of Scripture, yes, even the very words of Christ. Then the implications of its teachings begin to branch out – there can be no peace with God or a perfect conscience where this leaven is embraced (Rom. 5:1, Heb. 9:9).

[93] Another important point can be made regarding the fact that these seven churches actually existed at the time of the messages. Even though the literal view is not the proper prophetic view of the two chapters and

is not God's intention for giving the seven messages, the wisdom of God uses the messages to impress upon Christendom, even in the first century, what is the proper hope and constant expectation of the church (Rev. 2:25, 3:11). Christians are to be looking for and expecting the Lord's return for them, regardless of what century they find themselves in. (The removal of the true church from the earth is the subject of the second book of the Son of Man series, titled 'The Blessed Hope of the Church.')

[94] Seven is a prophetic number representing spiritual completeness, wholeness, or perfection. Yet with some prophetic subjects this number is divided into two divisions of three and four or four and three. This is the case with the seven churches. The first three are looking back and the corporate entity is being acknowledged by God. The last four are looking forward and the corporate entity is not acknowledged by God, being viewed by Him as corrupt. Also the first three have come and gone, while the last four exist in their distinct characters until the end.

In the book, the seven seals are divided into four and three (Rev. 6). The first four seals are providential in character, while the remaining three are quite distinct. If we look closely the trumpet and bowl judgments have a similar division. The seven parables that tell the prophetic story of the dispensation of the kingdom of heaven in Matthew 13 are also divided into four and three. The first four were spoken to the multitudes with the disciples present. The last three were spoken in private to the disciples only. Those spoken to the multitudes have a more worldly perspective. Those spoken to the disciples in private carry more of a divine perspective.

[95] The principle of God's government of the earth was with Israel all the time that Jehovah's presence was with the nation. This presence was directly related to the Ark of the Covenant, the throne of God between the cherubim (II Sam. 6:2, Ps. 99:1), where Jehovah dwelt. When the presence of God leaves the earth (Ez. 10), the Ark of the Covenant was lost forever. This was God's throne on the earth. The principle of the government of God was taken from Israel and given to the Gentiles.

We must see the connection and relationship between these three things: the shekinah glory of God, the Ark of the Covenant as the throne of God, and the principle of God's government of the earth. They all go together and they will not be separated. That is why the glory of God leaves the earth in Ezekiel 10. It is why the glory does not return back to the earth until Ezekiel 43. This is in the millennial temple in Jerusalem, which the Prince of Israel will build, and the glory of the Lord will come and fill (Zech.

6:12-13, Ez. 43:1-7). It is the Son of Man sitting on the throne of God's government over the entire earth.

The glory of the presence of the Lord is connected to the principle of God's direct government of the earth. I know that many believers pray and ask God to send down His glory, and many others testify of seeing His glory. Yet the Biblical principle is that the glory does not return until after the times of the Gentiles are completed. I do not believe that our prayers and desires will bring the glory down before the building of the millennial temple. There is a biblical principle involved with the glory.

96 The principle of calling begins with Abram. He was called by God and separated from the world (Gen. 12:1-3). This principle of calling continues in the flesh and by natural descent through the patriarchs, until God calls and delivers an entire nation out of bondage in Egypt. He brought them on eagles' wings to Him at Mt. Sinai, there to be the people of the Lord Jehovah by calling (Ex. 19:4-5). This earthly calling continued in Israel until the time of their rejection of Messiah. At that time many things relating to Israel were set aside by God, one of which was their calling as the people of God. This setting aside the principle of calling in Israel was sealed by the Romans destroying the city and temple in 70 AD. Israel's calling is according to the flesh and by natural descent, with circumcision in the flesh as a sign of that calling. Their religion is a walk in the flesh and a walk by sight. The law is not of faith, and therefore could not be a walk of faith (Gal. 3:12). Israel's calling has always been earthly, in the flesh, and involved the promised land. At this time the principle of calling is with the body of Christ. The church is being gathered by the Holy Spirit sent down from heaven. The church has a heavenly calling (Heb. 3:1).

97 Again, when we see the phrase, *"To him who overcomes..."* we automatically think an Arminian thought of human effort and struggle and accomplishment. 'Try more, do more, build more' should be the mantra. The believer is not labeled an 'overcomer' because he has accomplished a series of tasks assigned to him. If we would look at the Scriptures, without the bias of this corrupting doctrine, we will find a very different meaning to the term 'overcomer,' and this without the thought of human effort anywhere in sight:

1 John 4:4

"You are of God, little children, and have overcome them, because He who is in you is greater than he who is in the world."

1 John 5:1-5

(1) "Whoever believes that Jesus is the Christ is born of God, and everyone who loves Him who begot also loves him who is begotten of Him. (2) By this we know that we love the children of God, when we love God and keep His commandments. (3) For this is the love of God, that we keep His commandments. And His commandments are not burdensome. (4) For whatever is born of God overcomes the world. And this is the victory that has overcome the world—our faith. (5) Who is he who overcomes the world, but he who believes that Jesus is the Son of God?"

Those that are born of God are the overcomers. It is our faith that makes us overcomers, not our works or deeds. It is our position 'in Christ'. It is a position that is lifted up above the world, and is in the grace of God. In Christ we are apart from the world and thus have overcome it. The one who overcomes the world is the one who believes that Jesus is the Son of God. This is the Christian position. The overcoming has already been accomplished by Jesus when you are found to be 'of God, little children'. This is not an Arminian thought of human achievement. We are to be of good cheer, *because He has overcome the world.*

[98] The true Christian's hope is another Biblical teaching that is drastically altered by the Arminian leaven. Most Christian teachings today concentrate on life here on the earth and have all kinds of hopes and promises from God for this life that are ascertained by 'exercising' faith, praying harder, fasting longer, or waiting patiently on the Lord. However the Scriptures teach that the Christian's true hope is 'unseen' and hope that 'is seen' is not hope at all (Rom. 8:23-25). *We hope for what we do not see.* Doing this now, *then we eagerly wait for it with perseverance.* It is not by faith we make it happen now, or by much prayer and fasting we shorten the waiting time. True biblical faith is the means by which you eagerly wait 'in perseverance'. How is that? Now or presently, faith is the substance of things hoped for, the evidence of things not seen (Heb. 11:1).

Christ in you, the hope of glory. (Col. 1:27) Can't we see that our hopes are not of this world, are not to be found in this world? All the believer's proper hopes are in glory, and realized when we are physically present with Christ. Yet this isn't what people want to hear in the church world. You cannot build numbers by telling people they have to suffer with Christ now, so that they may be glorified with Him later (Rom. 8:18). *"For I consider that the sufferings of this present time are not worthy to be compared with the glory which shall be revealed in us."* People in professing Christianity don't want to hear this stuff about suffering at this present time with Christ. It is not a popular message, and they will certainly go somewhere else. The leaven of human achievement simply doesn't jive with 'the sufferings of this present time'. But why do you think all the promises to the overcomers in the seven messages refer to blessings in glory? It is true concerning every one of them! It is because this is what God promises, and glory is the time for which He promises it.

[I do not here speak of Christian virtues resulting from the new creation in Christ we have become, such as the fruit of the Spirit – love, joy, patience, etc. We may develop these now because we possess the seal of the Spirit as sons and we have the life of Christ. We have the firstfruits of the Spirit, but we still groan within ourselves and wait (Rom. 8:23). These virtues or fruit of the Spirit are not Christian hopes unseen, but are to be seen and developed in the walk of faith of every believer presently]

One more reference: *"These all died in faith, not having received the promises..."* (Heb. 11:13) Even though this specifically references Old Testament saints, it is true concerning every New Testament believer that has passed. Every Christian that dies, dies in faith, having not received the promises. The promises are in glory. And even at death they did not receive them, because their bodies went to the grave and were not glorified. The rest of this verse has a remarkable parallel to the walk of faith, which every true New Testament believer has in the wilderness of this world: *"...but having seen them afar off were assured of them, embraced them, and confessed that they were strangers and pilgrims on the earth."* We really do not have Christian hopes on the earth and in this world (II Cor. 4:17-18, Rom. 8:23-25). We are strangers to this world.

[Again, the present fruits and virtues of our redemption are ours to possess and develop in our walk of faith on this earth. The true believer is the new creation of God in Christ Jesus and we possess Christ as our life. Yet all our hopes are in glory. We walk by faith presently, with affliction and sufferings and persecutions as our current portion (II Cor. 4:17, Rom. 8:18, John 16:33, 15:20). The difference between the Old Testament saint and the New Testament believer is that our redemption is already accomplished and our sins are borne away, and we possess eternal life. We are similar to them in that they did not receive the promises, but walking in faith in God who promised, they were strangers and pilgrims on the earth. We also must wait for glory to receive the promises, and therefore walk by faith now.]

[99] When Satan is cast out of the heavens and down to the earth, all he will be able to do in retaliation against the heavens are the words he puts in the mouth of the Roman beast – *"Then he opened his mouth in blasphemy against God, to blaspheme His name, His tabernacle, and those who dwell in heaven."* (Rev. 13:5-6) This has no effect on God or those that dwell in the heavens (the church), but it is woe to the inhabitants of the earth and sea (Rev. 12:12).

[100] We may think of the last two churches in a way that follows the parable of the wheat and tares, and the results in that parable at the time of harvest (Matt. 13:30 and 13:37-43). In this view the corporate body in Thyatira is Jezebel, which is Romanism. It is completely corrupt. The corporate body of Sardis, which is distinct from Jezebel, is Protestantism, and is spiritually dead. There is a distinct small remnant existing in both. Jezebel came into influence by the sixth century, while Sardis comes about in the seventeenth century. This is approximately 1100 years of separation in which Jezebel is what the world views as Christianity. Now we come to the last two churches – Philadelphia and Laodicea – and all becomes simple. At the end of the age there are wheat and tares. The remnants of both Thyatira and Sardis exit their corporate entities and form the remnant church Philadelphia. This is the wheat removed from the world and placed into the barn (Matt. 13:30). Laodicea is the entire corporate structure of Christianity together at the end, as God views it. It is not together in any unity between Romanism, Protestantism, and Evangelical Christianity, but as God views the entire organized outer body as corrupt, dead, highly arrogant, and full of itself in pride as to what it thinks it has accomplished. Laodicea then is the tares bundled together and left in the field to be burned. Laodicea represents Christ removing the candlestick from Christendom and His spewing Laodicea out of His mouth.

Now I realize that I've gotten ahead of myself as far as the teaching goes in the chapters of the book, as it relates to specific messages to these churches. But I wanted to show how the parable of the wheat and tares fits in and is understood in view of the seven messages by Christ to the churches. It has to fit because the two are generally speaking about the same thing – Christendom on the earth in responsibility until the end of the age. The parable speaks of a spoiled crop in the world with evil growing and ripening in it. The seven messages have the same general theme. The parable has a separation of the tares from the wheat at the end. In the seven messages I believe Philadelphia and Laodicea represent this separation.

Chapter 6:
Ephesus: the Beginning of Decline and Decay

We do not find any reference to the active energy and power of the Holy Spirit to produce blessing in any of the seven messages to the churches. In the course of the messages we do not even find the Son of Man giving grace to the church world, as in, 'My grace is sufficient for you'. The messages are judgments of man's efforts and works in responsibility before God. They are not the assessment of God's efforts or sovereign work. The Son of Man is looking at the candlesticks that are on earth, and He is judging the form and condition of the professing church. Ephesus, the first church in the series, is the representation of the condition of the entire church world soon after the life of John. This is a time following Pentecost and its original blessings. It is the time after apostolic order and power in the early church.

The Active Energy of the Holy Spirit

It is not that there weren't any issues to be sorted out in the early church. But it was a time in which the power of the Holy Spirit was active – Peter is delivered from the hands of Herod, and Paul and

Silas set free from prison in Philippi (Acts 16:26). Philip is performing miracles in Samaria and later is translated from one place to another (Acts 8:5-6, 39). The energy of the Holy Spirit is found in audible messages in a number of instances (Acts 8:29, 10:19), as well as in visions, dreams, and detailed prophecies. There was also apostolic order through the Holy Spirit in Peter's dealing with Ananias and Sapphira (Acts 5:1-10). Apostolic authority is shown in Paul's ministry, especially in His dealings with the Corinthian church. The signs of an apostle were evident during the time of the early church (I Cor. 2:4, II Cor. 12:11-12).

The dynamics of this time are aptly described in the book of Acts by a Pharisee named Gamaliel, when the apostles were brought before the Jewish council:

Acts 5:34-39

(34) "Then one in the council stood up, a Pharisee named Gamaliel, a teacher of the law held in respect by all the people, and commanded them to put the apostles outside for a little while. (35) And he said to them: "Men of Israel, take heed to yourselves what you intend to do regarding these men. (36) For some time ago Theudas rose up, claiming to be somebody. A number of men, about four hundred, joined him. He was slain, and all who obeyed him were scattered and came to nothing. (37) After this man, Judas of Galilee rose up in the days of the census, and drew away many people after him. He also perished, and all who obeyed him were dispersed. (38) And now I say to you, keep away from these men and let them alone; for if this plan or this work is of men, it will come to nothing; (39) but if it is of God, you cannot overthrow it—lest you even be found to fight against God."

Ephesus: the Time after the Apostles

The church was started by the sovereign grace and work of God. The active energy of the Holy Spirit was present, as well as apostolic power. *"And the Lord added to the church daily those who were being saved."* (Acts 2:47) It was not a work of man in responsibility, but the outward manifestations of the Holy Spirit sent down to the earth to establish the beginnings of the church. By the grace and power of God a sure foundation was laid for the building of God (I Cor. 3:10). Now the time of the apostles was ending, and Ephesus, the first of the seven churches, represents this time. This is definitely the occasion when another man builds on the foundation in human responsibility. *"But let each one take heed how he builds on it."*

What could be expected in the church world after the apostles were gone? This passage spoken by Paul to the Ephesian elders seems unusually appropriate:

Acts 20:29-30

"For I know this, that after my departure savage wolves will come in among you, not sparing the flock. Also from among yourselves men will rise up, speaking perverse things, to draw away the disciples after themselves."

The candlesticks represent the corporate responsibility of the professing church. Even though John saw seven in his vision, symbolically it is only one candlestick seen seven times. We are looking at seven periods of time and/or distinct characters of Christendom on the earth. Ephesus is the first period of time. And I continue to use the phrase 'on the earth' because that is where responsibility is looked at and judged, and that is where the vision takes place.

Revelation 2:1-7

"To the angel of the church of Ephesus write,

"These things says He who holds the seven stars in His right hand, who walks in the midst of the seven golden lampstands: (2) "I know your works, your labor, your patience, and that you cannot bear those who are evil. And you have tested those who say they are apostles and are not, and have found them liars; (3) and you have persevered and have patience, and

have labored for My name's sake and have not become weary. (4) Nevertheless I have this against you, that you have left your first love. (5) Remember therefore from where you have fallen; repent and do the first works, or else I will come to you quickly and remove your lampstand from its place—unless you repent. (6) But this you have, that you hate the deeds of the Nicolaitans, which I also hate.

(7) "He who has an ear, let him hear what the Spirit says to the churches. To him who overcomes I will give to eat from the tree of life, which is in the midst of the Paradise of God."'

Ephesus: the removal of the Candlestick is threatened

The character of Christ to Ephesus is one in which He exercises judgment. In a sense I believe this character is applied to all seven churches in a general way, for He is walking in the midst of all seven candlesticks. I believe this is true also because this is the only church of the seven for which the candlestick is specifically mention in the message. This is not the presentation of a specific ecclesiastical character for the needs of Ephesus, but the general statement that Christ is judge of Christendom from beginning to end.

The Son of Man threatens Ephesus with the removal of their candlestick if they do not repent. The threat is to the professing church as a whole. The candlestick belongs to Christendom. If the candlestick is removed, it would mean the corporate body is no longer an acceptable testimony to the truth of God and the glory of Christ on the earth. So there are a few thoughts from the outset to keep in mind:

- For Ephesus, He begins to walk in the midst of the candlesticks, which is slightly different than the wording from chapter one (Rev. 1:12-13).[101] With Ephesus the Son of Man is beginning to exercise His judgment of the responsibility of the professing church.

- The removal of the candlestick is when the corporate body of professing Christianity is no longer a legitimate witness and testimony for God on the earth. This is when Christendom no longer properly shines as a light to this dark world. In the reality of the seven churches, this occurs with either Thyatira or Laodicea, or both. But its removal is what is threatened with Ephesus as the first church.[102]

- Unless there was repentance of the entire corporate body of Christianity, there would be the removal of the candlestick. Ephesus did not repent. Neither did the following two. By the fourth church this command to repent and return from where you have fallen is no longer entertained as a possibility for the corporate body by the Lord.

The Son of Man as Judge

He walks among the candlesticks in the character of the Judge, clothed with a garment down to His feet and girded about the chest with a golden band (Rev. 1:13). This is in contrast to His previous character as High Priest for the church, in which His loins would be girded about, and He would be washing our feet as a servant. As High Priest for the believer He removes all defilement and impurities from us resulting from our walk in this world (John 13:1-7, Heb. 4:14-16). But walking among the candlesticks the Son of Man's garment is girded about the chest with a golden band representing divine righteousness in judgment. It was to the Son of God as the Son of Man that the Father has committed the right to all judgment (John 5:26-27). He is here to see if the church world has an answer for the grace previously received, the sovereign work of the Holy Spirit. Holding the stars, He is the One with all power and authority in heaven and on earth (Matt. 28:18). Is the light from the candlestick burning bright?

The Son of Man is not blind to the good qualities and work that He finds (Rev. 2:2-3) and is quick to emphasize these good things. The professing church at this time would not allow evil to take up residence within, even testing all who say they are ministers of God.

He finds much that is acceptable, *"I know your works, your labor, your patience..."* Where He can find some good He always takes notice of it and encourage it. But the paramount question is what is the source and root of the labor? Is it still love for Jesus Christ? Is this a work springing forth from their love of the Lord, or has it become a labor in His name only?

The apostle Paul, writing to the Thessalonians, is continually reminded of their *'work of faith, labor of love, and patience of hope in our Lord Jesus Christ...'* (I Thess. 1:3) In the time of Ephesus the Lord finds works, labor, and patience, but it is no longer a work of faith, a labor of love, and a patience of hope in Christ Jesus. They had left their first love.

Ephesus: the Professing Church has lost its First Love

We must remember these are questions being asked of the corporate entity, and that the individual is not being addressed.[103] Has professing Christianity, as a whole, lost its first love? Has Christendom already decayed from the original position of the church? Has the candlestick dimmed from the amount of light it was given in its first position of blessing?

The question of our love for Jesus has to be viewed in the light of His love for us. Our love is in reciprocation to His love shown first. *"We love Him because He first loved us."* (I John 4:19) The question of the love of the corporate body for Him must be a reflection back to Him based on His love for the church, as a corporate entity.

Ephesians 5:25-27

"...just as Christ also loved the church and gave Himself for her, (26) that He might sanctify and cleanse her with the washing of water by the word,(27) that He might present her to Himself a glorious church, not having spot or wrinkle or any such thing, but that she should be holy and without blemish."

Ephesians 5:2

"And walk in love, as Christ also has loved us and given Himself for us, an offering and a sacrifice to God for a sweet-smelling aroma."

His love for the church went beyond death. Christ was the One who, being in the form of God, did not consider it robbery to change His state, but made Himself of no reputation, taking on the form of a servant, the likeness of sinful man (Phil. 2:5-8). He bore our sins and was made sin for us. The condemnation and wrath that we deserved was placed on Him. In the plan of God and in doing the will of God, He became obedient unto death, the death of the cross. He went down under death to deliver us from all the power of the enemy, and to release us, who through fear of death were all our lifetimes subject to bondage (Heb. 2:14-15). In order to bring many brethren to heavenly glory, it was fitting for Him, as the author of our salvation, to be made perfect through sufferings (Heb. 2:9-11). And now we have this:

Ephesians 5:29

"For no one ever hated his own flesh, but nourishes and cherishes it, just as the Lord does the church."

There is no question concerning the Lord's love for the church. It will never waver or diminish. This would be impossible. But can He be satisfied without the return of the Bride's love to Him? Isn't it true that only the response of love can satisfy the love first given? It does not matter what the professing church accomplishes in work and labor, if love for Christ Himself is not the motivation. Many great things done in the name of Christ would be judged wood, hay, and stubble if the true intentions and motives were known. He is the Word of God, the discerner of the thoughts and intents of the heart, and there is nothing hidden from His sight (Heb. 4:12-13). Having loved the church and given Himself for it, He desires her love in return. Any Bridegroom would have such an expectation of His betrothed. If there is no love for Him, it doesn't matter what we are doing. It is as a sounding brass or clanging symbol (I Cor. 13:1-3).

Ephesus: Christendom has left its First Position

There should be no question in any believer's mind that the professing church has lost its first love (Rev. 2:4). Christendom has left its first position of blessing. This constitutes decline and decay from its original state. The corporate body as a whole is not willing to remember from where it has fallen (Rev. 2:5). This is not a call for individuals to repent. It was the entire church world that was called on to repent and return to its first position. But professing Christianity would not and did not. It slowly became more interested in its own earthly glory than showing forth the glory of its missing Head in heaven. It would soon, as a corporate entity, start gathering earthly riches rather than laying up treasure in the heavens. The candlestick of witness and testimony for Christendom was destined to be removed, even from its beginning in Ephesus.

The feebleness of the church world's love for the One it professes is the first principle of failure of man in responsibility to God. The beginning of decline and decay in Ephesus would certainly lead to the predicted apostasy of the church world (II Thess. 2:3, I Tim. 4:1-3, II Tim. 4:3-4). When asked to 'do the first works' it is the Lord wanting to bring them back to their point of departure. Yet professing Christianity was heading in a certain direction, and even the exhortations of her Lord would not change her course. Decline and decay had set in. Apostasy would follow.

The Work of God – the Work of Man

Can Christendom be restored? When we understand the spiritual and moral impact of the seven messages, we realize that the possibility of restoration has long passed. Can the church world experience Pentecostal power and blessings again? Once more, according to the Son of Man's messages, this is foolish and pretentious thinking. It is the blindness of Laodicea, the refusal to see as God sees (Rev. 3:17), and ultimately declining to agree with Him.

There is an urgent need today for spiritual wisdom and discernment concerning the differences that exist between the work of God and the work of man. Because the Arminian and Judaizing leaven has so saturated Christendom today, it is almost impossible for the majority of Christianity to see any distinction. We said before that the work of God is what cannot fail. The work of man always does. The work that God does is eternal. The work that man does will pass away. The work of God will serve to glorify only Him. The work of man gives man a reason to boast. I pray that every believer will be able to see these differences. The Scriptures make these distinctions abundantly clear. But the leaven the church world has embraced exalts man, in human effort and human accomplishment, whatever it may be. We no longer accept the clear distinctions the Scriptures establish between the two. Men have to water down the truth of Scripture because it is so condemning of man's work.

Often our human thoughts are that we are doing the work of God. This is quite a presumption for anyone to make. Yet the leaven demands of us that we mix it up this way – the work of God 'depends' on man doing it. We are always doing something. What we can say about the church world is that it is always doing something. We would like to think it is the work of God. When God created the heavens and the earth, it was the work of God. In other words, the work of God was done by God. That is what makes it the work of God. And that is why He alone receives all the glory. He did not need man to do it. He did not 'depend' on man.

But you may say that God does depend on man for His will to be done. You may say that, at this time, God has chosen to become dependent on man to do His work. Do you really want to say that? Do you really want to teach that? Do you want to say that God is dependent on man for anything? Can the Creator become dependent on the created? Can He do this and still remain God? If you reason this way, then you do not know God. You do not know who God is, and what God is.

You may say God depends on us to preach the gospel. I agree that God has given the church the gospel, and has privileged us to be used as instruments of His grace to sinners. The preaching of the gospel is the common way God works in salvation. But if it severs His purposes, He will knock a man down on the road to Damascus and save him, and do it all without man's preaching. This is the work of

God, and it is God who does it. Whether it is by preaching or not, it is God working if a man is saved. Why? It is eternal life that is given to man. Only the work of God is eternal.

The corrupting leaven of human achievement has Christianity thinking and teaching that God truly needs our help or His plan is lost. Can the prophetic Scriptures be that unstable? No they are not! Prophecy is the infallible Word of God that cannot return to Him void, but will accomplish exactly His purposes (Is. 55:10-11). And for that very reason, prophecy – future things – cannot be, in any way, dependent on the responsibility of man.

What I see in prophecy is the 'times of the Gentiles' which involves Nebuchadnezzar's great image in his dream and the four beast world empires seen in Daniel's dream (Dan. 2:31-33, 7:2-7). Again, the coming of Christianity or the preaching of the gospel never changes the character of the four beasts. And what is it that destroys the great Gentile image? Is it the preaching of the Christian gospel? Rather, it is the stone made without hands, the coming of the Son of Man, which destroys the statue, grinds it into chaff, and then grows and fills the whole earth as the kingdom of the Son of Man (Dan. 2:34-35).

The corrupting leaven has Christians thinking that God places another person's eternal destiny in their hands, dependent on their actions and works in responsibility. There isn't another thought in Christian teaching that is more self-exalting in pride than this. But this simply is not true. The history of man in the Scriptures proves that man, in his responsibility, is always a failure. God would never base someone's, no, anyone's salvation on a principle that is destined to fail. It is God who gives eternal life, and He quickens whom He wills (John 5:21, 24-26, 17: 2-3). And when He does so, it is His work, and no one can snatch them out of His hand (John 10:28-29, 6:37-39).

The Sovereign Work of God

Creation was the sovereign work of God. The cross of Jesus Christ was the sovereign work of God. The Holy Spirit sent down at Pentecost was the sovereign work of God. Every sinner saved is the new creation of God, born of God, and the sovereign workmanship of God created in Christ Jesus (II Cor. 5:17, John 1:12-13, Eph. 2:10). The enlightenment of the Reformation was the sovereign work of God. The rapture of the church, her blessed hope, will be the sovereign work of God, the power of God by resurrection and change. When Satan is removed from the heavens and cast down to the earth, it will be the sovereign work of God. When he is bound in chains in the bottomless pit, and the Antichrist and Roman beast cast into the lake of fire, it will be the sovereign work of God. When all Christ's enemies are destroyed by the sword out of His mouth, this too will be the sovereign work of God. Daniel's interpretation of the king's dream refers to this as 'the stone made without hands' coming out of heaven to strike the feet of the great Gentile image – 'without hands' means divine sovereign power as the source or agent.

Israel saved and protected as a remnant during the tribulation is the sovereign work of God's choice and providential power. Israel restored in the land during the coming millennium, there doing all God's law in obedience, is another example of the sovereign grace and power of God – He writes His law on their minds and hearts, so they will do it and be the most blessed nation on the face of the earth (Deut. 28:1-13). *The point is:* God does His work, and He never becomes dependent on man. Also, the candlesticks are not His sovereign work, but rather the works of man in the professing church. The candlesticks are being judged by God. If they actually represented God's work, He would not be judging them.

The Question of Evil Within

"...you cannot bear those that are evil." (Rev. 2:2) The church was to be the manifestation of the power of God in goodness and truth in the midst of this evil world. In the professing church the conflict with evil would be within the corporate body. Early on Satan was allowed to come in and sow tares. The corruption and evil is there. It came in through the failure of men in responsibility (Matt. 13:25). The evil grows like weeds until it dominates the crop. This thing will spoil. The crop will ruin. Ephesus may have been a time when the evil wasn't tolerated, but they had left their first love. Where there

is decline and decay, there will always be the question of whether there is evil within. Eventually Christendom became comfortable with the corruption – it was even profitable in a worldly way for the church to embrace it.

"...you hate the deeds of the Nicolaitans, which I also hate." (Rev. 2:6) This involved a doctrine of outright evil acts in the name of Christ and in a false character of grace. It was connecting fleshliness with spirituality, and that Christians were released by grace from obeying moral law. It was a joining of Christ with evil. We are permitted to hate what Christ hates. We should always oppose what Christ opposes.

The Paradise of God

At the end of His message to Ephesus He speaks directly to the true believer – the overcomer. The promise He gives to the individual believer is that he will eat from the tree of life, which is in the midst of the paradise of God (Rev. 2:7). This is not the paradise in which God came down to visit man, to see what man was doing, and found sin. In that paradise man was thrown out. It was ruined by the sin of man. Rather what is promised is the paradise that God has made for Himself – God's rest, and God's heavenly glory. This is where the tree of life is – in God's paradise. By virtue of the redemption that is in Christ Jesus, God will take every believer there, to go out no more (Rev. 3:12). God does not swear in His wrath that the redeemed shall not enter His rest. It is to the redeemed it remains that they will enter in (Heb. 4:1, 6, 9-11). These are the justified in Christ, who no longer fall short of the glory of God (Rom. 3:23-24).

In God's paradise there are not two trees. Man gained the knowledge of good and evil in the garden, but this was through disobedience and under the mastery of sin. By our redemption in Christ we now possess a purged, sanctified, and perfect conscience – it is part of our redeemed nature (Heb. 9:9, 14, 10:1-2, 14). But while we are still on this earth, the principle of sin resides in the flesh. When we are brought to the paradise of God, sin will, of necessity, have been removed from our flesh, our bodies glorified. There we will possess the knowledge of good and evil according to the holiness of God. This being established, there is but one tree for the redeemed in the paradise of God – the tree of the life of God (Rev. 2:7). Man has had enough of the other tree.

Further, the paradise of God is not on the earth. The rest of God is not the millennium on earth. The millennium is the reign and kingdom of the Son of Man over the earth. But all that remains on the earth during that time in still man in Adam, man in the flesh, with the principle of sin in the flesh. And God's rest and paradise will never be where sin is present. During the millennium the glorified church will be in the kingdom of their Father in the heavens (Matt. 13:43).

In summary, what are the principles that are settled in Ephesus?

1. The assembly in this world and on this earth is subject to the judgment of God. Jesus would examine its whole existence and place before God as light-bearer in the world.

2. God would set the professing church aside on earth. He would remove its candlestick if it departs from its first spiritual energy and position in blessing.

God had placed the assembly (church) to be a true witness of what He had manifested in Jesus Christ, and what the Son of Man is when He is exalted on high. If it did not witness this, then the professing church is a false witness, and must be set aside. God may have patience and has shown tremendous patience with the corporate assembly. He may propose she return to her first love, and He does this. But if there is no return of the corporate assembly, the candlestick is removed, and Christendom ceases to be God's light-bearer to the world. The first estate must be maintained, or God's glory and His truth are falsified.

Ephesus had maintained consistency. Christ approved of that and He encourages her by showing His approval. But she could not forget herself and think only of Christ, which should always be the first results of receiving grace. The first fruits were gone. There were works of labor and patience, but missing were faith, hope, and love

– all to be in and of Christ. There was good to be commended, but still they had lost their first love. The assembly had fallen. The Son of Man asked the professing church to repent and return to its first position, to do its first works. This the corporate body, as a whole, would not do. The Gentiles grafted in by faith, have not continued in the goodness of God (Rom. 11:21-22).

The epistle to the Ephesian church represents the knowledge and intelligence of the body of Christ concerning the revealed counsels of God towards her (Eph. 1:3-12). The book of the Ephesians represents the expression of what the assembly of God was as originally established by God (Eph. 1:22-23, 2:11-22). It is ironic that the first decline and failure of the professing church is pictured in Scripture as the church of Ephesus.

The Ephesus of Paul's time is not the Ephesus that existed when John was on Patmos. The Ephesus of John's time becomes the demonstration on earth of the decay and decline of the professing assembly. God would eventually remove her candlestick. His patience would be shown towards the assembly as He had shown it in His longsuffering with Israel. The assembly would not maintain the testimony of God in the world any better than Israel had. The professing church eventually would cease to be a valid witness for God on the earth.

However, grace will always sustain the individual believer, even when the corporate body goes down in failure – in all seven messages there are promises 'to him who overcomes'. But a warning is in order here. Even though the believer is the workmanship of God, created in Christ Jesus and preserved in sovereign grace, he has responsibility to acknowledge evil and turn from it. The believer cannot be justified in simply sailing along in the stream of corporate corruption and failure in professing Christianity, just armed with the excuse that this is all there is, and there is nothing better to do. That is not the true believer 'having ears to hear' or 'overcoming by our faith'.

From the very first, judgment is pronounced on the church world. What proceeds from Ephesus are the differing states and conditions the professing church passes through to arrive at that judgment. The candlestick will be removed (Rev. 2:5).

Chapter 6: Endnotes

[101] In Rev. 1:10-13 Jesus Christ, the Son of Man is seen in the midst of the seven candlesticks and holding the seven stars in the power of His right hand. He is the One who lit the light of the candlesticks on the earth. He did so by sovereign grace and blessing, and as we have previously said, the house of God on the earth – the habitation of God in the Spirit – was begun as a sovereign work of God in original blessing. This was the power and energy of the Holy Spirit in the early church and apostolic power and order. The candlestick was originally lit by the Son of Man.

The character of Christ presented in the message to Ephesus is slightly different than what was found in chapter one. Here He is walking in the midst of the candlesticks (Rev. 2:1). This serves to bring out some subtle points in the use of the allegories. The candlesticks are the responsibility of the church world to be a light and testimony for God in this evil and dark world. His 'walking' in their midst also shows that responsibility is what is being judged. The professing church has a 'walk' in the wilderness of this world. It is a walk by faith (II Cor. 5:7). We are to walk as He walked (I John 2:6). Its 'walk' is the professing church's responsibility. The Son of Man is the Judge, and by walking in the midst of the candlesticks, He is beginning His judgments of the responsibility of the corporate body.

His walking in their midst also shows that the candlesticks are not a part of Him, that He is separate from them. He was responsible for lighting them in sovereign grace, but now responsibility has been turned over to man. But the candlesticks are not 'in Him'. All the wonderful truths and blessings concerning the believer/church are by sovereign grace found 'in Christ' and 'in Him'. But the candlesticks – the responsibility of professing Christianity – are definitely not a part of Him or His sovereign work. The responsibility of man is the works of man, and this is what He judges.

[102] The threat of the removal of the candlestick of the professing church is in the first message! The temptation is to look at Ephesus and ask, "What more can the Lord want or expect?" If we have this thought at all, we entirely miss the soberness and seriousness of what is being said. What the eye of faith sees in the professing church at this time is decline, decay, and failure – the root and beginning of apostasy. Will we have the ears of faith to hear what the Spirit is actually judging concerning Christendom? Listed below are the negative implications from the message to Ephesus:

- The implication is that in the professing church there may be evil already within.

- The implication is that there is falseness in ministry in the professing church already to contend with.

- The accusation is that the professing church has left its first love – the first principle of failure.

- The accusation is that the professing church has fallen, and that the corporate entity is asked to repent and return to its first position of blessing.

- The threat is made of removal of the candlestick of professing Christianity, if the corporate entity does not repent.

- The evil doctrine of the Nicolaitans is mentioned in connection with the professing church. By the third church (Pergamos) this appalling doctrine was now welcomed within the church world (Rev. 2:15).

[103] Even though we know the messages were spoken by the Son of Man to the corporate entity of Christendom as a whole, and it is the external body being told to repent, it does not prohibit the individual believer from profiting from the moral content of the messages. We will find that the Lord deals with the individual in the same way that He does with the professing church. He takes notice of any departure of the individual believer from their first love. His desire is to have you as His own, and that your love for Him to be genuine, the reciprocal of His love for you. It will not be in the perfection of His love for you, but the affections for Him and the desires to be with Him must be present and growing. If they are not acceptable He will point this out to you: *"Nevertheless I have this against you, that you have left your first love."* The individual's ability and opportunity to repent is also more simplified than the same for the corporate entity. When Christ asked Ephesus to repent, He was not speaking to the individual. Applying the message and the need for repentance to the individual, however, is an easier task.

Chapter 7:
Smyrna: the Time of Persecution

The professing church had fallen from its first position of grace. It did not stay in the original blessings of God. Through the responsibility of men, the church world was now on a course of decline and decay. It had fallen from God's expectations for it. It was to be a bright light and pure testimony for Him to the darkness of this world. When the corporate body was asked by the Lord to repent and return to its first position, she would not respond. The course was set. This decline and failure in Ephesus opened the door for trials and persecutions in the time of Smyrna that followed. The experience in Smyrna was a consequence of Ephesus losing its first love and falling.

Revelation 2:8-11

"And to the angel of the church in Smyrna write,

'These things says the First and the Last, who was dead, and came to life: (9) "I know your works, tribulation, and poverty (but you are rich); and I know the blasphemy of those who say they are Jews and are not, but are a synagogue of Satan. (10) Do not fear any of those things which you are about to suffer. Indeed, the devil is about to throw some of you into prison,

that you may be tested, and you will have tribulation ten days. Be faithful until death, and I will give you the crown of life.

(11) "He who has an ear, let him hear what the Spirit says to the churches. He who overcomes shall not be hurt by the second death."'

The professing church had lost its love and affections for Christ. Jesus loved the church and had given His life for her. It was reasonable for Him to expect her constant love and affections in return. But that state was short-lived in the early church. If it had fallen from true affection for Christ, its attention was being turned elsewhere. The professing church was in the world and the world itself was becoming an attraction.

God's use of Evil to bring Blessing

Ephesus, no doubt, was a time of great growth in numbers for the professing church. The crop had been enlarged and multiplied in the field of the world. There were far more churches in the world than the seven mentioned here. There was the natural tendency to rest and be satisfied with the results produced, instead of continual dependence on the Lord. The Lord loves the church too much to allow this to go on without a response from Him.

What we should understand is that God is willing to use Satan to accomplish certain results. His response to professing Christianity's departure is to use the persecution from the world to draw her back to Christ and to teach His lessons. Satan's power, acting through the hatred and ungodliness of the world, is used by God for two specific outcomes:

- First, to exercise divine grace in the saints in the corporate body of Christendom

- Second, to hinder the corporate body from departing any further from the Lord, and to separate it from the evil world around it

Sufferings used to bring out Grace

In the first point above the life of Jesus becomes our great example. His entire life on earth was filled with trials and sufferings leading to the cross – His redemptive sufferings and death. It wasn't that there were impurities and evil in His person that needed to be atoned for, but as the Scriptures declare, *"...He, by the grace of God, might taste death for everyone. For it was fitting for Him, for whom are all things and by whom are all things, in bringing many sons to glory, to make the author of their salvation perfect through sufferings."* (Heb. 2:9-10) This isn't speaking of imperfection in the Son of God. As God alone He would not have the experiences He gained as coming in the likeness of human flesh. Making the author of salvation perfect though sufferings speaks of the experience that He could not have in His divinity. So also the Scriptures say, *"And being found in the appearance as a man, He humbled Himself and became obedient to the point of death, even the death of the cross."* (Phil. 2:8) Again, even though being in the form of God and equal with God, in human flesh He showed obedience. This is His perfection through sufferings.

1 Peter 2:21-25

"For to this you were called, because Christ also suffered for us, leaving us an example, that you should follow His steps:

(22) "Who committed no sin,

Nor was deceit found in His mouth";

(23) who, when He was reviled, did not revile in return; when He suffered, He did not threaten, but committed Himself to Him who judges righteously; (24) who Himself bore our sins in His own body on the tree, that we, having died to sins, might live for righteousness—by whose stripes you were healed. (25) For you were like sheep going astray, but have now returned to the Shepherd and Overseer of your souls."

Hebrews 5:7-9

(7) "...who, in the days of His flesh, when He had offered up prayers and supplications, with vehement cries and tears to Him who was able to save Him from death, and was heard because of His godly fear, (8) though He was a Son, yet He learned obedience by the things which He suffered. (9) And having been perfected, He became the author of eternal salvation to all who obey Him."

The sufferings brought out the grace of God more fully in His life in the flesh and in the redemptive work as the Son of Man. The manifestation of all that was within Him was brought out through hardship and difficulty. The result is that there is now a Man in glory, the glorified Son of Man, who is the author of the only eternal salvation that is available for men. Having been perfected through sufferings, and having learned obedience as the Son of Man, He became the Author, as well as the Shepherd and Overseer of our souls.

Sufferings to hinder further Decline

The second effect of God's use of Satan in persecution is to separate the church from evil and to hinder the church from further decline and decay. There is a tendency for us to rest in worldly success and prosperous times. Professing Christianity had grown — by the grace of God, by the devil planting tares, and by man busy building in responsibility. The flesh naturally turns to what is agreeable in the world, and this wars against the Spirit within. The flesh desires to find rest in the world. The same is true for the house of God built on the earth, the habitation of God in the Spirit. Accommodating what the flesh finds rest in, leads to decay (Micah 2:10).

Persecution is the church's promised portion while on the earth and in the world (John 16:33). When the church world is beginning to rest in human endeavor, failing to even notice it has left its love for Christ as its motive, God brings in tribulation. It is opposition from outside, Satan using the world to bring trials and persecutions. But

God allows it and uses it to bring out grace in the corporate body, to separate her from evil and to hinder her decay. God uses Satan as an instrument to bring out blessing for the church.

Revelation 13:10

"He who leads into captivity shall go into captivity; he who kills with the sword must be killed with the sword. Here is the patience and the faith of the saints."

The saint's portion is to suffer and endure the continuance of evil, even its prospering for the time (Matt. 5:38-48). God permits evil in this age, even power given to it. This will not be true in the following dispensation. However, at this time the saints must not seek to avenge themselves or they will suffer the consequences of their actions. Patient suffering is the saint's place, like Christ when He walked in the flesh. Once Peter cut off the ear of the servant of the high priest. But later he would write, *"But when you do well and suffer for it, if you take it patiently, this is commendable before God."* (I Pet. 2:20) Vengeance is the Lord's. He will repay (Rev. 13:10).

I know that the above sounds strange and isn't taught much in Christian circles. God using Satan as an instrument would be denied and labeled blasphemous by many. But we should learn the wisdom of God from the Scriptures, and be taught of the Spirit. There are a number of elements that lead to this conclusion for Smyrna, which are important to keep in mind.

1. In the first three churches the messages are addressed to Christendom as a recognized corporate entity having testimony for the Lord. When the Lord says, *I know your works, tribulation, and poverty..."* he is not speaking to individuals, but to the external church body. The persecution is of the corporate entity and it is widespread, and would last, off and on, for a few hundred years. It was the existing Roman Empire, the Roman beast holding the throne of Satan in the world, which the devil was using.

2. While the church is on the earth, Paul describes its experience as *"...if indeed we suffer with Him...the sufferings of this present time..."* (Rom. 8:17-18) The professing church is on a walk in the wilderness. What professing Christianity seeks in the wilderness of the world is one thing. What the true church and true believers are to have in the wilderness is another. The history of Christendom has been the acquiring of earthly riches, power, and status. It is a history of seeking pleasure, vanity, and ambition. This is a relationship with the world (I John 2:15-17). Does that resemble Christ? Is that what He had on the earth? Riches, power, and a name? Are we not to walk as He walked? (I John 1:6) If indeed we are suffering with Him? The proper portion of the true church in this world is hatred (John 15:18-19). The proper portion of the true church in this world is tribulation (John 16:33). The proper portion of the true church in this world is sufferings (Rom. 8:18). The only way to avoid this is to become like the world.[104]

3. In the last four churches Christ doesn't recognize the corporate entity of Christendom and He alone knows those that are His. What I mean by this is that at that time only God can see the true body of Christ on the earth. Man no longer can see it. What the world recognizes is all of Christendom as the church. True believers try to have some vague acknowledgement of the body of Christ, but this vision is full of suppositions and judgments.[105] Today the persecution of Christians is individual and associated with certain places in the world. It is not of the entire corporate entity as it is referenced with Smyrna.

4. We have many examples in Scripture where God will use Satan or evil men as a rod of correction and chastisement for His people – the Assyrian, Nebuchadnezzar, and the Romans were all different groups or men used as a rod in judgment.

Scriptural Examples of God's use of the devil

Let us consider the example of Job. God used Satan in this case to bring circumstances and trials into his life. By these, God teaches Job the lessons he needed to learn, and in result, to bless him. It is God who initiates the conversation with Satan and asks him, *"Have you considered my servant Job...?"* God knows what He is doing by drawing the devil's attention to him. Satan is ready to act and bring trials, but by these actions God reveals the evil in Job's heart. Self-righteousness was creeping in and Job needed to learn what he really was in the presence of God. Job would not have learned this knowledge and lesson any other way. The goodness of God does not pass over iniquity, but will show us what we are and what we have done. Professing Christianity had left her first love and God would not overlook this, even if it meant using the trials and adversities of Satan.

Look at the example of Paul. He had spiritual experiences beyond everyone else. He was even taken up into the third heaven. In the Paradise of God he is prepared for the special ministry he would have for the church. He is given a revelation of Jesus Christ in glory that formed the gospel of the glory of Christ that he preached (II Cor. 4:3-7). He was fortified by the grace of Christ residing within, which sustained him through his many trials and persecutions (II Cor. 4:7-11) and energized him in his ministry. In the heavens he received an abundance of revelations (II Cor. 12:1).

A Messenger of Satan

Now Paul was just a man. His flesh would want to exalt itself over such things. There was a real danger for Paul, because of the abundance of the revelations, to be puffed up in human pride (II Cor. 12:7). God knew this, and so He gives Paul a thorn in the flesh. God uses a messenger from Satan to buffet Paul, to keep him humble. Paul's flesh doesn't like this, so he inquires of the Lord three times to have the thorn removed. God would not. Paul had to learn the lesson that he was nothing and that Christ and the grace of Christ was everything. It would have to be God working in him by God's strength, not Paul's. So he learns to glory, not in the confidences of the flesh, but in the weakness of the flesh, so that the grace of Christ is the only strength he has to rely on (II Cor. 12:7-9).

2 Corinthians 12:10

"Therefore I take pleasure in infirmities, in reproaches, in needs, in persecutions, in distresses, for Christ's sake. For when I am weak, then I am strong."

When Paul learned his own self, his own flesh in weakness, then Christ was the strength and power that rested upon him. God used a messenger of Satan to buffet him in order to get him to depend on Christ's grace and strength, and not in himself.

Paul is the greatest example of the sovereign work of God in a human being. He was made by God to be an instrument in the Lord's hands. I do not see God asking Saul for permission to do the things that He does in him. The words spoken to Ananias by the Lord at Paul's conversion speak volumes;

Acts 9:15-16

"But the Lord said to him, "Go, for he is a chosen vessel of Mine to bear My name before Gentiles, kings, and the children of Israel. For I will show him how many things he must suffer for My name's sake."

On the earth and in this world, Paul, the apostle of the glory of Christ, must suffer many things for the name of Jesus Christ. He was an elect vessel used by God. But in looking after this chosen instrument of His, God sees fit to give Paul a thorn in the flesh to keep him humble. Partly because of the things he suffered, his flesh and pride were humbled so that the power and grace of Christ would be upon him.

Present Sufferings, Future Glory

Paul's walk of responsibility on the earth becomes an example for all believers to emulate (Phil 3:15-17). His example teaches valuable principles to be learned and embraced by all Christians. He would only glory in the weaknesses of the flesh – in infirmities, in reproaches, in needs, in persecutions, in distresses (II Cor. 12:9-10). This was so the power and grace of Christ would be active in him. His thorn in the flesh taught him to glory only in the *weakness* of the flesh. All his *confidences* of the flesh he discards and leaves behind. The grace and power of Christ would never rest on these.

This is played out for us in the third chapter of Philippians. Paul says he cannot have any form of any of the confidences of the flesh, but these things are rubbish and dung and only fit for discarding (Phil. 3:3-9). He does this for the sole reason of gaining the knowledge and relationship of a person, Jesus Christ (Phil. 3:7-8). And he does nothing but press forward (Phil. 3:12-14). He purposely has no memory of things behind him. He has one calling, and it is upward and heavenly. This is all he knows! This is the only thing that is worth anything – *"I press toward the goal for the prize of the upward call of God in Christ Jesus."* (Phil. 3:14) Paul knows how this will be accomplished by God – *"...if, by any means, I may attain to the resurrection from the dead."* (Phil. 3:11) What was always before Paul, and that which motivated him so that he always was pressing forward, was the heavenly calling, the glory, and the resurrection as the means of getting there. All his pressing forward has the singular purpose of getting to where Jesus is, in the heavens. Then we find this statement:

Philippians 3:10

"...that I may know Him and the power of His resurrection, and the fellowship of His sufferings, being conformed to His death."

Knowing the power of His resurrection is the rapture of the church and the fulfillment of our heavenly calling (please see Eph. 1:18-23). But until then Paul is always pressing toward it. This is his responsibility and this is his walk while still on this earth. Not that he has already attained, or is already perfected in his walk (Phil. 3:12). This can never happen on the earth and in this flesh, but perfection can only be attained through Christ's resurrection.

What is the believer's portion on the earth while we press on towards the heavenly calling? Is it not the fellowship of His sufferings? Should we not, in our walk in the wilderness, exhibit a certain 'conforming to His death'?

2 Corinthians 4:7-14

"But we have this treasure in earthen vessels, that the excellence of the power may be of God and not of us. (8) We are hard-pressed on every side, yet not crushed; we are perplexed, but not in despair;(9) persecuted, but not forsaken; struck down, but not destroyed— (10) always carrying about in the body the dying of the Lord Jesus, that the life of Jesus also may be manifested in our body. (11) For we who live are always delivered to death for Jesus' sake, that the life of Jesus also may be manifested in our mortal flesh. (12) So then death is working in us, but life in you.

(13) And since we have the same spirit of faith, according to what is written, "I believed and therefore I spoke," we also believe and therefore speak, (14) knowing that He who raised up the Lord Jesus will also raise us up with Jesus, and will present us with you."

The Believer's Portion

This is so similar to the teaching from Philippians. In our walk we are earthen vessels in which the grace and power of God is contained. We already have been given eternal life. However our walk in this world is not the time in which the excellency of God's power and life will break out in open results. Notice how Paul speaks of the believer's portion in this present time as suffering, and always carrying about in the body the dying of the Lord Jesus. It is so that in this same body of flesh the life of Jesus may be shown forth to the world.

We should know there is a profound difference between the life of Jesus contained in a body of mortal flesh and this same life of Jesus in a body glorified by resurrection. We have the same spirit of faith that Paul had, and so our faith, like his, is the substance of things hoped for, the evidence of things yet to be seen (II Cor. 4:18). What are these things the believer hopes for? Well, it is glory – Christ in you, the hope of glory (Col. 1:27). It is the heavenly calling in Christ Jesus. It is the glorified body through resurrection or change – either way it is the exceeding greatness of His power toward us who believe (Eph. 1:19, I Cor. 15:50-53, John 11:25-26). Isn't this how the above passage ends? God raises us up with Jesus to be presented before Him (II Cor. 4:14). This presentation is in glory and after resurrection. To verify this understanding examine the passage that follows (II Cor. 5:1-7). It is all about resurrection, or the change that the life of Jesus will have on our mortality.

2 Corinthians 4:17

"For our light affliction, which is but for a moment, is working for us a far more exceeding and eternal weight of glory."

Here is the pattern and principle for the true believer that has been repeated in the previous passages. In this time of our walk on the earth our proper portion is to endure sufferings and afflictions. The Scriptures speak of persecutions and tribulations in the world. It speaks of suffering with Christ and for Christ, and filling up the measure of His sufferings. There are the trials of our faith and withstanding the wiles of the devil, quenching all his fiery darts. At this time we are to carry about in the body the dying of the Lord (II Cor. 4:10), being conformed to His death – the practical results and reality of that aspect of our redemption in Christ known as deliverance (Rom. 6:1-11). This allows the life of Jesus to be displayed in our walk of faith. The believer's portion now is to glory in tribulations, knowing that tribulation produces perseverance; and perseverance, character; and character, hope (Rom. 5:3-4). After this it will be the exceeding and eternal weight of glory. The believer's hopes are sure and steadfast, and have entered in behind the veil (Heb. 6:19). They are based upon a God who cannot lie (Heb. 6:17-18). Therefore, we rejoice in hope of the glory of God (Rom. 5:2), while we presently endure sufferings (I Peter 4:13, 5:10). This is the pattern and principle; this is the believer's portion.

The Trying of the Faith

It may be strange to contemplate, especially in the light of contemporary Christian teaching, that God would use Satan as an instrument of trial for the saints and the church. He does so without interfering or delivering. Christ will not prevent the believer from suffering. It is our portion on the earth. We must make up our minds to accept this in our walk.[106] The Son of Man says to Smyrna, *"Do not fear any of those things you are about to suffer. Indeed the devil is about to throw some of you into prison, that you may be tested..."* God could have stepped in and stopped this, however the trial was necessary. Ephesus had fallen. In the wisdom of God, Smyrna would be placed in persecution and tribulation to learn to be more dependent on Christ. There was still the possibility of the professing church returning to her first position.

Let us look at Peter's example. The Lord says to him, *"Simon, Simon! Indeed, Satan has asked for you, that he may sift you as wheat. But I have prayed for you..."* He does not pray to stop Satan from testing Peter, for God knew that Peter needed to be sifted. Peter had a great confidence in the flesh (Luke 22:33, Matt. 26:33). He could not believe he was capable of denying he knew the Lord three times. But the Lord had prayed for him that he would be sustained after his betrayal, and that his faith should not fail. Peter's heart had a hold on the Lord, but his confidence in himself often got in his way. God allowed Satan to sift him, but it proved a blessing to Peter, and by it God used him to strengthen his brethren (Luke 22:31-34). When confidence in self was broken down, Peter could be effective in God's grace. Peter eventually wrote:

1 Peter 1:6-7

"In this you greatly rejoice, though now for a little while, if need be, you have been grieved by various trials, that the genuineness of your faith, being much more precious than gold that perishes, though it is tested by fire, may be found to praise, honor, and glory at the revelation of Jesus Christ."

The World becomes an Attraction

When the professing church was walking in its first love, she had no desire for the world. But later on, other objects of attraction begin to hold power over the professing church, and Christ was no longer the center. The intentions of the heart no longer had Christ as their sole motivation, but she began to align with the course of this world. The flesh rose up and became interested in the evil world around it. She had to be put in tribulation. *"I know thy works, and tribulation, and poverty, but you are rich."* She was placed in the furnace of trials to keep her from joining to the world.

When the church is poor and insignificant, her spiritual reality is that she is rich beyond compare. In this state she is heavenly minded and has laid up divine treasures there. She is not to be resting in a false ease and pleasure in the world. She is not to be enticed by the allurements and trappings of the world. God would allow her to find sorrow in trials and persecutions. In poverty and weakness she would be dependent on Christ alone, *"My grace is sufficient for you, for My strength is made perfect in weakness."* (II Cor. 12:9)

The professing church has been left in this world and on this earth. She was not left here to build a habitation and dwelling place for herself and become a dweller of the earth. She is on a walk in the wilderness of this world, and is a pilgrim and stranger here. She should be a strange thing to the world and the world should be a strange place to her. However, what we will find as we progress through the seven prophetic messages is how the professing church is increasingly enticed into relationship and union with the world. In Ephesus, the professing church had left Christ, its first love. She embarked on a course toward the world. Her responsibility was to be God's shining light to the darkness of the world while she was here. As she becomes worldly over time, the light of the candlestick is diminished. She will no longer hold this position as the witness of God on the earth. In the time of Laodicea in the end, the character of Christ is that He alone is the Faithful and True Witness (Rev. 3:14). What Christendom should have been in witness and testimony all along, Christ takes back from her. The candlestick is removed (Rev. 3:16).

The Character of Christ for Smyrna

The character of Christ for the church world in this time of persecution is not only His divinity, but also as the One 'who was dead and came to life'. His character presented applies to the circumstances found at that time in the professing church. There would be much martyrdom at this time, and His character and His words encourage them, *"Be faithful unto death, and I will give you the crown of life."* (Rev. 2:8) All our blessings and privileges are with Christ, and He is not to be found in this world. He is not of this world. He is the Son of Man glorified to the right hand of God, and our relationships and life are only found there.

Colossians 3:1-3

"If then you were raised with Christ, seek those things which are above, where Christ is, sitting at the right hand of God. (2) Set your mind on things above, not on things on the earth. (3) For you died, and your life is hidden with Christ in God."

As believers, we cannot be looking to the world. You will soon be part of the world when you do. You will have left your first love, and you will not be looking at Christ. Christ is above, sitting at the right hand of God. Our mind must be set on things above. Christ is there. Our life is there. Our relationships are there. Our citizenship is there. Our inheritance and Christian hopes are there. Our God and Father is there. So then the Spirit tells us:

Philippians 3:20-21

"For our citizenship is in heaven, from which we also eagerly wait for the Savior, the Lord Jesus Christ, (21) who will transform our lowly body that it may be conformed to His glorious body, according to the working by which He is able even to subdue all things to Himself."

Where we are to look – at Christ at the right hand of God – is from where He will come for us. He will conform these lowly bodies of ours to be like Him, conformed into the image of God's Son (Rom. 8:29-30). Then He will take us into the heavens.

The persecution and tribulation allowed in Smyrna was to stop the professing church from being conformed to the world. Not only should we not cleave to the world, but we should not allow the world to cleave to us. There is always a pressure that the world exerts from without, to conform the believer into its image (Rom. 12:1-2). Often it is not a conscious decision the believer makes, but rather innocently, or by resting and letting our guard down. We start enjoying the world, its comforts and interests, and try to justify our actions. It is easy to rationalize the things we do in our own eyes, but God knows the motive and intentions of the heart. God knows the truth, even if we hide it from ourselves or make excuses.

The Judaizing of the Christian Faith

There was also an increasing danger from the Judaizers to the professing church at this time. They are also known in Scripture as the Concision. In the message to Smyrna these are *'those who say they are Jews and are not, but are a synagogue of Satan."* (Rev. 2:9)

Philippians 3:2-3

"Beware of dogs, beware of evil workers, beware of the mutilation! For we are the circumcision, who worship God in the Spirit, rejoice in Christ Jesus, and have no confidence in the flesh."

The Judaizing of the Christian faith is done by mixing Judaism with Christianity. The Lord Jesus identifies this as a religious work of the devil – a synagogue of Satan. The entire book of Galatians is written by the Spirit of God to combat this evil. We also find many other passages of direct warning (Col. 2, Phil. 3). It is this leaven of false doctrine that has also morphed into Arminianism. The two are the same, for they are both religion based on what man can do. It is the doctrine of human effort, human works, and human accomplishment, to one degree or another. It is humanism – man at the center. It results in human pride and boasting and self-righteousness (Phil. 3:9), always robbing glory from God. It is not God's work, but man's.

Judaism – the Beggarly Elements of the World

The religion God gave to man in Adam is Judaism. It is the religion of man in the flesh, of man in Adam. It is not the religion of the second Adam – Jesus Christ. Judaism is the religion of the earth and of the world. It is a walk by sight and physical senses, and all about the confidences of the flesh (Phil. 3:3-9). *"For the Jews request a sign..."* (I Cor. 1:22). Judaism is not of faith (Gal. 3:12), and is not a walk of faith (II Cor. 5:7). It is concerned with foods and drinks, various external washings, and fleshly ordinances imposed (Heb. 9:10). Judaism is not according to Christ, but rather according to the traditions of men, the rudimentary principles of the world (Col. 2:8). Judaism is the handwriting of requirements that no one could profit from, now nailed to the cross of Christ (Col. 2:14).

The believer who allows his faith to be Judaized is simply not holding fast to the Head, who is Christ (Col. 2:19). He is inviting something to stand between himself and the Lord, and is entering into worldly bondage.

Galatians 4:9-11

"But now after you have known God, or rather are known by God, how is it that you turn again to the weak and beggarly elements, to which you desire again to be in bondage? You observe days and months and seasons and years. I am afraid for you..."

The Bondage of Judaism

The weak and beggarly elements spoken of are Judaism. These elements of the world produce bondage and slavery (Gal. 4:3). The schoolmaster was the law (Gal. 3:24), under whose tutelage the Jews were always slaves (Gal. 4:1-3). The Galatians were being enticed by Judaizers to become circumcised, keep feast days and sabbaths, and observe fleshly ordinances. This would be a turning again to the weak and beggarly elements of the worldly religion of Judaism. It would be a desire to be in bondage.

The law, the covenant from Mount Sinai, gives birth to bondage (Gal. 4:24). The Jerusalem that was then, in the time of Paul, was in bondage with her children, the Jews (Gal. 4:25). The language concerning these things couldn't be any more direct and clear. So then the Spirit says:

Galatians 5:1

"Stand fast therefore in the liberty by which Christ has made us free, and do not be entangled again with a yoke of bondage."

The conclusion is obvious. Judaism brings bondage and slavery. Jesus Christ brings liberty. It is a freedom from the slavery of Judaism. The law is the yoke of bondage that believers are not to be entangled with. It was the schoolmaster that had its end when the promised Seed arrived (Gal. 3:19, 24-25, John 1:17). As a Christian, if you hold on to one observance of Judaism, you are a debtor to keep the whole law (Gal. 5:3). You are estranged from Christ and are falling from grace (Gal. 5:4). Why else would God remove Judaism and bring in Christianity? What other reason is there for His destruction of Jerusalem and its temple other than to end the practice of Judaism and to make Israel desolate? So then the Spirit warns again:

Colossians 2:20-23

(20) "Therefore, if you died with Christ from the basic principles of the world, why, as though living in the world, do you subject yourselves to regulations— (21) "Do not touch, do not taste, do not handle,"(22) which all concern things which perish with the using—according to the commandments and doctrines of men? (23) These things indeed have an appearance of wisdom in self-imposed religion, false humility, and neglect of the body, but are of no value against the indulgence of the flesh."

Judaism is of no value against the flesh. The law prohibited the flesh by many rules and commands. However, it never gave the individual any power to stop the flesh from acting out. Rather Judaism, the law, empowered the principle of sin in the flesh of man to act out all the more (II Cor. 15:56, Rom. 5:20, 7:7-13).

The believer has died with Christ from the basic principles of the world. In marriage we know the relationship continues until 'by death do you part'. If you died then you no longer have a relationship with the world. The relationship continued until you died with Christ. To take up Judaism is to take up a relationship with the world again, because it is God's religion of the world (Rom. 7:1-6). If you died with Christ, you are not of the world as He is not of the world. *Then why, as though living in the world, do you subject yourselves to the regulations of Judaism?* The God intended understanding here is, *"Then why, as though alive in the world..."* – for the believer has actually died to the world with Christ. You cannot be alive to something when you are dead to it already. This is redemptive truth of precious value. But the improper relationship and its results spoken of in the above passage are both the Judaizing of your Christian faith and the joining again with worldly religion.

The Evil Doctrine grows and spreads

This problem was an incipient evil in the church in Paul's time. In the time represented by Smyrna Judaizing had grown more widespread in the professing church. By the time Christendom progresses to the end of the age, the leaven will have saturated all of Christian teaching (Matt. 13:33). We notice that it is a subject brought up again by the Lord in a later message (Rev. 3:9). With this false doctrine so prominent in the professing church world, it may serve us well to list some of its salient characteristics and features.

1. Judaizing occurs when you muddle the distinctions between Judaism and Christianity. These are two separate religions. It is true that both are from God, but one was given to man in Adam, the other was given to man in the second Adam. God's intended purpose for Judaism was to test man in the flesh under the principle of human responsibility. This testing resulted in judgment and condemnation for man in Adam

(II Cor. 3:7, 9). When this testing was complete, there was no longer a purpose for Judaism (Gal. 3:19, 23-24). God's purpose in Christianity is to give eternal life in sovereign grace (John 17:1-3) and to bring man, in the second Adam, into the glory of God (Rom. 3:23-26).

2. Judaizing occurs when you confuse or merge the clear distinctions between Israel and the church. Israel is related to Judaism. The church is related to Christianity. The promises to Israel are not the promises to the body of Christ. The teaching and instruction of Israel is not to be confounded with the epistles to the church. Messiah, the King of Israel, is a prophetic promise to Israel. Messiah is a descendent of David, Judah, and Abraham according to the flesh. The church exists in union with Jesus Christ glorified, the Son of Man at the right hand of God. This last, for the church, is not a Christ known after the flesh (II Cor. 5:16-17).

3. Judaizing occurs when the two distinct callings of Israel and the church are confused or merged. Israel has a definite earthly calling, while the church has an equally distinct heavenly calling. Israel saved and restored in the land will be the center of the government of God in the kingdom of the Son of Man over the earth in the end. The church is seated in heavenly places in Christ Jesus in the kingdom of our Father in the heavens. Israel will be blessed with every physical blessing on the earth. The church is blessed with every spiritual blessing in the heavenly places (Eph. 1:3).

4. Judaizing occurs when the principle of the law (human responsibility) is confused and mixed with the principle of sovereign grace. Biblically, these two principles are diametrically opposed and are on opposite ends of the spectrum. Suffice it to say that grace is of faith, but the law is not of faith (Gal. 3:12). Therefore the law is not of grace. The Judaizing and Arminian doctrines create a middle ground between the two principles, a mixture of grace and some level of human effort, whatever that may be. In this false system, the grace of God always becomes a response to

some type of human effort or quality, a wage that God must pay because of what He saw, or sees, or will see in the man (Rom. 11:34-36, 4:1-5).

This middle ground simply does not exist. It is a creation of the human mind and thoughts. Man reasons as to what he thinks the system ought to be. He creates one in which there must be human effort, so there is a basis of boasting and receiving glory (Rom. 4:1-2). This smacks of humanism. In his reasoning, if he cannot put his finger on human effort, he points to intrinsic human value and quality as the reason God gives grace. But it remains the same evil system. This cannot be a definition of His grace. The source and cause of grace given is always from the inherent attributes of God Himself, not anything ever found in man. Grace does as it pleases in goodness, and is a reflection of the nature of Him who acts in grace. That is why any grace is always sovereign grace by definition. The middle ground does not exist!

The Arminian and Judaizing leavens are great evils readily accepted in Christian teaching in the professing church today. We have to remember that Paul said to Timothy that the professing church will not endure sound doctrine (II Tim. 4:3-4). It is false doctrine, and is an evil that will not go away. It will be part of the kingdom of heaven until the end of the age. It is the leaven that saturates the three lumps and characterizes the failure of the dispensation.

When Jesus Christ sat down at the right hand of the Majesty in the heavens, the work of redemption that saves and redeems us was completed and finalized. <u>Please note:</u> Any teaching requiring anything else, that adds something of men to complete the work, denies the perfection of the redemptive work of Jesus Christ. God has accepted the work of Christ and He will not have anything else added to it. This is verified by God raising Christ up from death. God has placed His approval and acceptance on Christ's work by resurrection. Christ has entered the holy of holies in the heavens with His blood. God simply will have nothing else but the death and blood of Christ (Heb. 9:12, 23-26).

The First and Second Deaths

The true church in Smyrna is promised they will not be hurt by the second death (Rev. 2:11). I can't help but think that this is still related to the tribulations and martyrdom at this time. The true Christian will not be touched by the second death, which is eternal judgment and condemnation (John 5:24). The first death is still a present judgment brought in by Adam's disobedience. It is both the power of Satan and part of the judgment of God. It was God who told Adam, *"... for in the day that you eat of it you shall surely die."* But Christ, through death, has destroyed him who had the power of death, that is, the devil (Heb. 2:14). This is verified by His resurrection from the dead. In the rapture, the church will experience this previously accomplished victory over the first death. The power of God to achieve this sovereign work on behalf of the church was already demonstrated in the raising of Christ from the dead (Eph. 1:19-21).

But the rapture is not yet, though it is our blessed hope and constant expectation. Now the question is asked, particularly in the time of Smyrna – are Christ and His promises of future blessing and glory worth giving up all for? Even one's own life? *"Be faithful until death, and I will give you the crown of life."*

2 Timothy 1:12

"For this reason I also suffer these things; nevertheless I am not ashamed, for I know whom I have believed and am persuaded that He is able to keep what I have committed to Him until that Day."

<u>Historical Note:</u> The amount of Satan's persecution of professing Christianity was allowed, but indeed measured by God – *"...you will have tribulation ten days."* (Rev. 2:10) This may directly refer to the ten years of severe persecution of the church under the emperor Diocletian (303-313 AD). The signing of the 'Edict of Milan' by Constantine and Licinius in 313 seems to bring an end to the generalized persecution of the professing church, and the time of Smyrna.

Chapter 7: Endnotes

[104] Christendom has sought rest in the wilderness of the world. When Israel first came from Sinai to the land, God swore that many of them would not enter His rest because of their unbelief (Heb. 3:15-19). One lesson to take from this is that being in the wilderness should not be mistaken for the rest of God. But Christendom has made this mistake and seeks rest in the wilderness of the world. God does the same thing with the professing church as Israel in the wilderness. He swears in His wrath that the tares of Christendom will not enter into His rest. Their corpses will fall in the wilderness and will not enter into the glory of God (Heb. 3:17, 4:1, 3, 6, 9-11, and Matt. 13:30). It is the flesh that seeks rest in the world.

[105] There are many ministers today that attempt to call out to the body of Christ to do certain things that they feel are the will of God. This is especially done in America, in the attempt to rally the troops to win and save a country that is progressing in the way of this world and age (Gal. 1:4). In this thinking there is a violation of a number of biblical principles and understandings. But let us consider the one under question here. How can you look and where do you look in America to see the true corporate body of Christ in order to address it? What I see is the spoiled crop in the field and what it has become under the responsibility and efforts of men. What we see is what the kingdom of heaven is like at this time. It is, in reality, wheat and tares mixed together as the corporate body of Christendom on the earth. It is the work of God *and* the work of the evil one. Don't you think that this similitude applies to Christendom in America? Only American arrogance would say that it doesn't. Only God truly knows that which is His – this is the solid foundation of God that stands (II Tim. 2:19).

In the seven messages to the churches there is a point in the progression in which the Son of Man stops acknowledging the corporate entity of Christendom. Do we think we have the ability to see and acknowledge the corporate body of Christ in America? Even the phrase 'the body of Christ in America' is often not correctly thought of in a proper biblical understanding. The true body of Christ is universal and always will be; *"There is one body and one Spirit..."* (Eph. 4:4) There are no nations in Christ (Gal. 3:27-29, Col. 3:10-11, I Cor. 12:12-13). All the earthly attachments and connections of man to the earth and the first creation have been removed and abolished in Christ and His body, the church. This is true of all earthly associations, even the abolishing of the earthly religion of Judaism (Eph.

2:13-16). There is no America in the body of Christ! The citizenship of the entire body is elsewhere (Phil. 3:20). The church is a corporate body with a pure heavenly calling (Heb. 3:1). It is not of this earth and not of this world, and never will be. Also Christianity is a heavenly religion in contrast to Judaism, because it carries the heavenly calling of the church/believer.

In the history of Christendom there are many instances of Christianity being nationalized. It was even the religion of the Roman Empire after Constantine. But professing Christianity is always the spoiled crop in the field of the world. The nationalizing of the religion afforded greater opportunities for the entrance of evil and the world, and promoted the spoiling of the crop to even greater lengths. Man was responsible for this, not God.

In the time of Smyrna, God was using persecutions and trials as the testing of the faith of the church (Jam. 1:2-4, I Pet. 1:6-7). This testing would purify the true church and have her again dependent on Christ to sustain her. The tribulations of this time actually made the true church stronger and healthier, even though in appearance to the world it looked poor and despised. The persecutions and martyrdom by the Roman Empire did not exterminate Christianity as they desired, but caused it to spread and become stronger.

When the empire was Christianized, for the most part it stopped the generalized persecution. This afforded a great opportunity for the world to enter into professing Christianity. It also motivated the church world to become interested in gaining and holding civil power. It also paved the way for Satan to bring false teachings and doctrine into the church. The contrast between Smyrna and the next church is obvious. In the time of Smyrna, Satan persecutes from without. In the time of Pergamos, Satan corrupts from within. There is no doubt the devil found a better way. If he can corrupt the church world from within and make it worldly, he does not need to expend so much energy in external persecutions by the world, especially if that wasn't producing his desired results.

As a nation, America goes the way of this evil age and there is really no stopping this. America is always the world from a biblical perspective. I can't fathom how any true believer, holding to the scripture for all his thoughts, could view America any differently than this. Then we have, *"Do not love the world or the things in the world. If anyone loves the world, the love of the Father is not in him. For all that is in the world – the lust of the flesh, the lust of the eyes, and the pride of life – is not of the Father but is of the world."* What is identified as 'of the world' can also easily be said to be 'of America'? It is the same. America is part of the world and goes the way of the world and this evil age.

Jesus gave Himself for our sins, that He might deliver us from this present evil age (Gal. 1:4). The believer/church delivered from this evil world or age is quite a different idea than the believer/church Christianizing the world or age, turning it from evil to righteousness. One of these two thoughts is biblical truth and comes out of Scripture. The other thought is all Arminian pretention and folly, and the misuse of Scripture, if it is attempted to support such a thought.

[106] We must make up our minds to suffer – I'm sure many ministers would have a problem with this statement. But it simply is true that it is the true believer's portion while here on this earth. *"For I consider that the sufferings of this present time are not worthy to be compared with the glory which shall be revealed in us."* (Rom. 8:18) Sufferings are our share in this present time.

Are you to reign in life as a king on this earth at this present time, through Jesus Christ? Reigning as a king in this present life would not include suffering, because kings do not suffer. As I previously said, that type of understanding of Romans 5:17 couldn't be farther from the truth. Jesus did not reign as a king in His life here on the earth. The Jews rejected Him as their King. The true believer is to walk as He walked (I John 2:6). Jesus walked as a servant. He said that in the kingdom of heaven the greatest would have to be the servant of all (Luke 22:25-27) He was among them as One who serves.

The believer will not reign in life as a king on this earth. You will have to wait for the time when Christ will get up off His Father's throne and take up His power and return to this earth and exercise dominion over it. Then you will be a king and priest in the heavens unto His God and Father (Rev. 1:6). But this is in glory and not of this present time (Rom. 8:18). The believer will reign in 'eternal life' in glory – that is the meaning of Romans 5:17.

When we look at the promises to be given to the overcomers in the seven prophetic messages to the seven churches, every one of them can only be found in glory. *What does that teach us?* Every proper Christian hope is beyond this present time we spend on earth. All Christian hopes are in glory, and are not to be found in this world. That is truly why 'faith is the substance of things hoped for, the evidence of things not seen'. It is why the true believer walks by faith. And it is not faith that makes it happen now, where we see it now. It is not grace enabling us to reign as kings now in this life. The things that God has promised to us we have to wait for. But the sufferings of this present time are not worthy to be compared with the glory which shall be revealed...

All the Christian's hopes are in glory because all the promises are the sovereign work of God, and according to His timing in His counsels. They are all after the rapture of the church, which will be the greatest demonstration of the sovereign power and work of God. But the professing church world doesn't want to wait for Christian hopes. The masses in Christendom want it now. So the Arminian leaven devises a way to bring the blessings in, as a present reality. By human efforts and human accomplishment, through exercising great faith or great understandings of grace, we teach that God wants you to have these things now, that God wants you to be satisfied now, and wants you to reign as a king now. The prosperity message is about having treasure in the world, not laying it up in heaven (Luke 12:33).

The true believer has been blessed with every spiritual blessing in heavenly places in Christ (Eph. 1:3). It is our God and Father who has done this. But this will not do for the majority of Christendom. We cannot put our hands on spiritual blessings. We cannot fathom what that even means. We do not understand heavenly places in Christ. We want earthly places and earthly blessings. And some land might be good as well. These things are the things we can see. These things we can touch and handle. The earthly things are the things that possess our emotions and comforts. We desire them now. So our faith and teaching becomes Judaized. By it we relinquish heavenly places in Christ Jesus and spiritual blessings. We forfeit heavenly citizenship, heavenly inheritance, and the heavenly calling. We exchange it for physical and earthly blessings, and a decidedly earthly calling. We forsake our proper heavenly position and are brought down low to the earth. We follow after things on the earth and the cares of life and the world. And you think we haven't lost our first love and fallen? Worse! The time of Ephesus has long past. Presently Christendom is committing fornication with the world.

There are some very simple but valuable Christian truths presented in the above paragraphs. When they are accepted and understood, they cut up by the roots the whole system of misguided thoughts, feelings, and judgments that so overwhelms contemporary Christian teachings and doctrine.

Here is another one of those simple truths. In the time of Ephesus the church had fallen (Rev. 2:5). These were the Lord's own words to the professing church. As soon as the church has fallen, it no longer is a secure place for the individual believer. I say secure in the sense of the fallen church remaining an authority and guide in faith and practice. From this point on the individual is guided by the Word of God itself, taught to him by the Holy Spirit. The individual believer has to make good his own security by the Word. That is why the individual is singled out from the first message on – *"He who has an ear, let him hear what the Spirit says to the churches."* The fallen church may have this right or that right, but it no longer is an authority. If you think about it, the church never was.

Chapter 8:
Pergamos: The World comes in

The benefits of refining the church world through external trials and persecutions would be a short-lived realization. Soon after the tribulations ended, the professing church is seen getting comfortable with the world. It would not be long before another notable event occurred in the world associated with the church – Christianity is promoted to the favored religion of the Roman Empire.

The Edict of Milan in 313 by Emperors Licinius and Constantine legalized Christian worship in the Roman Empire. The generalized persecution and martyrdom gradually ended. This was the end of the time of Smyrna and the beginning of Pergamos. At this time there were many changes affecting Christendom, from within and without. One of the major differences was a Christian Emperor within the church taking and holding governmental power and influence. In 380, by edict, the Roman Empire declared Christianity as its official state religion. For good or for bad, these are the general events of importance involving Christendom in the time of Pergamos.

It is an easy task to check the internet or history books to find this information. Man's opinion of these events is very high, even referring to this time as the 'Triumph of the Church'. However, as Christians, that which we should defer to and what should have greater significance for us has to be God's thoughts and opinion on this, especially the moral outcomes and results.

Revelation 2:12-17

"And to the angel of the church in Pergamos write,

'These things says He who has the sharp two-edged sword: (13) "I know your works, and where you dwell, where Satan's throne is. And you hold fast to My name, and did not deny My faith even in the days in which Antipas was My faithful martyr, who was killed among you, where Satan dwells. (14) But I have a few things against you, because you have there those who hold the doctrine of Balaam, who taught Balak to put a stumbling block before the children of Israel, to eat things sacrificed to idols, and to commit sexual immorality. (15) Thus you also have those who hold the doctrine of the Nicolaitans, which thing I hate. (16) Repent, or else I will come to you quickly and will fight against them with the sword of My mouth.

(17) "He who has an ear, let him hear what the Spirit says to the churches. To him who overcomes I will give some of the hidden manna to eat. And I will give him a white stone, and on the stone a new name written which no one knows except him who receives it."'

Dwelling where Satan's Throne is

Smyrna represented God keeping the assembly separated from the world by allowing her to be persecuted by the world. Pergamos represented the professing church becoming friendly with the world and allowing the world to enter in. In this time the general assembly becomes worldlier in its character and relationships. Christ says, *"I know your works, and where you dwell, where Satan's throne is."* This throne is in the world and part of the world. It is where the assembly was beginning to take up residence, dwelling with the world. This is beyond just being in the world, but rather the beginnings of becoming like the world.

Jesus says to Pergamos, *"I know your works, and where you dwell..."* He knows all we do, but also all our circumstances. He also knows the thoughts and intentions of the heart so that nothing is hidden from Him. We find the two-edged sword in Pergamos as well. All this should be a comfort to the faithful. He knows all the details about everything. *"I know your works..."* are the things we do. *"...where you live..."* are the circumstances we are set under. He takes all into consideration.

The time of Smyrna was when the world persecuted the professing church. But now, with the decrees of the Roman Empire, the world starts courting the church. The circumstances had drastically changed for Pergamos. But it is a comfort that Christ knows our circumstances, He knows our infirmities, and He knows all the things by which we are tempted. He knows where the professing church dwells. He provides His grace in every situation and for every circumstance to the faithful, so that He alone will be their strength (II Cor. 12:8-10).

So often we spend our time planning to do great works in the name of the Lord to glorify Him, thinking these things must be done and this is the will of God. What glorified God in Pergamos were those that remained faithful in the midst of circumstances that made being faithful very difficult. *"And you hold fast to My name, and did not deny My faith..."* This was the will of God, not the doing of great things. If you do not know how to remain truly faithful to Him and separated from the world, it doesn't matter what things you think you are doing in His name. And remaining faithful to God is problematic when there is increasing familiarity with the world (I John 2:15-17).

The entrance of the world into the professing church is a definite negative on two distinct fronts.

1. The believer is not of the world, just as Christ is not of the world (John 17:14-16). Therefore His body, the church, is not

of the world. The believer's relationship is with a Christ in the heavens, exalted to the right hand of God in glory. When the church was formed, her relationship with Jesus Christ in glory was the same as her individual members (Eph. 1:18-23). So then the assembly has a heavenly calling, a heavenly citizenship, and is seated in heavenly places. The assembly will be the recipient of the fullest measure of spiritual blessings in those heavenly places, as promised to the individual believer (Eph. 1:3).

Christ was rejected by the world when He was here in the flesh. He left the world and ascended up into glory. There He is accepted and exalted far above all principality and power and might and dominion (Eph. 1:20-21). At this time the world is not the place of His acceptance. It is to be exactly the same for the assembly. The church is not to be part of the world, but separated and rejected by the world as Christ was. We are not to find a dwelling place of acceptance with the world. Our place of acceptance is in the heavens. That is where He will eventually return from, coming to take the true church there (Phil. 3:20-21, John 14:1-3). In the world we are to be hated and have tribulation and sufferings. We are not of the world, and only strangers and pilgrims here. But be of good cheer, our Lord has overcome the world and the prince of it (John 16:33, 12:31-32), even though He has yet to take up His power and reign over it (Heb. 10:12-13, Rev. 19:11-16).

2. The book of Revelation places a particular emphasis on the phrase 'those who dwell on the earth' or 'inhabitants of the earth'. This is what is apostate from God and on which the wrath of God is poured out (Rev. 3:10, 6:10, 11:10, 12:12, 13:8, 17:2 etc.). When the professing church is noticed by Christ as dwelling where the throne of Satan is, there is the influence to take on the character of the world. The professing church would be tempted to become like those that dwell on the earth, and lose sight of the heavenly calling. Christendom has been 'living' where the throne of Satan is from the time of Pergamos.

The book of Revelation often uses prophetic language as allegories or symbols. Christendom committing adultery and fornications is its illicit relationship with the world. It is its worldliness. The true church is betrothed to Christ. Professing Christianity should not be seeking a relationship with the world.

The Judaizing Doctrines

Christ is judging the responsibility and works of the professing church. Which of these allowed the world to come in? If Judaism is God's religion of the earth, then by the Judaizing of the Christian faith the weak and beggarly elements of the world are invited in (Gal. 4:3, 9, Col. 2:8, 20). The thoughts that create doctrines of papal succession, the cult of saint and angel worship, priesthood, and church authority all originate in Judaism. There are many others from this source, such as the observance of festivals, sabbaths, holy days, and the eating of and restricting from certain foods, along with the use of holy water and incense.[107]

The heathen world had the worship of the mother of the gods. When the professing church declared Mary to be the mother of God at the council of Ephesus in 431, it opened the doors of the church for the heathen. This was a stroke of genius. Relating to popularity and numbers it was a great success. Of course Christendom had to allow heathen feasts and drunken festivals within to please the masses from the world, reasoning it was better to celebrate inside the church walls than outside. The policy of the church authorities was not to tear down heathen temples, but to convert them to places of Christian worship. The sprinkling of holy water and the smoking of incense would be all that was necessary to consecrate their new possessions. All this was the means by which the faith was judaized and the world entered the professing church. And from the time of Pergamos the world has never left her.

The two-edged Sword out of His Mouth

The character of Christ presented to Pergamos is interesting and makes for a valuable lesson for those who have ears to hear what the Spirit is saying. *"These things says He who has the sharp two-edged sword."* When the professing church had fallen and was increasingly more like the world, her worldliness had her desiring authority and power on earth. To combat the growth of this false and pretentious ecclesiastical authority, which had its beginnings in the time of Pergamos, we have the sword of the Spirit, the true authority of the Word of God:

Hebrews 4:12

"For the word of God is living and powerful, and sharper than any two-edged sword, piercing even to the division of soul and spirit, and of joints and marrow, and is a discerner of the thoughts and intents of the heart."

In Pergamos we have the Lord who possesses the piercing power which judges and discerns the secrets of the heart and conscience. The professing church is judged by the Word of God. It is not the professing church as judge. And it certainly isn't the professing church judging the Word of God. What we have in the messages of Christ to the churches is the individual Christian being impressed to give heed to the judgments pronounced *on* the corporate body of Christendom – *"He who has an ear, let him hear what the Spirit says to the churches."* The professing church cannot be an authority for me if Christ is asking me to listen and understand His reproofs and judgments of it. When the assembly is judged it cannot be a security of faith for the individual believer, or his guide. God sends the individual back to the Word of God for themselves. I am made aware of the corporate assembly's condition by the words spoken by the Spirit. *It is my responsibility to hear and understand this judgment.* The assembly cannot be an authority over me on the Lord's behalf in its fallen state and condition. The authority of God does not reside in the church, but in His word.

Jesus Christ holds All Authority

God is the only King in the kingdom of heaven. He has not given this position to anyone in His place. God has delivered us from the power of darkness and translated us into the kingdom of the Son of His love (Col. 1:13). This is the kingdom of heaven.[108] The character of the kingdom is the King in heaven, and the planting of the wheat all relates to the Son of Man dying and then being glorified (John 12:23-24, 13:31-32). Even though the King is in heaven, it is the King who holds and maintains the authority. As the King, God has given all authority to His Son, as the Son of Man. His death and resurrection were the basis of this.

Matthew 28:18

"And Jesus came and spoke to them, saying, "All authority has been given to Me in heaven and on earth."

The only one to whom God has given complete authority is the Son of God as the Son of Man. We may go in the name of Jesus and exercise privileges in the authority of that name, but the authority remains with Him. He was the one who was obedient unto death. He is the one who bore the cup of God's wrath and glorified God in doing so. He is the one who God raised from the dead, justifying it all (Rom. 1:4).

In a higher and more intimate relationship, Christ is Head of the body, the church. Jesus Christ always had the authority and always will. This principle is true for both the kingdom of heaven and the church, even though the two are not the same.[109]

The individual believer's responsibility is to judge all the teachings and doctrines of Christendom by the two-edged sword of the Word of God. His responsibility is to judge all the works of the church world by the words of Christ and the Spirit.

The Building of Christendom on the Earth

For centuries the church system has wielded ungodly authority on the earth, which it has unrighteously taken. It has declared infallibility for popes and church doctrines alike, and has avowed itself the sole interpreter of Scripture. It has purposely hidden the truth of God from the faithful, and has gained earthly riches and worldly luxuries by its corrupted teachings. It has committed fornication with the kings and governmental authorities of the earth, gaining and wielding civil power against the will and calling of God. It has done all these things in the name of Christ.

The effect of Israel's sin and rebellion not only proved man to be a lost sinner, but God having placed His name there, it connected sin with God's name. This is the same with the professing church. In Christianity it is the name of the Father and the Son. By the wickedness and worldliness of the church world their names are being blasphemed.

2 Peter 2:15

"They have forsaken the right way and gone astray, following the way of Balaam the son of Beor, who loved the wages of unrighteousness."

In the professing church at this time the Lord says, *"But I have a few things against you, because you have there those who hold the doctrine of Balaam..."* When Balaam could not curse and destroy Israel, he turned and counseled corruption to Israel as a friend. The message from Christ is symbolic in three areas.

1. *"...to eat things sacrificed to idols..."* is prophetic language for idol worship and the worship of Satan (Rev. 2:14). Idols and idolatry were being introduced into the professing church, along with religious relics and such. The merchandizing of these many objects of worship added wealth to the coffers of the professing church.

2. *"...and to commit sexual immorality"* is prophetic language for having a relationship with the world (Rev. 2:14). It is the entrance of worldliness into professing Christianity. It is an unholy relationship from which she was originally separated. *"Do not love the world or the things in the world. If anyone*

loves the world, the love of the Father is not in him. For all that is in the world – the lust of the flesh, the lust of the eyes, and the pride of life – is not of the Father but is of the world." (I John 2:15-16) The professing church began to concentrate on loving the world instead of Christ.

3. *"...have run greedily in the way of Balaam, for profit..."* is all the idolatry and all the worldliness for the gain of earthly riches and luxuries (Jude 1:11). It is hard to comprehend how much the professing church has chased after the wealth and riches of the world. And she has done a fair job in gaining them. When in Smyrna they were despised and poor, but spiritually rich (Rev. 2:9). Now they were on their way to becoming accepted and loved by the world. In time the church became rich in earthly treasures, but wretched in spiritual poverty. This reversal for Christendom increases in its dichotomy as it progresses from this point. The spirit of Balaam in the professing church makes her comfortable with the world.

False and Corrupt Doctrines

How much better was this for Satan? Instead of persecutions from without, which tend to push the soul closer to God, he is invited within the professing church to work his lies and deceptions. The wiles of the devil tend to separate the soul from God. These are the doctrines of Balaam now in the church world. When he could not get God to curse Israel, he brings in corruption by association with evil in the world (Num. 25). This is doctrinal corruption, and it was for financial gain.

The Lord also says to Pergamos, *"Thus you also have those who hold the doctrine of the Nicolaitans, which thing I hate."* This is teaching that sanctions evil works and moral misdeeds to be done in the name of Christ and excused by His grace (Jude 4). Now we see the progression of evil in the professing church. Previously in Ephesus the church hated the deeds of the Nicolaitans (Rev. 2:6). Now within the professing church there are those who embrace this doctrine.

With the doctrine of Balaam and the Nicolaitans we have corrupt teachings within. This is certainly the beginnings of the ecclesiastical character spoken of by Paul:

2 Timothy 4:3-4

"For the time will come when they will not endure sound doctrine, but according to their own desires, because they have itching ears, they will heap up for themselves teachers; and they will turn their ears away from the truth, and be turned aside to fables."

With Pergamos it was the ministry embracing and profiting from evil doctrines. The above passage implicates the masses in Christendom as having itching ears, and the teachings that appease their carnal desires. This is the reasoning of this ministry – appeal to the fleshly desires of the masses and give them what they want. That is how you build numbers. Today it is how you build mega churches with satellite campuses. Just make sure the organization and the ministry are financially profiting by it. Do we not see the full ripening of this philosophy today in the church world? Unsound and corrupt doctrines began to enter the church in the time of Pergamos. These doctrines had enough subtlety to still appear religious. If you have enough ignorance of Scriptural truth, many teachings can be passed off as Christian. These corrupt doctrines have only grown from that time.[110]

The condition of the professing church in Pergamos was still a progression from the time of Smyrna. There still remained much good and faithfulness in the church, a holding fast to Christ's name and not denying faith in Him, even in the face of death. But it certainly was the beginning of internal corruption. Ephesus resisted this, while the time of Pergamos embraced it. Unless those who held and practiced such doctrines repented, He would *"...come to you quickly and fight against them with the sword of My mouth."* This, I believe is the scene of His return and the white horse (Rev. 19:11-15) – *"...and His name is called The Word of God."* Then it will be physical judgment by His name and the sharp sword out of His mouth. He would fight against those of Pergamos who embraced these evils and taught others to do the same. He would fight against them and judge by His words (Rev. 2:16). The tares of the church world will be burned, and we see that part of Pergamos is guilty – *"Thou hast there them ... I will fight against them with the sword of my mouth."* It is the believer's responsibility to judge all by the Word of God.

Hidden Manna and the White Stone

To the overcomer, the individual promise is, *"...I will give some of the hidden manna to eat."* This promise points the believer's eyes to the heavens, the only place where the Christian's proper hope resides (Col. 1:5). The hidden manna speaks of a heavenly character when the world was entering in to the church. Before entering the Promised Land Israel was instructed to place a pot of manna inside the ark. Once in the land the hidden manna would serve as a memorial of their time spent in the wilderness and God's daily provision for them that sustained them. In the land they enjoyed the greater blessings of God, much more than a daily sustenance for their wilderness sojourn. Israel being brought into the land is type of the church being brought into the rest of God in glory.

When the church is found living where Satan's throne is, then Christ comes in and encourages the heavenly character of the believer. Now Jesus Christ is the bread of life, the bread of God that comes down from heaven. The manna with Israel was only a type of Christ, the true bread from God that gives eternal life (John 6:32-35, 48-50). The hidden manna for us speaks of an intimacy we will enjoy personally with Christ in the Father's house in glory. It is a heavenly character because it is hidden, not necessarily for our time in the wilderness. The manna in the wilderness was not 'hidden'. That which is hidden is specially reserved for our time with Christ in the rest of God. It is an exhortation from Christ for the true believer to remain heavenly minded, and not to be looking on the things of the world. In reality, the hidden manna will be our personal enjoyment of Christ as He is known in heaven, as having been in humiliation in the wilderness.

The second promise is more individually intimate and special. The white stone is given to the individual believer, and *"on the stone a new name written which no one knows except him who receives it."* (Rev. 2:17) This is Christ's personal vote of approval, the secret mark of favor.

There are many spiritual blessings in glory that will be common to the entire church. On the earth we presently share many joys in Christ. But Jesus would have our individual affections as well as the corporate and mutual affection of the body of Christ. All seven messages to the churches are spoken to the corporate professing church. In the time of Ephesus the corporate love for Christ was lost. However, all the promises in the messages are individual; "...to him who overcomes..." And the white stone has a name that only Christ and I will know. It is the expression of intimacy and affection we personally share between each other. This will be true for every believer, yet individually different in your joy and communion with Christ.

All the promises in the seven messages will only be true after Christ comes to take the church. They all form parts of our Christian hope and will only be realized with Christ in glory. The white stone and hidden manna are for such a time. We who have such hopes purify ourselves, even as He is pure (I John 3:3). You will not know the name written on the stone until in glory, but these hopes become a source of strength and joy and blessing now.

Pergamos is the time of the professing church progressing on from Constantine.

Chapter 8: Endnotes

[107] Roman Catholicism would have to be considered a form of Christianity that has been completely judaized. There is even in the Roman system the constant sacrifices, and the continual remembrance of sins as is at the heart of Judaism (Heb. 10:10-12). It is so earthy, it is so sensual. Yet this judaized system of Christianity remains the largest part of the professing church today. Its beginnings and doctrines are in Pergamos, but a fuller growth and ripening of its evil is Jezebel in Thyatira.

[108] The kingdom of heaven is presently the kingdom of the Son of His love. It is the kingdom that every believer has been translated into (Col. 1:13). The kingdom of heaven currently involves all the time of the slain Lamb is in the midst of the throne (Rev. 5:6). This is all the time that Jesus Christ, the Son of Man, is sitting on His Father's throne (Rev. 3:21). However this time will not last forever. Eventually, in His Father's timing, He will rise up from His Father's throne, and take up His power and reign on the earth, sitting as the Son of Man and King of kings on His own throne (Matt. 25:31), ruling over the earth.

[109] The kingdom of heaven exists presently as the spoiled crop in the field of the world (Matt. 13:24-26). The kingdom will experience a significant change and upheaval at the end of the age by the judgment of the tares and the removal of the wheat into the heavens (Matt. 13:30). The church is the body of Christ, and is the wheat in the crop in the field at this time. When the wheat is removed from the field and into the heavens, it will exist there throughout the millennium (Eph. 2:7, 3:10-11). The body of Christ never comes to an end, but will eternally exist as the habitation and tabernacle of God and the Lamb in the heavens, or in the eternal state as come down from heaven and now dwelling among men.

The kingdom of heaven eventually becomes the kingdom of the Father in the heavens (Matt. 13:43) and the kingdom of the Son of Man on the earth (Luke 22:28-30, Matt. 19:28). This is during the time of the millennium. After this, and after the great white throne judgment of the dead, the Son of Man gives up His kingdom to God, thus ending the last reign of man on the earth (I Cor. 15:24-28). In the eternal state, which is in the new heavens and the new earth, God is all in all in the divine glory. I say God is all in all as in Father, Son, and Holy Spirit.

I will make this one ecclesiastical correction: Peter was given the keys to the kingdom of heaven (Matt. 16:19). He was not given the keys to the church, the body of Christ. There is a huge difference between the two. The kingdom and the church are not the same. And further, you never build anything with keys.

[110] In contemporary Christendom the definition of words like corrupt, false, unsound, evil, apostasy, ungodly, etc. has changed. We tend to reserve these just for the devil or very extreme cases in the world. We would never think to use them in reference to Christendom or so called Christian teachings. Yet we simply have diminishing value for the word of God today. If our teachings appear close enough then they are good enough. We don't think twice about compromising the word of God, as long as it is working and growing and profiting – then we can say, "Look, God is really blessing this. We have money, numbers, and growth. God is with us in this and our prospering proves it."

This attitude sounds like it could be right and it sounds religious, but it is really worldliness and Jewish thinking. In the Jewish mind the measure of how much they prospered in a monetary and physical way was always the measure of their favor with Jehovah. The question becomes whether that is the measure of the blessing of God in Christianity? I know it is the Jewish measure, because they are dependent on a walk by sight. But is that Christianity? Is this truly the way God wants us to measure His favor? (Please see Luke 12:16-21. I believe Jesus told this parable to condemn and set aside this Jewish mindset by contrasting it with proper Christian thinking – being rich toward God.)

Chapter 9:

Thyatira: Christendom's Internal Corruption

The fourth church finishes the straight line prophetic progression of Christendom. The first three churches progress one after the other until we arrive at the fourth. The state and condition of Thyatira takes shape in the fifth and sixth centuries, and this particular form continues to exist and thrive all the way to the end of the age. This is Jezebel with all her worldliness and corruptions, her false teachings and idolatry. Early on she was given opportunity to repent, but would not. She is cast into the future great tribulation. There should be no doubt that this is the Roman Catholic form of professing Christianity.

In the previous three churches, the coming of the Lord is never mentioned. In those the corporate body was still acknowledged by the Lord, and therefore was asked to repent and return to the first position of apostolic order, power, and pureness. With Thyatira the public professing body of Christendom is utterly corrupt and past the point of any return. There is a change to be noted. The attention is directed to the coming of Christ as the individual or remnant's hope and strength, instead of any thought of return to Pentecost of the corporate body. In the last four churches, there is only instruction and encouragement in looking forward. From this point, the standard of judgment is their fitness for this future glory – that to which the believer is called.

With Thyatira we have the change of the structure of the messages; the change in the arrangement of the different parts of the message from the previous three. It demonstrates the reality of what I said above. The 'hearing ear' is no longer with the general testimony to the professing church, but is now placed at the very end of the message. It indicates that the corporate entity is no longer acknowledged by the Son of Man, and that only a faithful remnant is being singled out as the overcomers and heirs of the heavenly hope and promises (Col. 1:5). The corporate whole of professing Christianity is deemed hopeless, and the messages become decidedly individual. The individual's hope in Thyatira starts here, *"But hold fast what you have till I come."* The coming glory of Christ's return is held out as the remnant's encouragement.

Revelation 2:18-29

"And to the angel of the church in Thyatira write,

'These things says the Son of God, who has eyes like a flame of fire, and His feet like fine brass: (19) "I know your works, love, service, faith, and your patience; and as for your works, the last are more than the first. (20) Nevertheless I have a few things against you, because you allow that woman Jezebel, who calls herself a prophetess, to teach and seduce My servants to commit sexual immorality and eat things sacrificed to idols. (21) And I gave her time to repent of her sexual immorality, and she did not repent. (22) Indeed I will cast her into a sickbed, and those who commit adultery with her into great tribulation, unless they repent of their deeds. (23) I will kill her children with death, and all the churches shall know that I am He who searches the minds and hearts. And I will give to each one of you according to your works.

(24) "Now to you I say, and to the rest in Thyatira, as many as do not have this doctrine, who have not known the depths of Satan, as they say, I will put on you no other burden.(25) But hold fast what you have till I come. (26) And he who overcomes, and keeps My works until the end, to him I will give power over the nations—

(27) 'He shall rule them with a rod of iron;
They shall be dashed to pieces like the potter's vessels'—
as I also have received from My Father; (28) and I will give him the morning star.

(29) "He who has an ear, let him hear what the Spirit says to the churches."'

The Son of God, who has eyes as a flame of fire, and His feet as fine brass: Rev. 2:18; the character of Christ is again associated with the all-knowing and piercing judgment of God (eyes as a flame of fire). This is the declaration of divine judgment from the Son of God as the Son of Man (John 5:26-27). The corruption of Jezebel in Thyatira, as we should easily see, requires the judgment of God. The feet of fine brass represents the firmness and perfection of divine judgment as applied to men (the altar of burnt offerings and the laver were both covered with brass and in the courtyard outside the tabernacle). The character of Christ with Thyatira is as a Judge, and He will give to the guilty parties according to their works.

John's vision of the Son of Man in the midst of the candlesticks reveals the ecclesiastical character of Christ to the corporate professing church (Rev. 1:10-18). It needs to be observed that the term 'the Son of God' is personally who He is, and isn't mentioned as one of the characters describing Him walking among the candlesticks. However there is a merging of the Son of Man and the Ancient of Days as one and the same in chapter one, which is, in a sense, a greater development of what is found in Daniel (Dan. 7:9-10, 13-14, 22). Obviously Jesus, the Son of God, bears the title of the Son of Man. The Son of God is the Ancient of Days, and this refers to divinity, and this was definitely part of Jesus in the midst of the candlesticks.

"These things says the Son of God..." is the ultimate or most comprehensive ecclesiastical character. It is the confession that Jesus builds the church on – *"You are... the Son of the living God."* (Matt. 16:15-18) The reality of the church is solely dependent on this truth being acknowledged by faith. This confession is the rock upon which the church has its existence.

How appropriate for Jesus to present Himself to Thyatira in this character. His presentations throughout the seven messages are either for encouragement or warning. With Smyrna and Philadelphia His character is for encouragement. With Pergamos and Laodicea it is a definite warning. In Thyatira, the Son of God speaking to them is a threatening of the corporate church. The general professing body is what is built on the earth on this confession, and with Thyatira it is found to be corrupt. The Son of God refuses to acknowledge it. When Christ declares the corporate body of Christendom to be utterly corrupt, then He withdraws association with it. What He is in His person, which never will change and is incorruptible, now comes out.

Your love, faith, service, and patience...as for your works, the last are more than the first: Rev. 2:19; Jesus recognizes the good that He sees. He notices and commends their increase in devotedness, which continued on unabated. This would seem to be His commendation and approval of the faithfulness of the despised saints during the middle ages. It may be hard to find in some history books and they may not tell God's viewpoint of events, but many of those poor saints remained faithful in labors and service to God. They remained faithful while often being hunted down and punished by an increasingly corrupt ecclesiastical structure. This was not persecutions from a sparsely organized Gentile Empire as in Smyrna and Pergamos. It was the organized corporate entity of Christendom in its established Jezebel state, systematically searching down true witnesses of Christ's glory, attempting to force loyalty to the presumptuous authority of the mother church. There were many sorrows and sufferings inflicted on these despised ones, yet they persevered. They stood strong in their witness and devoted service, even unto death. It is devoted faithfulness of many for Jesus Christ in the face of a corrupt and power hungry church structure.

That Woman Jezebel: Rev. 2:20-23; She is the source of evil inside the professing church. She is heresy and false doctrines leading to idolatry and worldliness. The professing church 'allows' her to dwell inside as an established state and condition. She is a prophetess like Balaam, pandering the same corruption as he did. Balaam had the name and authority of Jehovah, yet he took his guidance from the devil. Jezebel does the same. The corruption is taught in the name of Jesus Christ, but its source is the world and the depths of Satan.

In Pergamos Balaam was not yet rooted in the body. Here however, this woman Jezebel is a greater development of evil in the church world.[111] She is now living within, freely committing her adulteries. She is the mother of illegitimate children, birthing her own in the evil, corruption being part of their nature. Her children are born in the general assembly, and they draw their faith and nature from her. Those of Christ's servants that become involved in her doctrines, or are led astray by them, will be given a chance to repent. If they do not they will be judged (sickbed) and thrown into the great tribulation with her. As for her children the judgment and wrath is certain – the Lord will kill all her children with death.

Jezebel is a false prophetess and teacher. She pretends to be God's authority in expressing His mind and will, and the sole expounder and caretaker of His Word. She teaches heresies and deceptions. Her sexual immorality is her relationship with the world. It is not merely a loss of first love, but now adultery practiced within. Worldly luxury and wealth are her specialty by which she beguiles. She courts the kings of the world and lusts after civil power and influence. She promotes the lust of the eyes and flesh, and the pride of life (I John 2:15-17). She capitalizes on idolatry and becomes rich by it: the cult of the saints, the cult of the popes, and the cult of the virgin. She knows and teaches the depths of Satan (Rev. 2:24).

Jezebel also promotes a false ecclesiastical position and a doctrine of successional authority that is born in Judaism. With the earthly priesthood and the eventual college of cardinals and bishops, this form of Christianity represents the complete judaizing of the Christian faith. Like Judaism, it is earthly, sensual, and ritualistic. It is dependent on fleshly ordinances for the supposed imparting of favor and grace from God (Heb. 9:9-10).

Jezebel is the general appearance of the condition of professing Christianity at this time. She represents the time of established ecclesiastical apostasy, and established idolatry within Christendom. She became the mother of her own children, born of the evil. In her form she is the Roman Catholic world, and the power and influence of Satan from it.

According to your works: Rev. 2:23: Whenever there is judgment in respect to man's conduct or works, this judgment is always condemnation. *"I will give to each one of you according to your works."* This is the case for all involved with Jezebel and her teachings. This is spoken to the corporate church, before the remnant is separated. If man leaves his first estate and enters into sin, this necessitates judgment. How can this judgment be anything but condemnation? The professing church left its first estate. (See Psalm 143:2)

"For the Son of Man will come in the glory of His Father with His angels, and then He will reward each according to his works." (Matt. 16:27) It appears that Jezebel and those with her will be treated much the same as the unbelieving world.

But to you I say, and to the rest in Thyatira: Rev. 2:24-25: Here in Thyatira we have the first separating of the remnant from the corporate body of the professing church. The hearing ear exhortation placed after the overcomer's promises serves to individualize the remnant from the corrupt general body. All connection to the external body is broken. The call to 'hear' is after the remnant is separated and acknowledged by the Son of Man. It places the remnant in the position of those to whom the promises are made.

Also all calls for the professing body as a whole to repent and return are dropped. The Son of Man knows this is impossible. Christ's coming for the true church is held out to the remnant as its hope to sustain it in the midst of the corruption – *"But hold fast what you have till I come."* No more looking back for restoration of the outer body. The remnant is looking ahead to the hope of the glory of Christ.

The remnant is encouraged to simply remain faithful, to hold fast to the good things they have. They are asked to remain separated from the evil and corruption of Jezebel. This is the assigned task from the Lord. They are not told to grow up from faith to faith or to walk in the power of earlier days, but to hold on and to hold tight to that which they have. The saints during the middle ages did not possess great spiritual knowledge and understandings. These were the times before the enlightening of the Reformation. But these are the ones exhibiting the growing devotedness to Christ in practice, while there was less and less of this shown in the general body (Rev. 2:19).

The hope given to them is meant to be more a refuge and comfort to the faithful in the midst of the evil. To be faithful to God we must separate ourselves from the evil around us, while in many respects we may not be separate from the consequences of corporate responsibility. Remember the example of Joshua and Caleb. They had the report of faith and were distinctly marked as separated from the rest, yet suffered the consequences of the corporate failure – they spent forty years in the wilderness with the unbelieving nation.

In the end there will be a Jewish remnant, chosen, sealed, and preserved by God, believing in Jehovah and having the Spirit of God poured out on them (Rev. 7:3-8, Joel 2:28-32). They also will exist in the midst of an unbelieving and apostate nation that has received the Antichrist and gone after idols (John 5:43, Matt. 12:43-45). This end-time Jewish remnant will suffer much during the time of Jacob's trouble, but will be saved out of it (Jer.30:7). In a similar manner this 'rest in Thyatira' is also a definite separated and numbered group. It is distinctly marked apart from the general public state of the outward church. However, this remnant in Thyatira endured the consequences and public results of the failure for hundreds of years. They were to turn away from Jezebel, but they still remained a 'rest in Thyatira'.

And he who overcomes: When the external body of the professing church is judged as corrupt, the coming kingdom and glory in hope is substituted for it. Jezebel desired civil power over this world, and she used her worldly connections to gain it. The outward church was like the world and lusted after power to falsely reign as kings. How does the church world justify this when Christ did not reign when He came in the flesh and presently sits patiently waiting? (Heb. 10:13) Christendom attempts to rule the nations without Christ being present. The outward church does all in the name of Christ, but acts in lust for power and influence. The overcomer in Thyatira is promised his part in the future rule and dominion of the Son of Man over the nations in the coming dispensation. This is part of the church's inheritance laid up for her in heaven.

The hope and promises for the believer/remnant are always a result of our association with Christ. If we are heirs of God, it is because we are co-heirs with Him. If He rules, we will rule with Him (Rev. 2:26-27). If He has received heavenly glory, then He shares it with us (John 17:22). If we are loved by the Father, it is with the same love the Father has for Him (John 17:23). The Father is our Father because He is His Father. God is our God because He is His God (John 20:17). We are one with Christ, joined to Him, bone of His bone, and flesh of His flesh (Eph. 5:30). This is the infinite measure of what Christ's love has done for us.

The promises to the faithful in Thyatira are general promises associated with the entire body of Christ – the true church will be found with Christ in His millennial glory. *"And He put all things under His feet, and gave Him to be head over all things to the church."* (Eph. 1:22-23) The true church will reign with Christ in glory. This is contrasted with the existing corrupted state of the professing church in Thyatira.

The Morning Star: II Peter 1:19, Rev. 2:28; Christ's coming for the church – the rapture, our blessed hope – is the Lord as the Morning Star. Christ appearing to the world in judgment is His full manifestation as the noon day Sun – supreme authority and power, full of glory (Col. 3:4, Rev. 1:7). The morning star is only seen by some who are waiting early for its light. It is gone before the world sees the sun, before the Sun rises, before the Day of the Lord appears.

He is the Sun of Righteousness to the world when He appears to the world for judgment (Mal. 4).[112]

As the Sun, Christ will rule over the world and we will rule with Him (Rev. 2:26-27). As the Morning Star He will be seen and enjoyed by those of faith. The Morning Star will never be seen or enjoyed by the world. The Morning Star always precedes the rising of the Sun to the world. We will have Christ and He will have us, as He will personally come for the church.

Who sees the morning star? – Those who watch while it is still the night. Christ is the morning star in the rapture of the true church (Rev. 22:16). If the coming of Jesus for the church is our blessed hope, then we should be looking for Him and expecting Him (Titus 2:11-13). If we have this hope, we will purify ourselves now. This is the practical effect. We will be looking up into the heavens, instead of looking around to this world. Having this hope will not restore apostolic power, but it allows the remnant to be faithful when the corporate entity is found corrupt by God. The night is far spent, and the day is at hand. We should be looking for that first light – Jesus Christ, our morning star.

If a husband is away, his wife normally would be looking and expecting his return, even preparing herself for it. Her thoughts and affections would be for him.[113] The bride alone hears the voice of the Bridegroom (Rev. 22:16-17), and responds in anticipation. She desires Him to return for her (v.17) and He in turn assures her that He is coming (v. 20). The Spirit is always the energy and animation of the bride, and so, *"...the Spirit and the bride say, "Come!"*

"And thus we shall always be with the Lord." (I Thess. 4:17) The believer who has learned to love the Lord cannot help but anticipate His coming. He will constantly be prepared and waiting for Him. If he loves the Lord and has affections only for Him, nothing more needs to be said. His looking and anticipation is not the result of knowing certain detail of Scripture, but of having learned to love the Lord in reciprocation of His love for us and the church (Eph. 5:25, I John 4:19).

The proper view of the coming of Jesus for the church brings light to hundreds of Scriptures. It changes the character of many previous understandings we had. Our calling is heavenly. We have to be taken there to fulfill that calling, and that must be in glory and as one body together. Our place is with Christ in heaven, where He is hid in God. With this understanding we know, by principle, many other truths. We are not looking for a place down here to live. We are not looking to find rest in the world. We are not looking for comforts and pleasures on the earth. We are pilgrims and strangers passing through. We find the body of teaching concerning the kingdom of heaven and the church overwhelmingly confirms these principles – we are not of the world, as Christ is not of the world (John 15:19, 17:14, 16).

It is a beautiful experience to be taught biblical principles from God's word by the Spirit. The Scriptures begin to make sense and all details fall into place. We get a spiritual understanding about the things in heaven and our association and connection with them. We see and understand what things are of the earth and world, and our separation from them. Our hearts must be set on Christ and He is hidden at the right hand of God. That is where our life really is (Col. 3:1-3).

At the end of Revelations, Christ declares to the church that He is the Morning Star, and by this calls out the affections of the bride for Him (Rev. 22:16-17). At the beginning of the book the mention of His name and what His work of redemption has accomplished for us, does the same (Rev. 1:5-6). At the end of the book it is not what He has done, but what He will do when He comes. This parallels the division of the seven messages and churches. The first three are called back to what Christ did at the beginning. The last four look forward to what He will do in glory.

Therefore, both the promises – the millennial kingdom and the Morning Star – answer to the particular testing and sufferings of the faithful remnant in Thyatira at this time.

He who has an ear: Rev. 2:29; Now that the outer body is found corrupt and in a state of evil (the woman), and God pronounces judgment on it, the hearing ear is not associated by God in the same way with what is being judged. The phrase is now moved to the very end of the message.

Thyatira – Corruption and Evil within Christendom

In a general way, Thyatira represents the end of the straight-line prophetic progression of the professing church. We can count one, two, three, four, and arrive at this point as one church succeeds the next. More specifically, the first four churches represent the history of what is called the 'apostolic succession' in Christendom.[114] Thyatira characterizes the final state of this history. We must remember that Thyatira contained two things: a corrupt and evil corporate body in majority and a distinctly separated faithful remnant.

The Jezebel state of worldly corruption continues to the end (the great tribulation) and characterizes the corporate mass of Christendom. She existed under the patience of God for a long time by herself, from approximately the seventh to sixteenth century. God gave her plenty of time to repent (Rev. 2:21) and she would not. This is marriage to the world and a much farther development of evil than what proceeded before. It is judged as utter ruin and corruption. This state of Christendom does not stand as the witness of God in the earth. Other states will be brought in for testimony. This ends the general prophetic history of the spoiled crop in the field. Thyatira represents the entire general assembly up to the time of the Reformation. Jezebel and those with her are unrepentant. She is Romanism continuing on to the tribulation.

Chapter 9: Endnotes

[111] The use of gender in allegories (typology) is a subtle thing but important to see and understand. Between Balaam in Pergamos progressing to Jezebel in Thyatira, you have a definite switch in gender in the type. Balaam is a false prophet who seduces the people of God to idolatry and worldliness, both of which are a departing from the proper relationship with God. Jezebel is the same, only worse. Females in typology seem to always represent an established state and position in general, whereas males are used to depict actions, behavior, circumstances, and characteristics. In Pergamos, the male false prophet was beguiling certain ones with his false teachings. But he is not yet established within as a general ecclesiastical position. Jezebel is the accomplishment of Satan in bringing professing Christianity to this established state. She produces her own children within the general assembly. There is no doubt that in God's eyes Jezebel is seen as the general overall corrupted state of Christendom now established. He does not ask Thyatira to attempt a return to the first position. This fourth church represents a change in God's ways in dealing with Christendom on the earth. You see this in many ways in this particular message to Thyatira. The gender change from prophet to prophetess is just one of the many clues embedded in the message. Now, instead of pointing back to Pentecost, the Lord only points forward to His return.

[112] If we look at Malachi 4 you find two groups being distinguished in the passage. There is the wicked and unbelieving world for which the Day of the Lord is like a burning oven of fiery indignation and the wrath of God (Mal. 4:1, Rev. 19:11-15). The other group is the Jewish remnant (Rev. 7:1-8) waiting for deliverance from their enemies, and is distinguished in verse two of the passage, *"But to you who fear My name..."* This would be the name of Jehovah, the specific Jewish revelation of God (Ex. 6:2-3). Jesus will be a Deliverer for them, their Messiah, coming to them in the name of Jehovah (Matt. 23:39). The remnant are the ones remembering the Law of Moses and looking for the prophet Elijah in type (Mal. 4:4-5, Rev. 11:3-7). You should know that the church is not the recipient of these earthly blessings or judgment, or involved, other than we appear to the world with Him in glory.

[113] Our union with the Lord through the power of the Holy Spirit (I Cor. 12:12-13) should be more intimate than that of husband and wife. We have four eternal relationships:

1. With the Father as sons of God (Gal. 4:6-7, Rom. 8:14-16); then our unity together as sons in the family of the Father (John 17:20-21)
2. With Jesus Christ as brethren individually (John 20:17, Rom. 8:29, Heb. 2:11); as His body and bride corporately (I Cor. 12:12-13, Eph. 5:25-32).
3. With the Holy Spirit, who abides with us and in us forever (John 14:16-17).
4. With each other as members one of another in His body (I Cor. 12:12).

The relationships associated with the first creation are not eternal. They are not part of the new creation of God. All these have their end in Christ as His body in the heavens: husbands and wives, parents and children, nations and nationalities, male and female, slave or free. All these have their end upon entrance into Christ (Gal. 3:26-28, Col. 3:9-11). These things have ended for all believers now, in title and position, and then after the rapture of the church as a true physical reality. We continue to acknowledge these relationships as ordained of God and part of the world and first creation. We do not deny them. They remain unchanged in the world. Yet we cannot deny that we are the new creation of God and part of a body that has no ties to the first creation. The believer's only connection to Adam and to the first creation is our bodies of flesh we have. That is why the rapture of the church is such a unique event – it severs the believer's last tie to the first creation and Adam. With and in the heavenly Man, the church is destined to live and abide in the heavens as the habitation of His Father.

However, during the millennium on the earth these natural relationships continue. Man on the earth during this time is man in the first Adam, and with natural bodies. The Son of Man, the second Adam, ruling and having dominion over the earth, is the one mediator between God and man. This has to be seen as mediator for man in the first Adam. The true believer is now in Christ and as Christ. The believer is in the mediator and as the mediator. During the millennium, in Christ we are kings and priests unto the Father in the heavens (Rev. 1:6). We are definitely involved through Christ in the mediation of the relationship between God and man in Adam on the earth. As priests we are part of the mediation, as kings we are part of the government of God over the earth. And this is by virtue of our position in Christ and before the Father.

[114] Apostolic succession deals with the passing of authority from man to man on the earth. In Jezebel, this is the cult of the popes, the college of cardinals and bishops, and the endowing of authority on the Roman Catholic church in general. It is the means for men and for the corporate organization to unrighteously usurp earthly power and authority in the name of Christ. But it is Jesus Christ alone who has this authority in the church, because He is the only one who builds the church – *"I will build My church..."* The building of the true church is a sovereign work of God, and man is not involved in it.

This is where the main issue has its importance – man thinks he does the work of God. But the Scriptures teach that when God works, He works alone. That is why the work of the Holy Spirit at Pentecost and the Reformation is not seen being judged by the Lord in Revelation 2 and 3. What is judged is the work of man. *This is the principle – God's work is never judged; man's works are always judged.* Yet men can't admit that we are not doing the work of God and that we are not building the true church. In the professing church, men have been given the responsibility to build the building of God, for which Paul laid the solid foundation through sovereign grace and apostolic authority (I Cor. 3:9-13). This building is built on the earth and eventually became the same entity as the crop in the field in the kingdom of heaven (Matt. 13:26). It is not the body of Christ. It is not the church. The building of God on the earth is now what we have to call Christendom.

Only Jesus builds the church (Matt. 16:18). The true church is the body of Christ (Eph. 1:22-23). Only true sons of God are gathered and baptized by the Holy Spirit into the body of Christ (I Cor. 12:12-13). And God knows those who are His, and the Spirit never makes a mistake in gathering and forming the body. Jesus builds the church and He never uses tares to accomplish this work. Yet when we see the crop in the field we see there are tares mixed in with the wheat. This cannot be the body of Christ. This cannot be the church. This is a greater and larger entity that contains the church.

Now the body of Christ is gathered on the earth, but it is destined for heavenly places. The Holy Spirit was sent down to the earth and abides on the earth for the purpose of gathering the church. He is the direct agent for God in accomplishing the work of God in the earth. The believer is the workmanship of God. I suppose we can rightly say the church is the workmanship of Christ, for He builds the church. Whether the individual believer or the assembly, the Scriptures speak of both as the creation of

God. We should fully realize that man never creates anything, that he can have no part in this work, and that only God can create. We should fully realize that man can have no real part in the workmanship of God.

Through the prophetic progression of the first four churches, men have believed that they build the church on the earth and they do the work of God. It follows then that man assumed he had to have authority in Christ's place on the earth to do all he does—his works, his building, and his doctrines. This comes through the Jewish thought of succession. For Judaism it is the patriarchs and natural descent through birth and many such earthly thoughts. For Romanism it is a continuation of one supreme apostolic leader, and the passing on of Christ's authority on the earth from man to man in a created line of leaders. Add to this the doctrine of infallibility and you have created an unholy and ungodly mess that is nothing but contrary to Scripture. This is what man has done.

There are quite a few peculiarities with the idea of apostolic succession that have no real Biblical basis.

1. Jesus alone is Head of the church, the body of Christ, and He alone builds the church. Peter was given keys to the kingdom of heaven, which is a different and distinct entity from the church. And you do not build anything with keys.

2. Apostolic succession would require apostles, and these continuing on. For the same reason the church world cannot return to apostolic days or the book of Acts, there does not exist any apostolic succession. There simply are no apostles today. The apostles and prophets were for the foundation of the church (Eph. 2:20). The apostles in particular were eye-witnesses of Jesus Christ. The foundation was finished long ago.

3. The choice by the Roman Catholic world of Peter as the head of the church and the first in this apostolic line of succession is simply an oddity. Peter was the apostle of the circumcision (Gal. 2:7-8) — that meaning the Jews. The church is basically Gentile and this by Paul, the apostle to the Gentiles (Rom. 11:13). It was Paul who was given to lay the foundation as a wise master-builder, that no one else could lay (I Cor. 3:10-11). Peter never labored in the open door of ministry to the Gentiles that was so miraculously presented to him by vision and audible voice from the Holy Spirit (Acts 10). God never records Peter having any positive involvement with the

Gentiles beyond Cornelius' household. There shouldn't be need to recount Peter's negative influence and hypocrisy among the Gentile Christians at Antioch (Gal. 2: 11-21). All Peter's epistles were written to the Dispersion (I Pet. 1:1). It seems the Roman Catholics have the wrong guy.

4. Apostleship doesn't come by succession. They were given by Christ Himself when He ascended up on high (Eph. 3). Paul shows conclusively that apostleship does not come from men or through man, but through Jesus Christ and God the Father (Gal. 1:1).

The bottom line on this issue is where does the authority reside? Is it with Jesus Christ, the Head of the church, or is it with the professing church having left its first love and fallen? The outward body of Christendom grew worse and worse in its corruptions and evil. It steadily progressed to the Jezebel state. It has no authority from God.

There is no such thing as ecclesiastical authority in the church with men. The church as an organization does not have any such authority, and men only pretend to have authority that does not exit. There is no such thing as apostolic succession. The doctrine is not worth the paper the list of popes is written on. Jesus is the one who ever lives. He is the one who is the Ancient of Days. He is the one who is the firstborn from the dead. He is the one with all authority in heaven and on earth.

The book of Hebrews teaches us a great distinction between Judaism and Christianity that is applicable to this discussion. The central point that produces all the doctrine of the book is the change in priesthood (Heb. 8:1). In Christianity we have such a great High Priest! *"For such a High Priest was fitting for us, who is holy, harmless, undefiled, separate from sinners, and has become higher than the heavens."* (Heb. 7:26) All these descriptions of Jesus are reasons why Christianity's High Priest is infinitely better than any priest or priesthood found in Judaism. Here is the point about earthly succession: *"And there were many priests, because they were prevented by death from continuing."* (Heb. 7:23) Judaism is the founder of succession. It is an earthly system that was forced by the flesh to embrace it. This is part of what makes Judaism earthly and inferior, the weak and beggarly elements of the world (Gal. 4:3, 9, Heb. 9:9-10). But what is the parallel point of Christianity that makes it so superior to Judaism? *"But He (Jesus), because He continues forever, has an unchangeable priesthood. Therefore He is able to save to the uttermost those who come to God through Him, since He ever lives to make intercession for them."* (Heb.

7:24-25) In Christianity there is no need for succession. Christianity has a High Priest who ever lives and remains so continually.

When Romanism came in with its doctrine of apostolic succession, it was the Judaizing of the Christian faith. It established an earthly priesthood like Judaism, based on fleshly and inferior principles. The other doctrines of infallibility and ecclesiastical authority flow out of this first error. It all is wrong. Coming out of the Reformation, Protestantism has not been able to throw off all the man-made ecclesiastical corruptions fashioned by Romanism.

Chapter 10:
Sardis: Protestantism is Dead

There was a sovereign work of God in the faithful remnant of the church world during the time of the Reformation. It was the energy and action of the Holy Spirit to bring enlightenment and rediscovery of certain basic divine truths. One was the divine authority of God's written Word as the only standard of faith and practice. Another was justification by faith for the individual. When Romanism placed divine authority with the established church structure and infallible popes, the light of God comes in and shows that it is still Jesus who has all authority in heaven and on earth. When Jezebel declared herself to be the sole interpreter of Scripture and systematically kept the written Word from the masses, God comes in to place His Word in the hands of the faithful. When the Roman Catholic church pretended to dispense the grace of God through fleshly ordinances, their priesthood always standing and continually ministering, God demonstrates His grace in justifying through the one time and eternal sacrifice and death of His Son (Heb.10:10-12). The Reformation was the work of God in sovereign grace.

However, like the first estate of the church that resulted from Pentecost, the Reformation is not found or judged in the addresses to the churches. God does not judge His own work, nor does Christ judge the work of the Spirit. Yet what is always judged (and this in relation to the earth) is the responsibility of man when he is given care for the work that God has done. The faithful remnant were despised and persecuted for hundreds of years during the rise of the Jezebel state in Christendom. They were called and labeled every irreverent and ungodly name that could be thought of by priests and popes. They were hunted and endured much suffering and isolation. But God would do a new work.

The Reformation: a new sovereign work of the Spirit

Jezebel was given time by God to repent, but she would not (Rev. 2:21). The Lord had to set Christendom aside as hopeless. This corrupt 'state' of the corporate body existed for more than nine hundred years before the Reformation. Sardis represents what resulted in Christendom out of the Reformation. This was separate and distinct from Jezebel and her corruptions. Although Jezebel continues on with barely an interruption, the woman represents a corrupted 'state' of professing Christianity that no longer was a light or testimony for God in the earth. The Reformation was God working anew and afresh by His Spirit in the faithful remnant. Sardis represents the time after the Reformation, from about the early 1700's, when God's new work is placed in man's hands, and the particular result of responsibility is produced. God is looking for fruit resulting from man's previous blessing.[115]

Revelation 3:1-6

"And to the angel of the church in Sardis write,

'These things says He who has the seven Spirits of God and the seven stars: "I know your works, that you have a name that you are alive, but you are dead. (2) Be watchful, and strengthen the things which remain, that are ready to die, for I have not found your works perfect before God. (3) Remember therefore how you have received and heard; hold fast and repent. Therefore if you will not watch, I will come upon you as a thief, and you will not know what hour I will come upon

you. (4) You have a few names even in Sardis who have not defiled their garments; and they shall walk with Me in white, for they are worthy. (5) He who overcomes shall be clothed in white garments, and I will not blot out his name from the Book of Life; but I will confess his name before My Father and before His angels.

(6) "He who has an ear, let him hear what the Spirit says to the churches."

The Characters of Christ in the Messages

The character of Christ presented for Sardis gives us hints that there was a new sovereign work of the Spirit previous to this state. The seven stars in His possession are similar to His character in the first church, which followed the sovereign work of Pentecost. I believe this is the sovereign spiritual representation of the church in the mind and counsels of God – what the church will be once glorified and found in the kingdom of His Father (Matt. 13:43). The stars in His possession show that He has all power and authority in sovereign divine grace for the church. It shows that Christ will build the true church and it will not fail, even in the midst of corporate corruption or spiritual deadness of the general body on the earth.

Ecclesiastical Characters	*Personal Characters*
Holding the seven stars in His right hand or in His possession (Ephesus and Sardis). This points to a sovereign work having previously been completed	The Son of God (Thyatira) – this is both personal and ecclesiastical and is used in the message to the transition church
Walking in the midst of the seven golden lampstands (Ephesus) – responsibility judged	He who possesses the seven Spirits of God (Sardis) – His providential and sovereign authority
The First and the Last (divinity - Smyrna)	He who is holy, He who is true (Philadelphia)

He who was dead and came to life (Man - Smyrna)	He who has the key of David, He who opens and no man shuts, and shuts etc. (Philadelphia)
He who has the sharp two-edged sword (Pergamos) – the authority of Christ and the Word	These things says the Amen (Laodicea) – personally all God's promises are in Christ.
He who has eyes like a flame of fire and feet like fine brass (Thyatira) – judgment of man's works of corruption in the professing church	The Faithful and True Witness (Laodicea) – the corporate church has failed in its responsibility of testimony and Christ takes back this title
There are others found in chapter one that are not used in the messages	The Beginning of the creation of God (Laodicea) – He is Head of both the old and the new creation

A Faithful Remnant Separated

When we saw the seven Spirits previously it was the providential power of God in the earth issuing forth from His throne of government in heaven (Rev. 1:4). When we see the slain Lamb in the midst of the throne possessing the seven Spirits, it is the perfection of power and intelligence for the exercise of the government of the earth, having Himself prevailed to open the book of inheritance (Rev. 5:6). But the character of Christ presented to Sardis is what is available for the faithful remnant in this particular corporate state. If God is working in the earth at this time, it would have to be in and through the vessel of the church and not the world. But the outward body is either corrupt or dead, so it would have to be through the small remnant that He keeps. The seven spirits of God in His possession speaks of the unchangeable fullness and perfection (the #7) of the sovereign grace of the Spirit in His control (John 16:13-15). Both the seven stars and Spirits speak of His divine power to bring forth a new sovereign work such as the Reformation.

Again we should observe that the character of Christ possessing the seven Spirits of God is not one of the ecclesiastical characters of Christ among the candlesticks. The seven Spirits do not represent the Holy Spirit dwelling in the midst of the church – the habitation of God by the Spirit (Eph. 2:22). Rather this speaks of the qualities and power of the Holy Spirit as the direct agent of Christ to bring about the will of God in the earth. It is that which is personal to Him, and in reference to His own power and rights, but even apart from the church world. It is comfort and assurance to the faithful that He alone is the real source of strength. His characters become more personal, indicating that the faithful remnant's security is not in the outward body of Christendom, but only now having Him personally. He alone has the power to sustain and support the remnant.[116]

Seeing clearly the Ruin of the Professing Church

Colossians 2:5-7

"For though I am absent in the flesh, yet I am with you in spirit, rejoicing to see your good order and the steadfastness of your faith in Christ.

As you therefore have received Christ Jesus the Lord, so walk in Him, rooted and built up in Him and established in the faith, as you have been taught, abounding in it with thanksgiving."

The 'steadfastness of your faith in Christ' has the meaning of faithfulness. Being 'rooted and built up in Christ' and 'established in the faith' is the same. The true believer must develop a deep understanding and appreciation of the value of all that is in Christ for the individual. This knowledge will open his eyes to the failure of the professing church and give him confidence in the midst of it. When he fully sees all that Christ has done for him, he will know that Christendom is not the faithful and fruit-bearing witness it had responsibility to be. His proper understanding and deep sense of the failure of the church world will enhance rather than weaken his confidence in the Lord. He will be steady and calm through all the pretense of the corporate institution. His confidence is no longer in man's work or the religious structure but in the grace that Christ personally gives that is sufficient for him (II Cor. 12:9-10).

When God finds the corporate structure of Christendom either corrupt (Thyatira) or dead (Sardis), then it remains that the individual believer is a testimony for Christ in the world. This is no longer a comparison to the book of Acts, Pentecost, and the apostolic church. All those comparisons ended with Pergamos. Christ does not look for or expect the remnant to do great and heroic things for God. He knows that this is not possible. Rather, it is in accordance to what the remnant has received in grace from Christ now, in their present situation and for their situation. His grace is always sufficient for the need, and He sees the present need as sustaining and supporting the faithfulness of the few in the midst of corporate failure until He returns.[117]

Protestantism: a Diverging Path from Jezebel

We should notice concerning the characters of Christ applied in the last four churches just how many of them are personal to Him. They are not the previous ecclesiastical characters.

The # of Ecclesiastical Characters in the Progression

Ephesus	Smyrna	Pergamos	Thyatira	Sardis	Philadelphia	Laodicea
2	2	2	2/1	1	0	0

On a technical note concerning the characters of Christ and how they are used in the structuring of the seven messages, we see that the first three churches have only ecclesiastical characters. In these three the corporate body is acknowledged by God as vital. The possibility of repentance and return are held out to them. Thyatira and Sardis both have one church character and one personal. These two churches represent times of transition. Thyatira is the total corruption of the original blessing of Pentecost, while Sardis is the responsible outcome of man's care for the second blessing of the Reformation. Sardis is immediately judged by God as spiritually dead. Both churches have a faithful remnant that God distinctly marks and acknowledges (Rev. 2:24, 3:4) because He chooses out of the world and knows those that are His (John 15:19, II Tim. 2:19). In the final two churches the character of Christ is all personal and there is no church character.

It is easy to see the progressive pattern and why we can say that Christ views the professing church, as it goes along in time, less and less as a corporate entity. Christendom loses any acknowledged church character. When the professing church has been found corrupt beyond any reasonable hope and no longer represents the glory of Christ before the world, then what comes forth as applied character is what Christ is in His person. His personal character is the resource and encouragement of the individual or small remnant. The general body of Protestantism had a certain outward profession and appearance of Christianity, but was spiritually dead, having no living power. The character of Christ presented stands in stark contrast to this condition. But His character is not for the outer body of Protestantism. It is for the few names in Sardis that have not defiled their garments.

The corporate church as Jezebel has been set aside, having no true testimony for God and having lost any true church characteristics that could be acknowledged. Therefore, except for the seven stars here in Sardis, the remaining churches see none of the original ecclesiastical characters of Christ. The general professing church that is Jezebel is not acknowledged; yet it exists, and remains, and goes on to the end. We have to be mindful that Jezebel is Romanism, and is the greater part of Christendom. Therefore, the Reformation starts a divergent path away from Jezebel, and Sardis is the human outcome in responsibility, so to speak, of the new work of God.

Protestantism: a Reputation and Appearance

Protestantism is the great public result that is looked at and judged by Christ in the time of Sardis. Protestantism is the work and responsibility of man resulting from the Reformation. It has a name, which is a certain reputation in the eyes of men. It has a name to be alive, but it is dead. It is not the corruption and evil of Jezebel. But it has no life and no fruit to answer to the previous work of God. All is spiritually dead. There is no moral power in the professing church. Jezebel is corruption. Sardis is a dead carcass.

The story of Sardis is easily told. It is not a state of corruption, although there was individual evil involved. Rather, it was a reputation of great moral activity on the part of men to deliver Christendom from the previous corruption and evil. That is what it was, just a name for something it really wasn't. The Reformation was the sovereign work of God's grace. If man takes credit for it as his work, then he has a reputation in the world and a reason for glorying.

The Exaltation of man and his Religion

Jezebel is Romanism, which is the complete judaizing of the Christian faith. By adding Judaism to Christianity man exalts himself by what he does and accomplishes, making his additions to the simplicity and efficacy of Christ. By adding Judaism man again has a religion he can perform by human effort and accomplishment, and the gaining of status and glory in the world. Man will desperately hold on to and fight for religion that he can accomplish by human effort. This isn't the case with true Christianity, and so man in the flesh will not be happy unless he can make it so.

In Sardis and with Protestantism men were prone to do the same, just not in such an outward corrupting degradation of the faith as is Jezebel. In Protestantism you eventually have the false leaven of Arminianism. It is a subtle form of judaizing, new and fresh, but accomplishes the same results – the glorifying of man in and by what he does. The Arminian leaven is everywhere in Protestant doctrines and teachings today, especially the Evangelical side of things. There is also the direct influence of Judaism, with its rituals, fleshly ordinances, earthly traditions, sabbaths, and holy days. One of the greatest impacts on Protestantism is the judaizing use of the teachings and doctrines of Israel, by which the separate and distinct callings of Israel and the church are confounded. We cannot leave Jezebel totally off this list. Although the Reformation was a divergent path away from her, man in his responsibility and care in Protestantism did not see it necessary to rid himself of all of Jezebel's ways and worldliness.

Protestantism, although having a great reputation, is spiritually dead. The orthodoxy in Protestantism is essentially this – a name, a reputation, a certain appearance, but no living Christ. There is no real life in it. When you establish state religions where entrance into the church is given to all with barely a commitment or profession, there will be no life of God in it. God calls, God chooses, and God works, not the state or country or empire.

The general body of Sardis is warned to *"Be watchful and to strengthen the things that remain, that are ready to die..."* Even what little spiritual life they had was about to be lost (Matt. 13:12). Their works were not truly Christian in character and pleasing to God. *"...for I have not found your works perfect before God."* God's standard is not being met and He will not compromise, in holiness and love. As it can be said, there are very many who profess Christ, comparatively few who live Christ.

"Remember therefore how you have received and heard." This is another reference to the previous sovereign work of God in the Reformation. Sardis is instructed to remember the previous blessing of God in grace and in a sense recover the truth of it. Yet the public body is found to have no answer to what they previously saw and heard. It is judged as failed and dead. They are to hold fast to whatever remains, and repent.

Sardis treated as the World

The most sobering part of the message to the corporate entity of Sardis is the threat that Christ *"...will come upon you as a thief, and you will not know what hour..."* Here Protestantism, as the corporate system, is reduced to equal status with the world (I Thess. 5:1-3). This is God's estimate of it. In I Thessalonians the contrast is between the true church and the world – between what is the light and what is in darkness. In Sardis it is the contrast between what professes and has a reputation in the eyes of the world and the faithful remnant. Sardis will be judged with the world.

Christ's Profession of the Remnant

The issue in Sardis is having the name, the reputation, the profession of Christ, and whether it is truly of God or not. This difference is observed when the faithful overcomers in Sardis are addressed:

- *He ...shall be clothed in white garments – the righteousness of the saints.*

- *Their names will not be blotted out of the Book of Life – in its use here it is a general archive of Christian 'profession' and all names written in it include all the wheat and tares of Christendom. This is not the book that God writes in before the foundations of the world. The one God writes in is the one of His eternal counsels and purpose.*

- *I will confess his name before My Father and before His angels – this is the profession that counts, where Christ Himself acknowledges and confesses you as His own.*

The hearing ear phrase is again found at the end of the message, indicating that the corporate body of Protestantism is not a witness for God in the world and its candlestick will soon be removed (Rev. 3:6). Only the remnant is acknowledged by Christ (Rev. 3:4). The corporate body is not.

Do not count on or rest in religious reputation. Listen and hear what the Spirit says, and act accordingly. Do not turn around and become a judge of God's Word.[118] This was Protestantism's demise. The Reformation holds God's word up as the sole authority on earth. When man is made responsible he sinks down into private interpretation of the word. This is soon perverted into men becoming judges of God's word, judges of its true meaning. This leads to the dividing of the body in denominationalism. Protestantism was a form of godliness without any life or power, and brought in the wholesale dividing up of Christ.

Chapter 10: Endnotes

[115] The principle of responsibility remains the same for Sardis as it was for Ephesus. A sovereign work of God and blessing by the energy of the Holy Spirit is done first. Now it is placed in the hands of men for the care of it. What is judged is man's care for the original blessing. Sardis is new ground, because it is man's responsibility following a new work of the Holy Spirit.

[116] Israel made the golden calf and failed before Moses brought the tablets down the mountain. As a consequence of this corporate corruption Moses moves the tabernacle outside and away from the camp of Israel. There the glory would come down and Moses would enjoy face to face communication with God (Ex. 33:7-11). In the understanding of intimate relationships, this was not the experience of the rest of Israel.

[117] The seven messages to the churches in Revelation 2 and 3 is God's judgment of the responsibility of the professing church in its time on the earth. This is the judgment of its work and its moral condition as a witness for God. Jesus Christ Himself is the One speaking the messages through the Spirit. He is the one walking in the midst of the candlesticks. In discussing and judging the responsibility of the corporate church He mentions certain subjects and categories – first love, false doctrines, evil deeds, worldliness, idolatry, and enduring suffering. Jezebel is the utter corruption and evil of the corporate body. Protestantism becomes the other part of the corporate body that is spiritually dead. When the corporate body failed, the remnant in the last four churches is then encouraged to faithfulness, holding on, and expecting and looking for Christ's coming for them.

My point is this: These are the things that God sees as important concerning the responsibility of the church and worthy of His notice. These are the subjects He chooses to discuss. This actually represents the responsibility of the corporate church. Why don't we understand this point? Why have we created other topics and things to emphasize as the will of God? Has God given an inadequate evaluation of the corporate responsibility of the professing church? Has He judged incorrectly or left important things out? Has He given incomplete instructions to His remnant as to what they should be doing in the midst of failure in order to sustain them?

Nothing in Revelation 2 and 3 is incomplete or needs any additions, especially adding the wayward thoughts and aspirations of men. It is the responsibility of the judged church world. We should have ears to hear what the Spirit is saying to the churches. Do you have ears to hear? Our problem is that we want the Spirit to say something different or something new. There isn't anything different from what we have in these seven messages or anything new that is different from what the Spirit has said. This is it. If you come up with something different, it isn't the Word of God. If you think you have something new from the Spirit, say from prayer and fasting, it isn't from God. Again, this is it. From the time of John on Patmos this is the history of the works and responsibility of the professing church on earth. This is the history of its candlestick until it is removed.

Further point: Why wouldn't we emphasize what God tells the faithful remnant to do? Why wouldn't we teach the same thing as God encourages the remnant with? I simply do not get it. We make up a new agenda with a different emphasis and call it the will of God. It doesn't agree with what God has said to do. By this we actually walk away from God. The remnant is what God counts as His and He preserves it to the end. Why wouldn't we pay close attention to what He says about it? His instructions are for the care of the remnant. He knows what it needs in order to keep it in His grace and faithful to Him.

Faithfulness to Christ is the key characteristic of the remnant. In Thyatira they are to keep free of the corruption of Jezebel (Rev. 2:24) and have no involvement with her. He says to the remnant,*"...I will put on you no other burden."* The only burden is faithfulness. They are told to *"...hold fast what you have till I come."* This is faithfulness in the midst of corruption (Rev. 2:25). In Sardis the remnant is marked out by the Lord as those who have not defiled their garments with the false profession and religious orthodoxy of Protestantism (Rev. 3:4). His encouragement to them is they are worthy and they should look forward to walking with Him in white. Again, not defiling your garments is remaining faithful to Him. When we get to Philadelphia, the remnant church, it is nothing other than faithfulness that He calls for – nothing else!

Over the course of our Lord's life here on earth, His 'reputation' in the eyes of men diminishes more and more until they hate Him and put Him on the cross. One friend betrays Him, one denies knowing Him, and all desert Him (John 16:32). He was the faithful and true witness of God always, but certainly of no reputation in the world. The believer's faithfulness to God will have a similar effect. Your faithfulness will lower other's opinion of you. It causes a certain amount of isolation. It will not give you a reputation in the world's eyes. You will be seen as odd and strange, even to other believers. Few will understand your walk. There are afflictions that are brought on by faithfulness: this is suffering with Christ because His faithfulness as the true witness of God caused the same for Him. *All who live godly in Christ Jesus will suffer persecution.* It is the believer's portion, while on the earth, to share in the sufferings of Christ. But through faithfulness you will walk closer to Christ and have more of His grace for others.

The final point: Faithfulness to Christ in the midst of the evil of the church body is what should be taught today. It is what Christ emphasizes. *"Hold fast what you have until I come"* is the other part of faithfulness. This is remaining true to Him while you are looking and expecting His imminent return for the body of Christ. His return to gather up the true church and take us to the Father's house needs to be taught more. The practical effect of this teaching is faithfulness to Christ and separation from the world and from worldliness (I John 3:1-3).

There are many teachings in the Christian world today about what the responsibilities of the church are. Very few of these teachings agree with what the Spirit has said to the churches when its responsibility is looked at, or even more importantly, how He instructs the faithful remnant in the messages. I see this as a real problem and a major disconnect. If we see fit to teach other things as our responsibilities, we are not agreeing with God. For example, if we do not see the general corporate body of Christendom as corrupt or spiritually dead, then we do not agree with God. God sees it as just this and He refuses to acknowledge it. He sees it as hopeless. But we teach that the corporate body has all kinds of hope and potential, all kinds of strength and power. If you take the corporate church body and wrap it up in Arminian thoughts of human achievement and great works to be accomplished for God, then I say you are not agreeing with God and are actually denying what God has said. But these are the things we actually teach, the winning of America and the winning of the world. The Arminian leaven sweeps us up into many pretentious thoughts which, when closely examined, do not have a true basis in the Word of God or the thoughts of God.

[118] One of the doctrines of Jezebel is that the authority of Christ on the earth resides in the church organization – church authority is held by the ecclesiastical structure and assumed by the men who controlled that structure. The infallibility of popes secured this earthly power and mechanism. With the Reformation God brings out, in sovereign grace and truth, the authority of Scripture alone – *sola Scriptura*. Protestantism diverges from the pretentious authority of the Catholic church, but soon

sank down into private interpretation and personal judgment of the Word of God. Both views are wrong. The authority of Christ does not reside in corrupt Jezebel. Neither do we possess a personal right to judge God's Word. If God has spoken, we do not judge it, only obey.

With Protestantism's premise of private interpretation, men devise 'crucial rules' in the so called 'science' of hermeneutics to 'properly interpret' the word of God. I see the wisdom of man and the world in this. God did not give these clever rules and drop them down to us. I do not see one hint of their existence or divine use in Paul's teaching in I Corinthians 2. These rules are not God's thoughts, the mind of Christ, or the Spirit of truth teaching the things of God. They amount to the wisdom of the world and the wisdom of the Greeks (I Cor. 1:19-31), and even a vague reference to the Greek god, Hermes. It is worldly intelligence and how the professing church copies and makes use of it. As I said before, this is where things break down in departure from the leading and teaching of the Spirit, and denominations were the result. Look what we have today. Christ is divided (I Cor. 1:13). And this was done by man, not by God.

Chapter 11:
Philadelphia: God Preserves a Remnant

Philadelphia is a remnant body that exists in Christendom in the end times. The true church has become a remnant. In God's view the remnant is the church and is what remains faithful to God. There may still remain some of the faithful in Thyatira and Sardis. Over time and with greater enlightenment from the Spirit and the Word the majority of the remnant will separate from the corporate body that is judged and no longer acknowledged by God. Jezebel is corruption. Sardis is spiritually dead. Together they make up the state of the corporate organized mass of Christendom.

There are a few different ways to look at the final four churches. In the prophetic element previously discussed I said they should be looked at as four parts existing at the same time forming the whole of Christendom at the end. In a sense this is a good way of viewing them because we are able to see each one existing distinctly at this present time. Jezebel is Romanism. The spiritual deadness of Sardis is Protestantism. Philadelphia is the faithful as a remnant body kept by God. Laodicea is Evangelical Christianity enveloped by the humanistic leaven.

Often with allegories, symbols, and prophetic language, you have to be aware of the possibility of double meanings. I'm not saying this is true of every symbol, but the majority of them have double meanings. Allow me to show you a few examples.

Daniel 2:36-38

"This is the dream. Now we will tell the interpretation of it before the king. You, O king, are a king of kings. For the God of heaven has given you a kingdom, power, strength, and glory; and wherever the children of men dwell, or the beasts of the field and the birds of the heaven, He has given them into your hand, and has made you ruler over them all—you are this head of gold."

The statue in the dream of Nebuchadnezzar, for which Daniel is given the interpretation by God, represents the four world powers that would dominate the 'times of the Gentiles' (Luke 21:24). The head of gold has two meanings. It stands for both Nebuchadnezzar himself as king and the Babylonian kingdom or empire. The statue in all its glory is the four world empires seen from man's perspective. When we are shown these same empires from God's viewpoint they are unruly beasts (Dan. 7:2-8). So when we look at each individual beast we should be first thinking that this represents a distinct civil world kingdom that would come forth on the face of the prophetic earth in time. But each beast also has its leader or head – Nebuchadnezzar, Darius, Alexander, and the Caesars. Notice what is said about the first beast.

Daniel 7:4

"The first was like a lion, and had eagle's wings. I watched till its wings were plucked off; and it was lifted up from the earth and made to stand on two feet like a man, and a man's heart was given to it."

The lion, the kingdom of Babylon, loses its character as a beast and is made like a man answering to God. The beast character is always such that it doesn't answer to God, but will go its own way and follow its own selfish will. The lion lifted up from the earth and made to stand like a man, having a man's heart, is the beast losing his beastly character. This was directly the personal experience of king Nebuchadnezzar (Dan. 4:10-37) which in turn changed the character and nature of his kingdom. He was directly judged by God for his arrogance and apostasy, made to act like a beast for seven full years, until he was made to acknowledge the Most High God.[119]

Sometimes an allegory or parable will have a very practical application separate from its symbolic meaning and interpretation. We find some examples of this in Matthew (Matt. 18:23-35 and Matt. 21:18-22). The practical application of the parable about the unforgiving servant is forgiveness (Matt. 18:35). With the miracle of cursing the fig tree the application is having faith in God to answer prayer (Matt. 21:21-22). But we have to realize that the practical application in no way deals with the allegories used or the interpretation they require. The main allegory in the parable is the unforgiving servant. Figuratively he represents the nation of Israel guilty of putting the Son of Man to death, but forgiven through the intercession of Jesus on the cross. After that, Israel is only a hindrance to any others receiving grace and forgiveness in the kingdom of heaven (Matt. 18:28-30, 23:13). The symbol of the fig tree is Israel serving as the test-case representing all mankind. It symbolizes man in Adam being tested in responsibility. God is looking for fruit in man, in Israel, but finds none. Both examples end with the setting aside of Israel, although the fig tree has deeper implications that go beyond Israel, reaching to the entire world.[120]

The Last Four Churches

Let us consider these thoughts in connection with the last four churches:

- Thyatira contains Jezebel. Sardis contains Protestantism. Jezebel is corruption and Protestantism is spiritually dead. These two represent the public outward body of Christendom as set aside, yet are very distinct corporate entities. There is a faithful remnant that Jesus personally identifies as existing in both Thyatira and Sardis (Rev. 2:24, 3:4). We can see these two remnants as distinct from the two general bodies.

- Laodicea is the last church in the list of seven. They are spewed out of the Lord's mouth. This seems to represent Christendom's candlestick finally being removed. This was the threat at the beginning with Ephesus (Rev. 2:5). If there is only one candlestick for all of Christendom, then the spewing out is the removal of the candlestick representing all of the professing church – all except Philadelphia, the small remnant body. This would be like Jezebel and Protestantism together making up the general body of Christendom, forming Laodicea. They aren't mixed together in themselves, but together make up the entire public body of Christendom spewed out. The remnants of Thyatira and Sardis are then viewed together forming Philadelphia. Jesus Christ alone is the Faithful and True Witness when the candlestick is finally removed (Rev. 3:14). Philadelphia is the wheat removed from the world (Matt. 13:30).

Revelation 3:7-13

"And to the angel of the church in Philadelphia write,

'These things says He who is holy, He who is true, "He who has the key of David, He who opens and no one shuts, and shuts and no one opens": (8) "I know your works. See, I have set before you an open door, and no one can shut it; for you have a little strength, have kept My word, and have not denied My name. (9) Indeed I will make those of the synagogue of Satan, who say they are Jews and are not, but lie—indeed I will make them come and worship before your feet, and to know that I have loved you. (10) Because you have kept My command to persevere, I also will keep you from the hour of trial which shall come upon the whole world, to test those who dwell on the earth. (11) Behold, I am coming quickly! Hold fast what you have, that no one may take your crown. (12) He who overcomes, I will make him a pillar in the temple of My God,

and he shall go out no more. I will write on him the name of My God and the name of the city of My God, the New Jerusalem, which comes down out of heaven from My God. And I will write on him My new name.

(13) "He who has an ear, let him hear what the Spirit says to the churches."'

The Character of Christ for Philadelphia

"He who is holy, He who is true..." This is the personal moral character of the Lord Jesus Christ. It is quite appropriate for this faithful remnant body. It is not a new sovereign work or ecclesiastical characters. The characterization of Christ for Philadelphia is not found in chapter one when He is in the midst of the candlesticks. Christ's character and Philadelphia as the remnant church is entirely outside that which is corporate and ecclesiastical. It is not a reference to outward power of seven Spirits and stars in his right hand, as in miracles, signs, and power of the Spirit. Rather it is what the faithful remnant can readily find for support and sustenance in the person of the Lord Himself. It is the proper character of Christ as found in the Word of God — He is holy and true.

"He who has the key of David..." This references His sovereignty. Soon the remnant will experience the exceeding greatness of God's power toward them, as was demonstrated when God raised the Son of Man from the dead (Eph. 1:19-21). It will be a great sovereign work of God on our behalf. Jesus is *"He who opens and no one shuts, and shuts and no one opens."*

The Open Door set before Philadelphia

The works of the faithful remnant are never questioned — *"I know your works."* The open door set before them is one based on His sovereign power — *"...and no one can shut it."* Many Christians interpret this to be an open door of evangelism for the church, but I believe that to be a misguided assumption going against the entire nature of His message to them.[121] The open door He sets before them will be the sovereign work in the rapture of the true church and taking Philadelphia into the presence of the Father. It will be a work done in sovereign power and grace on behalf of the true church (Eph. 1:19-23). It is Jesus Christ as the resurrection and the life for the faithful remnant (John 11:25-26). It is a door opened by Christ alone, and not by the help of man. *"After these things I looked, and behold, a door standing open in heaven. And the first voice which I heard was like a trumpet speaking to me, saying, "Come up here..."* (Rev. 4:1, I Thess. 4:16) John sees the same open door that is set before Philadelphia (Rev. 3:8).

Little Public Power in Philadelphia

"...for you have little strength, have kept My word, and have not denied My name." There is no apostolic power here. There is no great display of miracles. There is no return to the first position of Pentecost encouraged. The testimony here is that the public power is gone and it will not be recovered. You are of little strength. This is that by which you hold on, not win the world or the nation.

The Faithfulness of the Remnant Body

"Thy word I have hid in my heart..." The remnant is commended for keeping His word. This is especially characteristic of faithfulness in the last days – *"...you have kept My word..."* The security and sustenance of the remnant would not be in outward displays of power, but simply in hearing, reading, understanding, and keeping the written Word. This is the recognized means of blessing for the remnant.

It is the recognized authority of the Word and faithfulness to it which is the confidence of the remnant in perilous times. The last days are a time when evil men and seducers grow worse and worse. The seductive influence of the world must be met and resisted by each individual believer, holding fast to the written Word of God and not denying Christ's name. Everything found in the world is against this. It is purposed by Satan for the setting aside of the Word of God, its validity, its authority, its usefulness. But the faithful remnant keeps it when the entire world denies it. When the world is all about denying the name of Christ, the remnant does not. They are faithful in the midst of the unfaithfulness of the general body of Christendom, and this makes a special impression on the Lord. He commends their faithfulness.

The Judaizing of Professing Christianity

Those who say they are Jews and are not, but are of the synagogue of Satan I believed refers to the pervasiveness of the judaizing leaven in the professing church in the last days. Arminianism is a subtle form of the same humanistic leaven that exalts man in his works. These teachings inundate professing Christianity in modern times and the church world has become intoxicated by them, to the point that we no longer have the ability to distinguish between the work of God and that of man.

The mixing of the church with Israel is extremely hurtful in spiritual things. The church today is mostly taught with the teachings of the Jews and the instructions of Judaism. It is religion that is earthy and appeals to the senses and emotions – this is the nature of its attraction and is why the masses in the professing church crave it (II Tim. 4:3-4). It is God's religion of the world and therefore is according to the weak and beggarly elements (Gal. 4:3, 9-11, Col. 2:8, 20). It produces a walk by sight and physical senses, and incorporates fleshly ordinances and confidences (Heb. 9:9-10, Phil. 3:2-8). It is religion of human effort and accomplishment. It is a religion that man can do in order to fool himself into thinking he has right standing before God. It has no ability to produce a walk of faith (Gal. 3:12, II Cor. 5:7). There is little attempt to rightly divide the Word of truth today. There is very little understanding of the stark differences between Christianity and Judaism.[122]

While the mixing of the church with Israel has harmful effects on spiritual truth, it simply becomes the greatest of errors in the understanding of prophecy. By this mistake the true church loses its heavenly calling, its heavenly citizenship, and its spiritual blessings in heavenly places. The church is brought down low to the earth and all its hopes are rendered earthy and physical. The result of this is the church world's erroneous thinking and great human efforts to prepare and control the earth and world to make it a better place for its own glory and habitation.

Philadelphia understands the Sovereignty of God

It will only be the judgments of God at the end of the age that makes for a better world (Isa. 26:9-10). The presence of the church or the human efforts of professing Christianity does not make the world better. All the presence of the church on earth really does, and this by the habitation of the Holy Spirit in her, is hinder the full display of evil coming forth at this time (II Thess. 2:6-7). That is it. Our job is not the eradication of evil from the world and its conversion. We aren't permitted to do this work even in the confines of the professing church (Matt. 13:27-30). Shouldn't this tell us something? Christendom ripens its own evil and corruption to its end, just as the world does. And the mind of God, the will of God, is to leave it alone. In both cases – the professing church and the world – the entrance and growth of evil and corruption was through the responsibility of man. The Scriptures teach that the responsibility of man will not and cannot solve the problem.[123]

What are we taught in the Scriptures as to how the evil is dealt with and eventually removed from these two separate entities – Christendom and the world? For both it is a sovereign work of God at the end of the age, and not before that time. For professing Christianity it is the wheat removed from the field and the tares bundled together and left in the field to be burned (Matt. 13:30). This is the rapture of the church into the heavens and the separation of the remainder of the professing church to be judged with the world (Matt. 13:39-43). As for the world, although there are judgments proceeding from the throne in heaven coming down upon the earth, the removal of evil begins at the return of the Son of Man. He will destroy the two beasts and bind Satan. The judging of evil continues for the length of His millennial kingdom. He must reign until He has put all enemies under His feet (I Cor. 15:25).

We see how it is done – a sovereign work of God, and not by the work of man. So then, all the Arminian leaven that creates thoughts for doing great things and winning nations is found to be false, and not the will of God. He doesn't have some great thing for the professing church to accomplish on the earth. It was to be the light of God in the darkness of the world – a testimony of the truth of God – but it has allowed its own corruption, and has failed miserably in its corporate witness. 'Into the world' is not the calling of the true church. 'On the earth' is not the calling of the true church. Its calling is in the heavens, and there alone will you find her true purpose.

The Father's and Son's love for the faithful remnant

"Indeed I will make them come and worship before your feet, and to know that I have loved you." (Rev. 3:9) This will only happen when Philadelphia is in glory and believers sitting on endowed thrones ruling as kings. This is another of the many references to glory that we find in this message. Particularly this thought references a passage in the gospel of John:

John 17:20-23

(20) "I do not pray for these alone, but also for those who will believe in Me through their word; (21) that they all may be one, as You, Father, are in Me, and I in You; that they also may be one in Us, that the world may believe that You sent Me. (22) And the glory which You gave Me I have given them, that they may be one just as We are one: (23) I in them, and You in Me; that they may be made perfect in one, and that the world may know that You have sent Me, and have loved them as You have loved Me."

The world 'believing' in verse 21 above refers to the believer's present time in this world. The unity of believers as the Father's family was to be its testimony in responsibility and was to cause the world to notice and believe that Jesus Christ was truly of God. This unity of one family in the earthly testimony of believers to the world only happened early on in Christendom. Now such unity is nonexistent and impossible. But Christ's prayer to the Father goes on to the manifestation to the world of the true church in glory (Col. 3:4). This is when the world will 'know' the love of the Father for all the brethren as one family, because the world will see with their own eyes and they will know beyond any doubt. Christ assures the remnant of His love for them as well. He says to Philadelphia, *"...indeed I will make...them come and worship before your feet...to know that I have loved you."*[124] This helps to sustain our faith during the present time of suffering.

Jewish Opposition to the Kingdom of Heaven

It's possible to view this verse more from a literal sense (Rev. 3:9). In the time of Jesus and during the ministry of the apostles, the Jews hindered the preaching of the kingdom of heaven and the entrance of those wanting to come in. *"But woe to you, scribes and Pharisees, hypocrites. For you shut up the kingdom of heaven against men; for you neither go in yourselves, nor do you allow those who are entering to go in."* (Matt. 23:13) There are many passages that show this general attitude and behavior of the Jews (Acts 14:2). I have no reason to doubt that it continued for the first few centuries of the existence of Christendom, even after the destruction of Jerusalem and the temple. Those of Israel who professed Jesus Christ and were living in the midst of the nation before 70 AD, were those put under some of the greatest persecutions and hardships (Heb. 10:32-34). The epistle to the Hebrews must be read entirely in this light. *"Concerning the gospel they (Israel) are enemies for your sake (the Gentiles)..."* (Rom. 11:28; see also Gal. 4:29)

Orthodox Judaism, as well as those of Israel who have varying Jewish beliefs are in a difficult place. Their fathers rejected and killed the promised Messiah of Israel (John 19:19-22). They have to deny this. God has set Israel aside. God says they are not His people (Hosea 1:9, Heb. 8:9). They must deny this. God judged Israel and destroyed Jerusalem and their temple two separate times. How can they admit Jehovah did this? To maintain any portion of Judaism – their religion – they must deny the legitimacy of all Christian claims and foundations (I John 2:22). For their own feelings of preservation, particularly as a people and nation, they must emphatically deny Jesus Christ, and thereby deny the very God who sent Him (John 5:37-40, 8:42, 15:21-24). This is the same God they say they worship (John 8:54-55). One can easily see their denial of Christ is far more than individual, but national, and thus with these types of corporate implications and pressures.

When Jesus says, *"...who say they are Jews and are not, but lie..."* it is most likely Israel's propensity to rely on physical birth and circumcision. For the majority of the nation these were the only proper credentials for being the true people of God and favored by Him. They refused to acknowledge anything less, and by their religion and traditions certainly did not recognize Gentiles as having any status above that of dogs (Matt. 15:24-26). By birth they were Abraham's children. Their circumcision in the flesh was their proof of this. But God thought otherwise, as attested by His Spirit in the Scriptures (Rom. 9:6-16, 4:9-14, 2:28-29). Although knowing full well they were descendants of Abraham after the flesh, Jesus approached the majority of the Jews as a synagogue of Satan (John 8:33-59).

The Present State of the Kingdom of Heaven

"Because you have kept My command to persevere..." (Rev. 3:10) A different translation that gives a better sense of what He is saying is *"Because you have kept the Word of My patience..."* Christ's patience is that He sits at the right hand of God waiting until His enemies are made His footstool (Heb. 10:12-13, Rev. 1:9). At this time He is hidden in God and not manifested to the world (Col. 3:1-3). This is an important understanding when considering the present state of things on the earth and in the kingdom of heaven.

This kingdom presently has the king away in heaven. He sits on His Father's throne and not on any throne of His own (Rev. 3:21). He is hidden in God away from the world. The kingdom of heaven cannot be described as a king physically present on earth reigning in manifested power and glory, and sitting down properly on His own throne of power. As a consequence of the King being away (yet in greater measure to the failure of men in responsibility) the kingdom of heaven exists as a spoiled crop of wheat and tares in the field of the world. There is a big difference in Scripture between what happens while He is away and what happens when He is physically present. At this present time on the earth it will not be the winning of the world, the filling of the earth with the glory of the Lord through the preaching of the gospel, and the church creating a utopian state into which we invite the Lord back, presenting the kingdom to Him. This is the height of Arminian arrogance as to what good men are actually capable of accomplishing by their responsibility while still in these bodies of flesh. And here I am specifically referring to what the spoiled crop in the world is able to accomplish at this present time.

The absence of the Lord allows for certain effects. The goings-on in the kingdom have their basis upon His servants being given responsibility. From the beginning the servants failed and they slept (Matt. 13:25, 25:5). A great contributing factor as to why there is failure in Christendom and among His servants is the simple understanding that we are still in these bodies of flesh. We are the new creation of God in soul and spirit as believers, but the body of sin is still with us. We have not received yet the end of our salvation: the redemption of our bodies (Rom. 8:11, 23). There is a difference between our capabilities in responsibility now and after we are conformed into the image of His Son (Rom. 8:29). When we are glorified we will fulfill our responsibilities in the perfection of righteousness and true holiness. After the rapture of the true church there will be no failure in the individual believer or the true church. We will be perfectly like Christ. At this present time there is no perfection on this earth. No one has already attained (Phil. 3:12), although all believers are to reckon the old man as dead (Rom. 6:6-11). So then, there is failure in the flesh as concerning responsibility, and especially so in the corporate church.[125]

Another factor contributing to failure in the kingdom of heaven while the king is not present is the spoiled crop has its existence in the field. The devil is the god of this world. He showed he is active by coming in early on in the kingdom and planting tares (Matt. 13:25). The Son of Man's servants could have stopped this but they were sleeping. If Satan is active it would be in the world in which he is god over. The Son of Man is away in heaven, but His planting of the wheat was in the world where the devil is the god. Satan already rules over the sons of disobedience and unbelief, so his efforts will be against that which belongs to Christ. He cannot touch the wheat but he can bring about the spoiling of the crop in the field. He has accomplished this beyond any doubt.

The kingdom of heaven is a mixture of good and bad by the work of Satan. This does not tell the whole of the story. Evil grows, matures, and ripens wherever it is found. Right now it is found in the kingdom of heaven – in Christendom. It does not remain stagnant or dormant. Evil prospers in this world and during this present age, because Satan is the god of this present age and world. The full display of it may be restricted by the presence of the Holy Spirit in the true church (II Thess. 2:6-7), but it is growing and ripening to the end. And again, it is doing this within the professing church.

A third factor contributing to the failure found in the kingdom of heaven is an obvious one – there are tares present in Christendom. The tares are the sons of the wicked one (Matt. 13:38). They are present in the ministry, in the schools and seminaries, in the pulpits on Sunday. They are among the counselors and administrators in the organized church body, holding positions of importance and power. In times past they have argued in the great theological debates and held prominent seats on councils determining church doctrine. The effect of their influence in the kingdom over time and in the history of the professing church is seriously underestimated.

All this does not excuse the church's failure in responsibility. The professing church is guilty of its own lack of unity and oneness as a family and a body. It has failed in being the light of God left on the earth to shine to the darkness and wickedness of this world. The church has failed in its testimony to the glory of Jesus Christ, the Son of Man – the Head of the assembly to which the body is united by the power of the Spirit (Eph. 1:22-23, I Cor. 12:12-13). Simply put, the church has failed in its responsibility. The failure is non-recoverable, and the corporate body is without excuse.

Keeping the Word of His Patience

The three factors discussed above have no possibility of changing before the removal of the wheat from the world (Matt. 13:30). There is no possibility of improvement in the current situation and state of the kingdom of heaven. And so Jesus Christ waits until… This is the Word of His patience as it is revealed in the Scriptures. He waits for a kingdom and an inheritance, until His enemies be made His footstool. If we are to keep the Word of His patience as in Philadelphia, we will wait as He does. We do this by His Word, His promises, and the precious hope that He gives us. Through the Word and by the Spirit He guides us into the same mindset and thoughts that He has waiting, separated from the world and as united to Him. We will have the same inheritance He will have. We have the same hopes, joys, and expectations. His thoughts should be ours. We have the mind of Christ. It is our conformity to the position of Christ. If He is waiting, we are waiting with Him.[126]

We are also waiting for Him. As the Bridegroom has love and affection for the bride, she will, in earnest expectation, be looking for the Bridegroom (Heb. 9:28). The remnant is looking to heaven, eagerly waiting for the Savior from there, who will transform their lowly bodies that it may be conformed to His glorious body (Phil. 3:20-21). And so He says, *"Behold, I come quickly! Hold fast what you have…"* Having kept the Word of His patience, He, in turn, keeps them free and clear from the coming tribulation on the earth. He is not promising to preserve them through the hour of trial, as we see is promised in prophecy for a Jewish remnant. Philadelphia is His body and bride, and will not suffer such indignity (Eph. 5:25-30). They are not dwellers of the earth that need to be tested and tried or delivered through judgments (Rev. 3:10). They are not of the world and will not be judged with and as the world. He will give to them the crown of life.[127]

What should be noted with Philadelphia is that there is no instruction for maintaining the corporate position of testimony in the world. This thought is no longer addressed by Christ. Philadelphia is not viewed by the Lord as the corporate professing church. They are a small remnant in the midst of the gross corruption and unbelief of the mass of Christendom. Jesus tells them directly what their witness is to be before the world. Their testimony as the remnant church is that they have kept the Word of His patience (Rev. 3:10) and they are looking for His soon return.

The Heavenly Hope of the Remnant

When Jesus was raised from the dead He told Mary to tell His brethren (John 20:17),

"I am ascending to My Father and your Father, and to My God and your God."

When He says He is ascending to His Father, it is in relation to Jesus being the Son of God. When He says He is ascending to His God, He is speaking solely as the Son of Man and the relationship between man and God now being reconciled. This is the essence behind what He is saying in John 13:31-32 where this pairing is again found. When He speaks to Philadelphia concerning their hopes, He is speaking to them as the glorified Son of Man. He relates to them as having redeemed them and as having brought them to this position in which they enjoy the same relationship that He has with God as the glorified Man. Every hope He gives includes the phrase 'My God'.[128]

"...a pillar in the temple of My God..." (Rev. 3:12): When the remnant on earth had little strength, they had to be faithful and persevere (Rev. 3:8). In contrast to this, in glory they are each pillars of strength in the house of God. This is eternal, for he shall go out no more.

"And I will write on him the name of My God and the name of the city of My God, the New Jerusalem, which comes down out of heaven from My God." The name of His God written on us is the stamp of our heavenly citizenship. The city is our own proper dwelling place. The true believer is one who dwells in heaven while he presently walks as a pilgrim and stranger on earth.

"And I will write on him My new name." The Son of Man will be given a new name from His God for the millennium, and Jesus will write this name on every one that is His, as belonging to Him.

God the Father has associated everyone in Philadelphia with the object of His infinite and eternal delight – Jesus Christ. By being accepted in the Beloved, God will show us the exceeding riches of His grace throughout the ages to come without end (Eph. 1:6, 2:7).

Philadelphia is characterized by faithfulness in their individual walk which gave them inward strength. This is in contrast to having little in the way of an outward display of power. They were faithful to the Lord in the midst of generalized corruption and spiritual deadness in the outward body of Christendom. All dealings with the professing church as maintaining a position of testimony in the world is completely set aside. Philadelphia's testimony was that of keeping the word of His patience, and the expectation that Christ would come quickly. Philadelphia has little outward strength, but a greater nearness to Christ who has all the power and authority. They had greater affection for the Lord, greater intimacy of fellowship with Him, and the hope of the promises given to them has a greater identification with Him. The story of Philadelphia is the looking for the blessed hope of the church – the majority of His words to them point to His return for them and what they will have with Him in glory. *"I have set before you an open door...Behold, I come quickly!"*

Chapter 11: Footnotes

[119] Nebuchadnezzar's experience is a remarkable foreshadowing of the prophetic progression of the times of the Gentiles. His arrogance and failure to answer to God, when God had set him up in world power and dominion, leads to his judgment (Dan. 4:20-25). His behavior is typical of the general character of all four beasts during all the times of the Gentiles. Of greater importance for our spiritual understanding is not simply that four beasts will exist in progression as Gentile world powers, but that the character and nature of any beast depicted prophetically is that it has apostate behavior and does not acknowledge the Most High God.

Nebuchadnezzar is made to act as a beast for seven years. The number seven, in this case, definitely refers to the prophetic thought of 'wholeness' or 'complete'. His acting like an animal for 'seven years' is typical of the complete time span of the Gentile powers from the Babylonian empire all the way to the revived Roman empire seen in the future tribulation. At the end of seven years Nebuchadnezzar acknowledged the Most High God. At the end of the 'times of the Gentiles' the Most High God will be acknowledged as possessor of the heavens and earth (Gen. 14:18-20, Dan. 4:25-26).

The name of God as 'the Most High' is His millennial name and directly points to this time in which all Gentile rule will be destroyed. He will be the sole possessor of the heavens and the earth. At this present time Satan is still in the heavens and he exercises a two-fold influence there. From the heavens he rules the world as the god of the world, controlling the course of this world and the sons of disobedience (Eph. 2:2-3). Also in the heavens he is the anti-priest against the church and accuser of the brethren (Rev. 12:10). Although he cannot touch the wheat, his work has been the corruption of the crop in the field of the world. This he has accomplished beyond any doubt, and beyond any thought of its recovery. When the wheat is removed from the field to the heavens, there will soon come a time when Satan and his angels are removed from the heavens and cast down to the earth (Rev. 12:7-9). This is when the Most High is again fully the possessor of the heavens, and the true church positioned there, seated in heavenly places, is ready for their part in the government of the Most High over the millennial earth (Eph. 2:6). But as yet the Gentiles have not learned that the heavens do reign (Dan. 4:26).

Satan being cast down to the earth marks the remaining 3 ½ years of Gentile power and civil rule. All his efforts at this time are his struggle to remain god of the earth and in control of the earth. *"Woe to the inhabitants of the earth and the sea! For the devil has come down to you, having great wrath, because he knows that he has a short time."* (Rev. 12:12) It is the time for divine sovereign judgments to prepare the way for the Most High to take back possession of the earth. When the stone, made without hands, destroys the Gentile statue, the two beasts are cast into the lake of fire, their armies destroyed, and Satan is bound in chains in the bottomless pit for 1000 years (Dan. 2:34-35, Rev. 19:11-20:3). This is when the Most High takes back possession of the earth, and that is why the name 'Most High' points to the millennium.

This is also why the entire passage in Genesis 14:18-20 is a type that points to the millennium. Abram represents the Jewish remnant in the end physically blessed by the Most High through His Melchizedek priest, after the defeat of all their enemies. This Melchizedek priest is also a King, who will bring in peace through righteous judgments during the millennium (Heb. 7:1-3). This priest will be the means by which the Most High will physically bless Israel, restoring the Jewish remnant in the land. The dividing of the millennial earth is associated with a restored Israel in the land and the name of the Most High in Deuteronomy 32:8-9. So then, the lesson taught to Nebuchadnezzar is that the Most High rules in the kingdom of men (Dan. 4:25). His experience is an allegory depicting the lesson that the Gentiles will learn when the world comes to the end of the period of time known as 'the times of the Gentiles.' (Luke 21:24)

This allegory of Nebuchadnezzar's experience holds a double meaning. After the seven years the lion stood up like a man and was given the heart of a man (Dan. 7:4). This was true concerning the Babylonian kingdom when it existed (Dan. 4:28-37). The lion stopped acting like a beast. But the seven years also represents the entire time of the four beasts – the entire times of the Gentiles until they are fulfilled. The Most High God will then possess both the heavens and the earth during the millennium.

[120] The fig tree is symbolic of Israel. They were serving as the test case representing all mankind in Adam. God did not test all mankind under responsibility, just Israel. This was enough because there was no other nation or people as privileged by God. They were chosen and they were special (Deut. 7:6). God tested Israel in responsibility, looking for the fruit of obedience. This testing continued for a long time, from Mt. Sinai and the giving of the law, to the sending of Messiah to them so many years

later. When Messiah was rejected, God was finished with testing the state of man in Adam. God never found fruit on the fig tree (Israel). That is why when Jesus came to the fig tree that morning He found no fruit. In all that time from Mt. Sinai to Christ Israel could not obey. There was no fruit produced.

Jesus curses the fig tree. What does that mean? Man in Adam, man in the flesh, man in this particular state and position, was proven by God to be utterly depraved. The tree being cursed is man in Adam being judged and condemned. *"Let no fruit grow on you ever again"* shows that man in Adam, left to his own resources, could never, and more importantly to understand, will never produce fruit unto God. God proved this and the testing was now complete. Man in Adam had to be condemned. Man in the flesh was condemned to death at that time. This was the outcome of the testing of Israel. Again, Israel was the test case representing all mankind in Adam.

What do I mean by saying man in Adam is judged, and the judgment is condemnation? And the condemnation is death? *"And as it is appointed for men to die once, but after this the judgment..."* (Heb. 9:27) For all unbelievers this is what lies ahead of them – this is their destiny, this is their end. This judgment was settled at the time of the cursing of the fig tree. Man in Adam, man in the flesh, and all of Israel is condemned to death. Why Israel too? Because that is what the entire nation of Israel was – sinners in Adam. So we have the entire world condemned at that time (John 12:31, Rom. 3:19). We also have Satan defeated and judged by the cross at that time (John 12:31, Heb. 2:14), although the world does not see or realize his defeat as yet. We have Israel set aside and the kingdom of God taken away from them at that time (Matt. 21:43). The time of the cursing of the fig tree is also seen in Scripture as the end of the world (Heb. 9:26). Jesus suffered as a sacrifice for sin at one point in time – once at the end of the world. It was the end of the world because sin and guilt were complete as to human responsibility. The testing by God was complete. Man in Adam, man in the flesh, is condemned to death. These same thoughts concerning the end of the world are applicable to another passage found in Galatians 4:1-4, only here it is referred to as 'when the fullness of time had come'.

Allow me to show you one more insight related to the judgment of man in Adam. The fruit of man's failure in responsibility is death. This is the judgment of man in the flesh. However, for certain ones this judgment already has been met and death has been abolished for them (II Tim.

1:9-10). These certain ones are believers, those in Jesus Christ, the second Adam. Death has been abolished as judgment and condemnation for them, and life and immortality has been brought to light through the gospel of Jesus Christ. This will be *fully realized* in the rapture of the church – life and immortality – when the body of Christ is glorified and removed from the earth. This is not true for man remaining on the earth and living on the earth during the millennium. Man on the earth at this time is still man in the first Adam. Death as a judgment still remains on the earth until the end of the millennium (I Cor. 15:24-26).

These are biblical principles that clearly show you these differences and through which you may understand all of Scripture. Being in Christ, in the second Adam, is the difference between what is removed from the earth into the heavens, and what remains on the earth if it survives the tribulation. The body of Christ is what was purposed by God to be 'in Christ' before time began (II Tim. 1:9-10, Titus 1:2, Eph. 1:3-6, Rom. 8:29-30). The entire body of Christ will be removed from the earth, even the bodies of the dead in Christ (I Thess. 4:13-18). What remains on the earth for the Son of Man to rule over in His kingdom is man in the flesh, man in Adam. Even the Jewish remnant, restored in the Promised Land, is not 'in Christ' and not in the second Adam. They are ruled over by the second Adam, but they are never in the second Adam. That is why on the earth death remains as a judgment until the end of the millennium. Jesus Christ, the Son of Man, rules on the earth for 1000 years. This will be how long it takes to put all enemies under His feet (I Cor. 15:25), because on the earth is man in Adam, still possessing a sin nature from Adam. He will reign on the earth as the glorified Man, and will systematically put an end to all human dominion and government in the world. But this is not the position of the church.

[121] The open door set before Philadelphia is not the evangelistic opportunity to the church of winning the world or increased missionary work. It isn't an evangelistic opportunity at all. In the seven messages to the churches, Christ discusses and judges all the responsibility of the professing church. Not once in all the messages is the taking or preaching of the gospel into the world ever mentioned. Jesus never discusses with any church whether they are doing a great job in this area or chastens any church for failure. Don't you think that is odd? Why isn't this mentioned one way or the other when responsibility is discussed?

The reason for this is that the taking of the gospel into the world is not the responsibility of the church. It was the responsibility of apostles and evangelists, and now, without apostles today, just evangelists. The great commission is rightly labeled an apostolic commission, because that is who He was speaking to directly in sending them out into ministry (John 17:18). When the Father and the Son speak to the church it is by the Holy Spirit through the epistles. Never once in all the epistles is the great commission repeated, as responsibility given to the church. The Thessalonians and Corinthians are never told to pack up and move to Africa or Spain, as if this was in fact their responsibility. Therefore it is not discussed in Revelation 2 and 3, when all the responsibility of the professing church is discussed. Apostles are in fact told to go, as I would assume to be true of evangelists like Phillip.

Titus 1:2-3

"...in hope of eternal life which God, who cannot lie, promised before time began, but has in due time manifested His word through preaching, which was committed to me according to the commandment of God our Savior."

We can see in the above passage that the promise of eternal life from God is to all believers. However, the commission of preaching of the gospel into the world was committed to Paul (I would assume committed to all apostles and evangelists as well). There is no commandment given to the church (the body in general) to preach the gospel into the world.

Titus 2:11-14

"For the grace of God that brings salvation has appeared to all men, (12) teaching us that, denying ungodliness and worldly lusts, we should live soberly, righteously, and godly in the present age, (13) looking for the blessed hope and glorious appearing of our great God and Savior Jesus Christ, (14) who gave Himself for us, that He might redeem us from every lawless deed and purify for Himself His own special people, zealous for good works."

When Paul discusses in the same letter the responsibility of the believer/church upon receiving the grace of God in salvation, the preaching of the gospel and the making of disciples by the church is not included in their many responsibilities listed. He speaks of a godly walk and a constant looking for Christ to return. This is our responsibility. Also he discusses the believer/church should be zealous for good works, we are created in Christ for good works, and men should see our good works and glorify our Father in heaven by them. But the preaching of the gospel into all the world is not a commandment or mandate given to the church.

That does not mean that God never uses the individual Christian to share the gospel with unbelievers. The presentation of the gospel is the common way that God uses to draw to Christ those that He quickens (John 6:44). Whether it is apostles, evangelists, other ministers doing the work of an evangelist, or individual believers, the gospel is to be preached to the world. If God gives us an opportunity, it is because He wants to use us in His work. It doesn't mean we all, individually, have one of the five ministry gifts given when He ascended up on high. It doesn't mean the church has a calling to preach the gospel into the world.

If you look closely at the doctrine of the body of Christ presented by Paul in Ephesians 4:9-16, you should realize that the five gifts given have a threefold purpose:

1. For the equipping of the individual saints first
2. For the work of ministry (in a sense it refers to all ministry)
3. For the edifying of the body of Christ (the church)

Looking closely, we should also realize that the church is in the position of being taught and never in the position of teaching. The church is the learner that is being built up in stature and maturity, so it may withstand winds of doctrine and the trickery of false teachers – so she may be the pillar and ground of the truth (I Tim. 3:15). The purpose and intention for the body while on earth was to come into a unity of faith which can only involve the knowledge of the truth of God's word. It involves the knowledge of the Son of God, to a perfect man, to the measure of the stature of the fullness of Christ. The Holy Spirit was sent down into the world to gather the church. The church is not sent into the world to gather itself.

In the passage from Ephesians mentioned above (Eph. 4:9-16) we see what God's purpose and intention was for the assembly (church), consequent to the ascension of Christ on high and He receiving gifts to give her. *"...till we all come to the unity of the faith and the knowledge of the Son of God, to a perfect man, to the measure of the stature of the fullness of Christ."* I would ask any true believer to honestly evaluate how well the professing church has accomplished this responsibility? How does Christendom stack up in stature to the fullness of Christ? The assembly was given gifts so she could learn. By these gifts she was to be edified – growing up and maturing, and no longer a child. She was to possess the knowledge of the truth to keep her from being tossed to and fro and carried about by every wind of doctrine. How has the professing church fared in this respect? Throughout her history the assembly has constantly fell prey to the deceitful trickery of false teachers. Has she always spoken the truth in love and has she ever grown up in all things into Christ her head? The Scriptures themselves declare that she has miserably failed in all her responsibilities and that her failure continues and worsens to this day.

Now the leaven comes in and blinds her, telling her that in her history she has done a great job at fulfilling her responsibilities. What a grand deception the leaven of human effort and accomplishment perpetrates on the professing church. When the church world falls for this deception, then the leaven is free to create new responsibilities of human effort.

[122] For a more thorough discussion of the character and nature of Judaism I refer you back to the first book in the Son of Man series – 'The Son of Man Glorified'. That work contains extensive discussions on this particular subject, and Judaism contrasted with Christianity.

[123] This is the issue in the presentation of this entire book – what do the Scriptures say, what do they actually teach? What the Scriptures say is what God says. Will we be humble enough to submit to and place ourselves under what God has to say? Otherwise we go a different course, and most importantly, we go without God.

[124] This is another example of the failure of man in responsibility in a previous or present age that will be made good by the sovereignty of God in the age to come. This sovereign work towards the true sons of the Father's family will be God displaying them with Christ in His glory (John 17:22-23). Where the family failed in its responsibility to show unity in the present age, it will be made good when we appear to the world with Christ in glory (Col. 3:4). There will be no failure in responsibility at that time.

In Scripture we can make this distinction on the subject of unity in Christianity. The Father is Head over the Father's house. Individual believers are sons in that house, sons of the Father and sons of God. We are placed in this relationship with Christ after He accomplished the work of redemption. All the sons together make up the Father's family, the Father's house, the Father's heavenly city, as well as the Father's kingdom (John 14:1-3, Rev. 3:12, Matt. 13:43). We have this relationship with the

Father as sons of the Father and born of God (John 1:12-13, Gal. 3:26-28). We stand in this relationship along with Christ as His brethren, seeing He is the first born among many brethren (Rom. 8:29). We are co-heirs with Him of God and the Father (Rom. 8:17, Gal. 4:6-7). The unity of this family is spoken of in John 13-17, but specifically in John 17:20-23. John only speaks of individual believers and individual faith, and eternal life though this. The unity John speaks of is the unity of sons together in the Father's family and house (John 8:34-36).

The other unity spoken of in Scripture is that of the members of the body of Christ with each other. We are members one of another and the unity of the one body (I Cor. 12:12-27). The body is in union with Christ, its glorified Head in heaven, and this union was formed by the Holy Spirit. The church is the assembly, and is His body in union with Him. She is His bride or at least His betrothed bride waiting for the glory and the marriage presentation (Eph. 5:25-32, Rev. 19:7-9). Yet these relationships are more so with Jesus Christ Himself. It is Paul alone who speaks of the church as the body of Christ, and her responsibility for her unity on the earth (Eph. 4:1-4).

There is an importance placed in the message to Philadelphia as to the understanding of the sovereignty of God and of Christ, and the difference between the work of God and that of man. The character of Christ presented in this church is *"...He who opens and no one shuts, and shuts and no one opens."* His sovereignty is the key of David He possesses. The proper understanding of the sovereignty of God opposes all Judaizing and Arminian doctrine. It is the work of God alone and therefore only glorifies God. This understanding seems to be characteristic of Philadelphia, while the opposite will be found in Laodicea, the general body of Christendom.

[125] It is a much harder task to have the corporate entity of Christendom repent and return to its first position. At this time God views it as an impossibility that just will not happen. This is what is taught in His word, which is His judgment of the professing church. Individual responsibility is different from this. <u>The question will always be this</u>: Does God hold all of Christendom together, by its profession of Jesus Christ, responsible as a corporate body? Has He judged the corporate body as failed and in ruin? Can you see these important truths as taught by the Spirit in His word?

[126] Every blessing and hope for the believer is only experienced in Christ and with Christ, and is never apart from Him. We are His body, bone of His bone, flesh of His flesh. If He has not taken up His power to reign as King of kings and Lord of lords yet, then we do not reign as kings in this

present life in any respect. He has walked on this earth in the flesh, and in so doing, His walk is an example for us to walk in on this earth at this time – *"He who says he abides in Him ought himself also to walk just as He walked."* (I John 2:6) So also then, we ought to wait as He waits – this is the Word of His patience (Rev. 3:10).

[127] There is such a profound difference in the Scriptural character of Christ's relationship to the true church represented by the remnant body of Philadelphia, and that of the remnant of Israel in the end. *'Behold, I come quickly! Hold fast what you have, that no one may take your crown.'* This puts forth the true character and position of the rapture. It is personal and it is privilege. He is coming for her, His bride. She is looking for and expecting Him and her hope is to see Him soon. So at the end of the prophecy in chapter 22, He says, *"I, Jesus…am…the Bright and Morning Star."* This awakens the heartfelt cry of the Spirit and bride together saying, *"Come!"* Then He assures us with His reply, *"Surely I am coming quickly."* The church responds again, *"Even so, come, Lord Jesus!"* The taking of the church is such a personal thing between the Bridegroom and the bride. It is between Jesus Himself and the church.

This is not the case with His relationship with the end time Jewish remnant. They must be delivered through judgments in order for them to have their proper place in the earth. They are the earthly calling. The Lord's physical return to the earth will be associated with warring and righteous judgments, and the gathering out of His kingdom all things that offend (Matt. 13:41). In the end before Israel can have their blessing of being restored in the land and prospering, they will have to be delivered by the execution of judgments. This is the reason for the many examples of the crying out for vengeance found throughout the Psalms. It is the Jewish remnant crying out:

Psalm 94:1-3

"O Lord God, to whom vengeance belongs—
O God, to whom vengeance belongs, shine forth!
Rise up, O Judge of the earth;
Render punishment to the proud.
Lord, how long will the wicked,
How long will the wicked triumph?"

The believer and the true church do not need vengeance to be with Christ in glory. God has given us grace as our part. It is in this we live and walk. We are not crying out for the Lord to come and avenge us of our enemies. We expect to be gathered together unto Him and to be caught up together to meet Him in the air. The cry for vengeance as is seen throughout the Psalms and other portions of Scripture is associated with the physical return of Christ to this world. It is always the language of the Israeli remnant, and not that of the church. In the example of the widow and the unjust judge (Luke 18:1-8) she is crying out, *"Avenge me of my adversary."* The resulting interpretation is, *"And shall God not avenge His own elect who cry out day and night to Him, though He bears long with them?"* The widow is symbolic and characteristic of the end time Jewish remnant and the use of the word 'elect' identifies them as such. God bearing long with them is God bearing long with the crying out of this remnant. It is sad when this parable is misapplied to the church in attempts to teach us how to pray.

"That your foot may crush them in blood, and the tongues of your dogs may have their portion from your enemies." (Psalm 68:23) These are not the church's thoughts. This is not our blessed hope (Tit. 2:13). If I have partaken of the grace of the Lamb, then I will not be associated with what is considered as the wrath of the Lamb (Rev. 6:12-17). The church is associated with sovereign grace. The Israeli remnant is associated with righteous judgments. When the church is seen at the end of Revelation, it is the New Jerusalem whose trees have leaves for the healing of the nations.

Associated with the restored remnant of Israel on the earth is the government of God, which has its basis in the Jewish law and the outcomes according to judgments in righteousness – *"For the nation and kingdom which will not serve you (Israel) shall perish. And those nations shall be utterly ruined."* (Is. 60:12) The earth is destined to be delivered through judgments, but the church's portion is to be with Christ caught up in the air.

At the end of the passage referenced in Luke (Luke 18:1-8) Jesus makes this statement, *"Nevertheless, when the Son of Man comes, will He really find faith on the earth?"* Why such a question? The Jewish remnant will be like Thomas. They will believe only after seeing with their eyes – looking on Him whom they had pierced. If real bible faith is the evidence of things not seen, you can understand the Lord's question.

[128] You may notice that only the first part of the terms are used. To Mary He said *"... to My Father and your Father, and to my God and your God."* (John 20:17) However, in the book of Revelation the relationship of God

and Jesus Christ with the church is hidden. It is not the proper subject of prophecy, but rather the mystery of God. Therefore only half of the term is used – *'My God'*. In the book, when the term Father is used of God it is only in direct relation to Jesus Christ, usually as the Lamb slain (Rev. 14:1). When the name Father is used in close proximity to the church, as in the opening salutation of the book, it is still honoring the character of prophecy and the mystery by only using the term *"...His God and Father..."* (Rev. 1:6)

The terms, 'the body of Christ' and the 'church' are never used in the entire book. This shows you what the mystery of God is that was hidden from the prophets and prophecy. Jesus Christ, the Son of God, having the titles of Messiah or the Son of Man, was never hidden from prophecy. Neither was His suffering or death hidden, for He often said, *"The Son of Man indeed goes just as it is written of Him..."* (Matt. 26:24, Mark 14:21, Luke 22:22) So then in the book of Revelation the church is only referred to in allegorical forms – the twenty four elders or the bride of the Lamb. The rapture of the church is hidden in certain passages like Revelation 12:5 and 4:1.

It is also true that John was not the one who was given the dispensation or stewardship of the mystery. This was given to Paul (Eph. 3:9-10). So then John, Peter, and the others never use the terms, 'the body of Christ' or 'the church' in their writings or teachings (save Jesus being quoted in Matthew's gospel). Peter does make an allusion to the church in I Peter 2. Only Paul teaches the doctrine of the church. But I believe the main reason the church is treated as such in the book of Revelation is because the subjects of biblical prophecy do not include the church. The great subjects of prophecy are Israel, the earth, and the government of God over the earth. It is by knowing general biblical principles that we will understand the detail of Scripture, not the other way around.

Chapter 12:

Laodicea: Christendom's Candlestick Removed

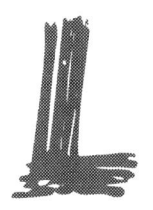

Laodicea represents the corporate Christian state at the end. After all the longsuffering and patience of God shown to Christendom, and the failure of the outer body of the professing church in its responsibility, Laodicea is spewed out and the candlestick is removed. Jesus is the Amen, the Faithful and True Witness, for there isn't a corporate witness for God on the earth in the church world (Rev. 3:14). The faithful remnant that is Philadelphia goes up through the open door that is set before them, while Laodicea becomes a dead carcass progressing toward the hour of trial which will come upon the whole world (Rev. 3:8, 10). But before these things take place Christ is seen standing outside Laodicea. He knocks to see if there remains any inside who have ears to hear (Rev. 3:20).

Revelation 3:14-22

(14) "And to the angel of the church of the Laodiceans write,

'These things says the Amen, the Faithful and True Witness, the Beginning of the creation of God: (15) "I know your works, that you are neither cold nor hot. I could wish you were cold or

hot. (16) So then, because you are lukewarm, and neither cold nor hot, I will vomit you out of My mouth. (17) Because you say, 'I am rich, have become wealthy, and have need of nothing'— and do not know that you are wretched, miserable, poor, blind, and naked— (18) I counsel you to buy from Me gold refined in the fire, that you may be rich; and white garments, that you may be clothed, that the shame of your nakedness may not be revealed; and anoint your eyes with eye salve, that you may see. (19) As many as I love, I rebuke and chasten. Therefore be zealous and repent. (20) Behold, I stand at the door and knock. If anyone hears My voice and opens the door, I will come in to him and dine with him, and he with Me. (21) To him who overcomes I will grant to sit with Me on My throne, as I also overcame and sat down with My Father on His throne.

(22) "He who has an ear, let him hear what the Spirit says to the churches."

The Character of Christ

As a gentle reminder the character of Christ presented to the final three churches is not ecclesiastical. The general body is corrupt or spiritually dead and ready to be spewed out. God is no longer recognizing proper church character in these final states, although He continues to warn and rebuke the general body. They are still addressed as the professing church body, or why would God bother with the threats? Though the outer body still subsists in a form, it is utterly rejected by God and declared to be so.

Jesus Christ standing before Laodicea is *The Faithful and True Witness* which the outward corporate body of Christendom had not been responsible in. The professing church failed as a light and testimony to the world. Laodicea is vomited out. The candlestick of light and testimony is removed. For the corporate body there is no hope for a different outcome. Christ takes back any title of witness for God. He is about to judge the professing church. The spewing out is not judgment being accomplished, as in the tares being burned in the field (Matt. 13:40-42). Rather this is rejection of its church standing. The judgment of the professing church is certain and assumed as set.

The Son of Man was the Faithful Witness of God when He walked upon the earth. He spoke those things He had heard above, He testified of what He knew and had seen (John 3:10-13). At the cost of great suffering, rejection, and isolation He bore witness to what God was, and perfectly revealed the Father in truth and grace.

John 1:17-18

"For the law was given through Moses, but grace and truth came through Jesus Christ. No one has seen God at any time. The only begotten Son, who is in the bosom of the Father, He has declared Him."

He was the perfect witness of God come into the world in which He was sent. He was the light of the world – *"As long as I am in the world, I am the light of the world."* (John 9:5, 8:12, 3:19, 1:9, 12:46) And yet the light of God was met with hatred, opposition, and darkness (John 15:22-25). This was His testimony:

1 John 1:5

"This is the message which we have heard from Him and declare to you, that God is light and in Him is no darkness at all."

Jesus was the manifestation of what He declared all the time He was in the world – the True and Faithful Witness of God, the light of God come into the world. So when men asked Him, *"Who are You?"* He could reply:

John 8:28-29

"When you lift up the Son of Man, then you will know that I am He, and that I do nothing of Myself; but as My Father taught Me, I speak these things. And He who sent Me is with Me. The Father has not left Me alone, for I always do those things that please Him."

But men could not comprehend the light and they preferred the darkness. The church was to be the light in the world, a city shining forth on a hill. But professing Christianity failed and Jesus replaces the church now as to any further thought in this testimony. The intention presented here to Christendom in this last message is that Christ alone, apart from the professing body, is the Faithful and True Witness for God.

Christ is the Great Amen – the only One in whom all God's blessings and promises reside (II Cor. 1:20). The church should have reflected this to the world. *"If you will not believe, surely you shall not be established."* (Is. 7:9) If the professing church will not confirm Christ, she will not be confirmed. Christ will seal up all the promises and prophecies. He is the stamp of Amen to the plan and purposes of God. The professing church had responsibilities and failed. The sovereign grace and power in Jesus Christ will never fail. The time draws near for Christ to take up His power and reign.

Jesus Christ *is the Beginning of the creation of God* – the firstborn over all creation. He is not this as God, but as the raised and glorified Man. God will set up creation according to His own purpose. Jesus Christ, the second Adam, will have the preeminence in it. He will be Head over all things when all things are new, which is soon to be manifested.

Colossians 1:15-17

(15) "He is the image of the invisible God, the firstborn over all creation. (16) For by Him all things were created that are in heaven and that are on earth, visible and invisible, whether thrones or dominions or principalities or powers. All things were created through Him and for Him. (17) And He is before all things, and in Him all things consist."

Colossians 1:19-20

(19) "For it pleased the Father that in Him all the fullness should dwell, (20) and by Him to reconcile all things to Himself,

by Him, whether things on earth or things in heaven, having made peace through the blood of His cross."

Through the blood of the cross He will reconcile all things back unto God, and accordingly all things created become His to inherit. He will not take one bit of His inheritance until His body is raised to be with Him. Except for His personal glory, He cannot take any other glory until the true church is with Him. We are the joint-heirs with Christ. All the heirs of God must be present (Rom. 8:17, Gal. 4:7) before He does, in fact, take up His power and reign in the counsels of God. His title here to Laodicea takes up the witness of God in the new creation, instead of the general church body, which is rejected.

Laodicea is lukewarm and will be spewed out of Christ's mouth. This is the general body of Christendom being addressed. What is spoken is not applied to individuals. The professing church had failed and the candlestick is removed. Christendom contains masses of people that have no true faith. Many simply bear the name of Christ without actually having the life of Christ (Gal. 2:20, II Cor. 4:10-11). Corruption began early on in the church. The mystery of lawlessness was present and growing (II Thess. 2:7). They had left their first love. The world soon entered within the assembly and the Scriptures speak, *"I looked in the place of righteousness, and behold, iniquity was there."* (Eccl. 3:16) This is Christendom's end. It had come to a spiritual state that was opposite to that which God had purposed. The corruption of what was intended for good and light is the worst of corruptions.

The professing church says *they are rich, wealthy, and have need of nothing.* (Rev. 3:17) It always has these great Arminian thoughts about itself and has become quite self-sufficient. If they have need of nothing, they don't even need the Lord or the presence of the Spirit. I have always been amazed that Laodicea thinks of itself diametrically opposite of what the Lord thinks of her. There is nothing more opposed to God than what this last state of Christendom is said to be.

1. No doubt Christendom is rich with earthly wealth. *"I am rich and have become wealthy..."* There is also no doubt that the

professing church in the end has a great profession that it is blessed and filled with the riches of God. There is great pretention concerning possessing spiritual riches. But Christ says they are wretched, miserable, and poor. Jesus says to them in order to be rich they need to buy gold from Him. This gold represents God's divine righteousness in and through Jesus Christ (II Cor. 5:21). This is the only wealth of value, for it is the foundation and standing of the saints.

2. *"...and have need of nothing."* In this state the professing church has made herself the source of blessing and grace. They have no dependence on the Lord. It is in essence a turning from the Lord and being full of self. Jesus finds them to be naked. They are instructed to buy from Him the white garments of the righteousness of the saints (Rev 3:4-5). *"And to her it was granted to be arrayed in fine linen, clean and bright, for the fine linen is the righteous acts of the saints."* (Rev. 19:8) These are the works of the saints which are the fruits of believing and receiving divine righteousness (Eph. 2:10).

3. The professing church is found to be spiritually blind and without any useful spiritual discernment. They were blind to the things of God, yet they were saying 'we see.' *They were to anoint their eyes with eye salve that they may see.* This is true spiritual wisdom and discernment in Christ and His word.

This is exactly what the church world lacks today. We cannot see the evil and corruption. We refuse to see it and will not admit it. We build with wood, hay, and stubble, but swear it is gold, silver, and precious stones. We divide up the body of Christ and create our own little kingdoms, and protect them at all cost. We step back and survey the Christian landscape and say, "This is all there is, it must be the sovereign will of God." It doesn't take much investigation of Scripture to show that it most certainly isn't. But we are spiritually blind to God's truth. *"For the time will come when they will not endure sound doctrine, but according to their own desires..."* We live in this time (II Tim. 4:3). It is the spiritual blindness of Laodicea. It is the spiritual blindness of the corporate body of Christendom today.

"Behold, I stand at the door and knock..." (Rev. 3:20) In the Lord's patient mercy He still acknowledges the possibility of any of the remnant existing within. As long as it is still possible for mercy to be shown in the Father's timing, He is still there. But His call goes out to individuals, for He says, *"...if anyone hears My voice and opens the door..."* The corporate state is beyond hope and is given up.

An important observation to be made with Laodicea is that there is no return of the Lord held out before them. The final exhortation of His return was with Philadelphia (Rev. 3:11). The final state of professing Christianity is morally hopeless and subject to judgment. Christ is truly standing apart and outside this final body. If there are any saints within, then the true testimony and words they may hear will come from outside that which they are involved in.

The promise to the overcomers is a simple one. It is the believer's part to reign with the Son of Man over the future millennial earth (Rev. 3:21). With Laodicea, the overcomers do not receive any intimate or personal promises from Christ. The hope given is that which the entire church will share in, in common. *"...I will grant to sit with Me on My throne, as I also overcame and sat down with My Father on His throne."*[129]

Laodicea is the professing church as a form of godliness, but no power or life or Spirit (II Tim. 3:1-5). They were lukewarm, and not hot or cold. They were not zealous for the Lord, but still maintaining an attachment to His name. They were this in-between state that had a certain need to be seen a certain way. They had an appearance and profession, but no true faith, passion, or zeal. This condition is nauseous to the Lord.

This is the time of the professing church saying, *"I am rich...and have need of nothing."* In truth everything is in need and they are completely blind to their actual condition. How dangerous is this spiritual blindness? Corruption and apostasy marked the history of Christendom.[130] As a dispensation on earth, the professing church would be cut off. It will be set aside as Israel was. Laodicea is the final state of the corporate body on earth. This is the present state of the corporate church. The Lord extinguishes its candlestick. It will be judged as the world.

Chapter 12: Endnotes

[129] This verse serves to clear up a lot of mistaken doctrine (Rev. 3:21). Jesus presently sits on His Father's throne. It is not His own throne that He sits on at this time. The character in which He sits is as the glorified Son of Man, who is the Head of His own body, the church. Also for the church He sits in the role of High Priest. These are His two roles and functions for those of faith in this current time of the kingdom of heaven in mystery, when the King is not present but away in heaven. Faith is the evidence of things not seen and therefore mystery. In relationship to the unbelieving world He was hated and rejected, and is the Lamb slain in the midst of the throne. He was the Male-child who is destined to rule the nations with a rod of iron, but now caught up to God and His throne (Rev. 12:5). As to the world, He is hidden there in God, and not manifested (Col. 3:1-4).

It is interesting how the two current roles of Jesus Christ for the church – Head of the body and High Priest – are completely hidden from the book of Revelation. It is because the church is the mystery of God hidden from prophecy, and the book is a book of prophecy. These two characters are noticeably missing in all the descriptions of Christ in the first chapter. Also missing from the book is the relationship of Father and the Comforter to the church.

It remains that Christ is currently sitting with His Father on His Father's throne (Rev. 3:21). It is not yet the Son of Man sitting on the throne of His glory or the Messianic throne of His father David (Matt. 25:31, 19:28). These thrones will be millennial and on the earth and in the earthly city of Jerusalem. This couldn't be any clearer from prophecy or this particular verse.

[130] Apostasy always assumes a previous position of profession (Heb. 6:4-9). The main body of apostasy is the professing church. It is the object of God's judgment and wrath. It is what should have been the light of God in the world when Christ ascended up on high. It should have been the epistle of Christ, known and read by all men (II Cor. 3:2-3). According to clear and proper Biblical principles, the professing church will incur the judgment and wrath of God. Judgment starts at the house of God (I Pet. 4:17). We see this principle borne out in God's dealings with Israel in their history. Now we see it in God's dealings with Christendom. The general body is corrupt and spiritually dead. It is now Laodicea. It is a nauseous and highly pretentious form of Christianity. It is full of itself instead of being full of Christ. Only a small remnant is identified by the Lord, separated and preserved in the grace of God. That is why chapters 2 and 3 of Revelation

precede chapter 4, where we see the preparations in heaven for the impending judgment of the earth and world. The professing church will be judged with the world and in the same manner as the world. With Thyatira it is said to the corporate body, *"Indeed I will cast her into a sickbed, and those who commit adultery with her into great tribulation...I will kill her children with death...and I will give to each one of you according to your works."* This is judgment as the world and with the world. With Sardis it is said, *"...I will come upon you as a thief..."* Again this is being judged as and with the world.

The final form of the general body of Christendom is spewed out of the Lord's mouth. It is a dead carcass that moves on into the tribulation period, still pretending to be approved by God. The spewing out of Laodicea sets the judgment of the professing church as certain in its future accomplishment. It isn't hard to see this final physical judgment in Scripture. Professing Christianity, minus Philadelphia, is the Babylonian harlot that is destroyed and burned by the ten Christian kingdoms, which in turn allows the fourth beast to come forth in character again, rising out of the bottomless pit (Rev. 17:16-17). The sobering realization is not the judgment of the Roman beast, its armies, the Antichrist, the last Caesar, and the binding of Satan. Instead it is that the judgment and wrath of God is precipitated by the professing church.

The apostasy in the end times with the Antichrist is the rejection of the foundations of the Christian faith. The character and spirit of all antichrists that have come from the church world is the rejection of the Father and the Son, and the denial that Jesus is the Christ (I John 2:18-23). It isn't hard to realize that the Antichrist in the end will arise from among the Jews. With the throwing off of the pseudo-Christianity of the whore, the character of the Antichrist, and the blasphemy of the Roman beast, it is not hard to see the world in the end as completely anti-Christian. This is the full apostasy of the world where it does not acknowledge God. What precedes it and leads to it is the rejection of all Christian doctrine. How soon did the spirit of Antichrist come in? John says they went out from among us (I John 2:19). The world will embrace the complete ripening of apostasy that is first found in the professing church.

Peter tells us the longsuffering of the Lord is for salvation. In His patience with the evil and corruption of the professing church, He is still gathering in individually. This doesn't mean that the judgment isn't set for Christendom. May the Lord graciously open our eyes to see the real character and nature of evil. Although His judgment is delayed at the present time, it is not changed. The only cure for the present condition is judgment.

Chapter 13:

The Babylonian Harlot: Christianity or Islam?

This portion of the book will look at a particular prophetic image that is found in the vision given to John in Revelation 17. Chapters 4 through 11:18 of the Revelation form a general account of the prophecy, with the portion from 6:1-11:18 giving a general progressing history of events that occur after the true church is removed from the earth. Chapters 17 and 18 are a separate vision and parenthetical section with parts that fit into the general history. I say this so the reader is not mistaken in thinking that each chapter of the book of Revelation simply follows one after the other in time. Along this line of thinking, chapters 12-14 is another parenthetical section and forms a separate but complete whole.

The harlot is an interesting prophetical symbol that attracts the attention of believers and prophecy buffs alike. In Christian circles it has recently been misrepresented as the religion of Islam. This is a misdirection of great importance. It becomes almost like the man attempting to remove a splinter from a friend's eye when there is a log in his own (Luke 6:41).

There are only two religions specifically considered and addressed by Scripture. There are only two religions that have any relationship with God – Judaism and Christianity. This chart gives a short review of what was taught in detail in the first book in this series, 'The Son of Man Glorified'.

Judaism	Christianity
The religion of man in Adam, man in the flesh	The religion of the second Adam, man in the Spirit.
The religion of the earth and the weak and beggarly principles of the world	The religion of the heavens and all that is not of this world.
A walk by sight and a religion that appeals to the physical senses of man in the flesh	A walk by faith – the substance of things hoped for, the evidence of the unseen
The testing of the principle of responsibility	The principle of sovereign grace
An administration of death and condemnation	An administration of life and justification
Self-righteousness, human righteousness	The righteousness of God
The religion of the earthly calling, the worship of Jehovah from a fixed physical location on the earth – the temple	The religion of the heavenly calling, the worship of the Father in spirit and truth.

God does not give man any other religion but these two. All other religions are man-made and are inspired by Satan, involving worship of false gods and idolatry (Rom. 1:21-23). God addresses idolatry coming into the world after the flood by calling and separating Abram from the world. His descendants are given the law at Mt. Sinai, after their external redemption and deliverance from Egypt (the world) and Pharaoh (the god of the world – Satan) in type. Judaism effectively separates Israel from the Gentiles, building up a wall of separation through the law. It was given by God and it separated Israel from all the false gods of the Gentile world. It gave them a certain worship and relationship with the one true God. However, by this separation God tested Israel as representing all mankind. By Judaism, God was testing the principle of human responsibility, looking for obedience in order to see if man in the flesh could have a relationship with Him.

Man in the flesh cannot please God (Rom. 8:8). Man in Adam cannot obey the law of God (Rom. 8:7). To say Israel was separated from the Gentiles as the people of God is one thing, but as a nation they remained in Adam and in the flesh and part of the world. God's presence always had to stay behind the veil. Man could never draw near. *God's purpose in Judaism was to prove mankind as utterly depraved and hopelessly lost.*[131] The law accomplished this with great results, for when the law entered in, sin abounded more and more (Rom. 5:20). But Judaism is a religion given by God. There should be no doubt that it was, and He had a certain divine purpose for doing so. In its Old Testament form, Judaism was nailed to the cross of Christ and abolished (Col. 2:14, Eph. 2:15). The destruction of Jerusalem and the temple in 70 AD brought a physical end to its practice.

Islam is not given by God. It is a man-made religion. God doesn't address it or deal with it. For that matter, He doesn't specifically deal with any other man-made religion in Scripture. It is all idolatry, apostasy, and worship of demons to Him. But some are trying to convince Christians that the Babylonian harlot found in John's vision is the religion of Islam and its spreading influence in the world. Some are trying to convince us that God takes notice of Islam in His word. If this is true, then Revelation 17 would be the first place in all the books of the Bible where God addresses the importance of a particular man-made religion. How out of character would this be, particularly waiting to do so until one of the last chapters of the last book of His revelation?

The Female Allegory in Prophetic Language

The Babylonian harlot is professing Christendom, or at the very least the Jezebel form of the professing body. It is what the professing church had become around the fifth century. Jezebel existed alone until around the sixteenth century and the development of Protestantism. For almost eleven centuries she was the corporate body of Christendom. She continues to exist today as the largest and most dominant form of the professing church.

The Babylonian harlot first and foremost does represent a religion or an ecclesiastical entity, as would be the proper prophetical category for interpreting the female. When we speak of civil world powers we should be referring to beasts and horns in the prophetic language from God's perspective, or splendid looking statues from man's perspective (Dan. 2:31-33, 7:1-7). The figure of a great tree seems to be used generically for a great earthly power (Dan. 4:10-12, Matt. 13:31-32). However, in prophetic language and allegories, the female will always be a religious entity.

- Jezebel is the form that the professing corporate church took on, known as Roman Catholic, in and around the fifth century. It took some time for her to fully develop all her false doctrines, idolatries, and corruptions, and for her to gain her influence with and over the civil kings of the Roman earth. She has done so with persistence. The official edicts of the Roman Empire in 313 and 380 helped pave the way for Christendom to more easily gain her worldly influence and wealth.

- In Revelation 12, the woman in the heavens is Israel as seen in the counsels of God, and when on the earth in that vision she is the Jewish remnant in the last days. Also the widow before the judge in Luke 18 is the elect Jewish remnant in the tribulation period crying out for vengeance against their enemies.

- The bride of the Lamb is a prophetic symbol representing the true church, the body of Christ, the bride of Christ. This has an obvious ecclesiastical meaning.

- Sarah and Hagar are used as types representing stark differences between Christianity and Judaism in their comparison in Galatians 4:21-5:4.

- Eve in the garden before the fall is a type of the church. The body of Christ is bone of His bone, flesh of His flesh (Eph. 5:29-32). The church is united to the second Adam, as Eve was to the first Adam. Adam is a type of the second Adam, Jesus Christ (Rom. 5:14). The type is always a lesser value or reality than the substance that fulfills it. Adam as a type of Christ and Eve as his help-meet has remarkable symbolism of the future glory of Christ and the church found with Him in that glory (Col. 3:4).

- Rebekah, Isaac's wife, is a type of the church. This is after Isaac was offered up by his father, where he becomes a type of Christ raised from the dead (Heb. 11:17-19).

All of the above females represent a religious or ecclesiastical entity and the same will be found true for the Babylonian harlot. But this point does not decide the case for differentiating between Christianity and Islam as the proper meaning of the whore. It remains true that God only deals with two religions in Scripture and this in a very specific and detailed way. But for some this is not enough of an explanation, and we must dig deeper.

Revelation 17:1-6

"Then one of the seven angels who had the seven bowls came and talked with me, saying to me, "Come, I will show you the judgment of the great harlot who sits on many waters, (2) with whom the kings of the earth committed fornication, and the inhabitants of the earth were made drunk with the wine of her fornication."

(3) So he carried me away in the Spirit into the wilderness. And I saw a woman sitting on a scarlet beast which was full of names of blasphemy, having seven heads and ten horns.(4) The woman was arrayed in purple and scarlet, and adorned

with gold and precious stones and pearls, having in her hand a golden cup full of abominations and the filthiness of her fornication. (5) And on her forehead a name was written:

MYSTERY, BABYLON THE GREAT,
THE MOTHER OF HARLOTS
AND OF THE ABOMINATIONS
OF THE EARTH.

(6) I saw the woman, drunk with the blood of the saints and with the blood of the martyrs of Jesus. And when I saw her, I marveled with great amazement."

John's Wonderment at the Woman

This is the vision. In verse six we have the first clue we will consider as to the identity of the women. Even though John is in the Spirit and having a vision, when he sees her, he recognizes what she is and is filled with amazement. The only plausible reason for his astonishment is because the woman is the corporate body of the professing church. If she is a harlot committing fornications, then her other known prophetic name is Jezebel (Rev. 2:20-23), and she is the Roman Catholic form of Christendom that has existed from the fifth century to today. John is connected to her as the last living apostle of the church.

John would not be astonished if the woman represented Islam. He wouldn't even be able to recognize Islam if he saw it. It comes into existence hundreds of years after his time. For John, the woman definitely represents something he is familiar with personally because it causes great amazement. Islam simply doesn't fit the bill here. The harlot is the professing church, and the evidence continues to mount up from this point.

The Blood of the Saints and Martyrs

The woman is drunk with the blood of the saints and the blood of the martyrs of Jesus (Rev. 17:6). This statement really needs no interpretation. This is part of the reason for John's amazement – the professing church that he was involved with and part of had become so corrupt and evil that God held it responsible and guilty of all the blood shed of the true church. God is assigning this responsibility. This accusation references the church's authority and control she had gained in her history, even her ungodly influence over governments and kings during the course of this age. The atrocities committed against the true wheat within her are inexcusable.

What is most hostile to the work of God and His truth? We would think it is Satan when he is using the world to persecute. But here we find it is more so when Satan has control of the professing church. When the Roman Empire became Christian, it was not the removal of Satan's throne from this world and the triumph of the church. Rather, it was Satan acquiring dominion and control over what is called Christendom.

How could John be amazed with Islam in this respect? Again, John had no knowledge of Islam as a religion. Besides, there is a Biblical principle in play that helps us make the correct association between the shed blood and the identity of the woman who is guilty.

Matthew 23:29-35

"Woe to you, scribes and Pharisees, hypocrites! Because you build the tombs of the prophets and adorn the monuments of the righteous, (30) and say, 'If we had lived in the days of our fathers, we would not have been partakers with them in the blood of the prophets.'

(31) "Therefore you are witnesses against yourselves that you are sons of those who murdered the prophets. (32) Fill up, then, the measure of your fathers' guilt. (33) Serpents, brood of vipers! How can you escape the condemnation of hell? (34) Therefore, indeed, I send you prophets, wise men, and scribes: some of them you will kill and crucify, and some of them you will scourge in your synagogues and persecute from city to city, (35) that on you may come all the righteous blood shed

on the earth, from the blood of righteous Abel to the blood of Zechariah, son of Berechiah, whom you murdered between the temple and the altar."

The blood of all the Jewish prophets is found in Judaism, with Israel being responsible. Israel, at the time of Christ, was guilty of all the righteous blood shed on the earth from the time of Abel. Jesus didn't look to anybody else being guilty of the killing of Jewish prophets other than Judaism and Israel. The principle is that the same parallel is used in assigning the guilt of the blood of the saints.

- Jewish prophets killed – Israel is guilty and responsible
- The martyrs of Jesus killed – the professing church is guilty and responsible.

The Character of the Harlot

The parallelism doesn't fit for the woman being Islam. The parallelism points to professing Christianity as being guilty. The Lord has already shown us Christendom's prophetic history on the earth by the seven messages to the seven churches. In those messages we easily see that professing Christianity grew corrupt and evil. Tares were sown early on in the crop in the field. Men with responsibility built with wood, hay, and stubble. The evil leaven came in and spread by which man exalts himself in the religious confidences of the flesh. Men did not heed the words of the Lord to leave the crop alone until the end of the age, but took up pretentious authority and unrighteously committed ungodly atrocities in the history of the professing church.

The symbol of the Babylonian woman/harlot is a religious entity of great worldly corruption and evil. It is filled with abominations and filthiness associated with her fornications (Rev. 17:4-5). The harlot's abominations refer to her idolatry. *This is the general character of Babylon.* A beast is a civil power in the world. We may assume the four beasts mentioned in Scripture are objects of Biblical prophecy because they were world powers that had conquered and taken possession of Israel and their land – prophecy always relating in some way to Israel. But the salient character of all beasts is apostasy – they are independent from God, they do their own will, and they say, "Who is Lord over me? (Dan. 8:4, 11:3, 16, 36). When Nebuchadnezzar was set up by God as the first Gentile beast, he made a great image of gold to be worshiped, joining civil power with religious idolatry (Dan. 3:1-6). This is the Babylonian character that was established.[132]

The Babylonian harlot has nothing to do with the physical location of the ancient city of Babylon, or with that part of the world being Islamic today. This is the mistake of those who teach that the harlot and beast are Islamic. The Biblical principle for understanding prophetic language has to do with the character and nature of the prophetic object when it is an allegory. Therefore, all beasts exhibit a general behavior of independence from God. All females are religious or ecclesiastical entities. And the descriptive adjective of Babylon involves idolatrous character, because Nebuchadnezzar originally linked idolatry with the civil power in the kingdom of Babylon.

The harlot's cup is full of abominations – her gross idolatries. The filthiness of her fornications is all the corruptions and worldliness associated with her idolatry. To those of faith and the spiritually minded, her character is described by the words written on her forehead. This character is as an idolatress, gaining influence over the mass of Gentile nations and committing fornication with the kings of the earth. She does as Nebuchadnezzar did. She joins religious idolatry to civil power to spread her influence. This is the character of Babylon.

The book of Revelation has already shown us something that looks like this harlot. She is what the corporate professing church became in the time of Thyatira (Rev. 2:20-23). This harlot is Jezebel, and Jezebel is the Roman papal system. Her form of Christendom has sought and gained civil power and worldly influence with the kings of the earth. The civil powers have been guilty of intimacy with her, seeking her nepotisms. Her religiosity and pretentions to being the one true representation of Christ on the earth gave her an intoxicating superstitious influence over the inhabitants of the earth. Those who dwell on the earth have lost their senses and any spiritual fortitude to her inebriating effect. Her ungodly abominations and spiritual fornications with the powers of the unbelieving world are clearly documented in her history.

Revelation 18:20

"Rejoice over her, O heaven, and you holy apostles and prophets, for God has avenged you on her!"

Revelation 18:24

"And in her was found the blood of prophets and saints, and of all who were slain on the earth."

Revelation 19:2

"For true and righteous are His judgments, because He has judged the great harlot who corrupted the earth with her fornication; and He has avenged on her the blood of His servants shed by her."

If God holds Judaism and Israel responsible for the blood of her prophets, then God holds professing Christianity responsible for the blood of her apostles, her saints, and her martyrs. We do not have to point the finger anywhere else. The misdirection will only make you, to a greater extent, blind and ignorant to the corporate responsibility of Christendom and its catastrophic failure to be the light of God.

One more point needs to be made from the vision John has, and before we take up the interpretation given by the angel. Verses one and two are introductory information given to John describing the woman (Rev. 17:1-2). The vision starts in verse three and continues through verse six (Rev. 17:3-6). The literal interpretation is given by God through the angel to John and fills the remainder of the chapter (Rev. 17:7-18). In the introductory material she is described as the harlot that sits on many waters. In the vision John sees her sitting on the seven-headed beast. Her 'sitting' is her influence, her control, and her power. Obviously God wants us to understand that her 'sitting' involves two separate locations or spheres of influence.

The Four Gentile Beasts

In the vision John says, *"And I saw a woman sitting on a scarlet beast..."* This beast is the fourth of the four beasts of Daniel 7, and is the Roman Empire (howbeit in a certain form that we will discuss later). What the reader should understand is that there are only four Gentile world powers that exist during 'the times of the Gentiles' (Luke 21:24, Dan. 7:17). These 'times' stretch from Nebuchadnezzar and Babylon to the return of the Son of Man coming with power and great glory (Luke 21:25-27). Daniel 7 depicts symbolically this entire time by describing four beasts. The great image of Nebuchadnezzar's dream also symbolically represents 'the times of the Gentiles' (Dan. 2:31-45).

the Great Image	the Beasts	the World Empires
Head of fine gold	The first was like a lion	Babylon Empire
Chest and arms of silver	The second like a bear	Mede-Persian Empire
Belly and thighs of bronze	The third was like a leopard	Grecian Empire
Legs of iron – as strong as iron, as iron breaks in pieces and shatters all things. That kingdom will break in pieces and crush all the others (Dan. 2: 33, 40).	The fourth beast, dreadful and terrible, exceedingly strong. It had huge iron teeth; it was devouring, breaking, trampling (Dan. 7:7)	Roman Empire in the time of Christ on the earth
Feet partly of iron and clay (Dan. 2:33, 41-43)	The same fourth beast in the end when it is judged and destroyed (Dan. 7:8-12)	A revived Roman Empire, having ascended up out of the bottomless pit (Rev. 11:7)

The point to be made is that there are only four beasts of Gentile world dominion. The interpretation of the king's dream by Daniel only counts up to the fourth kingdom (Dan. 2:40). The same is true concerning Daniel's dream of the beasts. In relating this dream Daniel says, *"...and behold, a fourth beast..."* There are only four beasts (Dan. 7:17), and the Roman Empire is the fourth beast. It is what was present in the time of Jesus Christ on the earth, as well as the apostle John at the time of his writing. But the fourth beast is the last beast, and its last form is clearly shown in Revelation 13. This is the revived Roman Empire having ascended up out of the bottomless pit (Rev. 13:1-7). This is the beast in the last 3 ½ years before the Son of Man returns to the earth.

The desire of some is to turn the scarlet beast, which the woman sits on, into some type of new Islamic beast made up of ten Islamic kingdoms. However, the beast with the harlot is the same beast that was present in the time of Jesus Christ, only then it was without the woman. We should resist attempting to create something different than what the fourth beast actually was – the Roman Empire. There is no fifth beast of Gentile world dominion. There will be no Islamic world empire. What clearly exists in the end will be a revived Roman beast.

The Harlot sits on Many Waters

The angel introduces the vision by telling John a little about the extended sphere of influence of its object, *"...the harlot who sits on many waters..."* (Rev. 17:1) Her impact goes well beyond the Roman beast. The waters would represent the remainder of the Gentile world beyond the Gentile earth – the land mass encompassed by the full extent of the reign of the four empires put together. This area would also be known as the prophetic earth. What is beyond this would be the 'many waters'. It stands to reason that the harlot has this extended influence and power beyond the territories of the four beasts.

Revelation 12:12

"Therefore rejoice, O heavens, and you who dwell in them! Woe to the inhabitants of the earth and the sea! For the devil has come down to you, having great wrath, because he knows that he has a short time."

In this verse we see a noticeable distinction between inhabitants of the earth and those of the sea. Have you ever wondered who the inhabitants of the sea are? This is still prophetic language and the use of allegories, and an interpretation is needed. The 'inhabitants of the earth' is a reference to the prophetic earth land mass and those nations that dwell within the boundaries of the four Gentile empires. This would include Israel and the Promised Land. The 'inhabitants of the sea' refers to the remainder of the Gentile nations. The removal of Satan from the heavens and cast down to the earth is a 'woe judgment' and an experience for the entire world – the inhabitants of the earth and the sea.

- **The Prophetic Earth** – the entire land mass and boundaries of the four Gentile world dynasties put together. The prophetic earth involves the regions and nations included in the extent of Scriptural prophecy.

- **The Roman Earth** – the physical boundaries of the Roman Empire in the time of Christ. It is that of the fourth beast without the extended lands associated with the previous three preceding it. This will also be the territory of the same beast in its last and final form, ascending up out of the bottomless pit. This very well could be what is meant in the book of Revelation when the phrase 'a third of the earth' is used (Rev. 8:7-12).

- **The Great Sea** – "...the four great beasts came up from the sea..." (Dan. 7:2-3). I doubt that this is a direct reference to the Mediterranean Sea. The Great Sea or sea is an allegory. It doesn't refer to bodies of salt or fresh water or water at all. The Great Sea is the mass of Gentile nations out of which the original four Gentile world kingdoms were formed. The territories associated with the Babylonian empire are added to the next empire that followed until you get to the Roman Empire. Their total amount of territories forms the prophetic earth. What isn't included in the prophetic earth is the 'many waters' (Rev. 17:1). However, we realize that all four beasts, when they appeared in their time, came up out of the unformed mass of Gentiles known as the Great Sea

(Dan. 7:3). We see that this meaning is confirmed by the angel in his interpretation.

Revelation 17:15

"Then he said to me, "The waters which you saw, where the harlot sits, are peoples, multitudes, nations, and tongues."

The understanding of how allegories are used in prophetic language and their consistent interpretations and meanings becomes a valuable tool for any believer in their attempts at understanding prophecy in general, and the book of Daniel and Revelation in particular.

Also understanding general Biblical principles is a key for studying Scripture. For example, consider the proper understanding of the principle of the government of God and what topics are related to this:

- the times of the Gentiles
- the four beasts
- the shekinah glory in the temple
- the presence of God leaving Israel
- God saying to Israel, *"For you are not My people, And I will not be your God"* (Hosea 1:9)
- the ark of the covenant, the throne of Jehovah
- the function of the Melchizedek priest
- the name of the Most High
- the two separate and distinct destructions of Jerusalem and the temple – one by the first beast, the other by the fourth beast
- the dividing up of the millennial earth by God – this division centering on Israel as a nation of God's favor and faithfulness (Deut. 32:8-9)

All these things and more are understood and become clear when general Biblical principles such as the government of God of the earth is comprehended.

The true church, the body of Christ, has nothing but heavenly citizenship, heavenly abodes, and heavenly glory. The great harlot has earthly glory and riches, though it is false glory and deceptive. Her conduct is ecclesiastical corruption on the earth, and the glory of the world associated with it. Her union with the world is her whoredom. The apostle John was mystified that the professing church, which he had oversight of as the last apostle, would take on this character and form. However, if we want to have more proof as to whom the harlot is, we must go to the interpretation given by the angel to John. This is what we will consider next.

Chapter 13: Endnotes

[131] The Biblical truth and teaching of the utter depravity of man after the fall and after being chased out of the garden is one of the most important truths of Scripture to fully comprehend and submit to. Without properly seeing this truth you simply will never correctly understand God or His sovereignty. You will never fully understand grace as it is given by God, nor the proper role of the gospel. You will not be able to clarify and separate the work of God from what man is doing. Finally, you will not be able to fully see the glory of God. All these doctrines and Biblical truths literally hang on this key understanding – man in Adam, man in the flesh, is utterly depraved and 100% lost, and without God and without resource in the world. There is nothing man can do. In and of himself, nothing. From the fall of Adam, man's will is a slave to sin. Sin is reigning as a king, in the flesh. Man's will is not free, not when it is a slave.

This state, as taught by Scripture, is 100% depraved, 100% lost. There is absolutely no middle ground, there is not a lower percentage, and there is no partial depravity or lostness. But this is just where the deception and evil of the Arminian and Judaizing doctrine raises its head. It creates a middle ground where no middle ground ever existed. It teaches a partial depravity of mankind where there exists only a full and comprehensive depravity of man. The leaven demands that man still has his resources intact and working for him. His will is still free, and by it he can reason and choose the good. He does not always love the darkness, but in the right situation is attracted to the light and will seek the light. He will seek after God and make the reasonable and intelligent decision (Rom. 3:10-11).

This is the reasoning that the false leaven brings in. But the experience of Israel in God's dealings with them proves this thinking to be utter nonsense. When God gave them the law, they broke it before the tablets were brought down the mountain. Israel, as man in the flesh, could never do the law of God (Rom. 8:7-8). Further, when God presented His Son to them as their Messiah, they killed Him. So when goodness, grace, and truth were presented to Israel by God coming to them in the flesh, man in Adam could only hate Him, despise Him, and reject Him. When God came into the very world that He Himself had created, man purposely and willingly chased Him back out. Without fully comprehending man's state of utter depravity in Adam, you will not be able to properly see the glory of God.

[132] Up to the point that Judah was taken captive into Babylon there remained two great Biblical principles of God with Israel – that of God's calling and that of God's government of the earth. These were introduced by God after He destroyed the world in the flood. The sword was placed into Noah's hand. This is the principle of God's government. Abram was called and separated from the world. This is the principle of God's calling.

After Israel was delivered from Egypt, the presence and glory of Jehovah came down at Mt. Sinai to live in the midst of the nation of Israel. Jehovah lived among them, in the tabernacle and later in Solomon's temple in Jerusalem. The basis of His presence there was that Israel was a called and redeemed people. This redemption was only external in the flesh, and through types and shadows, but still, Israel represented a redeemed people that God could live among. However He was still hidden behind a veil.

In Israel the two principles were united together by God – calling and government. Jehovah lived among a called and redeemed people, and ruled the world from His throne between the cherubim. These two principles remained united in Israel until their apostasy and idolatry forced Jehovah to remove His presence from the earth. At that time God allowed the destruction of Jerusalem and the temple, and the loss of the ark – the throne of God. Government of the earth was given to the Gentiles, starting with Nebuchadnezzar and Babylon.

Jerusalem would be rebuilt, its walls and streets. The temple would also be rebuilt. However, Nehemiah's temple was an inferior glory than the previous one. Solomon's temple had the ark, the throne of God, and the presence and glory of Jehovah was there. Nehemiah's temple never had this, nor did Nehemiah ever try to duplicate or mimic what was previously started and present through the time of Moses.

This is a lesson of great importance for us to see and understand today, especially Christian leaders. Nehemiah never assumes he has a right to the privileges of Moses' position. He never attempts to recapture Moses' power or glory. He never makes a new ark of the covenant to stick back inside the veil in the rebuilt temple. He never prays for the glory and presence of Jehovah to come back down from heaven and live among this remnant of Judah, now returned from Babylon. Along with this, Nehemiah realizes that the Gentiles are in control and rule over them, and it is God's will that it stays this way (Neh. 9:36-37). He never assumes he has the right to be a second Moses, and has a right to delivering power and miracles etc. He never assumes he has the right to call God's presence back from heaven, back to the earth and new temple.

Yet this is the mistake we make in the professing church. We read the passage in Luke 4:17-21 about the anointing of Messiah for His ministry in and toward Israel, and we mistakenly assume all believers by faith are privileged to have and walk in this same anointing and power. We are blind to Biblical principles that easily explain His position and title as Messiah and the scope and range of Messiah's mission (Matt. 15:24-26). We read the book of Acts and see the beginnings of the church, and again assume this is our right and God given privilege to walk in the same position and apostolic power they did, with the same blessings and miracles and apostolic authority. Do we not realize there are no apostles among us today? How can we possibly walk in apostolic power and authority? In the first three messages to Christendom in Revelation 2, Jesus held out to the church world the possibility of the corporate entity repenting and returning to its first position of blessing. After that He drops all thought of any return to Pentecost in the fourth church period. The professing church had become corrupt. Returning was no longer the will of God because Jesus does not see it as a possibility. Does that mean that in presumption, we should nevertheless hold it out as a possibility and teach it as our right and privilege? Are we going to continue to declare this return to Pentecostal power as the will of God and our right, and continue to encourage believers to give hours and years in prayer to make this happen?

I will be honest with you. A return to Pentecost for the professing church is not the will of God and not His plan. And further, the leap of presumption that the church will then rise up and change and save America is entirely out of the question. That is not His plan either. These thoughts and prayers only show the arrogance of Laodicea (Rev. 3:17). We show our lack of humility and show our spiritual blindness by refusing to recognize the evil and corruption of the professing church. It is the false Arminian leaven of human achievement that props up and inflates these very thoughts and blinds us to the purpose and plan of God. We essentially create our own plan out of our own wills, independent from God's. How is this not borderline apostasy? At the very least it is the religious confidences of the flesh that are found, when spiritual eyes are opened by the Spirit, to be mere rubbish and dung (Phil. 3:1-9).

The prophet Haggai was involved in the time of the rebuilt temple. He speaks for God saying, *"The glory of this latter temple shall be greater than the former...and in this place I will give peace."* But this is not a reference to Nehemiah's rebuilt temple, but rather to the millennial temple and the glory of Jesus Christ reigning on the earth in the latter days (Haggai 2:6-9).

When ministers talk of Nehemiah they talk of revival for the church, and come up with formulas to make revival happen. I simply don't get it. Where do we see revival with Nehemiah? There was no return to Moses' tabernacle, no glory and presence of Jehovah, no miracles or signs, and no deliverance from servitude to the Gentiles. There was the joy of Jehovah as their strength in blessing for this little remnant of Judah that was allowed to return from captivity (Neh. 8:10). There were more miracles and activity by God found with Daniel and his friends in captivity in Babylon than anything you see after the remnant of Judah was allowed to return to the land. There was no revival of Israel under Nehemiah. There was no Israel under Nehemiah for that matter. The ten northern tribes had long ago been scattered by the Assyrian into the Gentile world. A small remnant of Judah was what was with Nehemiah. God's plan was simple. The small remnant would rebuild Jerusalem and the temple over time, so that God could present Messiah to them according to promises and prophecy. They would reject the Messiah when He came, and God would destroy the city and the temple again in 70 AD. This time it was by the fourth beast.

God's separation of the two principles – calling and government – took place when god set up Babylon to rule the world. The principle of government was given to the Gentiles. This principle stays with the Gentiles for all the time known as the 'times of the Gentiles.' The principle of calling stayed with Israel. What distinctly marks God's separation of these two principles was the destruction of Jerusalem and the temple. When the principle of government was removed from Israel, Nebuchadnezzar and Babylon were used by God to bring destruction. When the principle of calling was set aside in Israel, God used the Romans to bring destruction. At the present time, and since the last destruction of the city and temple in 70 AD, Israel does not have either of the two principles acknowledged in them by God. God doesn't acknowledge them even as His people (Hosea 1:9).

When the principle of government was set aside from Israel and given to the Gentiles, God's intention and plan is not to unite these two principles again until the millennium. They are to stay separated until God acknowledges Israel again as His people. This will not be until the millennium. Both calling and government of the earth will then be centered in Israel with a Jewish remnant being saved. At this present time, the principle of calling is with the church, and government with the Gentiles. But make no mistake, the church wasn't given Israel's calling. The church's calling is heavenly. Israel's calling is earthly. And besides, all callings are without repentance. And further, God had to set aside Israel and their calling in order to bring forth the church and its calling. God will not deal with two different callings at the same time. As long as the true church is still on the earth, God will not recognize Israel as His people or their calling.

God's principle of calling rests with the church at this time, for as long as she exists upon the earth – until her rapture. What should be obvious is that the two principles are separated for the entire time of 'the times of the Gentiles' (Luke 21:24). God did this. God has separated them and man should not attempt to bring them back together. The professing church is guilty of committing adultery and fornications with the kings of the earth. Christendom seeking civil power has always been against the will of God. The professing church has never had the right to do this. It is all the filthiness of her fornications and her unholy uniting with the world (Rev. 17:2, 4).

Chapter 14:
The Babylonian Harlot: the Angelic Interpretation

The interpretation of the vision given to John by the angel follows the passages we considered in the last chapter. This portion fills the remainder of the chapter (Rev. 17:7-18). The angel gives a literal explanation of certain elements contained in the vision. The interpretation typically doesn't explain all the elements, but usually enough for a good understanding. What I find in all biblical interpretations, regardless of whether it explains a dream, vision, or parable, is that the content of the interpretation extends beyond the actual sphere of the corresponding element. This is always the case whether it is an angel, a man, or Jesus giving the interpretation. This is the case with what the angel shares with John.[133]

Revelation 17:7-18

"But the angel said to me, "Why did you marvel? I will tell you the mystery of the woman and of the beast that carries her, which has the seven heads and the ten horns. (8) The beast that you saw was, and is not, and will ascend out of the bottomless pit and go to perdition. And those who dwell on the

earth will marvel, whose names are not written in the Book of Life from the foundation of the world, when they see the beast that was, and is not, and yet is.

(9) "Here is the mind which has wisdom: The seven heads are seven mountains on which the woman sits. (10) There are also seven kings. Five have fallen, one is, and the other has not yet come. And when he comes, he must continue a short time. (11) The beast that was, and is not, is himself also the eighth, and is of the seven, and is going to perdition.

(12) "The ten horns which you saw are ten kings who have received no kingdom as yet, but they receive authority for one hour as kings with the beast. (13) These are of one mind, and they will give their power and authority to the beast. (14) These will make war with the Lamb, and the Lamb will overcome them, for He is Lord of lords and King of kings; and those who are with Him are called, chosen, and faithful."

(15) Then he said to me, "The waters which you saw, where the harlot sits, are peoples, multitudes, nations, and tongues. (16) And the ten horns which you saw on the beast, these will hate the harlot, make her desolate and naked, eat her flesh and burn her with fire. (17) For God has put it into their hearts to fulfill His purpose, to be of one mind, and to give their kingdom to the beast, until the words of God are fulfilled. (18) And the woman whom you saw is that great city which reigns over the kings of the earth."

Divine Truth: the Word and the Spirit

Before entering into the details it is good to remind the reader of an important understanding. God brings divine truths from His Word to the believer by the teaching of the Holy Spirit (I Cor. 2:7-12). *"Even so no one knows the things of God except the Spirit of God. Now we have received...the Spirit who is from God, that we might know the things that have been freely given to us by God."* And earlier in the same chapter (I Cor. 2:7): *"But we speak the wisdom of God...the hidden wisdom which God ordained before the ages for our glory."*

There are many people who attempt biblical interpretation and bible teaching. Ministry is often viewed as a potential career choice when trying to decide what to do with one's life and how to make a living. Many times certain ones with natural speaking talents and good story-telling skills will appear attractive, popular, and successful in this profession. What I want you to understand is that there is no truth of God taught from His word without possession of the seal of the Spirit. Further, there is no truth of God without the workings and doings of the Spirit through the word within the person being used of God to bring the interpretation or teaching. Most of us can't put our finger on what divine teaching really is, or what it looks like.

Does Christian teaching today have this character? If it doesn't, it's not likely to be Christian teaching at all. Is what you hear the hidden wisdom of God that is simply ordained by God for our glory? This is what divine truth is. This character is what forms the nature of divine teaching. *"But God has revealed them to us through His Spirit."* (I Cor. 2:10) Revealed what? The things of God that are ordained for our glory!

How do I know that unbelievers cannot receive divine truth, or that tares in Christendom do not teach divine truth? The world or the tares cannot receive the Spirit of truth. They cannot see Him or know Him. They do not have the Spirit of God dwelling in them (John 14:17). That is not to say that all true Christians only teach divine truth. There are many who have been sealed with the Spirit and belong to the Lord, yet do not rightly divide the word of truth (II Tim. 2:14-18). But the point is, tares exist in Christendom in large amounts. Worse yet is that the foolish virgins look exactly like the wise ones (Matt. 25:1-4). Tares are made to look very much like the wheat. Although you may not think or realize this, tares do hold positions in which they teach Christian doctrine. This is the main instrument by which the devil corrupts the professing church – false and misleading teachings and doctrines (Eph. 4:14). The history of Christendom is filled with this very issue. It stands then, that without having the Spirit of God, teaching divine truth is impossible.

If I gave you the term biblical scholarship or Christian scholarship, where would you go in the Scriptures to find God's idea or definition of this? His idea is found in I Corinthians 2 – the believer has been given the mind of Christ. We have been given the Spirit of God so that we would know the things of God, yes, the deep things of God. If all we do is mimic the scholarship of the world, their methods, ways, and practices, how is this distinctive to Christianity? How is it doctrine and divine truth from God if the world can do exactly the same thing? Hebrew and Greek words, root meanings and linguistics, structure of sentences, etc. Is this how the Spirit of God teaches? We may find Jewish rabbis that do the same, and often better.

All that remains today is the Word of God. Will we be taught the Word of God by the Spirit of God who has been given to us? Do we even know what that looks like, what that is? Can we recognize the truth of God and divine teaching in a time when the professing church will not endure sound doctrine? (II Tim 4:3-4) It is the discipline and faithfulness of Philadelphia that the Lord points out and commends in the end times – keeping His Word, not denying His name, and keeping the Word of His patience (Rev. 3:8, 10). That is it. That is our present assignment and responsibility according to the measure of grace given to us. Will we be faithful in these few things?

The False Bride of the Lamb

Often when we consider the detail of passages we miss out on the consequences and implications that are being taught. Often in the details we lose sight of the larger significance that is present. When we contemplate the Babylonian harlot we find there is a huge contrast being made. We need to see and understand this contrast. What the harlot pretends to be is the earthly bride of the Lamb. If we look we will see that the true bride of the Lamb is celebrated in the heavens. It is there that we eventually see the marriage supper of the Lamb (Rev. 19:7-9). But this marriage will not take place until that which is false on the earth, that which pretends to be the bride, is judged and destroyed.

This is the Biblical principle found in Revelations 17-21 that brings spiritual clarity to the interpretation of the angel – God judges the false pretentious bride of the Lamb and destroys her on the earth *before* the true bride of the Lamb is celebrated in heaven. The Babylonian harlot thinks she is the true bride of Christ. But she is only a false bride of the Lamb, living on the earth in her wealth and worldly luxury, committing her harlotry with the civil authorities established by God (Rom. 13:1-2, Rev. 17:2). The inhabitants of the earth are intoxicated with her earthly agenda and they lose all spiritual insight and direction. She is a harlot because she should have had a proper relationship with the Lamb and with Him alone. She should have been true to the Lamb. But she has been unfaithful, and she has committed her adulteries with the world. She is in relationship with the world and the kings of the earth.

Judgment starts at the House of God

The comparison and contrast between the false and true bride of the Lamb that is present in these chapters (Rev. 17, 18, 19, 21) ends when the Babylonian harlot is judged, burned, and destroyed (Rev. 19:1-6). At that point there is the greatest of celebrations in heaven. The order of these events is of significance and not a coincidence. Of particular notice should be that this judgment of the whore is carried out to completion before the marriage of the true bride and the Lamb, and before the Son of Man comes forth out of heaven to judge the world. *The biblical principle in this order is that judgment starts at the house of God* (I Pet. 4:17). This is why God uses the ten formerly Christian kingdoms and their ten kings (the ten horns) to throw the harlot off the beast and to accomplish God's will in judging her (Rev. 17:16-17). Also we can clearly see in chapter 17 that the harlot is judged and destroyed before the beast and the ten kings go off to make war with the Lamb (Rev. 17:12-14).

If the harlot is pretending to be the bride of the Lamb, and this comparison and contrast is the mind of God taught by the Spirit in these particular chapters, then the harlot could not be interpreted as the religion of Islam. There is no thought in Islam of any association with Jesus Christ. Islam cannot be a bride of the slain Lamb, even a false one. All thoughts of being a bride of the Lamb are only found in Christendom. The professing church alone could represent such deception. In order to pretend to be the bride of Christ the harlot would have to have a Christian profession. She would have to profess Christ. In all her worldly pride, Jezebel, as the Roman Catholic church, has been claiming to be the true bride of Christ for centuries. A harlot, on the earth, exalting herself by her corruptions and abominations, yet associated with Christ, can be no other than Jezebel.

The Six Allegories of John's Vision

There are many allegories in the vision, but only five that are directly dealt with in the interpretation by the angel. There is a sixth allegory related to the vision by the comparison and contrast the Spirit is making in the general overall background. This, as we have already discussed, is the true bride of the Lamb (Rev. 19:7-9). She has more than one association with the harlot as we will soon see. The true bride of the Lamb is celebrated in heaven only after the false bride of the Lamb is destroyed on the earth.

The Allegories	The Interpretation/Meaning
The bride of the Lamb	1. The bride of Christ, the body of Christ, the true church (Eph. 5:25-32, Rev. 19:7-9) 2. The heavenly city, the holy Jerusalem, the capital city of the government of God (Rev. 21:9-22:5, 3:12)
The Babylonian Harlot	1. The false bride of the Lamb on the earth, filled with abominations and fornications (Rev. 17:1-6, Rev. 2:20-23) 2. The great capital city of the Roman Empire; the capital city of the rule and dominion of man on the earth (Rev. 17:18)
The scarlet Beast	1. The Roman Empire that was, and is not, and will be present, ascending out of the bottomless pit (Rev. 17:8) 2. ...is himself the eighth (king, that is Caesar – Rev. 17:11)

The seven heads	1. They are seven (physical) mountains - geographical (Rev. 17:9)
	2. They are also seven kings, all Caesars, who all had come into power and now passed (Rev. 17:10)
The ten horns	1. They are ten future kings (Rev. 17:12)
	2. They are ten kingdoms, formerly Christian, in the western part of the Roman Empire.
The 'many waters'	The mass of Gentile nations not included in the prophetic earth (Rev. 17:15)

It is remarkable that five of the six allegories involved have a double meaning, and that this was the purpose and wisdom of God. It is equally remarkable how the double meaning of the heavenly bride perfectly answers to the earthly pretentions in the double meaning of the harlot. The Babylonian harlot exercised great affectation of being the true bride of Christ on the earth, with earthly glory and riches. However, she is a harlot actually joined to the world. In her second meaning she is the capital city of the Roman beast that was, and is not, and will be present. In this second meaning she is the city of Rome (Rev. 17:18).

The Seven Mountains

The separate allegory of the seven heads leads us to a similar conclusion (Rev. 17:9). The first literal meaning the angel gives is that the seven heads are, in fact, *seven mountains on which the woman sits*. This identifies a geographic location relating both to the beast and the woman. Her sitting on seven mountains makes her to be the capital city Rome (Rev. 17:18), the city of the seven hills. Also then, the heads actually belonging to the beast, confirms the beast is the Roman Empire, of which Rome is its capital city.

This is an important point. Error comes in when we do not follow the basic principles of Biblical interpretation in prophetic language. *The most basic of principles is that the interpretation actually gives you the literal meaning.* The interpretation does not introduce new allegories which in turn demand another distinct interpretation.

When the angel draws John's attention to the seven heads, the seven heads is the allegory/symbol he is about to give the literal meaning of. The first meaning is that they are actually seven physical mountains. We cannot take seven mountains and make an allegory out of it. We would be violating the basic principle of interpretation. Seven mountains is the literal meaning of seven heads. It is not the introduction of another allegory. Seven mountains do not mean seven kingdoms.

Therefore, in its first literal meaning, the seven heads refer to a geographic location where there are seven physical mountains. This location is Rome. One of the literal meanings of the woman is that she is this great earthly city, the capital city of the Roman Empire as well as the capital city of Christendom. We have to be able to see that this is part of the comparison and contrast between the bride of the Lamb and the Babylonian harlot. The bride of the Lamb is the great city, the holy and heavenly Jerusalem (Rev. 21:9-10). This is the capital city of God's government over the millennial earth yet to come. The woman is the earthly capital city of man's unrighteous government of the earth – Rome and the Roman Empire.

1 Peter 5:13

"She who is in Babylon, elect together with you, greets you; and so does Mark my son."

The spiritual name of the city of Rome is Babylon, and was commonly used from the time of Peter. The ancient city of Babylon had been destroyed and did not exist in Peter's day. The use of this label for the city of Rome speaks of its idolatrous character, not a physical location in Iraq. The character of Rome is Babylonian and therefore the city is spoken of by Peter as Babylon.[134]

The Wilderness

Except for the literal explanations involving the allegories surrounding the beast, which we will address in the following chapter, the last allegory we will briefly consider is the use of the word 'wilderness' (Rev. 17:3). *John was carried away in the Spirit by the angel into the wilderness.* This is where John sees the woman and the beast. The wilderness is where there are no springs or life from God. It is a dry and desert place. It is a virtual spiritual wasteland. The wilderness, as an allegory, represents the world, and it is used this way in Scripture.

The woman who bore the male Child in Revelation 12 is said to flee into the wilderness after her Child was caught up to God and to His throne. This catching up involves the rapture of the church, the Child's body. The woman, who bore the Child when on the earth, represents the Jewish remnant in the last 3 ½ years of the tribulation period.[135] In the world the sealed remnant is preserved and protected by God. In the wilderness she has a place prepared by God (Rev. 12:6, 14).

The believer/church is not of this world, as Jesus is not of this world (John 17:14, 16). In the wilderness we have no dwelling place, just as the Son of Man had no dwelling place in this world (Matt. 8:20, Luke 9:58). We walk in the wilderness as strangers and pilgrims, we are currently left in this world (John 17:15). But we are not of the world and should have no relationship with it. We should not emulate the Babylonian harlot in this respect – she is committing adultery and fornication with the world.

Christianity has been corrupted by man. It has never reformed the world, but rather the world has changed Christianity. The world entered into Christianity early on and long ago, and has never left, but only grown stronger within. The corporate body of the professing church is the greatest of all corruptions. It is where the light of God should have been burning strong.

If our eyes are opened by the Spirit to see and comprehend this unholy mess, we should not think that we can fix it and make it right. That is arrogance and the height of the Arminian leaven at work. Religious egotism is the biggest part of the problem. We can't be humble enough to admit the mess and we aren't humble enough to understand that we cannot fix it when we see it. Please, consider the harlot. God judges her, and He uses the evil world to do so – the ten kings with the beast do the will of God and destroy the harlot (Rev. 17:15-17).

Chapter 14: Endnote

[133] John only sees the woman sitting on the beast in the wilderness in his vision. Beyond the scope of the vision are the circumstances of how the harlot is eventually thrown off the beast and destroyed. Also what is additional is the ten kings giving their power to the beast and going off to make war with the Lamb. These understandings are not part of the vision itself.

[134] After God wrestled with Jacob, He changed his name to Israel. This nation would come from his twelve sons. However, the name change speaks more to the general character of the nation of Israel as reflected by Jacob's life and experiences. All Jacob's behavior, his wanderings, his wrestling with God, his fear of his brother, his fear of his father-in-law, and his desire, conniving, and deceptions to gain earthly blessings, are types and shadows of the experiences and behavior of the nation of Israel in general. Jacob is Israel's greatest type as to character and behavior in Scripture, and the name change confirms this.

Jacob wrestling with God is not some great example of faith, and not an example to be emulated in the church (Gen. 32:24-26). The church is to walk by faith, and faith is the evidence of things unseen. The wrestling was a 'human effort in the flesh' that is typical of the entire history of the nation of Israel, as well as typical of their religion. The angel Jacob wrestled with was right there and He wrestled with Jacob and Jacob would not let go until he received a physical blessing. Jacob wrestles and struggles all night and to the morning – this is a picture of Israel's entire history before God. This is not a principle of faith, but a walk by physical senses. Everything in Jacob's experiences leading up to this wrestling match was unbelief. Everything in his experiences that follows the wrestling match is fear and unbelief.

Jacob wrestles for himself and he struggles in the flesh. Jacob paid the price for this by being made to limp the rest of his life. Because there was nothing here of faith or communion with God, God refused to tell Jacob His name. Jacob's name change to Israel is simply God recognizing and acknowledging Jacob's relationship with God. It is a relationship in the flesh and one that is a constant struggle. In changing his name to Israel God is painting the picture of the future history of the nation. That history is nothing more than God testing the principle of responsibility with man in Adam and in the flesh.

This story represents God's dealings with a person that does not walk with Him. It represents how Israel, although highly favored and privileged by God as a nation, failed in their responsibility to walk in faith with God (Rom. 9:30-32, 10:1-4, 8:8). Israel never aspires to walk in the steps of the faith of Abraham, their father in the flesh (Rom. 4:12-22). Instead, Israel always lowers herself to the character and behavior of Jacob, with a walk by sight and in the flesh.

It remains that Jacob's name change to Israel speaks of character, behavior, and experiences that awaited the nation of Israel. Jacob serves as a remarkable type. In their history as a nation Israel always struggles and wrestles with God. It is only at the very end that Israel will receive a blessing from God – in the millennium, and this after wrestling in the flesh all the night.

So then, Rome being labeled Babylon speaks of its Babylonian character – idolatry is the abomination of Babylon and becomes the character associated with the name. In the times of the Roman Empire, Rome was the capital city enforcing its idolatries. Its most egregious idolatry is when the professing church corporately became Jezebel with her head located in Rome (popery – Vatican).

[135] The Jewish remnant is what God sovereignly saves out of apostate Israel during the coming tribulation. The overall condition of Israel and Judah at this time is described by the story Jesus tells in Matthew 12:43-45. Israel was delivered from the unclean spirit of idolatry by their being scattered into the world and by Judah being taken captive to Babylon. Their house has been swept clean and empty of idolatry for some time now, albeit a house in desolation because of unbelief (Matt. 23:37-39). What is certain is that their last state will be worse than the first. Seven other spirits with him is the completion and perfection of their idolatrous state under the Antichrist.

The woman on the earth in Revelation 12 represents the sealed and sovereignly preserved remnant of Israel. Her fleeing into the wilderness is her hiding in the world where God will protect what He has chosen and sealed. The Jewish remnant is important because it is what God sovereignly saves out of Israel. The remnant is what He will pour out His Spirit on in Israel before the great and terrible day of the Lord (Joel 2:28-32). The remnant is what God will place and restore in the Land. The remnant is what God will build a new nation from. The remnant is to whom all the promises and prophecies concerning Israel are actually promised to, and in whom the promises of God to Israel will be fulfilled. When Paul says, *"And so all Israel will be saved..."* he is speaking of this Jewish remnant only, not the idolatrous nation of Israel (Rom. 11:26-27). Concerning the promises and prophecies, and for the sake of the fathers, the Jewish remnant is the election (Rom. 11:28). You will find them called the elect in the prophecies of Jesus in the gospels. It is the Jewish remnant that will not be deceived by a false Christ, even when the remainder of the nation goes after the Antichrist. The elect remnant will not be deceived by false prophets that will come. This is what God will do, it will be His work alone, so that God alone receives the glory.

Chapter 15:

The Scarlet Beast; the Angelic Interpretation

In John's vision the harlot is seen sitting on the scarlet beast. It is the fourth beast seen by Daniel in his night visions (Dan. 7:7). Daniel's beast was the Roman Empire in the time in which Messiah was presented to Israel. You should remember Jesus answering the question asked of Him, *"Is it lawful to pay taxes to Caesar, or not?"* They attempted to trick Him in His words, testing Him. *"Render therefore to Caesar the things that are Caesar's, and to God the things that are God's."* (Matt. 22:15-22) We see that Jesus acknowledged the fourth beast. Why wouldn't He? The Roman Empire was brought into power and world dominion by the providence of God. It was according to God's plan. This is why Daniel saw the fourth beast, dreadful and terrible, and exceedingly strong. Daniel was seeing God's plan for Gentile world power from the time of the Babylonian kingdom to the second coming of Jesus Christ. Daniel sees the four world powers in prophecy, but it is the providence of God that brings these events and outcomes to pass.

As believers we not only walk by faith, but we must also see and understand, according to faith, the things that are not seen. Our faith is to be all the evidence we need of these things (Heb. 11:1).

The providential hand of God is one of those things not seen with the natural eye, but needs to be perceived by the believer with the eye of faith. It is easy to see the beasts. It is more difficult to see and understand the plan and providence of God that eventually brings such things to pass.[136]

2 Corinthians 4:18

"...while we do not look at the things which are seen, but at the things which are not seen. For the things which are seen are temporary, but the things which are not seen are eternal."

All the things of this world and on this earth are the things which are seen. They are the things that are temporary. And if so, why should I trust in them? Why should I desire them? The believer has no Christian hope in this world or on this earth. We have the promise of His grace being sufficient for us in time of need (II Cor. 12:9-10), yet we will have plenty of needs. We have the promise that we will not be tempted beyond that which we may withstand (I Cor. 10:13), but there will still be temptations. At this time we have a faithful High Priest who is indeed touched with the feeling of our infirmities, who can sympathize with our weaknesses (Heb. 4:14-16). However, the weaknesses and infirmities remain ours while we are in these bodies of flesh. If we indeed suffer with Him now, we have the promise that we will be glorified together with Him (Rom. 8:17-18). Therefore Paul says, *"...I take pleasure in infirmities, in reproaches, in needs, in persecutions, in distresses, for Christ's sake. For when I am weak, then I am strong."*

We all know the character of a mature person – they can wait patiently for the prize or reward. Children in general have a hard time being able to do this. They are impatient and want to be satisfied now. They do not understand the concept of waiting or holding out for something good or something better. This is typical of immaturity, and it produces a certain mindset and behavior. How much of Christianity is like this?[137]

Seeing with the eye of faith is the only way to understand the plan and counsels of God and His providential ways that order all things according to His will – even the four beasts. Are they not all civil world powers? Who is responsible for setting up all governing authority, if it isn't God? *"For there is no authority except from God, and the authorities that exist are appointed by God. Therefore whoever resists the authority resists the ordinance of God, and those who resist will bring judgment on themselves."* (Rom. 13:1-2)[138] God orders all things according to the counsel of His will (Eph. 1:11). These beasts have a part to play in His plan.

God's providential hand is hard to see and understand at times. It can truly only be seen by faith and by a believer who is familiar with the counsels and plan of God. Otherwise it will be confusion and heartache when we witness the growth and ripening of evil, both in the professing church and in the world. It will result in disappointment and frustration concerning prayers and the weakening of personal faith.

The Differing States of the Scarlet Beast

Many of the allegories associated with the scarlet beast are pointed out and discussed in the angel's interpretation. However, before addressing specific symbols, we would do well to first discuss the three different states of this fourth beast. This also is brought out in the words of the angel:

Revelation 17:8

"The beast that you saw was, and is not, and will ascend out of the bottomless pit and go to perdition. And those who dwell on the earth will marvel, whose names are not written in the Book of Life from the foundation of the world, when they see the beast that was, and is not, and yet is."

The last part of this verse where it says, 'and yet is' should read, 'and will be present'. This change gives a better understanding of the entire phrase. There are three parts to the phrase, as there are three states to the existence of the fourth beast. The third state of the beast is described differently, but this does not have a conflict in meaning. Here are the three states:

- The first state is described as the beast you saw 'was' or the beast that 'was'. This refers to the existence of the Roman Empire in the time of Christ and the time of John. This is depicted as the two legs of iron in the statue from Nebuchadnezzar's dream (Dan. 2:33, 40) and as the beast first appears coming up out of the Great Sea in Daniel's vision (Dan. 7:7).

- The second state of the beast is described by the phrase 'and is not'. Most people teach that this refers to the time when the Roman Empire was overthrown and it stopped existing as an empire. However, later on in the chapter I will show you why I believe the basis of this is wrong, and that the fourth beast never really stops existing. The beast in the 'is not' state has far more to do with the character of the beast than it does with the marking of time or existence.

- The third or last epoch of the beast is described as 'will ascend out of the bottomless pit and go to perdition' or as 'will be present' (Rev. 17:8). If the beast in this state is going to perdition or destruction, then it is his final or ending state. This state is depicted by what John sees in Revelation 13 after the dragon is cast out of the heavens and down to the earth (Rev. 12:7-12). The last epoch of the beast is the resumption of its formal beastly character under the direct influence of Satan, now cast down to the earth. The final state of the fourth beast is not until the ten horns have ten crowns on them (Rom. 13:1) – not until the ten kings are in full power over their ten kingdoms.

There is a reference to a time element in the phrase, *"...when they see the beast that was, and is not, and will be present."* The phrase uses the words was, is, and will be – past, present, and future. But what the time elements are relative to in their reference is of great importance. As I said, most would teach that it refers to the period of time of the existence of the Empire and when it fell. But let us consider the vision John was given. All of the proper interpretation relates directly to the vision. In it we have the scarlet beast in the wilderness, and the harlot sitting on top of it. One important question to be asked is which of the three epochs of the beast does the vision actually represent?

The Scarlet Beast that 'is not'

It is fairly logical and a simple process of elimination to find the answer. The Babylonian harlot that represents the professing church was not riding the beast in the first period. When the beast first rose up out of the Great Sea in Daniel's vision he didn't see a harlot on top of it. In the final period depicted by John's vision in Revelation 13, there is no harlot on the beast there either. The first and the third state of the Roman Empire do not involve the Babylonian harlot's influence. John's vision in Revelation 17 is a picture of the second state of the beast. It is a vision of the beast that is different and distinct from what Daniel saw and what John sees in Revelation 13. This period when the beast 'is not' begins when the harlot climbed up on top. It represents the time when the Roman Empire recognized Christianity as the state religion. The vision is of the time when the Empire was Christianized.

There is a biblical principle found in the book of Daniel that, if understood, explains why the beast is said to be in the state of 'is not' when the harlot is on board. We all know the story of Nebuchadnezzar's judgment from God for his arrogance, idolatry, and apostasy – he was made by God to crawl and live like a beast for seven years (Dan. 4:15-16, 24-33). During this time of judgment he personally has the character of a beast, and his behavior and lifestyle is that of an animal. The main distinguishing feature of a beast in prophetic language is that it has its own will that is independent from God.

When the time was over, God impressed upon Nebuchadnezzar's conscience the lesson of man in civil power properly acknowledging the Most High, and that He rules from the heavens in the kingdom of men (Dan. 4:25-26). He then received back his human character and senses.

Daniel 4:34-37

"And at the end of the time I, Nebuchadnezzar, lifted my eyes to heaven, and my understanding returned to me; and I blessed the Most High and praised and honored Him who lives forever:

For His dominion is an everlasting dominion,
And His kingdom is from generation to generation.
All the inhabitants of the earth are reputed as nothing;
He does according to His will in the army of heaven
And among the inhabitants of the earth.
No one can restrain His hand
Or say to Him, "What have You done?"

At the same time my reason returned to me, and for the glory of my kingdom, my honor and splendor returned to me. My counselors and nobles resorted to me, I was restored to my kingdom, and excellent majesty was added to me. Now I, Nebuchadnezzar, praise and extol and honor the King of heaven, all of whose works are truth, and His ways justice. And those who walk in pride He is able to put down."

How a Beast loses its Character

Nebuchadnezzar loses the character of the beast after seven years when he is made to acknowledge the Most High and His sovereignty from the heavens above. This loss of character is what is important to see. After seven years he stops acting like an animal. A beast has a will of its own independent from God. But now Nebuchadnezzar acknowledges the Most High. This principle is again emphasized in Daniel's vision of the four Gentile beasts.

Daniel 7:2-4

"Daniel spoke, saying, "I saw in my vision by night, and behold, the four winds of heaven were stirring up the Great Sea. And four great beasts came up from the sea, each different from the other. The first was like a lion, and had eagle's wings. I *watched till its wings were plucked off; and it was lifted up from the earth and made to stand on two feet like a man, and a man's heart was given to it."*

The lion is the Babylonian kingdom and the first Gentile beast. Its wings represent its speed of conquest as a world power. At its end the lion is lifted up from the earth and made to stand on two feet like a man. The lion is given a man's heart. This represents Nebuchadnezzar's personal experience as it had results in his kingdom. The lion standing on its two feet like a man is when Nebuchadnezzar was made to acknowledge the Most High. In its end Babylon became a world kingdom that acknowledged God (Dan 4:36-37). Babylon had lost its character as a beast. For this short time near its end the lion 'is not'.

This is the Biblical principle God is emphasizing in the two different passages in Daniel (Dan. 4, 7). This is the principle impressed upon the student of prophecy when God starts laying out His plan for the 'times of the Gentiles'. How does a beast lose its character or disappear? How then does a beast regain its character and become present again?

The Christianizing of the Roman Beast

This explains the second period of the Roman beast – the state in which it 'is not'. In 313 AD Constantine stopped the general persecution of the church by the Roman Empire. In 380 AD the empire declared by edict Christianity to be its state religion. The woman began to climb up on the Roman beast at that time. When she began to exercise her influence over the beast, the beast in a sense began to acknowledge God. This is when the empire loses its character as a beast and is said to be in a state described as 'is not'. This second period is all the time the harlot rides the beast in the wilderness. The second epoch ends when the harlot is thrown off the beast and the Roman Empire is free to resume its beastly character again, without in any sense answering to God. When the beast 'is not', it is not acting in the character of a beast.

The Final Epoch – the Return of the Beastly Character

In the first and third states, the Roman beast is in character and behaving as an unruly animal. However the final state is its worse. The second state is when the beast, in a sense, is playing nice, allowing the whore to have her place and time. The final period is when the beast 'will be present' and will ascend out of the bottomless pit. (Rev. 17:8). Just the thought of ascending out of the bottomless pit gives an ominous impression. This final state is the full ripening of civil evil and apostasy, and is when Satan directly gives the beast his power, his throne, and great authority (Rev. 13:2). The full display of imperial evil is easily seen in the Roman beast's rebellion and blasphemies against God and the true church in heaven (Rev. 13:5-6). Being free of the harlot, the beast has an openly public anti-Christian attitude.

The Times of the Gentiles

The beast never stops existing or 'the times of the Gentiles' would have to cease. Jesus never gave any indication that these 'times' would be suspended (Luke 21:24). The times of the Gentiles would continue until the return of Christ (Luke 21:25-27), until these times are fulfilled. The fourth beast that destroyed the city and the temple in 70 AD, as predicted by Jesus (Luke 21:20-24), is not just the same beast at the end, but of necessity it is the beast that continues to exist all through the remainder of the 'times of the Gentiles'. The Gentile beasts are the reason for the label attached to the age. If the fourth beast stopped existing, the 'times of the Gentiles' would have to come to an end.[139]

Nebuchadnezzar's entire experience is an allegory that has two specific meanings. It certainly shows how the beast character disappears when the Most High is acknowledged. It shows the principle that explains how the Roman beast has a state of 'is not' when the harlot is on top. However, his seven years in the character of a beast brings out a second meaning for his allegorical experience.

Nebuchadnezzar's Seven Years as a Beast

Often the number seven is used prophetically as representing completeness or totality. Nebuchadnezzar's experience represents the completeness of the 'times of the Gentiles' (Luke 21:24). The seven years he spent in the character of a beast is the entire time of the Gentile world powers and age. This time spans from the kingdom of Babylon, the head of fine gold in the Gentile statue, to the coming of 'the stone cut out without hands' that destroys the entire image (Dan. 2:31-35). After the destruction of the Gentile statue, the stone that struck the image becomes a great mountain that fills the entire earth (Dan. 2:44-45).

This is the time when the Most High is acknowledged as the possessor of the heavens and the earth (Gen. 14:19). It will be the time when the Melchizedek priest will represent the Most High on the earth, for the blessing of Israel and the blessing of the earth. This priest is Jesus Christ, the Messiah and Prince for Israel, and the glorified Son of Man whose reign and dominion will fill the earth as a great mountain. This Melchizedek is a kingly priest, whose rule and judgments in righteousness fill the earth with peace (Heb. 7:1-3). At the end of the seven years Nebuchadnezzar was made to stand up and acknowledge the Most High. This will happen when the times of the Gentiles are fulfilled (Luke 21:24) and the Gentile image is destroyed.

We see that instead of thinking of a specific time when the Roman Empire fell and stopped existing as an empire, we should more properly be thinking of the character of the beast and whether this character is hidden or displayed. We should have learned by now that the character of prophetic objects has more to do with properly understanding their role in prophecy, more so than specific points in time. Comprehending the moral character of the individual churches was of greater importance than knowing a specific time when Smyrna replaced Ephesus. Understanding the character of Babylon is more useful than knowing where its ancient geographical location is. Jezebel is corrupt. Sardis is spiritually dead. How important is it to be able to see and comprehend these moral realities of the professing church as judged by God? So then we understand the 'is not' period of the beast is not referring to the Empire being overthrown, but it being Christianized by the whore and the beast losing its character.

One further point can then be made to aid our understanding of the three epochs of the fourth beast. The time elements in the phrase describing the three different states, when simplified, are 'was', and 'is', and 'will be' – past, present, and future. The time elements do not relate to John and his time on the earth or his life. During John's life the epoch of the beast was the first state – the beast that 'was'. The harlot was not riding the beast in the time of John's life. So we find that the time elements describing the three states of the fourth beast are not in relation to John's life, but instead related only to the vision itself and what John actually sees. The vision – the harlot riding the beast – is itself in the present tense, and so, depicts the state of the beast that is described as in the present tense. This is the second period, the state that 'is' not.

The Double Meaning of the Seven Heads

We find in the angel's interpretation a few more allegories to speak of that are associated directly or indirectly with the harlot and the beast. The first meaning of the seven heads of the beast, as discussed earlier, was that they are seven mountains. This meaning points to the city of Rome, which is related to both the beast and the harlot. Rome is, in fact, the second meaning of the woman. She is that great city, the capital city of the beast as well as the central location of Jezebel (Rev. 17:18).

The second meaning of the seven heads is that, *"There are also seven kings. Five have fallen, one is, and the other has not yet come. And when he comes, he must continue a short time."* (Rev. 17:10) These seven kings are intimately connected to the Roman beast as heads. They are the Caesars as heads of the Roman Empire. In one sense 'seven kings' is the complete picture of the Caesars. However, the angel does begin counting. In this case I would think that the timing of these Caesars is related to John and the writing of the book of Revelation and his exile to the isle of Patmos. Five Caesars preceded

John's exile. One was present at that time and was responsible for John being on Patmos. If Caesars are being counted, it is important to remember they are being counted by God and not by man. I suspect that the Caesar yet to come is Constantine.

The King and the Kingdom: the Last Caesar

In contrast to the above there could be a different view of counting Caesars. If the time element refers to the harlot instead of John's exile, then I would think the one 'that is' would be referring to Constantine, who was instrumental in allowing the harlot to ascend the beast. He would be the Caesar most likely in the present tense of the vision – the one 'that is'. In this case Napoleon possibly would be the one yet to come. I know men do not consider Napoleon a Caesar, but possibly God does.

In the greatest sense, seven kings refer to the complete picture of Caesars to rule over the empire. The angel divides and counts only to distinguish the last two important ones from God's perspective – Constantine and Napoleon. The time element the angel gives in his interpretation relating to the seven kings more likely refers to the vision and not to John's life, as we saw to be true with the previous time elements involving the epochs of the beast. This would most likely be the proper understanding. So then, 'five kings have fallen' would be a simple reference to all the Caesars that preceded Constantine. He is the one 'that is' as to the present tense of the vision. He helped the harlot ascend and control the beast in the time that the beast 'is not'.

In the above explanation we may grasp insights into the double meaning of the prophetic number 'seven'. When we spoke previously of the seven churches we understood that together we see a complete picture of the entire time of Christendom on the earth. But we also saw there were seven distinct states through time forming this complete picture. This is a similar understanding of the seven kings. It is a complete picture of all the Caesars, yet when the angel divides and counts, it is for the purpose of pointing out certain individuals.

Regardless, I believe the seven kings are referring to Caesars, the heads of the Roman Empire and beast. Why else would the angel be listing a succession of seven? This understanding becomes important when we address the next verse given by the angel in the interpretation.

Revelation 17:11

"The beast that was, and is not, is himself also the eighth, and is of the seven, and is going to perdition."

Just as king Nebuchadnezzar and the Babylonian kingdom itself are both the head of gold in the Gentile image (Dan. 2:37-38), so the second meaning of the beast is that he is, in fact, also a Caesar. The beast is the Roman Empire as well as the last Caesar. *"The beast... is himself also the eighth, and is of the seven..."* The seven kings are Caesars and the beast is of the seven – he is part of the 'complete picture' of Caesars associated with the Roman beast. When God counts the Caesars, the beast himself is the eighth and last one that will ever come, for he himself will go into perdition. The double meaning of the prophetic term 'beast' is both the kingdom and the king (Dan. 7:17, 23).

This insight itself will clear up many misunderstandings associated with the current study of prophecy. I'll jump right into the fray by saying that I believe the last Caesar is distinct from the Antichrist. They are not one and the same. The Antichrist is not the head of the revived Roman beast. However, before delving into this distinction let us finish the interpretation given by the angel.

The Ten Horns: the Kings and their Kingdoms

Revelation 17:12-14

"The ten horns which you saw are ten kings who have received no kingdom as yet, but they receive authority for one hour as kings with the beast. (13) These are of one mind, and they will give their power and authority to the beast. (14) These will make war with the Lamb, and the Lamb will overcome them,

for He is Lord of lords and King of kings; and those who are with Him are called, chosen, and faithful."

The ten horns is the allegory being interpreted by the angel in the above passage. The double meaning of the horns is that they are both ten kings and ten kingdoms (Rev. 17:12). One thing that is both common and significant to all the different visions in Scripture of the fourth Gentile beast is that it always has ten horns. This is true when Daniel sees it (Dan. 7). It is true both times John sees the beast (Rev. 13, 17).

If we consider all the visions and prophecies that involve the fourth beast we should see that the ten horns serve a very specific purpose associated with its existence. The beast itself saunters through three states or epochs – this is its existence until it is destroyed. The ten horns have nothing to do with the beast that 'was' – the first period. The ten horns really haven't much to do with the harlot riding on top of the beast – the second epoch when the beast 'is not'. Where the horns become active is in bringing an end to the second state of the beast and the transition to the third – when the beast regains its character and ascends out of the bottomless pit. The power and prominence of the ten kings and kingdoms are shown during the third period of the beast.[140]

The allegory of the ten horns always points to the end, when prophecy will be fulfilled. The ten horns involve the final state of the Roman beast. The only part of the above quoted passage that isn't associated with the third and final epoch of the beast is the first part of verse twelve (12) – *"The ten horns which you saw are ten kings who have received no kingdom as yet..."* The remainder of the above quoted passage explains the involvement of the ten kings and their kingdoms in the activity of the Roman Empire and its last Caesar in the final epoch. During this time the horns have crowns (Rev. 13:1). During this time they have received their kingdoms and authority as kings. During this time the ten unanimously give their power and authority to the last Caesar (Rev. 17:13). They go off together with him to Armageddon, to make war against the Lamb and those with Him (Rev. 17:14). In the final state Satan has the ten kings along with the last Caesar thinking they can maintain possession of the earth away from God and the Lamb. The interesting thing is that we get greater detail of this rise to power by the Caesar and the Roman beast in the book of Daniel.

The Little Horn gains Power

Daniel 7:7-8

"After this I saw in the night visions, and behold, a fourth beast, dreadful and terrible, exceedingly strong. It had huge iron teeth; it was devouring, breaking in pieces, and trampling the residue with its feet. It was different from all the beasts that were before it, and it had ten horns. (8) I was considering the horns, and there was another horn, a little one, coming up among them, before whom three of the first horns were plucked out by the roots. And there, in this horn, were eyes like the eyes of a man, and a mouth speaking pompous words."

The last Caesar is the little horn that comes up among the ten horns and uproots three. This uprooting would have to be by war and conquest. Once he wins these three kingdoms the remaining kings and kingdoms of the ten relinquish their power and authority to him. This is what forms the power of the revived Roman Empire. These kingdoms are formerly Christian kingdoms, for when the ten have their power and crowns with the beast, the harlot has been destroyed. These help the Caesar and the Roman beast to manifest their blasphemous and anti-Christian character (Dan. 7:11, Rev. 13:5-6).

The Judgment of the Babylonian Harlot

The last portion of the angel's interpretation ends the chapter (Rev. 17). This passage reverts back to the second period of the beast, when the harlot was sitting on top and had her religious influence over the Empire. It concerns the judgment of the Babylonian harlot and the providential hand of God using the ten kings to accomplish His will (Rev. 17:17). This is an example of the Biblical principle that judgment starts at the house of God. God uses a greater evil and worldliness to judge that which should have represented Him in the earth and world. God judges His house first, *before* He judges the world. In historical time verses 15-17 occur *before* verses 12-14.

Revelation 17:15-17

"Then he said to me, "The waters which you saw, where the harlot sits, are peoples, multitudes, nations, and tongues. (16) And the ten horns which you saw on the beast, these will hate the harlot, make her desolate and naked, eat her flesh and burn her with fire. (17) For God has put it into their hearts to fulfill His purpose, to be of one mind, and to give their kingdom to the beast, until the words of God are fulfilled."

The influence that intoxicates the inhabitants of the earth is the same intoxicating influence she has over the inhabitants of the many waters. This is the Gentile world beyond the Roman earth. Jezebel's abominations and fornications stretch far and wide. The professing church is basically a Gentile church – until the fullness of the Gentiles has come in (Rom. 11:25).

The ten horns as John saw them in this vision were without crowns and without kingdoms as yet. Their rise to power in their individual kingdoms seems to be a result of an anti-Christian bigotry and persecution – the ten horns will hate the harlot. I believe that they come to power as kings and receive their kingdoms before the last Caesar becomes apparent (Dan. 7:8, 20, 24). But it seems they are kings in power in order to destroy the harlot's influence. Verse sixteen (16) above may better read, *"And the ten horns which you saw, and the beast, these will hate the harlot..."* Because the beast has a double meaning – the revived Roman Empire and the last Caesar – it is not clear whether the Caesar is present as yet and acting with the ten kings to destroy the harlot. Regardless, it remains true that the harlot is destroyed before the Roman beast is destroyed. Verse sixteen (16) occurs in the history of time before verse fourteen (14).

Chapter 15: Endnotes

[136] Ephesians 1:11 – *"...being predestined according to the purpose of Him who works all things according to the counsel of His will..."* Many people believe the majority of events and things are ordered by the human will or the will of the creature. Even many believers have this viewpoint. The Arminian leaven that exalts the free will of the creature, and human performance and accomplishment, helps us to accept this mindset. If we walk by sight we fall into this. We look around and see people making all kinds of decisions, and we reason that man has this free will by which he may seek God if he pleases, or reject God by simple human reasoning. This is an improper and unbiblical view of man's will as a fallen creature. I do not doubt that Adam in innocence had the freedom and ability to choose to obey God or listen to the devil. However, fallen man does not have this same freedom and ability. Sin in the flesh is his master, and he is its slave (John 8:34, Rom. 5:12-14, 17, 21).

The Arminian leaven will blind a believer to a proper walk of faith, and will encourage him to walk by his senses and to trust in some measure in the human condition. At its core is the stubborn belief that there is still good in fallen man, and by this good man can do right and do well and be saved. This is a Biblical fallacy. God spent four thousand years proving this thinking wrong. For four thousand years God tested fallen man in responsibility, looking for obedience. He found no fruit. And so we're going to nonchalantly take back up these thoughts of Arminianism and add them to all our Christian doctrines? After four thousand years? By them the believer is blind to who God really is, what God really is doing, what really is the work of God. By them the believer is blind to the understanding of the sovereignty and providence of God.

[137] There are doctrines and teachings in the Christian world that have this obvious mindset. They get the believer to focus on life in the world and on this earth. He stops being a stranger and pilgrim on a walk in a wilderness, and becomes a dweller on the earth. The doctrines often are innocent enough – emotions, relationships, family, and money. But they are crafted in such an earthly way that they subtly lead the believer away from his true calling and the true doctrines of the body of Christ. At times the teachings are obvious in what they are emphasizing and implying. Other times, as I said, it is very innocently presented as sound Christian teaching. But the lifestyle that is produced is unquestionably connected with this world.

This is the general warning and principle. As a believer you have to understand it and by it judge all that you hear and are taught. I cannot do it for you. You have to understand Christian maturity and Christian hope for yourself. You have to understand the believer's calling, the church's calling. Her calling is her purpose. You won't find her purpose anywhere else other than in her calling. Many modern Christian teachings deny this calling, or at least do a great job at obscuring it. It isn't done in an obvious evil way, but in a religious way. Modern Christian doctrine makes the listener a dweller of the earth and world.

[138] The beasts come forth by the providence of God and according to His counsel and plan. God is responsible for all civil authority. The believer should be able to see and understand the counsel and plan of God — it is found in His Word and we have been given the Spirit of truth and the mind of Christ. Only by these understandings will we be able to see the providential hand of God at work. At this time God allows evil to grow, ripen, and prosper. It will all serve His purpose. He may restrict its full display at this time, but He does not judge it directly (II Thess. 2:6-7). God acts in goodness and grace at this present time. For the most part, He uses the preaching of the gospel to accomplish His work. In the coming dispensation, by the use of His direct power, He will righteously judge all the evil and put it away. But we are not in that dispensation at this time, are we?

Other than knowing the plan of God, recognizing His providence, and understanding His authority in setting up civil powers, what should be our response? Should we buy guns and arm ourselves? Should we initiate civil unrest and protests against the powers God has set? Should the professing church seek civil power and office?

Revelation 13:10

"He who leads into captivity shall go into captivity; he who kills with the sword must be killed with the sword. Here is the patience and the faith of the saints."

It is patience and faith in the plan and sovereignty of God. Do we think Peter was justified in cutting off the ear of the servant in Gethsemane (Matt. 26:52)? Jesus corrects him by making a similar statement to him at that time.

What then should we be doing? We should learn how to be faithful to Christ in the midst of evil. Learn how to be mature and patient, endure sufferings now, and persevere. Learn how to keep the Word of His patience (Rev. 3:10). Learn how to be found in Philadelphia. This is the grace He gives for the present situation, for the present circumstances. This is the grace He gives for the present need. Don't allow some well-meaning brother to sway you that there is anything different, or something more (glory on this earth and great things to be done). The glory will only be realized beyond this world and beyond this physical earth.

[139] For a biblical understand detailing the 'times of the Gentiles' as the label assigned to the age, please consult the second book of the Son of Man series, 'The Blessed Hope of the Church' and read chapter thirteen (13), titled 'This Present Evil Age'.

[140] In Nebuchadnezzar's dream of the great image, the fourth and fifth distinguishing portions of the image represent the fourth beast (Dan 2:33). Although there are five distinct sections of the image, there are only four Gentile beasts (Dan. 7:17). The fourth beast is represented by the fourth and fifth section of the Gentile statue. The legs of iron, and the feet and toes partly of iron and partly of clay, are two separate sections, but in one sense treated the same—they correspond to the same fourth beast. The fifth section of the image, its feet and toes, represents the final period of the fourth beast. It is the final state because the stone made without hands strikes the statue in the feet and toes. The strike of the stone is the return of the Son of Man to this earth to judge and destroy the Gentile powers. My point is that the ten toes are seen only in this last state of the Roman beast. If you allow that the ten toes represent the ten horns, then it shows us when the ten kings have their power and kingdoms and activity.

Chapter 16:
The Last Caesar and the Antichrist

The common thought about Biblical prophecy and the instruments of evil that Satan brings forth at the end of the age is that the Antichrist will be the leader of the revived Roman Empire. I mentioned in an earlier chapter that I didn't believe this is what the Scriptures actually teach and that I would explain myself concerning this. However, regardless of whether there is to be a Caesar separate from an Antichrist, we should agree that the full power and display of evil on the earth occurs after Satan's removal from the heavens. The casting of Satan down to the earth is an event full of the purpose of God. That is when the world sees the full unbridled display of evil that issues forth from the god of this age, and his desperate attempt to maintain his control of the earth.

Satan's evil instruments that will be present on the earth at the end of the age are exactly what God will judge and destroy. Purpose? God orders all events according to the counsel of His will (Eph. 1:11). His sovereign work – providence, judgment, or grace – will serve to bring out the full manifestation of His glory. Whether it is sovereign judgment of the evil or His faithfulness to fulfill all His promises in sovereign grace to Israel, it will glorify God above all else.

The Transition at the end of the Age

These events point to the end of the age. There is a distinct understanding of what will exist and what will happen at the end. It is different from that of the present order and course of things. The end of the age is a period of transition to a new age – the millennium and the reign and dominion of the Son of Man over all creation. It would be helpful if we could list the major events that prophecy and the Scriptures tell us will take place in this period of transition between the two ages.

- The wheat will be removed from the field of the world (Matt. 13:30). The rapture of the true church to the heavens is the first significant event signaling the very beginning of this transition period. There is no prophetic event or any prophecies to be fulfilled before the glorification of the body of Christ. If the church is the mystery of God hidden from prophecy, then her rapture is hidden as well. Paul does say in speaking of the event, *"Behold, I tell you a mystery."* (I Cor. 15:46-54) This event will be one of the greatest works of God's sovereign power and grace ever known (Eph. 1:17-23).

  The true church is the heavenly calling. The remnant of Israel is the earthly calling. God will not and cannot recognize Israel in their calling as His people again until that which now has the principle of God's calling is finished and out of the way. When Philadelphia is taken and Laodicea is spewed out of the Lord's mouth and no longer acknowledged, then God can choose and seal a Jewish remnant on the earth. He has to stop acknowledging the church on the earth before He can recognize a remnant from Israel on the earth. The rapture of the true church must be first and precedes many things. Until Israel is acknowledged again in their calling, prophecy and time being counted cannot move forward or resume.

The rapture removes the true church from the earth and out of the way, in this regard.

- The tares of Christendom are bundled together and left in the field of the world. They are destined to be burned (Matt. 13:30, 40-42, 49-50). It seems certain that what remains of the professing church will be judged and destroyed before the judgment of the world (Rev. 17:16-17). Judgment starts first at the house of God.

- The rapture of the church is the realization of the heavenly calling of the church. After the rapture God then can turn back to Israel and deal with them in their earthly calling. When Israel rejected Jesus as their Messiah it resulted in the setting aside of Israel and their calling in the plan and counsels of God. It resulted in Messiah and all promises and prophecy associated with Messiah being set aside. Israel, as a house of God, will remain desolate until they physically see Jesus Christ again, and the remnant says to Him, *"Blessed is He who comes in the name of the Lord (Jehovah)."* (Matt. 23:37-39) *The principle is that until the heavenly calling is fulfilled, God will not turn back to the earthly calling in Israel.* After the true church is removed from the earth and during the transition period, God will choose and seal a Jewish remnant. He will preserve and protect them during the transition period, even pouring out His Spirit on them, *among the remnant whom the Lord calls* (Joel 2:28-32).

- The dragon will be cast out of the heavens and down to the earth, and he will know his time is short (3½ yrs.). There will be great rejoicing in the heavens by those (the church) now residing there, but it will be woe to the inhabitants of the earth and sea (Rev. 12:7-13). Satan will attempt to maintain control over the earth and world. He will bring forth two great and final instruments of evil in his desperation, and to them he will give all his power and authority.[141]

- The first instrument of Satan's evil in the end is the revived Roman beast and its corresponding Caesar. The beast represents both. The revived Roman Empire is the last form of the fourth beast of Daniel 7. The last Caesar is the little horn among the ten horns talked about in that chapter. The final form of the Roman Empire is that which 'will be present' and 'will ascend out of the bottomless pit' (Rev. 17:8, 11:7).

- The second instrument of Satan's final evil is another beast (Rev. 13:11). It comes up distinctly out of the earth as a contrast to the four beasts of Daniel that all come up out of the Great Sea (Dan. 7:2-3). This beast has two horns like a lamb, but speaks like the dragon who gave it authority. All beasts are earthly powers or kingdoms. All beasts are also the heads of their respective domain of power. This beast is no different – there is a sphere of earthly power and the head of it. This king is the Antichrist.

- Satan has a short time to bring forth the full perfection of his evil. Events take place. Judgments are trumpeted or poured out from the heavens upon the earth. The major players of the prophetic judgment of the world are found gathered at Armageddon (Rev. 16:12-16, 19:19) – the last Caesar, the kings of the earth and of the whole world, their armies, and the false prophet (Antichrist). All these are destroyed by the return of the Son of Man on the white horse with His armies.

- *These two* (the last Caesar and the false prophet – the Antichrist) *were cast alive into the lake of fire burning with brimstone. The rest were killed with the sword which proceeded from the mouth of Him who sat on the horse... Then I saw an angel...he laid hold of the dragon, that serpent of old, who is the devil and Satan, and bound him for a thousand years; and cast him into the bottomless pit..."* (Rev. 19:19 – 20:3)

These are the main events in the transition period between this age and the age to come. There are other things of course. God restores a Jewish remnant to the Promised Land. God deals with the remainder of unbelieving Israel as well as judging the remaining Gentile nations. These subjects are the main focus of bible prophecy for they deal with the earth, with Israel, and with God's government of the earth.

The Present Course of Things

When we talk of the course of this present age we can make four overall observations depicting its general characteristics as borne out in Scripture.

1. Israel is set aside at this present time. They are not God's people, and He is not their God. Judaism, as God's religion of the earth, is set aside as well. Jerusalem and the temple were destroyed. The principle of God's government of the earth is not with Israel. The principle of God's calling as a people is not with Israel. There are many consequences to the fact that Israel is set aside by God at this present time. The earth and prophecy are not being dealt with by God, and time is not being counted. Because Messiah was rejected by Israel, this title and the corresponding Messianic kingdom in Israel, and all associated promises to Israel are set aside for the time being.[142]

2. The principle of government is with the Gentiles and will remain that way until the return of the Son of Man to this earth. The label for this present age is 'the times of the Gentiles' and involves Nebuchadnezzar's great image and Daniel's visions of the four beasts (Luke 21:24, Dan. 2:31-35, 7:2-8).

3. The principle of God's calling is currently with the body of Christ. When the Son of Man was glorified to the right hand of God, then the Holy Spirit was sent down to gather in His body, the church, from out of the condemned world (John 7:38-39, 12:31). The present age is a time in which God shows goodness and grace. Jesus Christ builds His church in the heavens, by a heavenly calling and citizenship, and God's workmanship in this effort is incorruptible and eternal (Eph. 2:4-10). In contrast, on the earth man builds the house of God upon the foundation that Paul had laid as a wise master

builder (I Cor. 3:9-15). This is the work of man and is very corruptible, and has been proven corrupt by God.

4. The course of the age is that evil was present at the beginning, and that it grows and ripens to full fruit at the end. This is seen in both principles – the government of the earth in the Gentiles and the calling of God with the professing church. Both entities have failed miserably in their corporate responsibilities. Evil has entered in both and is spreading and growing. The only solution for both is the sovereign power of God that will be demonstrated either in judgment or grace. However, this sovereign work of God waits for the end of the age (Matt. 13:40-42, 49-50).

God presently restrains Evil

2 Thessalonians 2:6-7

"And now you know what is restraining, that he may be revealed in his own time. For the mystery of lawlessness is already at work; only He who now restrains will do so until He is taken out of the way."

God restrains the full display of evil in the church world at this present time. It is clear that the mystery of lawlessness was already at work in the church in Paul's days. This mystery of sin and corruption has been growing in Christendom from the first century. The full display of evil is hindered by the presence of the Holy Spirit in the true church on the earth – the habitation of God in the Spirit (Eph. 2:22). When the true church is removed to the heavens, the restraints on evil will then be lifted. What remains of the professing church will fall away (apostasy) and the man of sin will be revealed (II Thess. 2:3, 8-10).

The Two Beasts – one from the Sea and one from the Earth

But who is this man of sin and lawlessness spoken of by Paul? Is it the Caesar or the Antichrist, or are they one and the same? The passage in II Thessalonians does not definitively identify who the lawless one is (II Thess. 2:8-11). It could be a blasphemous civil power like a Caesar, who enjoys idolatry and self-deification. The second beast causes the whole earth to worship the first beast (Rev. 13:11-12). This would be the deifying of the first beast, and idolatry encouraged and enforced by the second. The man of sin does exalt himself above all that is called God and shows himself that he is God (II Thess. 2:4).

The first beast is worshiped along with the dragon (Rev. 13:4), and a mouth is given to him speaking great things and blasphemies (Rev. 13:5, Dan. 7:8, 11, 20, 24-25). The first beast is anti-Christian having rid himself of the harlot. He speaks blasphemy against God and God's name. He does the same against God's tabernacle and those who dwell in heaven (this is the church – Rev. 13:6).

The second beast is a bit different from the Roman beast. As a beast it will also be a king and an earthly power. But this beast rises up out of the earth. It does not come up out of the Gentile sea. This is an important distinction, for the terminology can easily be related to the Jews and Judaism. They have the earthly calling, and Judaism is God's religion for the earth and for man in Adam. Everything in Judaism is connected to the world and the first creation. Judaism is the vine of the earth, and as such the unbelieving Jews will be subject to the wrath of God (Rev. 14:19). This beast that comes up out of the earth is among the Jews and associated with Judaism. Doesn't John speak of similar things?

The Antichrist is associated with Judaism and a false Messiah

1 John 2:22

"Who is a liar but he who denies that Jesus is the Christ? He is antichrist who denies the Father and the Son."

1 John 4:3

"...and every spirit that does not confess that Jesus Christ has come in the flesh is not of God. And this is the spirit of the

Antichrist, which you have heard was coming, and is now already in the world."

2 John 1:7

"For many deceivers have gone out into the world who do not confess Jesus Christ as coming in the flesh. This is a deceiver and an antichrist."

In many respects the beliefs of the Antichrist are the same as the beliefs of the Jews. They deny the revelation of the Father given by the Son (John 15:22-24). They deny that Jesus is their Messiah and King. They deny that Messiah has already visited them. The Antichrist is a religious Jewish entity associated with Judaism.

John 5:43

"I have come in My Father's name, and you do not receive Me; if another comes in his own name, him you will receive."

The Antichrist is who Jesus is referring to in this passage. He will be the other one who will come in his own name to the Jews. He will not have witness and testimony as to who he is, but the nation will receive him as the Messiah.[143] An interesting contrast is that when Jesus came to Israel, the small Jewish remnant received Him, while the nation as a whole rejected Him. When the Antichrist comes in the end it will be the opposite – the unbelieving nation will receive him, while the elect Jewish remnant rejects him (Matt. 24:24).

The second beast in Revelation 13 is of the earth and looks like a lamb. This is an imitation of Jesus Christ, the slain Lamb. This is a false king, a false Christ, and false Messiah. He doesn't have seven horns as Jesus, the slain Lamb in the midst of the throne (Rev. 5:6), and thus the divine perfection of power. But he has two horns giving him title to his earthly power. This will most likely be in Judah.

Pilate and Herod in Type

There is another significant parallelism I want to point out on this subject. In the time Jesus came to Israel the Roman Empire was in power with Caesars as their kings. The representative of the Romans in Jerusalem was Pilate. But there was another king in Judah of the Jewish persuasion – Herod. He was mostly a false king of Judah, but he was there. Jesus was taken before him during His trial (Luke 23:7-11).

When Jesus comes a second time there will again be these two authorities. There will be a Caesar over the revived Roman Empire, but also there will be a false king in Jerusalem among the Jews. This will be the Antichrist. He will exercise power in the presence of the Roman beast and its Caesar, just as Herod did of old. Herod serves as a type of what is to come.

The Power, Signs, and Lying Wonders

Revelation 13:13-15

"He performs great signs, so that he even makes fire come down from heaven on the earth in the sight of men. (14) And he deceives those who dwell on the earth by those signs which he was granted to do in the sight of the beast, telling those who dwell on the earth to make an image to the beast who was wounded by the sword and lived. (15) He was granted power to give breath to the image of the beast, that the image of the beast should both speak and cause as many as would not worship the image of the beast to be killed."

The calling of fire down from heaven mimics the contest between Elijah and the prophets of Baal (I Kings 18:17-39). Elijah demonstrated that, *"The Lord, He is God."* In the end with the Antichrist, Israel will turn back to idolatry and apostasy rather than away from it. Israel as a whole will follow after the Antichrist. Their spiritual condition at the end of the age will be seven times worse than at first with Baal (Matt. 12:43-45). The fire from heaven is particularly a Jewish sign. And what is the character of Judaism? *"The Jews request a sign."* (I Cor. 1:22)

The Unholy Trinity of Evil at the End of the Age

After Satan is cast down from the heavens to the earth and the restraints to evil are removed, there will be a trinity of evil on the earth. Satan as the god and source of evil, the first beast having been given his throne and all his authority and power on the earth, and the second beast exercising that power and authority in the presence of the first beast. This is a direct mimicking of the trinity of the Godhead – the Father, Son, and Holy Spirit.

Mark 13:22

"For false Christs and false prophets will arise, and give signs and wonders to deceive, if possible, even the elect."

The Jewish remnant will not be deceived by the Antichrist or others. They are looking for and expecting the fulfillment of the promise of Messiah to Israel. Jehovah will keep these elect ones from being fooled (Matt. 24:4-11). They are chosen and preserved by the sovereign grace of God. They will be a marked remnant in the midst of a deceived and idolatrous nation (Rev. 7:1-8).

The Character of the end-time Remnant

They are also the remnant that will have the Spirit of Jehovah poured out *on them* (Joel 2:28-32). However, 'on them' is very different than the Spirit of God 'in them' as a seal of redemption in Christ. The former is very Jewish, while the latter is the seal of the sons of God in Christianity (Gal. 3:26, 4:6, Eph. 1:13-14). Poured out on them is like the Jewish prophets of old, and leads to Jewish signs like visions and dreams and prophesying. These things aren't Christian signs? No, they are the result of the Spirit poured out on a person, as Daniel had dreams and visions, and Isaiah and Jeremiah prophesied. It is the Spirit of God on them and by measure (John 3:34).

John 4:48

"Then Jesus said to him, "Unless you people see signs and wonders, you will by no means believe."

Remember Judaism is a walk by sight and signs. It is the character of Judaism and the character of the Jewish people. When the Jewish remnant is sealed by God at the end of the age, He will deal with them in Judaism and by Jewish ways. This remnant will not believe until they see. They will not receive any false Christs and false prophets. But they will not believe in Jesus as their Messiah until they look on Him whom they have pierced and they say, *"Blessed is He who comes in the name of Jehovah."* (Zech. 12:9-10, Matt. 23:37-39) They will be like Thomas in their faith (John 20:26-29). For that matter, they will be like all eleven disciples who did not believe until they saw with their eyes Jesus raised from the dead. It is remarkable how the twelve disciples are often used in Scripture as a type/shadow of the Jewish remnant at the end of the age. They are used as a type in this way quite extensively.

The Gospel of the Kingdom

We should not be looking for a Jewish remnant in the tribulation period going throughout the entire world evangelizing with a Christian gospel, and achieving remarkable results (Rev. 7:4-10). This thought is such a mismatch of Biblical principles and characteristics, and is a contradiction of sound spiritual reasoning.

The gospel of the kingdom preached in all the world at the end of the age is not the Christian gospel. It is a message of warning from God of impending judgment on the world (Matt. 24:14). The gospel of the kingdom is that God is soon to make the world and the earth His kingdom (Rev. 10:15, 12:10, and 14:6-7). The Jewish end-time remnant may in fact have this message and be spreading it, but it is the gospel of the physical kingdom of God coming on the earth that the Jews have always expected from prophecy. The gospel of the coming kingdom is a very Jewish message and a very earthly message. It is a witness and warning to the nations, not the means of converting and saving them. The same is true of the testimony of the two witnesses in Jerusalem – they testify on behalf of Jehovah, the true Lord of the earth (Rev. 11:4). Their testimony for 3½ years doesn't attract positive attention from anybody except the remnant inside of Israel (Rev. 11:1). Think of the years that Noah preached. It was a warning of approaching judgment and by his faith he condemned the world (Heb. 11:7). We only see eight people enter the ark (II Pet. 2:5).

The Character of the Jewish Remnant in the Psalms

The Jewish remnant will have a certain character according to Judaism. They are the elect ones crying out day and night for deliverance and vengeance during Jacob's trouble. *"Avenge me of my adversary."* (Luke 18:1-8) This describes the Jewish character and a walk by sight, and a certain looking for vengeance. It is also this future Jewish remnant in the Psalms crying out to Jehovah, asking how long will the wicked prosper, and how long will Jehovah remain silent (Ps. 94, 83, 79, 74, 73, 68-71, etc.). The Psalms cannot be properly understood without having the character of the future Jewish remnant in mind. In many instances it is their crying out for vengeance and deliverance, as well as Christ identifying with the sufferings of the remnant.

Psalm 59:1-13

"Deliver me from my enemies, O my God;
Defend me from those who rise up against me.
Deliver me from the workers of iniquity,
And save me from bloodthirsty men.

For look, they lie in wait for my life;
The mighty gather against me,
Not for my transgression nor for my sin, O Lord.
They run and prepare themselves through no fault of mine.

Awake to help me, and behold!
You therefore, O Lord God of hosts, the God of Israel,
Awake to punish all the nations;
Do not be merciful to any wicked transgressors. Selah

At evening they return,
They growl like a dog,

And go all around the city.
Indeed, they belch with their mouth;
Swords are in their lips;
For they say, "Who hears?"

But You, O Lord, shall laugh at them;
You shall have all the nations in derision.
I will wait for You, O You his Strength;
For God is my defense.
My God of mercy shall come to meet me;
God shall let me see my desire on my enemies.

Do not slay them, lest my people forget;
Scatter them by Your power,
And bring them down,
O Lord our shield.
For the sin of their mouth and the words of their lips,
Let them even be taken in their pride,
And for the cursing and lying which they speak.
Consume them in wrath, consume them,
That they may not be;
And let them know that God rules in Jacob
To the ends of the earth. Selah"

The distinct signature of the character of the future remnant is seen all over the above psalm. However, this is not Christian character. It is not the way to teach Christians to pray (Luke 18:1). In the time of grace and the gospel we tolerate evil prospering around us, and never cry out for vengeance upon it. How do you turn the other cheek if you are crying out for vengeance on the one who slapped you? True believers suffer persecutions now and endure trials with perseverance, knowing that we are in Christ and will be found in glory with Him. We can suffer reproaches and distresses now, for His grace is sufficient strength for our present need. And He has gone away to prepare a place for us in the Father's house, in the heavens and in glory.

God will avenge His elect Jewish remnant that cries out constantly to Him, though He bears long with them (Luke 18:7-8). But God bears long with them because they have no walk of faith or heavenly Christian hopes. God preserves them and eventually avenges them on the earth because God has to remain faithful to keep His promises to Israel. It is toward the elect remnant of Israel that His sovereign grace is shown. The true church, which had the walk of faith on the earth, is now gone. So then, Jesus asks the question, *"...when the Son of Man comes, will He really find faith on the earth?"*

The Character of the coming Age

All of this will take place during the transition period between the two ages. The present age has the character of a walk by faith by the true church in the wilderness. Our faith is the substance of the things we hope for, and all our hopes are in glory. Christ in the believer, the hope of glory (Col. 1:27). The age that is coming upon the earth is one where every eye will see Him.

Revelation 1:7

"Behold, He is coming with clouds, and every eye will see Him, even they who pierced Him. And all the tribes of the earth will mourn because of Him. Even so, Amen."

In a certain sense this gives you the character of things on the earth in the coming age – every eye will see (Matt. 24:30). Allow me to ask this question. Is this the character of Christianity or Judaism? In the coming age and on the millennial earth certain truths will be manifested, very different from the previous age involving the church and gospel and a King hidden away in heaven.

1. God will make a new covenant with the two divided houses of Israel, finally bringing the two back together (Jer. 31:31, Heb. 8:8). The two sticks will be joined as one (Ez. 37:15-20). This is at the beginning of the new age, the millennium, when the Jewish remnant is restored in the Promised Land.

Ezekiel 37:21-28

"Then say to them, 'Thus says the Lord God: "Surely I will take the children of Israel from among the nations, wherever they have gone, and will gather them from every side and bring them into their own land; (22) and I will make them one nation in the land, on the mountains of Israel; and one king shall be king over them all; they shall no longer be two nations, nor shall they ever be divided into two kingdoms again. (23) They shall not defile themselves anymore with their idols, nor with their detestable things, nor with any of their transgressions; but I will deliver them from all their dwelling places in which they have sinned, and will cleanse them. Then they shall be My people, and I will be their God.

(24) "David My servant shall be king over them, and they shall all have one shepherd; they shall also walk in My judgments and observe My statutes, and do them. (25) Then they shall dwell in the land that I have given to Jacob My servant, where your fathers dwelt; and they shall dwell there, they, their children, and their children's children, forever; and My servant David shall be their prince forever. (26) Moreover I will make a covenant of peace with them, and it shall be an everlasting covenant with them; I will establish them and multiply them, and I will set My sanctuary in their midst forevermore. (27) My tabernacle also shall be over them; indeed I will be their God, and they shall be My people. (28) The nations also will know that I, the Lord, sanctify Israel, when My sanctuary is in their midst forevermore."

The new covenant will reunite the two houses of Israel as one (Jer. 31:31). It is for the purpose of blessing and prospering this Jewish remnant in the land.

2. The new covenant in its formal sense and plain language is a Jewish covenant. It replaces the first covenant they had long ago that passed away. As most of the covenants are in their formal character (the letter of the covenant), the new covenant is for Israel when they are restored in the land. Concerning this new covenant Jehovah says, *"Behold the days are coming...when I will make a new covenant with the house of Israel and with the house of Judah."* (Jer. 31:31, Heb. 8:8) This new covenant replaces the old covenant they were given at Mt. Sinai (Jer. 31:32, Heb. 8:9). The old covenant was written in tablets of stone and, as we said, has already ceased to exist (Heb. 8:13). The old covenant's final passing was when the Romans destroyed Jerusalem and the temple. That is why in the time of Paul writing the epistle to the Hebrews, he says concerning the old covenant, *"Now what is becoming obsolete and growing old is ready to vanish away."*

The old covenant was defective and had Moses as a mediator (Heb. 8:5, 7, Gal. 3:19). The old covenant was given only to Israel and not to the Gentiles. The old covenant created a wall of separation between Israel and the Gentile nations. The new covenant is a better covenant, with a more excellent Mediator (Heb. 8:6). The new covenant is also given only to Israel. The new covenant *maintains* the wall of separation between Israel and the Gentile nations. During the millennium the Gentile nations will serve Israel, and be gathered to this nation for blessing (Isa. 49:6, 23, 60:1-12, Zech. 14:16-17). Israel is separated out of the nations and restored to the land (Isa. 11:11-12, 49:5-6, Jer. 3:17-18, 31:7-12, 31:36-40, 32:36-44, 33:6-9, Ez. 20:33-44, 28:25-26, 34:11-14, 34:27-31, 36:2-11, 36:22-38, 37:11-14, 37:21-28, 39:21-29, Zech. 10:6-12). These words of prophetic scripture cannot be taken any other way but literally. To spiritualize all of this to apply it to the church is simply an impossible task. It cannot be accomplished with any sound spiritual thinking. These prophecies speak of the nation of Israel – on the earth and restored in the land – having the new covenant. Israel becomes the greatest, most blessed, and most favored nation on the face of the earth. But the new covenant maintains the wall of separation for Israel on the earth, and maintains it eternally. This is the point. The new covenant, bringing the two kingdoms of Israel back together as one nation, is an eternal covenant. Israel will eternally be maintained before God as a separate nation from the Gentiles.

The Davidic Throne

Jeremiah 33:14-17

"Behold, the days are coming,' says the Lord, 'that I will perform that good thing which I have promised to the house of Israel and to the house of Judah:

'In those days and at that time
I will cause to grow up to David
A Branch of righteousness;
He shall execute judgment and righteousness in the earth.
In those days Judah will be saved,
And Jerusalem will dwell safely.
And this is the name by which she will be called:

'THE LORD OUR RIGHTEOUSNESS.'

"For thus says the Lord: 'David shall never lack a man to sit on the throne of the house of Israel."

That 'good thing' that Jehovah will perform is the gathering of the Jewish remnant out of the nations and restoring them in the Promised land by sovereign power and grace, and then formally making a new covenant with them for their blessing and prosperity. This is easily understood by the use of the phrase 'behold the days are coming' and the direct reference to the two distinct houses, for these particular phrases are the same used in the promise of the new covenant (Jer. 31:31). Jerusalem is called 'the Lord our Righteousness' because Jesus, 'the Branch of Righteousness' growing up unto David, will be physically present on the Davidic throne of the house of Israel. In order for Him to sit on this throne in earthly Jerusalem, He will have to return to the earth from where He presently is – hidden from the world at the right hand of God (Col. 3:1-4). There can be no mistaking that the Davidic throne is on the earth, in the earthly city of Jerusalem, and in the house of Israel. There can be no mistaking that Jesus is not presently sitting on any Davidic throne (Rev. 3:21).

The passage quoted above gives us another understanding that further proves this point. When Jesus returns to this earth and does sit on the Davidic throne in Jerusalem, His reigning at that time is described as, *"... executing judgments in righteousness in the earth."* Some say that He reigns now, and that He does so as the King sitting on the Davidic throne. If this were true you would see Him executing judgments. But this is exactly what you do not see at this present time and in this present evil age (Gal. 1:4). The phrase depicts the *character* of His reign over the earth in the coming age – when He is physically present on the earth.

The Davidic Throne and Peter's preaching

Many people use the preaching of Peter on the day of Pentecost, with his references to the words of David, as proof for their belief and teaching of the present fulfillment of the Davidic throne and covenant (Acts 2:22-36). But these are misguided human conclusions that result from not attending closely to God's word. If we take the assumption of a fulfilled Davidic throne, existing now for the past 2000 years, and compare this conclusion to the above quoted passage from Jeremiah 34, we immediately see how much is missing. The assumption falls to the wayside as all human thoughts and systems should, when analyzed in the light of Scripture. The only portion of Peter's words that actually speaks of the throne of David is verse thirty (v. 30). But this becomes the launching board for all the mistaken assumptions concerning the remainder of the passage, and these assumptions are used to support a human system of doctrine.

Now let us consider what proper relationship the Davidic throne has with Nebuchadnezzar's dream of the Gentile statue. In his dream we see a stone cut out without hands, which strikes the image on its feet of iron and clay, and breaks them in pieces. All the different portions of the statue were crushed together and became like chaff (Dan. 2:34-35, 2:44-45). The stone that brings this judgment on the last form of the Gentile civil world powers is Jesus Christ and His return to this earth. Are we willing to say that the establishing of the Davidic throne has nothing to do with this stone cut out without hands coming out of heaven? Are we willing to say that David's throne in Israel has nothing to do with Gentile power and rule being thrown off of the Jews? Yet at the time of Peter's preaching in Acts 2 the Romans were firmly entrenched in their civil world dominion – this according to the statue's two legs of iron. The place where the stone strikes the statue has never come about yet in the history of these Gentile powers. The feet and toes of iron and clay are yet future in time. I am perplexed that anyone could think that the fulfillment of the covenant of the eternal throne of David could co-exist at the same moment in time with Gentile world dominion. How does that make any biblical sense?

If our Lord sits on a Davidic throne today, then we are in the millennium. But alas, the 1000 years has expanded to 2000, give or take a few – another forced spiritualized explanation to accommodate the human system. The millennial reign of the Davidic throne is *characterized* by judgments in righteousness that put away all evil. Where do we see anything today that resembles these actions or this character? We live in a present evil age where evil grows and prospers in the world (Gal. 1:4). It does the same in God's house of Christendom on the earth. The full display of the evil is only restricted by the presence of the Holy Spirit on the earth (II Thess. 2:6-7). Yet we are not mistaken in saying the principle of sin was well entrenched in the church world from its beginning. How is this present age the character of the throne of David?

The King on the present Throne is the Father

The current form the kingdom of God takes in this evil age is what Matthew's gospel speaks of as the kingdom of heaven in mystery. There exist two main components in this kingdom:

- *the field which is the world*
- *the spoiled crop that is in the field.*

We understand that the wheat in the crop in the field was planted by the Son of Man. These are the true sons of the kingdom as it is in this present form (Matt. 13:37-38). It is also clear that the kingdom of God stays in this general form until the end of the age (Matt. 13:30, 39-42, 47-50). When Jesus gives us the teachings of the kingdom of heaven, believers are portrayed as the sons of the Father who is in heaven (Matt. 5:45). These teachings center in upon the relationship of the sons of the kingdom with their Father in heaven (Matt. 5, 6, 7). In all honesty, the King of the kingdom of heaven is the Father and not Jesus, the Son of Man. This is why Jesus presently sits on His Father's throne (Rev. 3:21). The King on that throne is the Father, and He has that present relationship to the kingdom of heaven and with the wheat in the crop in the field.

There are so many Christians who want to have Jesus as their King. For the believer and true church this will always be a misguided and unscriptural thought. The church is always His body and His bride (Eph. 5:25-32). He is Head of the body, and the church is His helpmeet as Eve was for Adam. Individually we are His brethren and joint-heirs with Him of God (Heb. 2:11, Rom. 8:17). Individually we are sons of God with Him, and when we are glorified, we will be conformed into the image of God's Son (Gal. 3:26, Rom. 8:29). When Jesus takes up the title of 'King of kings and Lord of lords' it is in manifestation to the world. This is who He is to the world and for the earth, but it is never a title that describes His relationship with the believer/church.

3. The new covenant made with Israel during the millennium is the same law of Jehovah given to Israel at Mt. Sinai, only instead of writing on tablets of stone, it is written in the Jewish remnant's hearts and minds (Jer. 31:33, Heb. 8:10). They will

not need to teach one another the law for they all will know the Lord Jehovah, from the least to the greatest among them (Jer. 31:34, Heb. 8:11). Israel will again be recognized as His people and Jehovah again as their God (Jer. 31:1, 33). This is Israel with the new covenant during the coming age.

Israel's New Covenant

How will Israel be blessed on the earth during the millennium? They are blessed above all nations through their new covenant. God will forgive all their iniquity and sin (Jer. 31:34). He will enable them by divine power to do the law written now on their hearts and minds and be blessed.

Ezekiel 11:16-20

"Therefore say, 'Thus says the Lord God: "Although I have cast them far off among the Gentiles, and although I have scattered them among the countries, yet I shall be a little sanctuary for them in the countries where they have gone."' (17) Therefore say, 'Thus says the Lord God: "I will gather you from the peoples, assemble you from the countries where you have been scattered, and I will give you the land of Israel."' (18) And they will go there, and they will take away all its detestable things and all its abominations from there. (19) Then I will give them one heart, and I will put a new spirit within them, and take the stony heart out of their flesh, and give them a heart of flesh, (20) that they may walk in My statutes and keep My judgments and do them; and they shall be My people, and I will be their God."

This passage succinctly tells the story of Israel's scattering in 70 AD, Jehovah preserving a physical seed of Abraham in the nations, and then gathering the remnant back at the beginning of the millennium. He gives them a new heart and spirit by which they will walk in His commandments and law. And look how the passage ends – *they will be My people, and I will be their God.* This phrase, commonly found in prophecy, always points to Jehovah again recognizing Israel after having set them aside and having disregarded them (Jer. 31:1, 33, 30:22, 24:7, 32:38, Ez. 14:11, 34:30, 37:23, 37:27, Zech. 8:8, Heb. 8:10). When Israel receives their new covenant in the millennium, their blessings as a nation will be according to this passage:

Deuteronomy 28:1

"Now it shall come to pass, if you diligently obey the voice of the Lord your God, to observe carefully all His commandments which I command you today, that the Lord your God will set you high above all nations of the earth."

Please continue to read Deuteronomy 28:2-14. These are the physical blessings of Israel for their obedience during the coming millennium.

4. The law will be the basis of God's government of the earth during the millennium. We must remember that the law is God's perfect rule for man in Adam. The law represents human righteousness for man in the flesh, and all that is on the earth at that time will be man in the flesh. The Son of Man will rule the world and will righteously judge the nations, putting down all evil. Israel will do the law and Jerusalem will be the capital city of Jehovah's government of the earth. Judaism is God's religion for the world and man in Adam. The millennium will prove this to be true.

The Final Caesar and the Antichrist

When the dragon is cast down from the heavens he empowers the first beast and the world follows after it – *"And all the world marveled and followed the beast. So they worshiped the dragon who gave authority to the beast; and they worshiped the beast, saying, "Who is like the beast? Who is able to make war with him?"* (Rev. 13:3-4) But the second beast is the one who sets things up for the first. He is a false Messiah in the east who compels the inhabitants of the earth into idolatry (Rev. 13:14-15). While civil power is in the hands of the first beast, religious deception and wickedness are exercised by the second.

What are the results? The first beast is both the revived Roman Empire in the last 3½ years of the tribulation period, and the civil head of this Empire. He is the last Caesar of Rome. He is given generalized imperial power by Satan. He is associated with the ten kings and kingdoms, having overthrown three of them as the little horn of Daniel 7. He is blasphemous of God and Christianity, having thrown off the Babylonian harlot and destroyed her.

In Palestine there will be the second beast. He is the Antichrist, the false Messiah. He denies all basic Christian truth among the Jews, denying the claims of Christ as do the Jews. He deceives men by false miracles and wonders. He sets up an image of the first beast and forces open subjection to the Caesar by extreme governmental tyranny. He enslaves the wills of men by his great deceptions. His sphere of influence will be in the east, in Palestine. He is the little horn of Daniel 8, coming up out of the territories of the Grecian empire in the east. He grows exceedingly great in the direction of the south and east, and toward the Glorious Land (Dan. 8:9). This little horn stops the daily sacrifices in Israel and casts truth down to the ground (Dan. 8:11-12). He will magnify himself and through his cunning he will cause deceit to prosper (Dan. 8:23-26).

There are two little horns in the book of Daniel. The little horn of chapter seven is directly associated with the fourth beast. This beast is the Roman Empire but also, I believe, an end time Caesar. The little horn in chapter eight is in the east and from the confines of the previous Grecian empire. I believe this little horn to be the Antichrist. I do not believe these two entities are one and the same. I believe the two little horns of Daniel to be the two beasts of John's vision in Revelation 13. It is not difficult to conceive of the second beast proclaiming to be the Messiah for Israel – as a beast he has the prophetic image of a lamb.

Chapter 16: Endnotes

[141] When Satan is removed from the heavens and cast down to the earth he loses his anti-priestly character as the accuser of the brethren (Rev. 12:10). On the earth, all he is left with is his anti-kingly and anti-prophet character. He gives the first beast his power, his throne, and great authority. This is civil power. The first beast is the anti-king character of Satan. The second beast has religious power and deception. He is a false prophet and a false Messiah (Rev. 16:13). This is the anti-prophet character of Satan.

There is an even greater parallel found in this. Jesus was the true King and Prophet rejected on the earth. It is on the earth at the end of the age that Satan will be allowed to imitate these two offices – king and prophet. Jesus is currently in the heavens as the High Priest for the church (Heb. 7:26). Satan is in the heavens currently and is there as the anti-priest against the church. He is cast down to the earth after the church is taken to the heavens. He loses any anti-priestly influence against the church. Of course the true church, having been raptured, glorified, and conformed into the Son's image (Rom. 8:29-30), and now holy and blameless before the Father (Eph. 1:4), will have no need for Jesus to continue to function in His High Priestly ministry for her (Heb. 4:14-16). Why? Having been glorified, the church will no longer have weakness, infirmity, and needs.

The role of the true Prophet was fulfilled by Jesus when He first came to Israel. He was the Prophet that Moses referred to that would rise up after him, to whom Israel was to listen. In the heavens He is currently High Priest for the church (Heb. 4:14-16). He will be King of kings and Lord of lords to the world when He returns to the earth.

[142] All the Biblical understandings concerning Judaism and the law of Moses are thoroughly discussed in the first book of the series, 'The Son of Man Glorified'. God's purposes and reasoning for giving the law to Israel and that nation serving as a test case for all mankind is discussed there. Judaism as God's religion for the earth and man in Adam is also explained.

[143] Jesus had a fourfold testimony and witness as to who He was:

1. John the Baptist testified (John 5:33-35)
2. The works the Father gave Him to do were testimony (John 5:36)

3. The Father's voice from heaven testified as to who He was (John 5:37)

4. The Scriptures testify of Him (John 5:39, 46, and 47).

Yet Israel believed none of this and rejected Him (John 5:40). The Antichrist will come to Israel without such testimony as to who he really is, but Israel will receive him (John 5:43).

Chapter 17:
The Olive Tree

The olive tree is a symbol found in Romans 11 that stands for the promises and privileges of God in the earth. I want to make a few points concerning this symbol because there are so many confusing ideas and teachings that involve its use. A large number of teachers and theologians err in making the tree either the church or the nation of Israel. They would have us believe that God cut off the nation of Israel from the body of Christ, or that born-again believers are grafted into the nation of Israel. Both of these ideas are misleading and do not agree with what the passage speaks of. These errors are not just damaging to the proper understanding of Bible prophecy, but also do serious harm to the doctrines of the church.

Romans 11:12

"Now if their fall is riches for the world, and their failure riches for the Gentiles, how much more their fullness!"

Romans 11:17

"And if some of the branches were broken off, and you, being a wild olive tree, were grafted in among them, and with them became a partaker of the root and fatness of the olive tree."

The olive tree produces fatness and blessings from God (Rom. 11:17, 22). It is symbolic of the promises and goodness of God on the earth. Because of Israel's failure, the fatness of the olive tree means riches for the world and riches for the Gentiles. The world enjoys this fatness when Israel is cut off and the Gentiles are grafted in.

The Natural Heirs of the Promises

As long as Israel was acknowledged by God, through natural descent and on the ground of Judaism (birthright and their old legal covenant and law), they were the heirs of the promises through Abraham (Rom. 9:3-5). God honored Israel's fathers by all of His dealings with the Jews. He chose them as a people and a nation. He delivered them as a people and a nation. By their redemption His presence dwelled in their midst (Ex. 29:45-46). He eventually brings them into the land according to the promises He made to the forefathers. The land itself was called the land of promise. He had given Israel His law and when they failed in responsibility He promised to send them a Prophet greater than Moses. God promised them the throne of David as an eternal throne and reign to give them hope, with the son of David after the flesh pledged to sit on it eternally.

God eventually does this and sends the Messiah of promise to the Jews (Acts 13:23). *Jesus Christ became a minister of the circumcision for the truth of God, to confirm the promises made to the fathers* (Rom. 15:8). These were the fathers of Israel and this was Jesus as come according to the flesh – a Jewish Messiah. When He came to them as the Anointed One of Jehovah, He preached to them the glad tidings of promises being fulfilled (Luke 4:17-21). *The extent and scope of His mission was limited to the lost sheep of Israel.* God was faithful and did nothing to deny the prophecies and promises (Matt. 10:5-6, 15:24, Luke 4:42-44). As long as God recognized Israel in this way He could not turn from them to the Gentiles, or do anything that denied them as heirs of the promises (Rom. 9:4-5). That is why it is said quite directly, *"...Israelites, to whom pertain...the promises."*

But Israel failed to receive the promises. Often they simply relied on their physical birth and national ties to Abraham (John 8:33-47,

Matt. 3:9, Rom. 9:6-8). This was not pleasing to God. Being under the law in human responsibility they failed to attain righteousness, which was necessary to receive the promises (Gal. 3:10-12, 18, Rom. 9:30-32). Their law was not of faith and therefore not of grace, and could not justify them. Their law could not help them maintain their hold on any of the promises. When God sent His Son to them in goodness and grace, they rejected Him, threw Him out, and put Him to death. They rejected the one Seed of Abraham in whom all the promises resided (Gal. 3:16). Israel was set aside by God from the promises. They stumbled at the stumbling stone God had set in Zion (Rom. 9:30-33). Romans 11 describes it as a temporary fall by Israel (Rom. 11:11-15). The kingdom was taken from them and with it all the promises were gone (Matt. 21:43). This is the breaking off and casting aside by God of the natural branches from the olive tree.

Reliance on the Flesh

What were the things that Israel relied on in thinking they obtained the favor of God and the promises? The answer is threefold:

1. Israel relied on and boasted in natural birth and descent. They were the physical children of Abraham, according to the flesh. They were the heirs of the promises by birth.

2. Israel relied on and boasted in the works of the law, which law was given to them by God. By doing the law they felt they merited the divine favor of God.

3. Israel relied on and boasted in religious forms of worship and carnal ordinances. The main emphasis of the former is the temple, the later was circumcision. The males in Israel were circumcised as an outward sign, showing the world they belonged to God and were the only heirs of the promises.

It isn't hard to see Israel's reliance on the flesh, and their human pride in doing so. All three things listed are what Paul calls religious confidences of the flesh. They are called confidences for man because he embraces them as the means of gaining God's favor.

Phil. 3:4-6

"...confidence in the flesh...circumcised the eight day, of the stock of Israel, of the tribe of Benjamin, a Hebrew of the Hebrews; concerning the law, a Pharisee...concerning the righteousness which is in the law, blameless."

This portion of Scripture perfectly matches the above list. Israel wholeheartedly embraced the religious confidences of the flesh in order to please God. But if we look at God's word we will see exactly how far down this path they were able to travel.

1. Natural birth and descent — *"For they are not all Israel who are of Israel, nor are they all children because they are the seed of Abraham...that is, those who are the children of the flesh, these are not the children of God..."* (Rom. 9:6-8) Then John the Baptist says, *"...do not think to say to yourselves, 'We have Abraham as our father.'"* (Matt. 3:9) And finally when the Jews remarked to Jesus, *"We are Abraham's descendants, and have never been in bondage to anyone..."* they were lying, for at that moment the Romans ruled over them. And further, they were not speaking the truth because Jesus replies to them, *"You are of your father the devil..."* (John 8:31-47)

2. The works of the law — first we should understand that Abraham preceded the law by 430 years and could not actually become a doer of the works of the law. But it becomes clear that Abraham and David, the two fathers most recognized by the nation, were not justified before God by doing works (Rom. 4:1-8). *"Therefore by the deeds of the law no flesh will be justified in His sight..."* (Rom. 3:19-20, Gal. 2:16)

3. Religious forms of worship and carnal ordinances — if the temple was set aside by God as *the* place of worship, then all the religious service and forms of worship in Judaism would be equally set aside (John 4:21, Matt. 23:37-24:2). And circumcision, as a carnal ordinance, was not the means by which Abraham was blessed (Rom. 4:9-12). All the remaining

carnal ordinances of their religion fall to the wayside along with circumcision (Heb. 9:9-10).

The confidences of the flesh that the Jews relied upon were useless, and gained them no favor with God. There were three things necessary for Israel to receive the promises – justification, righteousness, and the principle of grace through faith. Yet they could not attain these very things through their law. It may be helpful to break these thoughts down and distinguish them in another list.

- The issue of justification – *"But that no one is justified by the law in the sight of God is evident..."* (Gal. 3:11) Israel could not be justified through their religion.

- And we know that the justified shall have life through the principle of grace and faith, *"...for the just shall live by faith."* (Gal. 3:11)

- *"Yet the law is not of faith..."* The law is not according to the principle of grace and faith, but rather the opposite principle. The man who does all the commandments and statutes of the law shall have life by the doing of them (Gal. 3:12). *"...but the man who does them shall live by them."* The working principle of the law is human responsibility.

- The issue of righteousness – we read also, *"For Moses writes about the righteousness which is of the law, 'The man who does those things shall live by them.'"* (Rom. 10:5) So the law given to Israel, by its own working principle, could not justify or make righteous, and could not give life. This is the law, and this is their religion.

- The principle of grace through faith – *"...but Israel, pursuing the law of righteousness, has not attained to the law of righteousness. Why? Because they did not seek it by faith, but as it were, by the works of the law."* (Rom. 9:31-32)

- The principle of grace through faith – *"Now to him who works, the wages are not counted as grace but as debt. But to him who does not work but believes on Him who justifies the ungodly, his faith is accounted for righteousness."* (Rom. 4:4-5) In this passage we have all four words – justify, righteousness, grace, and faith. We see how they are connected together while other words are excluded – law, curse, works, wages, debt, and boasting. We also read, *"And if by grace, then it is no longer of works; otherwise grace is no longer grace. But if it is of works, it is no longer grace; otherwise work is no longer work. What then? Israel has not obtained what it seeks...but... were hardened."* (Rom. 11:6-7)

- The sending of Messiah to Israel – *"For the law was given through Moses, but grace and truth came through Jesus Christ."* (John 1:17) When Jesus came in grace, Israel rejected Him. They would have had all the promises if they received Him. Even after the crucifixion and after Pentecost Israel was offered an invitation of grace (Matt. 22:1-7). But they refused it, made light of it, and went their way.

Israel set aside by God

These were God's reasons for setting aside Israel and casting them off from the olive tree as the natural branches. Israel never receives the kingdom nor maintains the promises. Yet we see that the promises made to the Jewish forefathers were secured in Jesus Christ by His resurrection (Acts 13:30-34, Rom. 15:8). We should not fail to see both the irony of these events as well as the wisdom of the plan of God in them. Israel's hatred by crucifying Jesus Christ is their stumbling and falling on the stone God had set in Zion (Matt. 21:42-44). It is the reason for God temporarily setting them aside, while at the same time, His death and resurrection secures for them their future restoration in the land with all the promises. This will be done, the nation grafted in and accepted, according to the fulfillment of all promises based on the faithfulness of Jehovah. This will include the return of the Messiah to them whom the nation had previously killed (Acts. 2:22-24). But Israel must wait until God acknowledges them again as *His people, and He as their God* (Jer. 24:7, 31:33, 32:38, Ez. 11:20, 37:23, 37:27, Zech. 8:8, Heb. 8:10 – every verse listed here uses this phrase and points to the millennium when Israel is again acknowledged and restored by God. At the present time *they are not His people, and He is not their God* – Hosea 1:9).

Israel is cut off from the fatness of the tree. *"For if the inheritance is of the law, it is no longer of promise; but God gave it to Abraham by promise."* (Gal. 3:18) *"Now to Abraham and his Seed were the promises made."* (Gal. 3:16) His one Seed is Jesus Christ, in whom all the promises of God are found (II Cor. 1:20). Abraham is the root of the olive tree. In him were all the promises deposited (Heb. 7:6). His one Seed, Jesus Christ, met and fulfilled all the conditions for blessing. Israel's law could not make them fit for the promises and then they crucified the one Seed. They are set aside by God and hardened, except for a very small Jewish remnant that remains as natural branches in the tree (Rom. 11:5-10). And now the Gentiles come in (Rom. 11:11-13).

God turns to the Gentiles

Matt. 22:8-10

"Then he said to his servants, 'The wedding is ready, but those who were invited were not worthy. Therefore go into the highways, and as many as you find, invite to the wedding. So those servants went out into the highways and gathered together all whom they found, both bad and good. And the wedding hall was filled with guests."

God turns to the Gentiles in a general and dispensational way. *"That Gentiles, who did not pursue righteousness, have attained to righteousness, even the righteousness of faith."* (Rom. 9:30) And later in Romans Paul says, *"But through their fall, to provoke them to jealousy, salvation has come to the Gentiles."* (Rom. 11:11) Israel's failure and fall from the olive tree means riches for the Gentiles and riches for the world (Rom. 11:12). Not once is Paul directly speaking of the church seated in the heavens or the believer in glory with Christ. But he speaks of the Gentiles in general. He speaks of God turning to them with the offer of blessing and grace by the gospel of salvation through faith. In the above verse it is through the gospel that the servants gather in the Gentiles both good and bad. It is similar to the net cast into the sea or the spoiled crop in the field in the kingdom of heaven. The Gentiles are grafted in, standing in a profession of faith, in order to be partakers of the root and fatness of the olive tree (Rom. 11:17-20). The availability of salvation and the promise of the Spirit, as well as God's general favor, are part of the present fatness and blessing of the olive tree that the Gentiles currently are offered and enjoy (Gal. 3:14).

"...salvation for the Gentiles," is a vague and general statement only to be understood as a change in the dispensational dealings of God (Rom. 11:11). In fact, not all Gentiles are saved and we will not find all Gentiles in heaven. *"Now if their fall is riches for the world..."*, again is a phrase that can only be understood by dispensation (Rom. 11:12). God cuts Israel off from the promises and turns His attention and dealings to the rest of the world – to the Gentiles.

The future Millennial Fullness of Israel

We should understand that the full measure of Romans 11:12 is pointing to the millennium when Israel will be grafted back into the fatness of the olive tree and will finally be restored and have 'their fullness'. If the blessing was so great for the world with Israel 'fallen' and in failure, how much more will it be blessing and riches for the Gentile nations when Israel is restored in 'fullness' in their land? It is during the coming millennium that Israel will grow to be the greatest and most blessed nation on the face of the earth and the Gentiles, the world, will be blessed through them. Israel, as a formed nation, will be back from the dead (Rom. 11:15).

But notice the verse says, *"...their fullness."* During the millennium Israel is still a separated people and nation, distinct from the Gentiles. It will be Israel in the land, it won't be the Gentiles or the church living there with them. The Gentile nations will be blessed from the overflow of blessings, but Israel will remain a separated nation. [Please see Deut. 32:8. The name for God as the Most High points to the millennium. This verse shows that God will make Israel the center of the millennial earth.] It will be at the beginning of the millennium that God will say to the saved Jewish remnant in the land (Rom. 9:27), *"...I will be their God, and they shall be My people."* God will form a nation from this elect and chosen remnant (Isa. 10:20-23, 66:6-9, Rev. 7:3-8). This is where the new covenant comes in, at the time when God again acknowledges Israel as His people. The new covenant will be instituted when God again recognizes Israel's calling (Rom. 11:29).

Hebrews 8:6-13

"But now He has obtained a more excellent ministry, inasmuch as He is also Mediator of a better covenant, which was established on better promises.

7 For if that first covenant had been faultless, then no place would have been sought for a second. 8 Because finding fault with them, He says: "Behold, the days are coming, says the Lord, when I will make a new covenant with the house of Israel and with the house of Judah— 9 not according to the covenant that I made with their fathers in the day when I took them by the hand to lead them out of the land of Egypt; because they did not continue in My covenant, and I disregarded them, says the Lord. 10 For this is the covenant that I will make with the house of Israel after those days, says the Lord: I will put My laws in their mind and write them on their hearts; and I will be their God, and they shall be My people. 11 None of them shall teach his neighbor, and none his brother, saying, 'Know the Lord,' for all shall know Me, from the least of them to the greatest of them. 12 For I will be merciful to their unrighteousness, and their sins and their lawless deeds I will remember no more."

13 In that He says, "A new covenant," He has made the first obsolete. Now what is becoming obsolete and growing old is ready to vanish away."

If I may be direct, there are a few points to be made here that are hard to dispute. The first point is that what is called the 'new covenant' is a second covenant made between God and Israel. Regardless of what your thoughts are of the 'new covenant' and who you think is involved in the agreement, the above passage is fairly clear. It stands to reason that if the first covenant was made between God and Israel, and the second replaces the first, then the second covenant is made between God and Israel. The new covenant will be made with the house of Israel and Judah, bringing them back together as one nation and one people before God. Therefore He says, *"...I will be their God, and they shall be My people."* The first covenant was not formally made with the Gentiles. The first covenant separated Israel from the Gentiles.

When Israel was set aside by God and He ended the practice of the first covenant by destroying Jerusalem and the temple, the remaining Jews were scattered into the nations (Luke 21:24). They are no longer separated from the Gentiles. From God's viewpoint they live among the Gentiles as the Gentiles, and so doing, they defile His name (Ez. 36:19-24). They do not currently have a covenant, for if they did, it would separate them from the rest. The obvious conclusion is this: there is no recognition from God of the Jews being His people, no separation from the Gentiles, no land, and no covenant.

God will have to return Israel to the land in order to make the second or new covenant with them. The formal implementation of the new covenant will once again separate Israel from the Gentile nations. Then God will acknowledge Israel as His people, they will be separated from the Gentiles, they will possess the land, and the new covenant will be formally made with them. Jehovah will hallow His own name by doing this for Israel. If their 'new covenant' re-establishes the nation as distinct and separate from the Gentiles, how can we think the new covenant is made with the Gentiles?

The Common Character of God's Covenants

If I may be direct again in speaking of the character and nature of covenants in general:

- Covenants are agreements made by God. They explain God's dealings in blessing with the earth and man on the earth and in connection with the first creation. Scripturally this is man in the first Adam and man in the flesh.

- Except for the first covenants (those made with creation and the ones made with Abraham), all the remaining ones are made with Israel after they became a nation. This explains why the Scriptures say, *"...Israelites, to whom pertain...the covenants..."* (Rom. 9:4)

- The covenant with creation, for which the rainbow is a sign, involves God preserving the earth for future blessing. During the millennium the curse on creation, which God placed at the fall of man, will be removed. The first creation is currently under futility and corruption because of Adam, but placed there in hope (Rom. 8:19-22). We see that God deals by covenant with the first creation and the earth.

- The covenants with Abraham all deal with blessing in the earth, the dividing of land for inheritance, or the building of nations on the earth. One particular promise from God says this, *"In you all the nations or families of the earth shall be blessed."* (Gen. 12:3, 18:18) There is more to this particular covenant than meets the eye. Some previously hidden blessings come in, related as auxiliaries to the original words of promise made to Abraham. The explanation of this is found in the understanding that the Spirit has been sent down from heaven. He reveals the mystery of Christ and the glory of Christ, who is Himself the one Seed of Abraham (Eph. 3:1-6, Gal. 3:16). The believer comes into association with Abraham through the gospel and its founding principle of grace through faith – the same principle that distinguished Abraham (Gal. 3:6-9, 14). However, for this particular point in reference to Abraham, if we speak of nations or families of the earth, we are referring to relationships connected with the world and the first creation (Gen. 12:2-3). In the plain words of the promise it references the world and the earth, not the church. Through Abraham the Gentile nations will be blessed during the millennium.

- All the remaining covenants that exist were made directly with Israel. As a nation on the earth they have two major covenants. God found fault with the first covenant and made it obsolete (Heb. 8:7, 13). The second covenant, the 'new covenant', has yet to be made with them. It is a covenant made with a future Jewish remnant after they are brought into their land. By this covenant they will be physically blessed and all their sins will be forgiven (Jer. 31:31-34).

- Of all the covenants God ever made, only one was the basis for God's testing of man in the flesh in the principle of human responsibility. That covenant was made at Mt. Sinai with Israel. It is the essence of Judaism and that which the Scriptures call the law. In the above passage from Hebrews 8 it is referred to as 'the first covenant'. It is significant that this particular covenant has passed away – it is the only covenant that God makes that will ever do this. You must see the connection between God completing His testing of man in human responsibility, looking for fruit, and this covenant passing away (Heb. 8:7, 13). <u>Now this is a great teaching point</u>: Of all the covenants God made, this one alone, made at Mt. Sinai, has ended. It clearly shows that human responsibility on its own can never sustain anything. Even when God highly privileged Israel and showed them favoritism, there was no good fruit produced, only failure.[144]

The common character of covenants is for the blessing of the earth, and the blessing of man in Adam on the earth. These are essential characteristics in the foreground of every covenant God has made – whether He makes it with creation (Gen. 8:21-22), with Abraham by promise (Gal. 3:16, Gen. 12:2-3), or with the nation of Israel (Deut. 28:1-14, Jer. 31:31).

Regarding the individual believer and the body of Christ, covenants are a lot like the subject of prophecy. The church is hidden, it is mystery and obscure. It is clear what the covenants will do for a future Jewish remnant. It is equally clear what the covenants will do for the remaining nations on the earth who survive the coming tribulation and judgments. In Abraham all the families of the earth will be blessed (Gen. 12:3). However, the believer will be conformed into the image of His Son. There isn't a covenantal agreement spelled out in Scripture that will do that. God predestined it to be before the world was created, before man existed, before Adam was in the garden and sinned – bringing the entire human race under the dominion of sin. God settled in His eternal purpose and counsels what He would do for the believer before there was man in paradise and a need for covenants with a cursed creation and a fallen man (Eph. 1:3-6). Covenants come into existence after the foundations of the world and therefore are part of the world – arrangements from God for man in the world and connected to the first creation. This is easily seen in the plain and straight forward language of all the covenants (the letter of them). They are earthy in their character and for physical blessing. They never specifically deal with the believer being blessed with every spiritual blessing in the heavenly places in the second Adam (Eph. 1:3). The believer in Christ and the body of Christ are in the counsels of God before the foundations of the world (Eph. 1:4). They are wholly set apart from the world. They are wholly set apart from the first creation. They are as Christ, who ended all relationship with this world by His death and resurrection (John 12:24, 32).

The Olive Tree – God's favor on the earth in Dispensation

If we turn our attention back to the olive tree we will find a similar character in God's dealings – blessings on the earth for man in Adam. The tree represents God's dealings with two different groups – the nation of Israel and the Gentiles (Rom. 11:1-15). The broad wording found in Romans 9-11 is what gives this passage its dispensational character, rather than covenantal.

Romans 11:19-22

"You will say then, "Branches were broken off that I might be grafted in." (20) Well said. Because of unbelief they were

broken off, and you stand by faith. Do not be haughty, but fear. (21) For if God did not spare the natural branches, He may not spare you either. (22) Therefore consider the goodness and severity of God: on those who fell, severity; but toward you, goodness, if you continue in His goodness. Otherwise you also will be cut off."

Please forgive me if I repeat myself, but the proper understanding of the olive tree will clear up much confusion of doctrine. The entire eleventh chapter of Romans is speaking about these two dispensations – the Jewish dispensation in which Israel is acknowledged by God in calling, and a subsequent general Gentile dispensation with the spoiled crop in the world (Matt. 13:24-30). The Jewish dispensation ends when Israel, as a whole, is cut off from the olive tree of the promises of God in blessing and goodness (Rom. 11:15, 20-22). Israel is hardened (Rom 11:7). One thing is clear – Israel is not the olive tree. As a nation, Israel was cut off from the tree and hardened.[145]

The Progression of Israel as associated with the Olive Tree

What is the final outcome for Israel? Has God cast away His people for good? (Rom. 11:1) The chapter clearly answers these questions. Israel's final outcome will be exactly according to the Old Testament prophecies, fulfilled by the faithfulness, the sovereign grace, and the power of God. This chapter presents the prominent elements found in those prophecies and God's counsels toward Israel.

- There is an obvious setting aside of the nation where they have not attained what they sought – Rom. 11:7-10. Israel at this present time is not acknowledged as His people. They have no existing covenant with God. He does not recognize their calling.

- There are Jewish remnants that God is pleased to save by sovereign grace – an election of grace. This is the only way you can ever define the biblical use of the word 'grace'; this shows what the grace of God actually is, in its character, as always the sovereign election of God – Rom. 11:2-6

- God will turn back to Israel at a future point in time. He has to do this. He has to be shown to be the faithful God and Israel's Jehovah, who keeps covenant with Israel for the sake of their forefathers (Ex. 3:6, 15, Ex. 6:2-4, Ex. 32:12-13, Deut. 7:9) It will be when the Gentile dispensation is cut off and ended, when God's fullness of the Gentiles has come in – Rom. 11:25. The Gentiles will not continue in the goodness of God – Rom. 11:21-22. He will acknowledge Israel again as *'His people, and He as their God'* – Rom. 11:23-27. In the end it will be done by God in His faithfulness to Israel, because the gifts and callings of God are without repentance – Rom. 11:28-29

- The phrase *'the fullness of the Gentiles'* refers to the time when the Gentile dispensation will end. The Gentiles *'not continuing in the goodness of God'* refers to Christendom as a spoiled crop in the world associated with the olive tree of God's favor. The first thought has a positive connotation, while the second has a negative one. *'The fullness'* refers to the dispensation, while *'the continuing'* refers to the corporate responsibility of the external body of Christendom. God's purpose and counsels involve the dispensation and its timing. He has patience and longsuffering with human responsibility and Christendom's failure. In the chapter we see that both, out of mutual necessity, must end at the same time. Then God turns back to acknowledge the nation of Israel.

- Israel will be saved as a remnant, according to the many Old Testament prophecies and the book of Revelation. God always has a remnant of Israel according to the election of grace. When the chapter speaks of all Israel being saved in the end (Rom. 11:26-27), it is as a final distinct remnant (Rev. 7:1-8, 14:1-4, Rom. 9:27-29, Isaiah 6:13, 8:18, 10:20-23, 11:11, 16, 37:31-32, Joel 2:28-32, Dan. 12:1). This Jewish remnant forms national Israel for the millennium (Isa. 66:6-9). *Shall a nation be born at once?* Israel will realize their fullness in blessings, being grafted back in and partaking of the root and fatness of the olive tree (Rom. 11:12, 17). Their acceptance by God will be, for the nation, life from the dead (Rom. 11:15, Ez. 37:1-14).

God turns to the Gentiles in a Dispensation

If there was a Jewish dispensation (and there was), then it is now set aside by God (Isaiah 8:14-17, Heb. 8:9, Matt. 21:42-44, 23:37-39). According to this chapter (Romans 11), when He cut Israel off and hardened them, He turned to the Gentiles. Israel being cast aside, as far as God's ways and dealings, means the reconciling of the world, the accepted time, the day of salvation (Rom. 11:15). This general turning away from Israel and turning to the Gentiles by God is seen in this earlier passage.

Romans 9:30-33

"What shall we say then? That Gentiles, who did not pursue righteousness, have attained to righteousness, even the righteousness of faith; (31) but Israel, pursuing the law of righteousness, has not attained to the law of righteousness. (32) Why? Because they did not seek it by faith, but as it were, by the works of the law. For they stumbled at that stumbling stone. (33) As it is written:

"Behold, I lay in Zion a stumbling stone and rock of offense, And whoever believes on Him will not be put to shame."

If we read Romans 9-11 closely we see that God's ways and dealings in history first involved Israel, then the Gentiles, and then Israel again. These dealings are very distinct in timing with little overlap. This portion of Romans gives us a general understanding of two groups and God's dealings with them, separately and distinctly, but in a dispensational arrangement. God's general turning to the Gentiles is also confirmed in a passage at the end of Acts (Acts 28:23-29). The Jewish dispensation ended and a Gentile dispensation began. It will continue until the fullness of the Gentiles comes in and the Gentile dispensation is cut off (Rom. 11:22, 25). Romans eleven (11) views

Christendom, in a sense, as consisting of a small Jewish remnant (Rom. 11:7) and an overwhelming majority of Gentiles. It is such a majority in composition that the chapter refers to the dispensation as that of the Gentiles (Rom 11:11-14).

The Body of Christ is not the Olive Tree

The olive tree is never a picture of the body of Christ and its doctrines. The church is the body united to the Head in heavenly glory by the power of the Holy Spirit. The church's union is with the glorified Son of Man at the right hand of God. There is no thought of this with the olive tree, for it is on the earth. When anyone looks into the world what they see is Christendom (Matt. 13:26-30). They do not see the body of Christ (Matt. 13:44). Israel is cut off from the tree, except for a small believing remnant (Rom. 11:5). The church is not the olive tree and Christ is not the olive tree, because the nation of Israel was never in Christ or in the church.

The Gentiles will be cut off later. This cannot be the true church because God's work – the body of Christ – cannot fail in His eternal purposes. The true church cannot be broken off. But the spoiled crop in the field can be cut off and will be cut off. The Gentile dispensation will come to an end. The Gentiles did not continue in the goodness of God. The olive tree is on the earth and not in heaven. It represents the administration of God's promises and blessings on the earth in a dispensational way.

Rom. 11:24-26

"For if you were cut out of the olive tree which is wild by nature, and were grafted contrary to nature into a good olive tree, how much more will these, who are the natural branches, be grafted into their own olive tree? For I do not desire, brethren, that you should be ignorant of this mystery, lest you should be wise in your own opinion, that hardening in part has happened to Israel until the fullness of the Gentiles has come in. And so all Israel will be saved..."

1. God sets Israel aside. They are cut off. They are hardened (Rom. 11:7).

2. God turns to the Gentiles, after Messiah's rejection and after Stephen's death.

3. The Gentiles are grafted in. Christendom grows up in the earth as a spoiled crop.

4. The Gentiles fail to continue in the goodness of God and their dispensation ends.

5. Israel is acknowledged again by God. *"You are My people, and I am your God."*

The nation of Israel was heir of God's promises according to the flesh and natural descent (Rom. 9:3-5). They were the 'natural' branches. The wild branches of the wild olive tree were the Gentiles, who were aliens from the commonwealth of Israel and strangers from the promises (Eph. 2:11-13). *The olive tree recognizes Jews and Gentiles. The body of Christ does not (Gal. 3:28).* The church was formed by Jews and Gentiles brought together creating a 'new man' in Christ (Eph. 2:11-15). This new man is where there is neither Jew nor Gentile (Col. 3:10-11). The olive tree does not represent a new position or a new man, but rather the previous position of Israel on the earth and associated with the favor of God. The body of Christ does not recognize Jews and Gentiles while the olive tree does recognize them. The olive tree is not the true church. The true church is a new position, a new man created in Christ (Eph. 2:15).

Israel is not the Olive Tree

Is the olive tree Israel, and is the church grafted into Israel? The Jews and their law and religion may recognize Gentiles, but only in a negative way by keeping away from them. The law and Judaism is a wall of separation from the Gentiles. A wall of separation is the opposite from the thought of Gentiles grafted into Israel. *The wall of separation is abolished in the body of Christ, but it is always present in the nation of Israel.* The basis of God's government of the world during the millennium is the law. All through the millennium Israel will be in their land, separated from the Gentile nations.

Is the Olive Tree the family of God?

Romans 9-11 is a portion of Scripture that has caused much confusion in Christian teaching and doctrine. We see the tree is not the church or Israel. Does the olive tree represent the general family of God? It would seem that the details of the passage would support this idea until the point the Gentiles are cut off, allowing all Israel to be saved. Gentiles cut off from the family of God? I can't comprehend the thought of the tree representing God's family, and have it make sense for the entire passage.

It also is very difficult to call the body of Christ a dispensation. The true church has a heavenly calling. One of the features of dispensations is that their character involves God's dealings with man on the earth. This thought should be further qualified as God's dealings with man in Adam and the first creation. In this way dispensations are similar and have common character with covenants. Christendom is the spoiled crop on the earth and is easily seen as a dispensation. The crop is a mixture of three different works – that of God, of the devil, and of man. Christendom will end in the same way as all the other dispensations that preceded it – in human failure. Laodicea is spewed out. The Gentiles are cut off.

As soon as an unbeliever becomes a believer, God moves him out of the first Adam and the first creation and into the second Adam and the new creation of God (Rom. 8:9, Gal. 3:26-27, II Cor. 5:17). As soon as he is sealed by the Spirit (Eph. 1:13), he is baptized by this same Spirit into the body of Christ (I Cor. 12:13). The individual believer and the body of Christ are not of the earth or world (John 17:14-16). The Gentile dispensation that Romans 11 speaks of is that of the spoiled crop in the field of the world or the dispensation of the kingdom of heaven in mystery (in profession). These are the things that are on the earth and of the world, and may be viewed as a dispensation concerning the time period in which the Gentiles are grafted into the olive tree.

The Olive Tree and Human Responsibility

It remains that the olive tree speaks of a 'position or place' that Israel originally held by natural birth and descent. It is a position that is maintained in human responsibility. Israel failed in this responsibility and has not kept her place. The nation is now cut off from the tree. It is crucial to see that this is not a failure in sovereign grace on God's part. Grace cannot fail, and when paired together with God's calling the two are said by Scripture to be without repentance (Rom. 11:29).

Presently God gives the Gentiles this position or place of blessing as wild olive branches grafted into the original olive tree. But they only stay grafted in by human responsibility – *if they continue in His goodness* (Rom. 11:22). This is a key understanding for the olive tree. The Gentiles were not grafted in by sovereign grace and they are not secured in place by sovereign grace. They only remain in the tree if they continue in the goodness of God, that is, by human responsibility. This entire book documents with Scripture Christendom's failure in this present dispensation. Christendom has not continued in the goodness of God. It is safe to say it will be cut off and the Gentile dispensation will end. Christendom will come to an end on the earth (Matt. 13:30, 40-43, 49-50).

The entire teaching of Romans 11 centers around the question asked at the beginning of the chapter – *has God cast away His people Israel, the ones He foreknew* (Rom. 11:1-2). God forbid! Those He did foreknow form a Jewish remnant that is part of the true church. As for the nation, the gifts and callings of God are without repentance. He has cast them off temporarily, but they will realize the promises in the end – through God's faithfulness and sovereign grace, which cannot fail. Israel will not be cut off from the olive tree a second time. When the Jewish remnant is restored as the nation in the land and they have 'their fullness', this final dispensation will be sustained in the sovereign power and grace of God through the rule and reign of the Son of Man on the earth. From beginning to end this final dispensation will not fail (Eph. 1:10). It is known as *'the dispensation of the fullness of times'*. This stands in contrast to all the dispensations that preceded it.

In the above passage the Gentile dispensation is assumed to exist in apostasy. This is based on the fact that *its continuance depends on maintaining itself by responsibility* in the goodness and blessing of God (Rom. 11:21-22). Are the popes, the cult of the saints and virgin, infidelity, worldliness, divisions and denominations, cathedral building, state churches, and inquisitions, the continuing in the goodness of God? Is the minding of earthly things, which they who do such things are enemies of the cross of Christ (Phil. 3:18-19), the continuing in the goodness of God?

Will there be Revival?

We should also notice that the dispensation has no promise of general revival during its course or at its end.[146] Failure to continue in God's goodness is ruinous without hope of recovery. It is easily said that professing Christianity is anything but a continuance in the goodness of God in which it was started. Ephesus did not repent and return to its first state from which it had fallen (Rev. 2:5). Before the end of the age there may be an extraordinary testimony of warning to gather out the remnant before the judgments. However this is not the promise of revival.

We have not continued in His goodness, for if we had, such a corrupt state of things would not exist. When apostasy comes in, God's true people suffer in it, and are contained in it, though they did not begin it.[147] The true church is scattered and divided, and in many things it is worldly. We are not as Jesus prayed, *"that they all may be one... that the world may believe that you sent Me."* Christendom does not stand as one. It has been divided up by man in every imaginable way. The world does not believe that Jesus was sent by God into this world, this based upon the unity and testimony of the professing church (John 17:20-21). Christendom will soon be cut off from the olive tree.

Chapter 17: Endnotes

[144] There are further points to be made, associated with man's constant failure in human responsibility. Judaism, as a religion, is the 'first covenant'. Judaism passed away as a religion when God ended the first covenant (Heb. 8:6-8, 13). Now it all passes away for a very specific reason – it was based *entirely* on the principle of human responsibility, and this principle always leads to failure.

How important is it for you to be able to distinguish between human responsibility and sovereign grace? How important is it for you to be able to recognize the difference between man's work and God's work? How important is it to realize when something is based *entirely* on a certain principle, and to have the spiritual understanding – that which only those who possess the Spirit of God and are taught by that same Spirit can be given – of that principle, to the point that we readily see the guaranteed outcomes and results consequent to the action and effect of that principle? The entire basis of the 'first covenant', and therefore the same for Judaism as a religion, is the principle of human responsibility. The guaranteed outcome was failure. It depended on man's obedience.

Now we can look at this other principle – sovereign grace. What is this the basis of? It is the foundational principle of all God's work, except for that which is known as God's strange work – His judgment and wrath. If we exclude judgment, then all God does is based on the principle of grace. It is the basis of the wheat in the field, as planted by the Son of Man. It is the principle by which the wheat is preserved in the field as wheat. It is the basis by which the wheat will eventually be removed from the field, all together and at once, and placed in His barn. And so, what are the outcomes of this principle of sovereign grace? It is nothing short of the fact that God's work cannot fail and is always eternal in its results. This is also what the apostle is saying in reference to grace, as well as the principle of calling, when Paul says these two are without repentance concerning God's counsels (Rom. 8:29). The two being irrevocable means that God will never waver from them and that they cannot be stopped. Both calling and grace will accomplish God's full intended purpose. Both must be viewed in the sovereignty of God.

It should be profitable to compare the two dispensations – the Jewish dispensation and the dispensation of the kingdom of heaven in mystery that replaced it. We know the Jewish dispensation failed and ended, being entirely based on human responsibility and God testing this principle in man. God ends the testing. God ends the Jewish dispensation. God ends their 'first covenant'. God ends the practice of their religion. God destroys their city and temple. The kingdom is taken from them. God sets Israel aside – they are not His people. They are cut off from the olive tree. Scripture cannot be more clear in the teaching of these things.

What of the kingdom of heaven, the dispensation that replaced the Jewish one? Well, it would be odd and senseless if the new dispensation was based entirely on the same principle that doomed the Jewish dispensation to failure. And so we find that it isn't. As I said previously in the book, the kingdom of heaven is a mixture of three separate works – that of God, that of man, and that of the devil. Only the work of God that is the wheat is based on the principle of sovereign grace – the wheat is planted, the wheat is preserved, and the wheat is removed from the field. This sequence of the specific effects and outcomes of sovereign grace cannot fail at any point – it is the work of God.

Yet man's work is always based on human responsibility and will fail. Satan's work is of himself and is evil, deceitful, beguiling, and untruthful. His intentions are to corrupt the work of God if he can. But he cannot touch the wheat. Man's work and Satan's work is subject to the judgment of God. But God will never judge His own work, for He is not a workman that needs to do so. In the kingdom of heaven then, we find that which is based on the principle of sovereign grace and will not fail, right alongside and mixed in with that which does fail and will be judged. This is the spoiled crop in the field. At the end of the age the wheat is removed from the world and the tares are bundled together to be burned.

[145] The olive tree is not Israel. As a nation, Israel was cut off from the tree as 'natural' branches. This gives the impression that the olive tree was the promises of God and that Israel, as the chosen and privileged people of God, naturally had the promises (Rom. 9:4). Also the olive tree could be seen as the kingdom of God in general, as it develops upon the earth, and the possibility of entrance into the kingdom of God. The parable of the vineyard in Matt. 21:33-44 shows Israel's failure in their responsibility and they could not produce fruit pleasing to God. This passage concludes with the kingdom of God being taken away from them as a nation. Here, in a sense, Israel loses the promises of God and the kingdom, and is cut off.

The very next parable shows how Israel, as a whole, refused the invitation of grace offered to them after the cross (Matt. 22:2-14). This is the parable of the wedding of the king's son, and speaks of the time of the kingdom of heaven as a progressing development of the general kingdom of God. This time follows after the previous parable showing Israel's failure in responsibility. They now refuse the offer or invitation of grace from God. Israel's failure is double. First, as privileged above all other nations, they failed in responsibility. Second, when invited in grace, they refuse and reject grace. *"Israel has not attained what it seeks, but…were hardened."* (Rom. 11:7)

God turned away from Israel with the offer and invitation of grace and the kingdom, and turned to the Gentiles in general. This is the essence of Romans 9-11. It is God's dealings with these two different groups at separate times, but in a general dispensational arrangement. I say this because God's dealings in Romans 9-11 are with the two groups, not with individuals. The church, the body of Christ, is not one of the two groups. It is excluded from any consideration in the three chapters. And so, the olive tree represents the promises of God. In the Old Testament the promises were through Abraham, and the covenants made with him. Israel was in the olive tree by 'natural descent'. They were the natural branches as for receiving the blessings of God. But they rejected the one 'Seed' of Abraham, to whom the promises were confirmed in that very covenant. Therefore Israel was cut off and hardened after they rejected the one Seed of Abraham (Gal. 3:16-19). Then God turned to the 'wild' olive branches, which were the Gentiles in general and dispensationally.

[146] There is no evidence or promise of recovery and revival to be found in the Scriptures concerning this present time or dispensation. The implied course of things in Romans 11 is that the Gentiles will not continue in the goodness of God. The Gentile dispensation will be stopped and cut off. The general course of the kingdom of heaven is good and evil mixed together until the end of the age, and men not holding to their responsibilities. The crop in the field is ripening in evil and corruption. As for the candlesticks, they are dimming and are removed. In the seven messages of the Son of Man to Christendom there is not one indication of recovery and restoration before the end – no general revival of the corporate entity. In Philadelphia, the best of the seven, they are weak with little power, and hanging on and holding fast to what they have, remaining faithful and looking for the Lord's return. Philadelphia represents what the Lord wants us to be about, here at the end. But this is not the message we are hearing from our ministers.

[147] At the time the law was given to Israel and before the tablets were brought down the mountain and into the camp, Israel had begun its apostasy by fashioning a golden idol. It was the zeal of Moses that rescued Israel from the consequences of their departure from Jehovah. Instead of acting towards them by the just consequences of the law, God acts in goodness and mercy, forbearing the sins of some by passing over them (Rom. 3:25). Even though Israel was sustained by the intercession of Moses, the apostasy had come in and was present. In His sovereignty Jehovah showed mercy and compassion on whomever He willed (Ex.33:19, Rom. 9:14-16). Nevertheless the law was still present and many were destroyed in the wilderness (Jude 5, I Cor. 10:5-10). As for this Jewish dispensation the patience and longsuffering of God was not exhausted until Israel rejected His Son, although at many times and in many ways Israel tested God and angered Him.

One of those times was when the twelve spies were sent out into the land. Ten returned with an evil report while Joshua and Caleb had the good report of faith. Yet what were the consequences for the two of faith in the midst of the evil majority? They had to suffer in the wilderness for forty years with those in apostasy, until all those in unbelief died. God sustained Joshua and Caleb and those with them in faith, but they still spent forty years in the wilderness. **This example becomes very important to understand, for it shows and proves the existence of corporate responsibility and its consequences when there is failure in the majority.**

These events are all types and shadows for our present instruction. The true believer is on a walk of faith in the wilderness of the world. Israel as a whole, when in the wilderness, represents professing Christianity in the world. Israel consisted of wheat and tares, just like the corporate body of professing Christianity – the spoiled crop in the field. God will bundle together the tares of Christendom and eventually burn them in judgment in the wilderness (the world), just as He did with the unbelief associated with the nation of Israel (Heb. 3:16-19). The remaining Israelites, after the forty years of wandering, did cross the Jordan into the land under Joshua. This represents the wheat removed from the field (the wilderness), the rapture of the true church (crossing Jordan) and our entrance into the rest of God (the land – Heb. 4:1-11). Jesus Himself (Joshua) will come for us to take us into the presence of our God and Father. Nevertheless, the point is that true believers will live in the midst of the apostasy of professing Christianity while all the time this corporate body exists in the wilderness. Joshua and Caleb were not exempt from suffering just because they gave the report of faith. **There is such a thing as corporate responsibility, where the entire body as a whole is held responsible before God.** In this sense, Joshua and Caleb partook of the circumstances and conditions of failure, in that they could not change it. They may have been preserved through the conditions, but they definitely experienced the consequences of corporate failure for forty years.

Modern teachings in Christendom on the topics of grace and faith would have us question why Joshua and Caleb didn't receive what they desired. Why would they have to wait forty years? Why not use the principles and methods and laws of faith that we are taught today to get what they desired? They certainly had the correct report and right confession! In these modern teachings there is a serious lack of depth of understanding of any true biblical principles from God's word. They are filled with the leaven of humanism – human effort and accomplishment. I believe Joshua and Caleb had great faith. But their faith was not based on principles, methods, and following laws, but rather it was *faith in God.* In faith they were preserved by God and kept strong for forty years in the wilderness.

Here is another example. We are taught that we have great authority as believers in the name of Jesus. But this is often presented as a broad blanket statement without any understanding of biblical principles, parameters, or circumstances. We are taught that we have this authority in the name of Jesus and we should use it to bind Satan, bind enemies, bind certain avenues of thinking, change things, etc. We justify our use of His name by referring to what He said to His disciples after His resurrection – *"All authority has been given to Me in heaven and on earth."* (Matt. 28:18) But we should realize that at this present time Jesus is sitting hidden and in patience at the right hand of God, and that He hasn't taken up His power and authority, as in actively and directly using it, in order to reign on this earth (Col. 3:1-3, Heb. 10:12-13). He sits hidden from the world and He sits waiting in patience. I do not doubt that when Paul preached the gospel wherever he went, he did so in the name of Jesus. So Paul says this concerning his preaching of the gospel, *"But even if our gospel is veiled, it is veiled to those who are perishing, whose minds the god of this age has blinded..."* (II Cor. 4:3-4) The thought, in view of our modern teachings, would be to ask why Paul didn't just use his 'great authority', not only as a believer, but also as an apostle. Why didn't he use the name of Jesus to stop Satan from blinding unbelievers?

There are many teachings in the church world that are unsound doctrines simply because there is no understanding in them of these biblical principles. We do not exhibit much understanding of the kingdom of heaven, what it is, how it exists, or how it is judged by God in the end. We do not understand the spoiled crop in the field, the enemy sowing tares among the wheat, and how these things progress in time on the earth (the history of Christianity). We do not comprehend the corporate responsibility of the spoiled crop in the field, and consequences, and that all the works of man on the earth done in human responsibility will be judged by God. The dispensation of the kingdom of heaven exists in apostasy, and true believers are in the midst of it, just like Joshua and Caleb, like Elijah, and again like Jeremiah.

Chapter 18:
The Ruin of Professing Christianity

It alters the believer's entire state of mind to recognize that we live in a church world in apostasy that is hastening to its final consummation and judgment. It is a sobering spiritual realization. Instead of a church world or dispensation being sustained by God in sovereign power, as will be the case in the succeeding one, we have the present one dependent on man's faithfulness and responsibility. It is ready to be cut off in judgment, bringing it to an unceremonious end. When the Jewish dispensation failed, judgment soon came from God in the form of the Roman army. God started a new work, a new planting, in the new revelation of the kingdom of heaven. It is obvious from the parables that tell the story of this new dispensation that evil entered in early on, and that in time it too would end in failure and judgment.

God's Testimony of Apostasy in Christendom

Here is the testimony of Scripture concerning the end of the age. Before the Son of Man is revealed, it will be like the days of Noah and the days of Lot (Luke 17:26-30). There will be eating and drinking, buying and selling, planting and building, marrying and giving in marriage. There will be all the general things and cares of life that are easily found in the church world; and that day will come upon them as a thief in the night. This passage references the days in the past just before great judgments and destructions were brought on the earth by God. Clearly the last days will be marked by this 'life going on as usual' attitude. This will characterize the state of the dispensation at the end. It describes a general malaise and disconnection from God and spiritual realities. You can almost hear it being said already, "Peace, safety..."

We may say emphatically by the authority of Scripture, *"...for that Day will not come unless the falling away comes first..."* (II Thess. 2:3) In the church world it will be apostasy first – this leaves little room for a day of blessing and revival that so many want us to believe in and look for. The Scriptures tell us that apostasy will precede the end of Christendom. The consequence of this will be a cutting off of the Gentile dispensation. It will not be restoration or recovery. Those that speak such things are not speaking in faith, but in pretention, and their promises are unfounded.[148]

"But know this, that in the last days perilous times will come: For men will be lovers of themselves..." (II Tim. 3:1-5) This is the authority of God's Word. It is the testimony of the Holy Spirit through Paul concerning professing Christianity's return to a state of heathenism. The Spirit is not speaking of the world, but of that which will *'have a form of godliness but denying the power.'* It is Christendom He speaks of. We are instructed by the Spirit to turn away from such religious evil (II Tim. 3:5).

"Little children, it is the last hour; and as you have heard that the Antichrist is coming, even now many antichrists have come, by which we know it is the last hour. They went out from us..." (I John 2:18-19) This is not speaking of antichrists coming from the evil world, but from among us. The antichrists and the apostasy are within the church world, this was set in place in John's time. True Christians will know, and this passage is the proof of it, that it is the last days, that apostasy is here, and antichrists are present.

"Now the Spirit expressly says that in latter times some will depart from the faith, giving heed to deceiving spirits and doctrines of demons..." (I Tim. 4:1) Also the Spirit says, *"For the mystery of lawlessness is already at work..."* (II Thess. 2:7) There remains a hindrance at this time to the revealing of the man of sin, but the basic principle and mystery of iniquity was already at work early on in the church world. When the hindrance is finally removed, the great agent of this mysterious principle of sin comes forth. He will be the unhindered ripening in the fullness of this principle of iniquity that is now everywhere working in professing Christianity. The man of sin will be destroyed by the Lord's appearing (II Thess. 2:8). The Scriptures prove that the dispensation is prone to apostasy. The consequences must be the judgment of God and a cutting off of the Gentile dispensation.

Christendom is not expecting the Coming of the Lord

The Spirit of God through Peter predicts that in the church world there will be widespread derision concerning the expectation of the Lord's second coming (II Pet. 3:3-4). *"Scoffers will come in the last days, walking in their own lusts, saying, where is the promise of His coming?"* This is like the evil servant who says, *'my master delays his coming'* and begins to beat his fellow servants and to get drunk with the drunkards. This is the Lord's own prediction of ecclesiastical abuse and worldliness in Christendom (Luke 12:45-46). This has been going on in professing Christianity for hundreds of years. The church world has lost the expectation of His soon coming, and has become very comfortable with life in the world.

This is what things are like today: *"They ate, they drank, they married wives, and they were given in marriage..."* (Luke 17:27) This is life in the world. It does not have the thoughts of God or faithfulness to God, or the expectation of His coming. It does not have the consideration that the sufferings of this present time are not worthy of comparison with the glory which shall be revealed in us (Rom. 8:18). It is a mindset about today and life on this earth, and what is mine and how I can be happy, and at all cost it doesn't want to suffer with Him. This is what many of our Christian teachings amount to today—it is all about life in this world and on this earth and how we can improve this present time. It is a funny sort of Jesus who can help make life better for you, get control of your emotions, and improve your self-worth and self-confidence. But the real Jesus said, *"He who loves his life will lose it, and he who hates his life in this world will keep it for eternal life."* (John 12:25)

How about this: *'They ate, they drank, they bought, they sold, they planted, they built..."* (Luke 17:28) This is occupation with the things of the world and an emphasis of life on this earth. We sit back and say this is spoken of the world. But I say the world is thoroughly found throughout the professing church, and that this looks just like the church and what she does now. The teachings of Christendom emphasize this present life, but unfortunately not sufferings, and not suffering with Him so you will share in the glory with Him later. Rather, by emphasizing our lives, we can learn to reign as kings through the faith and grace teachers and their assorted doctrines.

Unsound Doctrine for Itching Ears

2 Timothy 4:3-4

"For the time will come when they will not endure sound doctrine, but according to their own desires, because they have itching ears, they will heap up for themselves teachers; and they will turn their ears away from the truth, and be turned aside to fables."

This is not a warning of what might happen. It is the Holy Spirit declaring what definitely will happen. The church world will not endure sound doctrine. It will not endure the truth of God or the words of Jesus Christ. It will have its own teachings by which the ears of the masses of professing Christianity may be scratched. They will have their own flavor and brand of Christianity. They will not adhere to the Word of God.

What characterizes the dispensation of the kingdom of heaven is apostasy, perilous times, departure from the faith, and a mystery of iniquity growing and ripening. *"But evil men and imposters will grow* worse and worse, deceiving and being deceived." (II Tim. 3:13) Peter says, "...there will be false teachers among you, who will secretly bring in destructive heresies... And many will follow their destructive ways, because of whom the way of truth will be blasphemed. By covetousness they will exploit you with deceptive words." (II Pet. 2:1-3) Paul tells us again, "For many walk, of whom I have told you often, and now tell you even weeping, that they are enemies of the cross of Christ: whose end is destruction, whose god is their belly, and whose glory is in their shame – who set their mind on earthly things." (Phil. 3:18-19) All of these unsavory characters and characteristics find a continuance in the church world because 'corrupt men were allowed to creep in unawares' (Jude 4). The mystery of iniquity was already working in the church in the first century. It has only been ripening and growing and increasing since that time. The church world is in apostasy now! It is only by the gracious patience of God that things continue on, His longsuffering meaning salvation for some (II Pet. 3:9, 15).

Christendom and Denominationalism

In the beginning of the dispensation there was apostolic power and spiritual energy in the church body to either suppress evil or cast it out. The presence of Paul delayed the display of apostasy early on. We know this because he said that after his death, "... savage wolves would come in among them, not sparing the flock." He said that, "... evil men would rise up from among them, speaking perverse things, to draw away disciples after themselves" (Acts 20:29-31). Hasn't this already taken place long ago in the church world? Aren't these things repeated today in Christendom? Haven't men divided up Christianity with self-righteous impunity, creating their own callings and kingdoms, all contrary to the very Word of God? Where is the one Lord, one body, one Spirit, one baptism? (Eph. 4:1-5) Where is the unity of the one body of Christ when we justify more denominations than we can possibly count? How is this not dividing up Christ? How is this not a violation of the Word of God? How then is it not evil and corruption? It does not matter if you can find good men and good hearts in every denomination. That does not justify what man has done in dividing up the body of Christ and in direct violation of God's word.

1 Corinthians 1:12-13

"Now I say this, that each of you says, "I am of Paul," or "I am of Apollos," or "I am of Cephas," or "I am of Christ." Is Christ divided? Was Paul crucified for you? Or were you baptized in the name of Paul?"

Is Christ divided? This was the startling appeal of Paul in the first century church, questioning such a possibility. It only took a few centuries before the dividing up of Christ was the norm. And today the denominations of Christendom are exactly this. They are an offence against the Word of God and the revealed doctrine of the true church. In no way can we justify them as the will of God revealed in Scripture. It is evil and corruption introduced by man.

The Beginnings of Division

Historical Note: There were undeniable divisions and schisms in Christianity early on. When Paul was at Antioch with the Gentile Christians, men came down from the Jerusalem church (Acts 15:1-2). This was the very beginning of divisions. They came to spy out the liberty of the Gentile Christians (Gal. 2:1-5). This serious problem and potential splitting of the early church was averted by the intervention of the Holy Spirit. The Spirit gives direct revelation to Paul to go up to Jerusalem to settle the matter (Gal. 2:2). He was directed by the Spirit to speak in defense of the true gospel, and his ministry and work among the Gentiles. God also reminds Peter of the vision and audible voice of the Spirit in the matter of Cornelius' household and conversion of the first Gentiles (Acts 15:7-12). The power of the Holy Spirit was present to keep the early church from splitting in two – a Jewish church and a Gentile church. But there is no doubt what the root cause of this potential division was:

Acts 15:5

"But some of the sect of the Pharisees who believed rose up, saying, "It is necessary to circumcise them, and to command them to keep the law of Moses."

This is the judaizing of the Christian faith. The problem is spelled out clearly for us by the Spirit. This was the main issue at the Jerusalem council. There was potential for the splitting into two churches: a church bound by the law in Jerusalem, and a church free from the law at Antioch. It was settled by the Spirit and the wisdom of God, the Jerusalem leaders declaring the Antioch Christians free from observing the law. Unity of the body of Christ was preserved, but the judaizing influence would continue to fester underneath the surface, even among many that were at this early council. This is the evil leaven that is ongoing in Christendom in some measure or form, and penetrates throughout to the end (Matt. 13:33).

Years later in Antioch, when Peter was visiting and enjoying fellowship and communion with the Gentile believers, even eating many meals with them, the judaizing leaven rears its ugly head again (Gal. 2:11-19). This time the judaizers were sent by James from the Jerusalem church. Peter is found at fault and playing the hypocrite, not holding to the truth of the gospel, bowing under the pressure of the scrutiny of the concision (Phil. 3:2-3). Barnabas is also involved in their hypocrisy (Gal. 2:13). But in this case the power of apostolic authority in Paul settled the issue, at least on the surface.

The Jerusalem Church

It is fairly obvious from this example the direction the Jerusalem church was heading, and that the Spirit of God was no longer going to halt this pattern. Peter's hypocrisy was denying the reality of his earlier visions and obedience. James, in his position in the church at Jerusalem, was becoming the main proponent of the leaven. Barnabas, Paul's partner in ministry, is in the middle of the deception. Basically Paul and the Gentile Christians are left to themselves, excluded. Even the Jewish Christians at Antioch followed Peter's example (Gal. 2:13).

For a time God allowed the church at Jerusalem to play a prominent role in the beginnings of His new work and planting. Jerusalem was where the sovereign work of the Holy Spirit began at Pentecost – the beginning of both the kingdom of heaven and the church. Yet the Jerusalem church always had its Judaism, and Jewish ways, and temple use, etc. In the beginning they were more in the character of a believing Jewish remnant in the midst of an unbelieving nation. In many ways this is how the Jerusalem church should be viewed. It is how the twelve disciples are viewed, in types and shadows, in many of their circumstances (John 20:24-28).

The Jerusalem church served God's purposes during a time of transition between the Jewish dispensation and the dispensation of the kingdom of heaven. This church was instrumental in presenting God's last invitation of grace to the nation of Israel (Matt. 22:2-7). It served God's purposes for the transition between Judaism and Christianity. It is understandable for the church at Jerusalem to be so Jewish in character and ways. God allowed it for a time – this time of transition. And this explains why James' epistle must be seen as inspired by the Spirit and part of the cannon of Scripture. In a sense it explains Peter and John's epistles. Please look to whom these letters were written. Peter, James, and John do not write to the Gentile church.

But God would not permit the Jerusalem church to go on indefinitely in its Jewish ways. Paul's epistle to the Hebrews is a warning. It was written to Hebrews who had a profession of Christ, but because of severe persecution, were considering renouncing their profession and returning to Judaism. The eventual instruction of the Spirit for them is to come outside the camp, where Jesus is (Heb. 13:11-13). This camp is Israel and Judaism (the law). As Christians they were to quit the camp and to bear the reproach of Christ outside the gate. This was timely advice. God would soon have the Romans destroy Jerusalem and the temple. This event not only stopped the practice of Judaism and effectively set Israel aside in their calling, but also served to put an end to the Jerusalem church and its influence. This was God's intention and plan. However, beyond the destruction of Jerusalem, the professing church still had the judaizers spinning their deceptions. The church world continued to have its problems with unity (John 17:20-21, Eph. 4:3-4).

When Christendom was split between east and west in the eleventh century, the Roman part claimed to be the universal church in its label – Catholic. But this action of splitting from the eastern orthodox part guaranteed there would no longer be a universal body in Christendom. Man had allowed schisms to enter in despite his pretentious claims of unity. In the professing church world there would never again be one body.

The Reformation, then Protestantism

From the time Ephesus left its first estate, the professing church has been declining into apostasy according to the clearest and most unmistakable testimonies of Scripture. The church world is not capable of restoring what existed in apostolic times – unity, power, and love. The evidence that proves this point beyond doubt is the existence of Protestantism. In the Reformation we have the energy of the Holy Spirit bringing forth enlightenment and rediscovery of certain lost Biblical truths. This was the sovereign work of God. But when man was given responsibility to care for the grace of God given and the work God had done, what were the results? – Divisions and denominations. Protestantism is filled with many forms, churches, and organizations. All of this is contrary to the authority of the word of God – that same authority the Reformation had rediscovered.

We foolishly think that a church on every street corner is a sign of Jesus Christ being exalted and the church growing and prospering. Every church feels they have a right to be there, making up their own callings and justifying their own purpose. *Is Christ divided?* Protestantism is a smorgasbord of choices where the individual is guaranteed to find something he likes or something that comforts him. We think and judge in human and worldly ways. How can all this division and schism possibly return to Pentecostal power? It represents the failure of man when given responsibility for the care of God's work in the Reformation. The professing church and Protestantism is not the pillar of the truth of God in the world (I Tim.

3:15). Christendom in general and Protestantism more specifically, is the work of man.

What does it mean that the professing church is in ruin? I ask anyone to show me the unity of the body of Christ today? The unity of the Spirit in the bond of peace does not exist in Christendom. Therefore the corporate entity cannot have a walk worthy of its calling – that is, to be the habitation of God through the Spirit on earth as the one body (Eph. 2:22). Such unity has not existed for centuries in Christendom and cannot exist today. The conscience of the believer cannot be satisfied with this sinful state.

Ephesians 4:1-4

"I, therefore, the prisoner of the Lord, beseech you to walk worthy of the calling with which you were called, (2) with all lowliness and gentleness, with longsuffering, bearing with one another in love, (3) endeavoring to keep the unity of the Spirit in the bond of peace. (4) There is one body and one Spirit, just as you were called in one hope of your calling."

Can we return to the days of Pentecost and apostolic order? Such an attainment is outside the range of possibility today. The renewal of an apostolic church would make the restoration of apostles an absolute imperative. Then also the denominations of Christendom would have to unite and act as one, voluntarily laying down all divisions and differences. The possibility of such a desire does not exist. The restoration of the first estate is not possible. But you say, with God all things are possible! But you ask amiss, and God will not do it. We would be asking God to compromise Himself, His own integrity. He will not give divine power to the unholy mess we have created.

A Form of Godliness

Matthew 15:7-9

"Hypocrites! Well did Isaiah prophesy about you, saying:

*"These people draw near to Me with their mouth,
And honor Me with their lips,
But their heart is far from Me.
And in vain they worship Me,
Teaching as doctrines the commandments of men.' "*

I know this was spoken to Israel, but it characterizes Christendom today. In the church world in the last days, perilous times will come. Men will have a form of godliness, but will deny the power of life in Christ (II Tim. 3:5). The professing church draws near to the Father and the Son with their mouths and lips, but the heart of the corporate church world is far from God. We teach the teachings of men as if it were the Word of God and sound doctrine (II Tim. 3:12-4:4).

Christendom and Man's Responsibility

Paul's desire and vigor was to keep all perfect for the coming of the Lord, presenting every man perfect in Jesus Christ (Col. 1:28, I Thess. 3:13, 5:23, I Cor. 1:8). Yet at the end of his ministry he says, *"...I have no one like-minded, who will sincerely care for your state. For all seek their own, not the things which are of Christ Jesus."* (Phil. 2:20-21) This is what has been going on in the church world from Paul's days. Men are basically motivated to seek their own, and not the things of God. Men are self-motivated to build their own, and not to enter in to the true work of God. Has every man heeded how they have built on the foundation that Paul laid?

While men slept the enemy came in and sowed tares (Matt. 13:25). This was in the beginning of the kingdom of heaven, and the crop of professing Christianity has been spoiled in the field ever since. However, in our teachings in the church world we do not even acknowledge that a spoiled crop exists. If this is true, then we are not acknowledging the evil and corruption around us. We are blind to these realities, as blind as the multitudes were to whom He spoke these parables (Matt. 13:13-15).

The spiritually-minded believer will see the spoiled crop of Christendom and realize it is ruined. The Scriptures instructs us to turn away from evil and have no part in it. But the temptation is to think you can do something about it and remedy the situation. Yet this is only spiritual pride and arrogance, and the evil leaven working. In the actual parable Jesus says, *"Let both grow together until the harvest..."* The question becomes, where do you get your commission to fix the spoiled crop? How is this according to the will of God? You say, "Well, at least I will try!" I'll remind you again of the words of the parable. The servants of the owner asked, "Do you want us then to go and gather them up?" His response was, "No, lest while you gather up the tares you also uproot the wheat..." The Lord is saying, do not try to do this or you will be guilty of doing something even more irresponsible than your sleeping at the beginning. You say, "What about revival?" I do not see the Lord promising that, certainly not to the spoiled crop. There is no promise of revival or success of the dispensation.

The book of Jude describes the history of the apostasy in the church world. (v.3) *"Beloved, while I was very diligent to write to you concerning our common salvation, I found it necessary to write to you exhorting you to contend earnestly for the faith which was once for all delivered to the saints. (v.4) For certain men have crept in unnoticed, who long ago were marked out for this condemnation, ungodly men, who turn the grace of our God into lewdness and deny the only Lord God and our Lord Jesus Christ."* The evil had crept in by the neglect of men in the church in the apostles' days. Jude couldn't speak to them about what he intended, but has to exhort them to contend for the faith once delivered to the saints! He then says (v.5), *"But I want to remind you, though you once knew this, that the Lord, having saved the people out of the land of Egypt, afterward destroyed those who did not believe."* The book of Jude shows the progression of the apostasy in the church world.

- Cain – natural evil and enmity against God (v. 11).
- Balaam – religious corruption for wealth and profit (v. 11).
- Korah – open hostility and rebellion to the priesthood and royalty of Jesus Christ (v. 11). In Korah's rebellion they all perish.

What had already found its way into the church world would become the target of the direct judgment of the Lord at His coming (vs. 14-15). It was the 'coming in' of these and not the 'going out' of them that would elicit the wrath of God in judgment. The 'coming in' was early on, in the days of the apostles. It remains present and growing until the judgment at the end of the age, that is, the entire time the church is on the earth. They were 'spots' in their feasts of charity in the church, among the Christians, and there without fear. They exalt themselves to places of importance, and loved the best places as the Pharisees did in Israel (v. 12).

If we look at the book of Acts we see the work of God at the beginning of the church. We read, *"...and the Lord added to the assembly daily those that were to be saved."* If we look at the present picture we have of Christendom, there exists little similarity in comparison to the book of Acts. What we find are opposites and that the church failed to keep its first estate. Through mercy and sovereign grace God has maintained a witness to Himself in the earth. However man, given the responsibility for the care of God's house has failed as he has in every previous dispensation.

The Principle of Responsibility

Here is this great Scriptural principle again: **Responsibility attaches itself to every creature that can be conscious of a relationship with God, the Creator. Whenever there is awareness of this relationship, there is obligation in it to God. The Creator expects obedience in the creature, and therefore looks for the production of this fruit or result.**

1. In the creature that has a holy nature preserved by God, responsibility is seen as obedience delighted in. These are the elect angels, who have not left their first estate.

2. In a nature in innocence, where thankfulness for the goodness of God is displayed as was seen in Adam and Eve before the fall. Responsibility was tested by obedience to the one command from God.

3. In a state of sin of the fallen nature of man – a man in Adam, in the flesh, and a sinner – which does not alter the fact that he has been placed in relationships with God and his neighbor, and responsibility is to be met in those relationships.

When the law was given to man (given only to Israel as representing all mankind), we see the first five commandments dealing with man's relationship with God (Deut. 5:6-15). If man obeyed the first five laws he would have produced a certain 'human righteousness'— an obeying or 'doing right' in his relationship. Man also had been placed in a relationship with his fellow creatures – his neighbor. We see the second five commandments address responsibility in this relationship (Deut. 5:16-21). If man obeyed the second five laws he would produce a certain 'doing right' toward his neighbor. We then can see that the law presents a standard or measure for man 'doing right' and it was given to him as required responsibility.

When Jesus was asked concerning the law as to which commandment was the greatest, He sums up the whole essence of the law in two distinct areas – man's responsibility to first love God and then his responsibility to love his neighbor as himself (Matt. 22:36-40). In this biblical sense, it is interesting that sin in man at the beginning becomes complete by Adam sinning against God and then Cain sinning against his neighbor.

Sin entered the world through Adam. Man was chased out of the garden as fallen and a sinner. Yet the presence of sin in the flesh, and the fruit of sin in the committing sins or acts of unrighteousness, never changes the original relationships man was placed in. And it never changes his responsibility in those relationships. If the relationship still exists, then the responsibility is still present. What then are the consequences of sin entering the world through the first man? It is simply this – it is now impossible for man to obey or 'do right' in any and all of his relationships.

What the Scriptures teach is the utter depravity of fallen man in his ability to obey and 'do right'. He cannot fulfill his responsibilities as required – not in obedience and not in 'human righteousness'. Why would God say all man's righteousness is but filthy rags in His sight if any of it is acceptable to Him? (Isa. 64:6) Why would God say of the children of men that there are none that do good, no, not one? (Ps. 14:2-3) God's nature is holy and righteous. We should always consider the true nature of God before declaring what they think should be acceptable to Him.

But this is where the leaven comes in to appeal to man's pride and emotions. Satan is the source of the lies and he whispers in man's ear, "Has God really said this? Utter depravity? That sounds harsh and extreme. Surely this isn't what God has declared. Surely this is not the correct understanding!" We believe the beguiling words of the deceiver in order to feel better about 'self' and to improve our self-esteem. It is trusting in mere humanism, where man at all times is at the center and is the focus of attention. It props man up to be something in his own eyes that he is not (Rom. 12:3). God spent 4000 years prior to the cross testing man's responsibility, proving man's depravity in principle. Yet almost immediately after the cross we take back up the evil leaven in our Judaizing and Arminianizing ways. We refuse to be instructed by God. We may as well rebuild the tower of Babel! These are all the same ungodly corruptions of God's word and truth. It is as if we are completely ignorant of what God was doing for the 4000 years between the promise of the seed of the woman and the time when He arrived. Even in the making of this promise in the judgment of the serpent, God shows that the first Adam was wholly passed by. The first Adam was not the seed of the woman. God didn't place the promise of hope in him. Man in the flesh, man in Adam, is utterly depraved. This is what God proved; this is what the Scriptures teach.

The Failure of Man in Responsibility

The history of man in responsibility shows a pattern of 100% failure. This is the story of mankind in Scripture:

- Adam in paradise failed in his responsibility to obey the one command of His Creator. Adam sins against God.
- Cain killed his brother Abel. He sinned against his neighbor. Early on man's sin was complete in regards to the relationships

he was placed in, and the responsibility attached to these relationships.

- The world from Adam to Noah becomes so evil God had to destroy it by a flood.

- Noah got drunk after exiting the ark when the principle of government and the sword is placed into his hands, his son disparaging his authority.

- God sovereignly chose Abram out of a world filling with idolatry – the new abomination that Satan brings forth in the earth after the flood (Josh. 24:2-3).

- When Moses brings the tablets down the mountain the first time, Israel already has the golden calf and is worshipping it.

- The priesthood fails in its first order of service. Aaron's sons offer strange fire. They are judged immediately and destroyed.

- Royalty fails in Saul, Israel's king chosen after fleshly appearance. David steals another man's wife. Solomon, the son of David, has many wives, and with them many gods to serve and please. Israel is divided into two kingdoms.

- The prophets are discarded, starting with Samuel, because Israel wanted a king to rule over them. Most of the true prophets are abused, beaten, imprisoned, and killed (Matt. 21:35-36). False prophets fill up the void for Israel, ones who will prophesy good and pleasant things for the kings and nation.

- Israel uses the law contrary to its purpose, and thinking they are doing it they believe they are righteous and have life. God's purpose for giving it was death and condemnation. Israel excels in human pride and accomplishment.

- Israel's idolatry and apostasy against God becomes so bad that God says to them, *"For you are not my people, and I will not be your God."* (Hos. 1:9) God removes His presence from them, and the Ark of the Covenant, the throne of God, is lost forever.

- When the Gentiles are given responsibility for world government it fails in the idolatry of Nebuchadnezzar, the blasphemy of Belshazzar, and the self-deification of Darius. What ensues from responsibility in government given to the Gentiles are four beasts – wild, ravenous, unruly, idolatrous, and apostate in character. What characterizes the beasts is a mind of their own will in which they do not answer in responsibility to God.

Jesus tells a parable about the vineyard of God that represented the nation of Israel. In it He directly implicates the failure of Israel in responsibility over time (Matt. 21:33-40). Their final failure was the rejection and killing of God's Son, when He was sent to them (vs. 37-39). Look at the failure and evil that surrounds this parable:

- The King of Israel, their promised Messiah, enters into Jerusalem (Matt. 21:1-11). Immediately He clears the temple of its consumerism and profiteering, and addresses the indignation of the leadership (Matt. 21:12-16).

- The next morning He curses the fig tree, symbolic of Israel specifically, and all man in Adam in general. These cannot produce fruit unto God and must be condemned (Matt. 21:18-19).

- In the literal explanation of the parable, the kingdom of God is taken away from Israel for rejecting the Son, and judgment is pronounced (Matt. 21:42-44).

- In the following parable (Matt. 22:1-14) the Jews are those who reject the free invitation to the wedding of the king's son. This parable speaks of the time from Pentecost to the destruction of Jerusalem in 70 AD (v. 7). The servants of the king who were spitefully treated and killed are the disciples (v. 6).

- *"Is it lawful to pay taxes to Caesar, or not?"* Their evil attempts to trap Him in His words (Matt. 22:15-18). But the reality is evident – Israel's king is Caesar.

- The present generation of Israel is pronounced guilty of all the righteous blood shed on the face of the earth, from Abel to Zechariah (Matt. 23:29-36)

- Israel is set aside and made desolate as the house of God (Matt. 23:37-39).

- Pilate presents Jesus as King of the Jews (Matt. 27:11, 29, 37). Israel would have no other king but Caesar, and says, *"His blood be on us and on our children."* (Matt. 27:25) The fourth beast, the Roman Empire, represented by Pilate, rejects Him as do His own. Yet Jesus was the true King of Israel and the world.

Man was tried in his innocence in the garden, listened to the serpent, and fell. He was tried without law and sin reigned. When man was given the law and he lived under it, he was guilty of transgressing it. Afterwards, when man was fully shown to be a sinner and a transgressor, God came in goodness, not imputing his sins to him, and man would not have God (II Cor. 5:19). The history of responsible man was ended at that point in time – at the cross. Israel also had lost all claims to the fulfillment of the promises and kingdom of God by rejecting Him in whom the fulfillment of promises and the kingdom was to be found.

Is Christendom any different?

We think there is a better outcome in Christendom, when man is given responsibility there. But this is not the case and we deceive ourselves. *The professing church has not escaped the common pattern of disobedience and ruin any more than what came before it.* The responsibility of man on the earth will be judged – this is an unwavering principle of Scripture. The fact is that the professing church in this world is subject to judgment and its performance is judged in Revelation 2 and 3. The biblical conclusion is that it has lost its position as a light-bearer in the world. God had to do this when the general assembly departed from its first position. His action of removing the candlestick is part of the overall principle. If professing Christianity does not show Jesus Christ to the world, then it is a false witness for God and has to be set aside. God may have patience with the general body, and has done so, showing remarkable longsuffering with it. He may propose its repentance and return to the first estate, but if this is not done, then the candlestick is removed. The first position must be maintained or God's glory and truth are falsified.

God judges the performance of the professing church as a failure. When God looked in the place where there should have been righteousness, He found iniquity. The corruption of that which should have stood for the good is the worst of all corruptions. We clearly find in Scripture and in the history of man that all responsibility fails and is judged. Against this record there is only one exception – that which will be sustained and upheld by the power of the Son of God reigning as the last Man in the dispensation of the fullness of times (Eph. 1:10).

The Faithfulness of God

Man has been unfaithful. Man has failed consistently and comprehensively when tested in responsibility. Israel, God's chosen people and nation, have failed miserably. The professing church has followed this same pattern found in the history of mankind. The professing church has failed as the light and witness for God on the earth. However, none of these things change God. None of these things hinder the faithfulness of God. God will do everything He has promised to do. He cannot do otherwise. He is the one true living God.

Romans 3:3-4

"For what if some did not believe? Will their unbelief make the faithfulness of God without effect? Certainly not! Indeed, let God be true but every man a liar. As it is written:

*"That You may be justified in Your words,
And may overcome when You are judged."*

Regardless of man's failure and unfaithfulness, God will remain faithful. And guess what? None of these things touch the sovereignty of God. His counsel and plans move forward unhindered. They continue on in His patient mercy and sovereign grace. They continue on in His hidden providence, until all is fulfilled in Jesus Christ.

In contrast, man's continual failure in responsibility serves to glorify the faithfulness and sovereign grace of God. There are difficult but important biblical lessons to learn here as a result – that God must be everything, and man is nothing. That God receives all the glory, and there is no reason for boasting in man whatsoever. God will do all things in the future by His sovereign grace and power. When Christ returns it is the destruction of evil by righteous judgment and fiery indignation (Rev. 19:15-21). The coming millennium is the rule of Christ in power and righteousness (Rev. 12:10, Mark 9:1). This is what qualifies as the work of God. Its results stand in stark contrast to the actions, performance, and will of man. The entire counsel of Scripture proves the utter failure of man in his works.

Man in Adam is fallen and utterly depraved. There is no redeeming value in him. God never saw value in him, which we assume would require God to respond in kind. God did not set His love on the believer because of something in him, but rather, He set His love on us because of what is in Himself, what is in God. God is love – it is an intrinsic attribute of His. God chose, in Himself, to set His love upon us. This is the simple biblical truth, but for contemporary man it is a very difficult thing to admit.

The Dispensational Pattern

Every previous dispensation as well as the present one follow the same pattern:

- Man fails in responsibility, and that failure is usually immediate. The failure is apostasy, in one or more of its various forms. There may be a period of decay or decline from the starting point, but apostasy is established and sets in.

- The dispensation continues on in the grace, longsuffering, and mercy of God until the full ripening of the apostasy has come. It must be judged by God. This is the point where the longsuffering of God is exhausted.

- There is never a recovery midstream or before the end. The patience and longsuffering of God never undoes the apostasy that is established in any dispensation, but rather, carries the dispensation on in grace and mercy. The consequences of the first failure are never undone.

The Last Four Church States

The progression of professing Christianity in responsibility on the earth is shown to us in Revelation 2, 3. Jesus judges the responsibility of the spoiled crop in the field. The two chapters clearly show in detail the apostasy and failure of the church world and the dispensation. The addresses to the seven churches are very much threats of judgment, except for the encouragement given to the faithful remnant (Philadelphia).

The last four churches survive the progression of time in the messages. They are four distinct states we can see forming Christendom at its end. Thyatira, the fourth church of the seven, is the last church given ecclesiastical character. She existed on her own as the 'professing church' for over 1100 years previous to the Reformation. The remaining three churches are associated with Protestantism. However, the final three are never acknowledged as having any proper corporate church position. The characters of Christ associated with the last three are never anything John saw of Christ in the midst of the candlesticks.

1. Jezebel in Thyatira is Romanism. She teaches corruption and idolatry. She knows the depths of Satan in her worldliness and births her own children in the corruption. She influences

many others to accept her teachings. She goes on to the tribulation.

2. Sardis is spiritually dead, having no life, and is Protestantism after the Reformation. It results in denominationalism and personal judgment of the Word of God.

3. Philadelphia is the weak but faithful remnant, holding on to His word and name, and practicing the word of His patience. His exhortation to them is, *"Behold, I come quickly! Hold fast what you have..."* He basically tells the believing remnant to hold true to Him in the midst of all the corruption of the professing church, and that He will be with them soon.

4. Laodicea is upside down. Its impression of itself is the opposite of Christ's impression of it. For Laodicea, evil is good and good is evil. It has earthly wealth and a high opinion of itself. But Christ says it is spiritually wretched, miserable, poor, blind, and naked. This is the evangelical church world.

These are the four distinct entities that Christ gives. Together they form the present state of Christendom. My question to you personally, one believer to another – which of the four looks like what you are involved in? Which of the four is your local church a microcosm of?

The first four churches tell the history of what men call 'the apostolic succession' of the professing church. This is man pretending to hold the authority of Christ, passing it on from man to man in its corruption and evil lust for power. This results in the harlot Jezebel and the list of popes in the Roman church. Certainly the Greek Orthodox Church is included in Jezebel and 'succession', for the split of west from east did not occur until the turn of the millennium (@1000 AD). In Thyatira the judgment will come on Jezebel, all her children she birthed in her corruptions, and all those who hold to her doctrines.

The Reformation brings a divergent path from Jezebel. The last three churches can easily be seen as representing the history of Protestantism.

The Last Two Churches

Perhaps there is a better way of looking at the four ending churches. Corporately both Romanism and Protestantism exist in Christendom. Jezebel is corruption and Sardis is spiritually dead. Both Thyatira and Sardis had a remnant surviving within. These two small remnants form Philadelphia, the remnant church. Then Romanism and Protestantism, along with the development of Evangelical Christianity, form Laodicea and has its candlestick removed. In this view, which I believe to be the most scripturally sound, there are only two representative churches at the end – Philadelphia and Laodicea. Together the two form the whole of Christendom. One is wheat, and the other is nothing but tares. Christ stands outside Laodicea knocking on its door, but no one inside hears Him. The wheat is removed from the field. The tares are bundled together and left behind, to be burned (Matt. 13:30).

Failure at the Beginning

When the Lord was ready to leave this earth and ascend back to His Father He gave a commandment to the apostles, *"Go ye and make disciples of all nations."* This was their special commission from the Lord who chose them. He had been raised from the dead, and had been given all power and authority in heaven and earth. Where is the fulfillment of these words by the twelve apostles? Jesus also instructed them, *"Behold, I send you out as sheep in the midst of wolves...when you are persecuted in one city, flee to the next."* But when the great persecution arose in Jerusalem at the time of Stephen's death, all of the church was scattered throughout Judea and Samaria, except the twelve apostles (Acts 8:1). Where is the fulfillment by the twelve? There is no account recorded by the Holy Spirit in all of Scripture of the twelve going into all the world and preaching the gospel to every creature. This shows that the command given on which the dispensation balanced, as to the revealed testimony of Scripture, remained unfulfilled by those to whom it was committed.

God does intervene in an extraordinary way in sovereign grace, and a new arrangement is made. The twelve would be apostles to the circumcised (Gal. 2:6-9). God chose Paul in sovereign grace, and used him to be the apostle to the uncircumcised, that is, to the Gentiles. He was raised up by God as 'one born out of due time,' totally distinct, and 'not of man, nor by man.' (Gal. 1:1) He was not an apostle with the twelve, nor an apostle from the twelve, but one entirely independent from them in all his qualifications (Gal. 1:11-23). He was the apostle to the nations (Rom. 11:13).

The critical point is not just that Christendom is in a bad state now. But like all dispensations, it failed at the beginning, not long after man was given responsibility to care for the sovereign work of God. Failure then will bring in certain judgment from God. He will not allow the evil to go on indefinitely, though He now bears long and patiently with it. As I said previously, this does not impugn the faithfulness of God. It exalts His faithfulness and glorifies Him. God will always keep and preserve a remnant. They will prosper according to the measure of faith and grace God has given them. His grace is sufficient for them in all situations and circumstances. *These are those who have ears to hear all the Spirit is saying and the Son of Man is judging concerning the churches* (Rev. 2:7, 11, 17, 29, 3:6, 13, 22).

The Failure of man vs. the Sovereign Work of God

It is the failure of man in responsibility that is the central issue. We must recognize it and be willing to admit it. This failure has been consistent and comprehensive by man, from the beginning of time. It is not a difficult task to trace this failure in Scripture, as we did above. The important point is this: the failure is no different in the church age or the time of the covenant and gospel of grace, or whatever label we put on present things. But this is exactly what I find the leadership in Christendom unwilling to see and admit. Covenant theologians, dispensationalists, and the ministry in general, all point to a future feat of great human exploit in winning or changing the world. A feat of winning or fundamentally changing America by man's preaching and spreading of the gospel. These aspirations are beyond the Scriptures, and contrary to God's thoughts and plan.

What is the essence of God's thoughts on the return of Jesus Christ to this earth? He rides a white horse in glory with a double-edged sword out of His mouth by which He strikes the nations. He will rule them with a rod of iron. He Himself treads the winepress of the fierceness and wrath of Almighty God (Rev. 19:11-15). Satan is bound for a thousand years, the heads of the two beasts thrown into the lake of fire, their armies completely destroyed. He separates the sheep from the goats, and rules the nations. His judgment in righteousness is a rod of iron by which He rules until every enemy is put under His feet (I Cor. 15:24-25). The overriding thought of God concerning these things is this – God will do by His own work what man has always failed in doing by his work and responsibility.[149] This failure also includes the time of the church on earth. These events I described are the sovereign work, power, judgment, and wrath of Almighty God. They come about because of the growing and ever increasing evil and corruption of the world and man. It is not a world getting better or changing for the good. <u>My point is this:</u> it doesn't describe a world changed by grace, by the turning of the other cheek, or by the preaching of the gospel. The world doesn't change by the influence of these things. Improving the world for good is not the purpose for preaching of the gospel.

The Gates of Hell

There is another important point that needs to be brought up concerning how predictable the failure of man in responsibility is, even during the time of the church on earth. Our temptation is to think the church should be able to succeed where Israel so miserably failed, because the church was founded on true redemption and grace. One part of this statement is true. The true church has title to position and privileges in Jesus Christ that Israel would be envious of – if they had any spiritual knowledge or comprehension of this. But, as believers, we are still in our bodies of flesh, and we do not have the end of our salvation yet. There is no perfection for the church short of her rapture and glorification. This makes all the difference.

What are the three great evils for the believer to contend with? They are the world, the flesh, and the devil. The first Adam fell to the wiles of the devil when he was innocent, and when there was no world or flesh. His sin was the greatest of sins and the human race was condemned in him (Rom. 5:16-19).

Jesus said, *"I will build My church, and the gates of hell will not prevail against it."* The gates of hell prevailed against man when he was innocent. They prevailed against man when he was in the world without the law. When man received the law of God, the gates of hell prevailed again. When the Gentiles were given civil rule of the earth, Satan inspired them from his place in the heavens above. When God comes into the world by goodness and grace, the gates of hell motivates the Jews to hand Him over to the Gentiles to put Him to death.

Satan cannot touch the body of Christ, the true church. The planted wheat remains wheat.[150] But we see the gates of hell have prevailed against the crop in the field and it is ruined. The professing church has failed in its responsibility. Please note that despite true redemption and grace positioning and privileging the church, Satan is still in the heavens as god of this world and he influences the course of this age. I have previously shown that he is in the heavens to corrupt professing Christianity and its testimony on earth. This he has done well. The gates of hell have prevailed against Christendom. Its candlestick is all but snuffed out.

As long as Satan is not bound in the bottomless pit, man will always be found to fail when given responsibility on the earth (Rev. 20:1-3). I believe every believer should be able to see and admit this reality. You can easily see this in the Scriptures. I do not speak of the individual responsibility of the believer, but rather the corporate responsibility of the professing church as represented by the candlestick. It is ruined and cannot be recovered. Only the patience and longsuffering of God allows the continuance of the age and the church on earth.

As a student of the Scriptures, just ask yourself these questions: Why is Satan bound in the bottomless pit for the entire time of the thousand years? What is the importance of this difference in the coming age from the previous one? Why remove him from the heavens? Why not allow him to roam the earth? It isn't the work of the church that accomplishes these things. It isn't the preaching of the gospel of grace. It is the sovereign power and work of God. All these events have their purpose in the counsels of God. I pray that all readers will have eyes to see and understand these truths by the teaching of the Spirit in God's word.

Only God's Judgments can change the World

How will the earth be filled with the knowledge of the glory of the Lord, as the waters cover the sea? How is this going to happen? Many say by our efforts in preaching the gospel. But where do you find that? The passage below explains how it actually happens. The earth and the world do not change by grace or the gospel – not for righteousness.

Isaiah 26:9-10

"For when Your judgments are in the earth,
The inhabitants of the world will learn righteousness.
Let grace be shown to the wicked,
Yet he will not learn righteousness;
In the land of uprightness he will deal unjustly,
And will not behold the majesty of the Lord."

Unless the judgments of God are brought to the world from heaven above, the world will not be changed and will not learn righteousness. The world is not changed by grace. The world is not won by the gospel. The world will only change after Christ physically returns and judges it. When He appears and establishes His kingdom, it will be a time of judgment. The Psalms speak of His millennial kingdom as the time when, *"...judgment shall return to righteousness, and all the upright in heart will follow it."* (Psalms 94:15) This is the truth of Scripture. I would rather agree with God than jump on the bandwagon of presumptuous human thoughts and endeavors.

The cross of Christ, by His blood and God's grace, has wrought divine righteousness for every believer. But the cross has not produced righteousness for the world. Rather it was quite the opposite. Righteousness was in the person of Christ. Judgment was with Pilate and the leaders of the Jews. However, when Christ appears again, righteousness and judgment will be joined together in the millennial earth. *"For He is coming, for He is coming to judge the earth. He shall judge the world with righteousness and the peoples with His truth."* (Psalm 96:13) And we read (Acts 17:31), *"because He has appointed a day on which He will judge the world in righteousness by the Man whom He has ordained. He has given assurance of this to all by raising Him from the dead."*

The professing church is corrupt. Satan has planted evil in her, by tares and leaven. She has invited the world inside, the throne of Satan. She is beyond recovery. This is the Son of Man's actual appraisal of her. She cannot save herself, let alone save the world.

What is the judgment of the Son of Man? Jezebel of Thyatira, and those with her, will be cast into the great tribulation and He kills her children (Rev. 2:21-23). He comes to Sardis as He comes to the world – as a thief in the night (Rev. 3:3). He spews Laodicea out of His mouth (Rev. 3:16). All three of these are sobering judgments and endings.

Matthew 13:40

"Therefore as the tares are gathered and burned in the fire, so it will be at the end of this age."

This is what the kingdom of heaven looks like – wheat and tares mixed together in the crop in the field. The crop is the work of the Son of Man and the work of Satan. It has been this mixture of good and evil for some time, as it is now. It remains like this to the end of the age.

Christendom and the Individual Believer

This is the final question to be decided with respect to the condition of professing Christianity. Will we be held individually responsible, and are we judged as such, in light of having been warned, if we continue to walk in that which the Lord has already declared judgment on? The answer to this question must weigh heavily on every believer. And particularly the question must weigh upon every minister, for these are the ones Paul is speaking to when he implores, *"But let each one take heed how he builds on it"* (the foundation of God's building – I Cor. 3:9-10). If we entertain hope of re-establishing the church through recovery and revival, then we deny at the very same time the unity of the body of Christ and the responsibility of the professing church.

"He who has an ear, let him hear what the Spirit says to the churches." Rev. 2, 3

These are the words of Christ spoken after each of the seven messages to Christendom in Revelation. The messages are His judgments of the professing church. This phrase tells every true believer that it is his personal responsibility to hear and understand what Christ is saying. We are responsible to recognize Christ's judgment of the state and condition of the church, and to heed His words at all times. We are called upon to be guided by His words and to act upon them. This is obedience to God's word and obedience to Christ. And it is hearing what the Spirit is actually saying.

We also realize that it is the professing church that is being judged. The church can no longer be an authority for us if Christ is judging it. If there is evil and corruption within (we are told by the Scriptures it is evil growing and ripening), how can the outer public body be a safe haven for us? The church is a judged object, not an authority or safe refuge. Jesus expressly tells us to heed what the Spirit is saying, not what the church is saying.

We must notice the irony of Ephesus being the first of the churches looked at. The decline and decay begins with her. She is the one in whom Christendom's candlestick is threatened. In the beginning Ephesus had the highest level of knowledge, blessing, and privilege. She was the vessel of great grace, yet represents the church's departure from its first estate. The soberness of this reality should not be lost on any believer. It serves to prove whether you have ears to hear Christ and the Spirit.

- There's an old man that has been preaching for years the same depressing message of judgment from God on the horizon. How edifying is that? He really is an odd bird. Now he and his small family are over that hill and across the valley building a large boat they call an ark. They say that God will bring the rain. Now who has ever heard of such a thing? That cannot be of God. What they are saying and what they are doing is simply madness! It cannot be of God because there are only six of them and there are a thousand with us. That proves it. We'll just keep doing what we've been doing (Luke 17:26-27). We know God is blessing this.

- There's this odd character hiding out in the cave over there. He must be afraid and running from something. He must be guilty of doing something really bad. Get this – He thinks he represents God and the rest of the nation is against him! Talk about visions of grandeur (I Kings 19:9-10).

  In this case we know that God preserved an elect remnant of 7000 that had not bowed their knees to Baal (I Kings 19:18). But we have to admit that this was a remnant that stayed hidden, and preferred it that way. They did not come to the support of the man of God standing up to the ungodly nation given over to idolatry and apostasy.

- There is the message of Jeremiah in the midst of unbelieving and ungodly Judah. The succession of kings had become accustomed to gathering prophets who would speak only good and pleasing things to them. They heaped up prophets to themselves, according to their own desires, having ears that needed itching (II Tim. 4:3-4). They were guilty of turning away from the truth, and turning to lies and deceptions. Standing up for the true message from God, Jeremiah ends up in a deep dark hole in the prison – his present reward and reality for his faithfulness.

I wish I could teach something different to you, and bring you a different message, but the Spirit of God and His Word will not allow this. In this chapter I have set before you the testimony of Scripture concerning the ripening evil of Christendom in the last days. God allowed the evil to begin and show itself early in the history of the professing church. His purpose for this was to include in His word His thoughts concerning the nature and character of the evil. What was already manifested in the early church becomes the ground for final judgment. This is the testimony of the Spirit found in God's word. God saw fit to make arrangement for this before the cannon of Scripture was complete. It is intended for the church in the last days.

You judge the message, if it is of God and of His Word. Having read, you will be responsible for this, and then to act according to your spiritual judgment, whatever it may be. I have tried my best to be responsible to speak and to teach from the word of God. I attempt to write only God's thoughts and this from His Word taught by His Spirit. The question remains: Will you acknowledge the ruin of the corporate body?

Chapter 18: Endnotes

[148] Often the carnality of the human mind in the flesh (in Adam) or the untrained spiritual mind of the believer will see things and teach things opposite of what God's mind is and what God's Word teaches. Examples of this are such things as the law of Moses. This is clearly taught in the epistles of Paul as the administration of death and condemnation (II Cor. 3). In its Old Testament form it can never be anything different than this. It should never be represented as having the ability to provide life and righteousness. It is neither good for the believer's justification or for his walk of faith on this earth. If the law is not of faith (Gal. 3:12), how can it produce a walk of faith for the true Christian? It simply cannot. The law of Moses is the religion of the Jews. It is Judaism. In many ways Judaism is the opposite of Christianity. It is a walk by sight, by physical senses. It is not Christianity. When our teachers use the teachings of Judaism (which are decidedly different in character and principle from Christianity, and which cannot produce faith which is the basis of Christianity), and mix them with the teachings for the church, you have the evil leaven of the Judaizing of the faith.

Another example of these contradictory understandings from the truth of God's Word is the proper biblical teaching of the principle of grace in redemption, delivering from the principle of sin (Rom. 6:1-7). Yet we are accused of giving the believer a license to sin – licentiousness. The proper teaching of grace will never lead a true believer to licentiousness. The true believer will eventually know that by God's grace he has died and has been freed from sin (Rom. 6:7). The life he now has is the life of Christ raised from the dead. By it he lives to God as Christ does (Rom. 6:7-13). This is hardly the teaching of licentiousness to the believer. The only ones that will take God's grace as a license to sin are the tares in professing Christianity. Those who accuse the proper teaching of grace as a license to sin are often true believers simply demonstrating an ignorance and carnal understanding of sound biblical doctrine. They have no knowledge of the power of grace to deliver from the slavery and dominion of sin – something the law or Judaism could never do for anyone (Rom. 6:14).

A third example of this contradictory understanding is the biblical teaching of the sovereign choice of God. The Scriptural basis for all the choices of God is the exaltation of His own glory. The vessels of mercy are prepared beforehand for glory – this is the believer, those that He called, those that He chose, and those that He prepared (Rom. 9:20-24). Yet the carnal understanding sees unfairness and unrighteousness in the choice of God (Rom. 9:14).

I said all the above to get to the example we find in the chapter. ***It is a contradiction of the truth of God's word and counsels to believe and teach that we will experience revival and recovery in the current dispensation, and that man, by the gospel, will win nation after nation, and will fill the earth with the glory of the Lord.*** This is opposite of the mind of God and is not in agreement with God's Word. There is not one dispensation in the history of Scripture, when placed in the responsibility of man, which did not end in failure and the judgment of God. It didn't matter if it was God's government of the earth, the law, the prophets, priesthood, or royalty. When man was tested in responsibility he failed every time, as he originally did in the garden when in a far better position. The Jewish dispensation ended with Israel crucifying their Messiah and King!

The only dispensation that will not fail is the dispensation of the fullness of times, the millennium. It will be sustained by the power of God over the earth in righteous judgment in the kingdom of the Son of Man. This coming dispensation is a dispensation of judgment on the earth. It is very much in contrast to grace and the longsuffering of God's patience. That is why it is the last dispensation! Regardless of dispensation, it is always true that the individual is saved by the sovereign grace of God. The children of promise, whoever they may be individually, walk in the steps of faith as Abraham as being heirs of the promises (Rom. 4:11-16, Gal. 3:6-9, 14, 22, 29). In the present dispensation the church has not seen and yet she believes (John 20:29). In the coming dispensation the future Jewish remnant must see with their eyes in order to know their Messiah (John 20:27-29, Zech. 12:10-14). It is a dispensation where every eye will see (Rev. 1:7).

But the present dispensation of the kingdom of heaven in mystery is in apostasy and corruption, headed for failure, and will incur the just judgment of God. The opposite of this is not possible, regardless of the many prayers of the few faithful.

We often begin to think and teach that we can accomplish anything if we try hard enough and organize enough. That is Arminian thinking and it is wrong. If we pray long enough God will do it. That is Arminian thinking and it is wrong. If we fast and pray this entire month for our nation, we will see miraculous things and God will save America and heal our land. That is definitely Jewish thinking with an Arminian effort. It is all wrong. What is all important is the mind of God, the will of God, and the purpose of God's counsel found in His Word. He will accomplish all His counsel in His sovereignty. It will be His glory alone that is exalted.

[149] We have noted and documented man's failures in responsibility from the beginning of time in the garden. God will truly accomplish all of what man could never be responsible to accomplish. This will be done through His Son, and the rule and reign of the Son of Man over the millennial earth. Where the first Adam ruined the 'rest of God' with man on the earth, the second Adam will establish rest for man on the earth, bringing peace through His rule in righteousness. Where the first Adam succumbed to the temptation of the evil one, the second Adam overcame him and spoiled his goods. Through death Jesus destroys him who had the power of death. Adam fails in responsibility, but the Lord Jesus fulfills Adam's responsibilities for the glory of God as the second Adam. Where government failed in Noah, it will succeed in the kingdom of the Son of Man. Where the law, written on tablets of stone, could not be accomplished by Israel for their blessing, God will do in a new covenant by writing His law on minds and hearts. Israel will fulfill it, and be exalted and prosper in the land. Where priesthood failed in Aaron's and Eli's sons, it will be found most excellent for Israel's blessing by the Melchizedek priest in their temple, who had neither beginning of days nor end of life. Israel's blessings will be realized as was Abraham's, after the defeat of their enemies (Heb. 7:1-3). Also Christ is High Priest for the church, and will save all its members to the uttermost by the end of His ministry (Heb. 7:25-27). Also the Gentile supremacy of civil dominion will be put down and reversed by the King of kings and Lord of lords destroying all Gentile rule (Dan. 2:34-35), and in turn, ruling over the Gentile nations with a rod of iron (Rev. 2:26-27). It will be in Christ the Gentiles will trust. Where Solomon, the son of David failed in faithfulness, Jewish royalty will be gloriously fulfilled by the true Son of David in the Messianic kingdom over Israel.

So also the church (although separated and no part of the above dealings of God with man on the earth), having failed in showing forth God's glory in its time of responsibility, will be raised up by God in the rapture, and will be made perfect, holy, and blameless in the presence of God eternally (Eph. 1:3-4). She will be the accomplishment of the heavenly glory of Christ through the ages to come (Eph. 2:6-7). It is the same principle and pattern from beginning to end. First, the responsibility of man ends in failure, then divine success in sovereign grace and power in the second Adam.

We easily trace through Scripture the record of the failure of man. In every circumstance of testing responsibility in man God has never found obedience. Man's failure has been 100%. It is complete and proven to be so by God Himself. In the end God makes good all the failure of man by and through His own sovereign work. In the end all is made good by God in and through the second Man, Jesus Christ – this is to the praise of God's glory. These are the two great facts of the testimony of Scripture – man's complete failure in his work and responsibility (100% - utter depravity), and God's own workmanship in sovereign grace to undo and make good all of the failure. The realization of these two biblical truths serve to meet the pride of the human heart, whether believer or unbeliever, whether the world or the professing church. The natural tendency of the human heart is to self-dependency. This is the evil leaven that has infected and saturated all of the doctrine of Christendom and has produced its results – the corruption and ruin of the professing church. Yet the full realization of these two truths should have destroyed long ago all the leaven – all the Judaizing and Arminianizing influence. But it has not destroyed it. Rather the professing church has taken the leaven back up and fully embraced it. It has done this to its irreconcilable ruin.

Even though the professing church is in ruin and with no recourse, still the spiritual believer can fully realize the two truths and their consequences. He may walk with God individually, and do so faithfully, even in the midst of a ruined Christendom. Jesus Christ gives His grace to the believer, which translates into His strength in us, when we remain conscious of our human weakness and infirmity (II Cor. 12:9). This is similar to the critical understanding that every unbeliever must realize before coming to faith in Christ – he stands before God as a sinner and enemy of God, who is utterly depraved and lost and without any hope or strength (Rom. 5:6, 8, 10, Luke 19:10, Eph. 2:12). It is necessary that the unbeliever should feel himself condemned before God, and learn that from this point on all depends on God's unmerited grace. The unbeliever cannot be saved through self-dependence. Neither can the believer walk with God while maintaining any trace of self-dependence. This is why the professing church is in ruin.

[150] The true church is the body of Christ. Individual believers, sealed by the Spirit of God as sons, are baptized by this same Spirit into the one corporate body of Christ (I Cor. 12:12-13). All believers are gathered unto Him as to a living stone. We also as living stones are built up a spiritual house (I Pet. 2:4-5). The illustration here is to the resurrected life of Christ and all are living stones in Him and built up with Him. There are no dead stones here. There are no tares – the sons of the wicked one – in this allusion. This is what Christ builds, the body of Christ, and is the sovereign work of God. The exceedingly great power of God that raised Christ up and set Him at the right hand of God, is the same sovereign power that raised up the church and exalted it far above all principalities and powers. The members of the body are the members of Christ, and livingly secure in Him. This is the work of God. This cannot fail and Satan cannot touch it.

Chapter 19

What in the World are we to do?

The professing church is in a ruined condition. What should the true believer do? Are we to labor and pray for its restoration? What course should we pursue? What hope do we have? When our eyes are opened by the Spirit and He lays bare the realities of the professing church to us, the faithful will be found at a crossroads. Will you admit the evil is present and growing in the professing church and will you acknowledge the ruin? Further, will you then admit that there is no present solution or cure for the circumstances we find in Christendom? Our consciences can't be satisfied to rest in a sinful state and be content to continue in the failure.

I have spoken to a few who tell me, "This is all there is, this is all we have." This is our common excuse to continue on in the evil and corruption that has been created. Many Christians have developed an innate ability to be able to fashion an alternative spiritual reality in their thoughts and mind from that which is actually present. They do this in the guise of exercising faith, hope, or a sincere desire for things to be different. They refuse to admit that they are fooling themselves and trusting in the wrong things.

It is not a question of sincerity. It is not a question of dedication. Many people are admired for leading lives of great devotion, yet they are devoted to false principles. There are many loving people who work hard in the things they are doing. There are good people to be found in every local assembly. But these attributes – goodness, hardworking, dedication – are not the means by which the truth of God's word is determined. More often than not Satan will use the admiration of them as a snare for others into false doctrines. What we must have in these last days is an understanding of God's word, and then a willingness to obey.

It is the easiest thing to say, "This is the will of God…" Rarely will anyone challenge such a statement. Yet this whole book is a challenge to those making such claims. If you do not see and understand the counsel and plan of God, then you do not know the purpose and will of God. If you do not understand the course of the present age or the character of the age to come, you will not be able to recognize the providential hand of God or the actual workings of God. If you do not know what God will do, then you shouldn't be guessing at it and sounding authoritative. You shouldn't be making the above statement, "This is the will of God."

The Will of God does not always stay the same

Many have pride in their work and the things they are doing. Even if the work is wrong and compromised, they will not forsake it. They are like captains going down with their ships. This may be a form of American pride, but I'm sure it is not Christianity or the mind of God. Will we admit the ruined state of the professing church? Will we allow its ruin to be present on our conscience? Will we be humbled by its reality? Will we find the humility to admit it is wrong and corrupt, and confess it as sin and evil?[151] Then can we turn from it and truly depend on God instead of ourselves? We desperately need humility of faith and conscience to properly understand the real condition of the professing church and to keep us from pretentions. Yes – pretentions – that compel us to be involved in activities upon activities which are unauthorized by the word for the present circumstances we find ourselves in.

Allow me to share a biblical example that is applicable to this topic. In the time of Isaiah's ministry the Assyrians came against Judah, Jerusalem, and king Hezekiah. The Assyrians were the same people who had scattered the ten tribes of Israel – the northern kingdom. Now they come against the southern kingdom – Judah and Jerusalem.

Isaiah 37:33-36

"Therefore thus says the Lord concerning the king of Assyria:

'He shall not come into this city,
Nor shoot an arrow there,
Nor come before it with shield,
Nor build a siege mound against it.
(34) By the way that he came,
By the same shall he return;
And he shall not come into this city,'
Says the Lord.
(35) 'For I will defend this city, to save it
For My own sake and for My servant David's sake.'"

(36) Then the angel of the Lord went out, and killed in the camp of the Assyrians one hundred and eighty-five thousand; and when people arose early in the morning, there were the corpses—all dead."

Years later (during the time of the prophet Jeremiah) Nebuchadnezzar and the Chaldeans come against Judah and Jerusalem. This is in the time of king Zedekiah. What is important to notice is that this time God's instructions through the prophet are opposite from what they were in the previous example. It now was the moment of God's judgment of the southern kingdom.

Jeremiah 21:8-9

"Now you shall say to this people, 'Thus says the Lord: "Behold, I set before you the way of life and the way of death. He who remains in this city shall die by the sword, by famine, and by

pestilence; but he who goes out and defects to the Chaldeans who besiege you, he shall live, and his life shall be as a prize to him."

Jeremiah 27:12

"I also spoke to Zedekiah king of Judah according to all these words, saying, "Bring your necks under the yoke of the king of Babylon, and serve him and his people, and live!"

The king never believed Jeremiah. He had other prophets, false prophets, telling him comforting words of success and deliverance. Why did he need to listen to this one who was kept away and locked-up in a dark hole in his prison? The outcome was that the king's eyes were cut out by the Chaldeans, and he was taken bound in brass shackles to Babylon (II Kings 25:7). Many people lost their lives in Judea and Jerusalem because they did not heed the word of the Lord. There was a remnant from Judah, which included young Daniel, that listened to Jeremiah. Their lives were spared, howbeit as captives in Babylon.

God Himself doesn't change, but His ways change

What would have happened if all the people of Judah would have said, "God delivered us before in a miraculous way from the hand of the Assyrian, and He will in like manner deliver us, His chosen people, from the hand of Nebuchadnezzar! After all, this is our right and Jehovah hasn't changed, He is always the same." That would have been a ridiculous statement showing scriptural ignorance of God and His ways. The above passages show and prove that God's ways in His dealings with man do change, even though God in His person always remains the same. In the first example above the *will of God* was for the people to stay in Jerusalem and see the salvation and deliverance of Jehovah. The second example is different, even though it's the same city, basically the same people, the same Lord Jehovah, and very similar circumstances. This time however, *God's will* is for the people to go out of Jerusalem and defect to the Chaldeans, and they would save their lives. Jerusalem and Judea were under judgment by

God. The instructions are very different. Under Hezekiah they were protected; under Zedekiah they were to submit to the judgment. The ways of God do not remain the same. I refer to these circumstances as a testimony of this principle from Scripture. While the relationship of God with Israel in this world is unchanging, yet their conduct had to be the opposite at one time to that at another. There are many other examples of this truth in Scripture.

John 1:17

"For the law was given through Moses, but grace and truth came through Jesus Christ."

This verse depicts the greatest, most important *change* in the ways of God in His dealings with man in the history of the human race. The principle of the law is the polar opposite of the principle of grace. The law was always limited in its revelation of the truth of God, because when Israel was under law, God stayed behind the veil. However Jesus came to reveal God to us, showing us the Father, and this in divine perfection and grace. In His ministry He removed every evil and consequence of man's sin among the people. There is a great *contrast* being made in this verse. God's ways are changing, but He always remains the same.[152]

So here is the point. God has visited us in grace through the redemption founded on the shed blood of Jesus Christ. There are many great principles by which God has made the Christian accepted in the Beloved Son (Eph. 1:3-8). These principles are the same for all believers. However we have to understand in our thinking what are the present results of the measure of grace He has shown us. We must hold fast the great principles under which we are set, while at the same time be able to apply those principles to the circumstances in which we find ourselves. The circumstances vary. The ways of God will vary depending on the circumstances and the actual state we find ourselves in along the way. We have to know where we are, and, at the same time, to learn what the path of God is in our current circumstances.

Look at the beginning of the church in Acts. There was evident power, one heart and mind, all things in common, and the buildings were shaking where they gathered. But look at the church world now. If we would acknowledge the corporate whole (including Romanism) and all the evil at once, we will admit that God cannot possibly send Holy Spirit power to bless it. He will not sustain us in corruption and evil. Although God's thoughts never change and He knows His people, yet we need spiritual discernment to see where we are, and what the ways of God are in the circumstances.

The ways of God have changed in His dealings with the professing church on earth, even though He ever remains the same God. How have His ways changed towards the professing church given her present circumstances? His remaining the same – holy and righteous – is why He cannot do the same things He did in Holy Spirit power at the beginning. He will not bless the ungodly mess that man has allowed. God's working and ways will be according to the state and condition the professing church is in. It is not according to the state she is not in. The professing church is in irrecoverable ruin. That is her present state.

How will we respond?

When we open our eyes to the possibility that something may be seriously wrong in the professing church, then there will be one of four available options to choose from.

1. You may still pretend that nothing is wrong and that things are not so bad. After all, what does the Lord really expect from us, perfection? God will have to be satisfied with what man has brought forth in the professing church on the earth. We are satisfied with what we have done. Therefore we assume that God is satisfied. By a false principle forced on us by the Arminian leaven we place a positive sanction on the ruin of Christendom. This is the same leaven by which the Jews produced self-righteousness by doing their law. This is very similar to the deadly mistake the unbeliever makes in contemplating standing before God one day and assuming

things will be judged in his favor or that God will wink at his sin. You go on in the condition of the present things. Your eyes are blind to the spiritual reality.

2. You may readily see the evil and corruption, but assume you have no choice but to go on in it. You throw your hands up and say that there is nothing you can do about it. This is true. There is no changing the corporate mess. However this does not replace the need to obey God on an individual basis as the Spirit leads in His word. Individually, His grace is always faithful and sufficient for the believer's present need and circumstance. The Holy Spirit is still on earth to teach the word and guide the believer. Listlessness is not a godly option.

3. You may see with spiritual eyes the ruin of the professing church and become despondent, thinking that the plans and purpose of God for the church are also in ruin. If God's plans depended on man cooperating with them or depended on man in an Arminian way for his works, then all would be lost and Satan has defeated the purpose of God. But God's plans and purpose cannot be stopped or defeated, and do not depend on the will of man or Satan for cooperation. Jesus will build the church, the body of Christ. What man builds on the earth is no longer the divine purpose of God and is not God doing the building. Despondency is not the appropriate response.

4. You fully see and acknowledge the corporate evil and ruin of the professing church world. You also realize that the word of God does not teach an improvement or revival for the ruined condition. Your action is mainly individual and according to the mind and thoughts of God as revealed by His Spirit in His word.

The Religious Confidences of the Flesh

If you say this is all there is and we cannot do otherwise, then you will be content to go on in it as before, most likely for the rest of your Christian walk. You are likely to refuse to acknowledge the evil or have a less than biblical perspective of it. You will have to practice your excuses and have them ready, especially when the eye of the Lord is upon you. I'm not sure how one explains the evil and corruption as good, and does so in the presence of our Lord. But many will decide, even when their eyes are opened, to continue on. It is the easy thing to do. It is most convenient. You settle for the evil condition and are content with it. The leaven will give you all the reasons and explanations you need to justify your position. However, when Paul's eyes were opened to the reality of the glorified Christ, he could not continue on in the religious workings of the flesh.

Philippians 3:4-10

"...though I also might have confidence in the flesh. If anyone else thinks he may have confidence in the flesh, I more so: (5) circumcised the eighth day, of the stock of Israel, of the tribe of Benjamin, a Hebrew of the Hebrews; concerning the law, a Pharisee; (6) concerning zeal, persecuting the church; concerning the righteousness which is in the law, blameless.

(7) But what things were gain to me, these I have counted loss for Christ. (8) Yet indeed I also count all things loss for the excellence of the knowledge of Christ Jesus my Lord, for whom I have suffered the loss of all things, and count them as rubbish, that I may gain Christ (9) and be found in Him, not having my own righteousness, which is from the law, but that which is through faith in Christ, the righteousness which is from God by faith; (10) that I may know Him and the power of His resurrection, and the fellowship of His sufferings, being conformed to His death."

The religious confidences of the flesh are such a deceptive path to be on. They are self-righteous confidences in what man does. For the most part he does them in innocence and with good intentions. *They are the things that are done for God but are not of God, and in fact, turn out to be against God.* Saul could boast of many religious accomplishments, even his physical birth and circumcision. As concerning zeal he persecuted this new sect of Judaism that had arisen. He was an intelligent man, serving God and his religion in great efforts and without blemish. He put many believers in chains and was personally responsible for putting others to death (John 16:2, Acts 26:9-11). Without any doubt, in his mind Saul thought he was serving God above the efforts of all others. When God takes hold of him, Saul realizes that he is the worst of all sinners, that he was actually the enemy of God (I Tim. 1:15, I Cor. 15:8-10). When God awakens him and turns him in sovereign grace, he realizes that his Judaism, his birth, his circumcision on the eighth day, Hebrew of the Hebrews, his Phariseeism, all is rubbish, filth, and dung. And he leaves it behind, never to count on it again (Phil. 3:12-14).

If you are a pastor, you are at the crossroads. You see glimpses of evil and corruption, and much of the workings of religious flesh, but you think – what can I possibly do? Too much depends on me continuing on in this. I cannot possibly change now. I have family, friends, and responsibilities. There are bills to pay, committee meetings to chair, boards to meet with. My schedule is full and I have little time. I have been faithfully serving this denomination for thirty years. You want me to admit, to myself and to others, that this is all the confidences of the flesh? You want me to forget those things that are behind me? Those things are all the things I have built and I have accomplished. Leave them behind? Well, the decision is yours, and I do not say it is an easy one. Nothing here is easy. When God stopped Saul in his tracks, he was blind for three days and took no food and water (Acts 9:9). Yet this is the one thing you *must* do to go with God (Phil. 3:12-13). Do so only if you want to truly have Christ (Phil. 3:7-8).

Depart from the Corruption

So what is the individual believer to do? What course are we to take? The epistles to Timothy give us a guide to answering these questions. The first epistle in general speaks of the proper order of the church as God intended it to be. The second epistle shows the ruin of the church in its earthly position and directs us how to act individually when the church has failed. It individualizes the duty of the Christian in the last days, when the public body has taken a form of godliness, but denies the power of life (II Tim. 3:1-5).

2 Timothy 2:19-22

"Nevertheless the solid foundation of God stands, having this seal: "The Lord knows those who are His," and, "Let everyone who names the name of Christ depart from iniquity."

20 But in a great house there are not only vessels of gold and silver, but also of wood and clay, some for honor and some for dishonor. 21 Therefore if anyone cleanses himself from the latter, he will be a vessel for honor, sanctified and useful for the Master, prepared for every good work. 22 Flee also youthful lusts; but pursue righteousness, faith, love, peace with those who call on the Lord out of a pure heart."

"The Lord knows those who are His..." This is the sure foundation of God's work, and it is a truth to be known particularly in these last days. We are His workmanship created in Christ Jesus (Eph. 2:10). This is stated by the Spirit because the state of Christendom exists as a mixture of wheat and tares. Yet this condition of the great house on the earth cannot frustrate the sure purpose of God's sovereign calling. The Lord knows who His wheat are. However, the remainder of the verse speaks of the individual responsibility of everyone in the spoiled crop of the field – *"Let everyone who names the name of Christ depart from iniquity."* Also if we are truly His we will cleanse ourselves from dishonor. Then we are to join with those who call on the Lord out of a pure heart.

The Remnant trusts in the Word

The Spirit directs us to the two safeguards God has for the believer during the evil of the last days.

1. First believers are to continue in the truths you have already learned in the Lord, considering from whom you have learned them. Paul was the spiritual father and teacher for Timothy (II Tim. 3:14). It is not a commendation to follow so

called church authority or 'fathers' that would rise up in time. When we go back to Paul, Peter, and John, we are going back to the beginning (I John 1:1). Why is this important? Because it is what God has given! Now we know from whom we are learning (I John 2:24).

2. The first could only solidify the second safeguard which is the authority of the Holy Scriptures (II Tim. 3:15-17). It is what we have individually between ourselves and God, where nothing else is permitted to enter in – not any man, not any church authority, not superstitions or teachings of men. It is the word of God alone that is the believer's true safeguard in the time when the public body will not endure sound doctrine (II Tim. 4:1-5). Seeing the corruption and evil of the public body of Christendom we want to be found in faithful Philadelphia, instead of in 'full of itself' Laodicea. When Paul speaks for the last time to the elders of the church at Ephesus, revealing the evil and corruption that would come in among them after his death, he commends the faithful to two things: *to God and to the word of God* (Acts 20:32).

What can the believer do in obedience?

- Recognize the corporate evil and turn from it (II Tim. 3:5). If you name the name of Christ in true faith, depart from iniquity and dishonor (II Tim. 2:19-21). Evil is growing in the church world and the disobedience of the corporate body cannot be remedied.

- Gather with those who call on the Lord out of a pure heart (II Tim. 2:22). This is the simple obedience of the faithful remnant in the midst of the public professing body. The basis for believers gathering has always been, *"For where two or three are gathered together in My name, I am there in the midst of them."* (Matt. 18:20) These are His words. This is His promise. The Lord spoke it for the church before her beginning. I have no doubt His words are intended for the remnant church (Philadelphia) in the last days. Gathering like this in obedience to His words can be accomplished in integrity and purity. It is the true gathering of the assembly. It can be done as frequently as the Lord leads. It can be done with the Lord's table as its center, for this speaks of the unity of the body (I Cor. 10:17).

When three thousand were added to the disciples on the day of Pentecost, the fellowship and praying centered around their gathering from house to house and the breaking of bread, along with holding all things in common (Acts 2:41-47). Here we see the general direction of things concerning the assembly. I seriously doubt that this early group of three thousand plus were ever called to assemble in one physical location after that day. Their use of the temple to gather would prove to be temporary. Although this was certainly the church in infancy, this assembly can be understood as a believing Jewish remnant in the midst of unbelief, holding out and looking for the repentance of the nation, so that God would send back their resurrected Messiah to them (Acts 2:36, 3:12-21). They were definitely the beginning of the church, yet also they were a believing Jewish remnant serving this final purpose on behalf of unbelieving Israel.[153]

- His grace is sufficient for every need that a gathering of two or three will ever have. God is faithful and the Lord is present. The true gifts Christ gives for the edifying of the church will be known and obvious over time to the faithful (pastors, teachers, evangelists). Christ is the head of the church. There will never be any need or reason for any one person to dominate, or a group of individuals to struggle over control (Matt. 20:24-28). Jesus Christ never stops nourishing and caring for the true church, the body of Christ (Eph. 5:29-30). This just isn't true concerning the spoiled crop in the field.

- All true believers in one locale should desire and should be free to assemble together as one body. Except for excommunication or schisms, all could assemble as one if possible, a microcosm of the universal body. In the first century, at Antioch, Corinth, and Ephesus, there was one assembly reflecting the overall universal body. All the different assemblies in the differing locales together made up the house of God on the earth. This is what is according to Scripture.[154]

- If there is an assembly already in a particular locale that adheres to these Scriptural principles of one body and the unity of that body, and teaches sound Scriptural doctrine, then there is never a justification for starting something new.

To be in Philadelphia you make sure you distinguish yourself as a Philadelphian. Make sure you know the character of those found there. Pay close attention to the words the Lord speaks to this remnant church. It is His instructions given to the faithful for the end times and is the measure of His grace given to them for this present need.

The Philadelphian Character

- Christ's character for Philadelphia is that He is holy and true. He has the sovereign power of God. When God shows His exceeding great power toward us in the exalting of the true church to His right hand (Eph. 1:19-23), then we will be made like His Son – holy and true (Rom. 8:29-30). This is what the faithful attempt to emulate in their walk on this earth, to walk as holy and true with Christ (Rev. 3:7)

- We have little strength or power, and we are fully aware of this present state. His grace is sufficient for our every need. We are faithful to keep His word. We do not deny His name. We are faithful to Him (Rev. 3:8).

- We are attentive to keep the word of His patience (Rev. 3:10, 1:9). We are vigilant to be looking for Him, expecting Him (Rev. 3:11). His coming for us is the sole object of our minds and hearts. If we have the spirit of the bride, we will desire with all our heart the coming of the Bridegroom. There is no doubting the love and desire of the Bridegroom for the bride (Eph. 5:25-32). In turn, the bride looks to see the Bridegroom coming for her, and has the appropriate desire and affections for His presence. *The Spirit and the bride say "Come".* This is distinctly Philadelphian character.

- We remain faithful now knowing that in the coming age we will be glorified together with Him. All His promises to us are to be found in glory with Him. So we wait and endure the present time and sufferings (Rom. 8:17-18). We do not act like immature children desiring immediate satisfaction and personal ease. Christ in us is all the hope we need. His Spirit in us is the guarantee of us with Him in future glory (Col. 1:27).

- Those in Philadelphia are totally dependent on Christ. Those in Laodicea are quite independent of Christ.

This is what Christ tells us to be and do. He doesn't add anything else. This is it. There is no great Arminian work to be accomplished by the church in the world at the end of the age. Where do we find such aspirations, such visions of grandeur? I only see the crop in the field spoiled and growing worse (Matt. 13:26-29). The work at the end of the age is done by the Son of Man and his angels (Matt. 13:30, 39-43, 49-50).

I am content to believe that Jesus has given Philadelphia His full instructions for what He wants from them and what He wants them to do. I am confident He left nothing out. That wouldn't be like Him to make such mistakes. No, it is all there for you and me to read and know. These are His instructions for the faithful in the last days of the church on earth.

In the described character of this remnant church the singular object of faith and faithfulness is the Lord's coming for us. There may be much ignorance as to what we should be doing, but our relationship and affections for Christ must be genuine. The bride that is actually looking for her Bridegroom will seek to be pure for Him, to be prepared and readied for Him by the washing of the water of the Word. We should realize we are for Jesus Christ and Him alone.

There is Philadelphia, the remnant church. This is the wheat, the sons of the kingdom (Matt. 13:38). Christ sets an open door before them that no man can shut (Rev. 3:8). There is Laodicea, the corporate form of Christendom. The tares are gathered together and left in the field to be burned. This is spewed out of the Lord's mouth and the candlestick is removed. Even Philadelphia has no power to maintain the candlestick. The church on earth is no longer acknowledged by God in its responsibility. After this, the very next verse is:

Revelation 4:1

"After these things I looked, and behold, a door standing open in heaven. And the first voice which I heard was like a trumpet speaking with me, saying, "Come up here, and I will show you things which must take place after this."

Philadelphia goes up into the heavens through the open door in front of them. The tares are bundled together and left on the earth. Revelation 2 and 3 are the present things, the things which are (Rev. 1:19). After the true church is taken to the heavens, the present things are complete. The prophecy of the book can now begin – the things which must take place after this (Rev. 1:19, 4:1). Prophecy is the future things, and the church is always the mystery hidden from prophecy. That is why the church was only involved in the present things or the second section of the book. The things that must take place after this, the third section, is God dealing with the world in judgment – that is prophecy.[155]

As for answering the question as to what is our hope, we know from Scripture that all the believer's legitimate hopes are in glory and beyond this present time. This does not mean that Christ does not give grace now to the faithful to meet our present needs. He has promised and He is faithful. The measure of His grace is our strength to persevere under any present trials.

Chapter 19: Endnotes

[151] In captivity Daniel confessed the sins of his people, even though these weren't necessarily his own sins. He felt he was part of the corporate responsibility of the nation (Dan. 9:3-19). God would allow a remnant to return to the land, rebuild the walls of the city and eventually rebuild the temple. God providentially brings these events to pass in order that years later, according to the counting of time in Daniel's 70 week prophecy, He may present Messiah to them in Jerusalem (Dan. 9:24-26).

What should the believer do at this present time? Admit the ruin and corruption of the professing church and confess it as evil and sin, asking God to forgive us. Then turn from the evil and have no part in it. And then depend only on God and His word. Isn't that like Daniel? Both Caleb and Joshua partook of the corporate failure of Israel, wandering in the wilderness with Israel for 40 years. They did so as part of Israel, and so exercised grace, patience, and love towards the people who sinned. God was faithful in keeping them, while the rest fell in the wilderness. This is the believing remnant's place – in the spirit of love, patience, and humiliation, we are to always take the place of those who sinned. The sin and evil of Christendom should be confessed by the remnant, though they were not partakers of it. The remnant suffers in all the affliction. They do so with true sympathy and fellowship.

[152] John 1:17 also shows the transition between the two dispensations. The Jewish dispensation ends and the dispensation of the kingdom of heaven in mystery begins. The Jewish dispensation involves the law of Moses (Judaism) and the testing of mankind in responsibility. The kingdom of heaven in mystery involves God acting in sovereign grace and the truth of God in Jesus Christ found in Christianity.

[153] I do not think it is a stretch of the imagination to see the group of disciples after the day of Pentecost as both the beginning church body and a believing Jewish remnant in the midst of the nation. The prophecy of Joel that Peter quotes, directly points to a yet future Jewish remnant having the Spirit poured out *on* them before the great and terrible day of the Lord (Joel 2:28-32). If you read the entire 32nd verse you will be convinced the prophecy only refers to a Jewish remnant. The future Jewish remnant before this terrible day is the only group by which this prophecy may be completely fulfilled. Yet for what can only be considered a partial fulfillment of the prophecy at Pentecost, and not that specific remnant

to which the prophecy actually refers, this group of 120 disciples was a Jewish remnant to which the prophecy could be applied by the Holy Spirit.

Room was left by God for the group in the upper room on the day of Pentecost to serve as a Jewish remnant. God's purpose was to give Israel a last chance at that time concerning the kingdom, their promises, and their Messiah – all this according to Jewish prophecy. This final chance was after Jesus was on the cross asking the Father to forgive them, for they know not what they do. Yet this was based solely on human responsibility in the nation and could only fail.

We see a similar double meaning found again in Peter's preaching in Acts 2:22-23. The nation of Israel was guilty of putting Jesus to death by lawless hands, and God holds the nation accountable. Yet at the same time Christ's suffering and death was according to the determined counsel and foreknowledge of God. Both thoughts come to pass during the same action, so to speak, of the cross. Therefore both thoughts are harmonious with each other and are fulfilled at the same time. Man's sin and hatred only brought about the accomplishment of God's counsels. That is the beauty and the glory of the cross, and only seen on God's side, when man's offerings were only sin and enmity.

When the disciples walked with Jesus during His 3 ½ years of ministry, they were in fact a believing remnant in the midst of the unbelieving nation (Matt. 13:9-16). They were His own sheep that He goes through the gate of the sheepfold of Israel to retrieve and take out (John 10:1-5). This remnant of Israel was not yet mixed with His sheep from another fold (the Gentiles – John 10:16). During this time the disciples, in many ways and circumstances, foreshadow in type the final Jewish remnant that God will choose and preserve in the coming tribulation (Rev. 7:3-8, Joel 2:32). It is quite remarkable (Matt. 14:14-21, 14:22-33, John 6: 5-15, 6:16-21, 20:24-29, 21:1-13). It isn't hard to see that the 3,120 disciples after the day of Pentecost were both the beginning of the assembly (body of Christ) and a Jewish remnant used for God's certain purpose.

[154] Jesus Christ said He would build the church, which is the body of Christ (Eph. 5:23, Col. 1:18, 24). God builds this without any help from man, so that it is God's work alone and cannot fail. This is an important point and distinction. Jesus saying, *"...I will build My church, and the gates of Hades will not prevail against it"* shows at the same time God's sovereignty in His work and the understanding that God's work cannot ever fail. When you mix Arminian thoughts and leaven with this passage, inevitably you have man thinking he

is doing the work of God and building the body of Christ, the church, on the earth. He also thinks that what he builds cannot possibly fail and that God will sustain and uphold it. You can see how the Arminian leaven constantly leads one further and further from the truth of Scripture and God's thoughts.

In contrast, what God started on the earth and then turned over to men in responsibility, is viewed in Scripture as the house of God, particularly those aspects of the body of Christ on earth that involve the responsibility of man (I Cor. 3:9). By sovereign grace and in using the apostle Paul as the instrument of that grace, God laid a masterful foundation on the earth for this house (I Cor. 3:7, 9-11). This was God starting the building and He started it well. Everything on earth given over to the responsibility of man, to maintain the glory and purity of God's initial work and blessing, always fails and is corrupted. Again, this is not the body of Christ failing. This is not the church failing. It is the house of God on the earth – started in sovereign grace by God, initially God's work, now turned over to men to build and maintain in responsibility, men sleeping and the enemy entering in to plant tares and spread leaven – which is failing.

Knowing this failure and ruin of the house of God on the earth, it is hard to speak of a local assembly as being a microcosm of the universal body of Christ. Inevitably we are looking at what is on the earth, which is the house of God built by man. We see the spoiled crop in the field, and only with the eye of faith do we understand it is spoiled. The unbelieving world, as well as many Christians, sees the crop as the good influence of Christendom in the world, and that it is all the work of God. They don't see that it is spoiled. The unbelieving world and many Christians see the great tree that has grown up in the field and extol the wonderful influence of this great worldly power. They don't see the birds flying in to roost (Matt. 13:31-32). The house of God built up by men on the earth is not the hidden treasure in the field (Matt. 13:44). The house of God built by men is the spoiled crop and the great expansive tree. These are easily seen in the world and by the world with the naked eye. What is hidden in the world and out of eyesight is the body of Christ, the church. The body of Christ – the work of God – is God's hidden treasure in the world.

The differences I speak of between the parables in Matthew thirteen (13) fall into three categories:

- First, what is seen with the natural eye.
- Second, what is seen by the believer's eye of faith.
- Third, what is hidden and only God sees, or the spirit realm sees.

The natural eye sees the great crop in the field, the great tree in the field, and the three measures of meal. The natural eye sees all that was told to the multitudes (Matt. 13:34-35). The eye of faith of the believer sees and understands much more (Matt. 13:11). This involves seeing the crop as spoiled, the great tree harboring every kind of bird, and the leaven saturating all three measures. Also the eye of faith knows the treasure exists in the field, but as the treasure is hidden, the believer cannot really see it. God sees the body of Christ, for He knows those that are His (II Tim. 2:19), and bought the field in order to hide the treasure there. The pearl of great price is the body of Christ as well (Matt. 13:45-46). The Son of Man paid a great price to possess it. But this pearl is yet to be displayed for the entire world to see (Col 3:4). The pearl is unseen and in His possession at this present time.

In the house of God that man built on the earth, there is no longer any church unity, church discipline, one faith or doctrine, etc. The example and reality of a local assembly being a microcosm of the body existed in the first century and was valid then, but for the reasons mentioned above, it doesn't exist today. In the first century, Paul could legitimately send an epistle to *"...the church of God which is at Corinth, to those who are sanctified in Christ Jesus, called to be saints, with all who in every place call on the name of Jesus Christ our Lord..."* A local assembly represented the whole of God's assembly. Today however, there is no apostolic power or care for the maintenance of the general assembly. Local assemblies should not think or pretend that they gather every true believer in a specific locality. They should be open for all true believers to gather and not deny any, but they cannot declare themselves to be the only true representation of the body in that locality. The unity of the universal house does not exist any longer. How can a local assembly be a legitimate microcosm of what no longer exists?

When people are asked to think of churches today, they would think of what is called churches in the religious world. You have the Southern Baptist church and their churches, the Presbyterian church and their churches, the Catholic church and their churches, the Church of God and their churches, etc. If the believer is scripturally minded and asked to think of churches, he will think of Corinth, Antioch, and Philippi – one assembly in a place, which was God's assembly. This latter is what is found in Scripture, the former is not. Today there exists such a disconnection from the word of God. If what we see is not in agreement with Scripture, how can church unity and power in the Holy Spirit exist?

I will say this. The basis of gathering has always been, *"For where two or three are gathered together in My name..."* (Matt. 18:20) This is especially valid for the end times, and the Lord may have had the end of the church on earth in mind when He said this. Certainly it is the basis for gathering from beginning to end of the history of the church. Yet this is especially valid and useful now when one sees the corruption and ruin of the professing church. How precious it is that Jesus promises He will be present among us.

[155] The integrity and perfection of the Word of God is an amazing thing to see and behold. The book of Revelation is a remarkable work that soundly and masterfully maintains this integrity, in the midst of very detailed circumstances. There are three subjects I will point out that the book itself treats and handles in a very unique way – the character of the prophetic word, the body of Christ as the mystery of God hidden from prophecy, and the general inerrancy of God's Word.

- The book of Revelation is a book of prophecy (Rev. 1:1-3). The character of prophecy is three fold – it is about Israel, it is about the earth, and it is about God's government of the earth. According to this character then, the body of Christ is never found to be the proper subject of prophecy. It is not just that God tells us the church is the mystery hidden from the prophets (Eph. 3:1-11), but that it also doesn't fit the character of prophecy. The church is not Israel. The church is not of the earth in her calling. She is seated in the heavens as having any connection with God's government over the millennial earth. We find that prophecy is never about the church and is never about the heavens. The only point in time when the church is seen as directly a part of the prophecy of the book is at the end, when the bride of the Lamb is seen at the marriage feast and also seen as the heavenly city. The New Jerusalem is God's capital city of His government over the millennial earth and is now finally related to the character of Biblical prophecy. Nowhere before this is the body of Christ, the church, directly referred to in the book. Even at the end it is still seen as an allegory (the bride of the Lamb), and the words 'body' or 'church' are not used.

- The names for God as found in the book are those found in the Old Testament – the prophetic writings of the Jewish prophets. These are all God's names as He revealed Himself to Israel or their forefathers, and this fits the character of prophecy. However, His name for His relationship with the church is our Father, and this will be hidden in the book. We do find the name Father, but it is never the Father of the church or the Father of the believer as is established in the epistles (Rom. 1:7, I Cor. 1:3, II Cor. 1:2, Gal. 1:1, etc.). It is always the Father of the Lamb or His Father (Rev. 1:6, 3:5, 3:21, and 14:1). If you hold that the church age is not properly a dispensation, then these Old Testament names are the dispensational names for God.

- Even though Revelation 2 and 3 is about the responsibility of the professing church on the earth, the words 'body' and 'church' are never directly used. The closest you get is the Spirit speaking to the churches, which becomes an allegory for Christendom. This section of the book is labeled 'the things which are' or the present things. As I said earlier, prophecy is about future things, not present things. The seven messages were in fact spoken to seven existing churches or seven 'present' churches. You see the lengths taken to maintain the character of prophecy and to keep the mystery hidden. If it refers to the church, even indirectly or hidden, these are then the 'present things'. Then God has to stop acknowledging the church on earth in order to move on to the things that must take place after this (Rev. 4:1) – the prophetic part of the book, its third division (Rev. 1:19). We know that the second division concerning the candlesticks is prophetic and gives a prophetic picture of the progressive history of the church on the earth. Yet it is delivered to us in 'present time' and concerning 'seven present and existing Asian churches'. It is all allusion and allegory and requires the mind of Christ to properly see the prophetic picture and message. In this way, in this division of the book, the character of prophecy and the integrity of the word of God are maintained. At the same time the mystery remains hidden in allegories and symbols.

- The general meaning of the labels for the second and third divisions of the book serve to maintain the three points mentioned above. "The things which are" and "the things which will take place after this" simply are distinct from each other in the character of their content. The present things involve the body of Christ, howbeit indirectly and allegorically. The things after this is prophecy – about the earth, God's government of the earth, and God's dealings with Israel.

- The names and titles for Jesus Christ used in the book also serve to maintain this overall integrity. His present titles as they relate to the church – Head of the body and High Priest for the church – are not found in the entire book. Again, this is because the church is hidden from this book of prophecy. Therefore, her established relationships with the Father, with Jesus Christ, and with the Holy Spirit as the Comforter are hidden. In the book Jesus is pictured in one of two general ways – both as divine and merged with God in attributes, or as the Son of Man with His connections to the earth. As divine He is seen as the Ancient of Days and the Eternal One, the Alpha and Omega (Rev. 1:11, 14, 17, 22:13). As the Son of Man, He is on the earth in the midst of the candlesticks, judging (Rev. 1:13). He says He is the One who lives, and was dead, and behold, I am alive forevermore. His death and resurrection occurred on the earth. This connection to the earth, and therefore prophecy, has a greater emphasis in the introduction of the book (Rev. 1:5). He was the faithful witness of God on the earth, perfectly revealing the Father. He is the firstborn from the dead in physical resurrection, which took place on the earth. He will be ruler over the kings of the earth in the coming age. Finally in verse seven (7) it shows His appearing to the world and earth, where all the tribes on the earth will mourn. These descriptions of Christ at the beginning of the book entirely skip over what He is presently for the church – High Priest and Head of the body – partly because the church has a heavenly calling with no connection to the earth and the character of prophecy. The descriptions entirely pass over what Jesus Christ is in heaven presently. Heaven and the things of heaven are not the proper subject of prophecy or the counting of time. The descriptions only refer to Christ's connection to the character of the book itself. Yet regardless of what descriptions are used, when the church hears His name spoken she answers, *"To Him who loved us and washed us from our sins in His own blood, and has made us kings and priests unto His God and Father, to Him be glory and dominion forever and ever. Amen."* Although Christ is referred to in His connections to the earth and world, the true church knows Him for what He is for her and what He has done for her. We know Jesus Christ for what He is for us, and this cannot be hidden in the introduction of the book.

- In the book the Holy Spirit is never seen as the Comforter to the church. The closest you get to this relationship is what the

Spirit says to the churches. However even the Spirit's reference to the churches is cloaked in allegory. His words are mostly chastisements and judgments, and not comfort. When the Holy Spirit is acknowledged in the introduction it is not as the Comforter to the church, but as the seven Spirits who are before the throne (Rev. 1:4). There are three words or phrases used in the book to describe associations with certain things, particularly the throne – in the midst, around, and before. The word 'before' never really means physical location, but rather moral relationship and connection, while remaining on or in the earth. The seven Spirits before the throne is the Holy Spirit as the perfect (7) instrument of the providence and judgment of God and His government of the earth from the throne. He is the agent of God's power, judgments, and dealings in the earth.

- The order in which the trinity is acknowledged in the introduction is worth noting (Rev. 1:4-5). It is God who sits on the throne, the Holy Spirit before the throne, and then Jesus Christ mentioned last. This is because Jesus is seen here as the Son of Man and in His humanity, not in His divinity, and in His connections with the earth that is about to be judged.

- The last unique circumstance found early in the book that maintains the three points mentioned above is the position that John is found in. He is immediately viewed as a servant and Old Testament prophet (Rev. 1:1-2). When the vision begins he is looking out to the judgment of the world and earth, according to his position and the character of prophecy. But Christ is behind him and among the seven candlesticks. John is made to turn around and view what concerns the responsibility of the professing church on earth. He has to turn around because the candlesticks involve the church, which is not the proper subject of prophecy and the prophet. *"...I heard behind me a loud voice... saying...Then I turned...And having turned..."* (Rev. 1:10-11)

- You should be able to realize the spiritual value of being able to rightly divide the word of truth by the Spirit (II Tim. 2:15). In the fine detail of Scripture God refuses to ever violate His overall Biblical principles. This is the overall integrity of God's word and this perfection is a beautiful element to see maintained. God has privileged the believer/church to know all His counsels and plans, and to be His confidant (John 15:15, I Cor. 2:6-16). This knowledge gained from the Spirit and the word is part of 'our reasonable service' (Rom. 12:1). Reasonable means intelligent. This plays a big part in the book of Revelation. Whenever a question needs to be answered or an explanation needs to be given, it is the twenty-four elders that do so. This is the church in the heavens. These are the ones in the book who give reason for their worship, and intelligent explanations and answers (Rev. 4:11, 5:5, 8-10, and 7:13-17). This is our reasonable service.

Chapter 20

The True Calling of the Church

The body of Christ has a calling in which we easily discover God's true purpose for the church. We are members of the heavenly calling. Our purpose, in the counsels and plan of God, is contained in this calling. The church is to be in the heavens, seated in Christ in heavenly places, forming the habitation of God our Father. There we are destined to be blessed with every spiritual blessing. We are to be found there, exalted above all principalities, powers, might, and dominion. In the ages to come our Father will show the exceeding riches of His grace in His kindness toward us in Christ (Eph. 1:3, 21, 2:6-7).

Hebrews 3:1

"Therefore, holy brethren, partakers of the heavenly calling, consider the Apostle and High Priest of our confession, Christ Jesus."

Our calling is heavenly and our citizenship is in heaven (Phil. 3:20). Jesus went away to heaven to prepare a place for us there. In the heavens is the Father's house. We are the sons destined and predestined to dwell in that house (John 14:1-3). We are those, along with Paul, in possession of the upward calling of God in Christ Jesus

(Phil. 3:14). We are instructed to always look there, into the heavens. Our thoughts are to be there, as heavenly minded (Col. 3:1-2).[156]

Our Calling: Holy and Blameless in His Presence

The church will be in the presence of the Father. We are closest to Him and we approach the One who dwells in unapproachable light. We are the ones who, being in Christ and united to Him, will look upon the glory on the face of God – that which was forbidden for Moses. This is our calling and the result of our redemption.

All true believers are called according to His purpose – *"For whom He foreknew, He also predestined to be conformed to the image of His Son, that He might be the firstborn among many brethren. Moreover whom He predestined, these He also called; whom He called, these He also justified; and whom He justified, these He also glorified."* (Rom. 8:28-30) God's purpose is for the believer to be conformed into the image of His Son. It does not yet appear what we will be, but we know that when He appears, we will be like Him, for we will see Him as He is (I John 3:2). As we have borne the image of the earthy, so also we will bear the image of the heavenly (I Cor. 15:49). Our earthly bodies of flesh will be fashioned like His glorious body (Phil. 3:21). This will be a body given to us that is suited for heavenly places and glory. God has prepared us for this very thing, who has also given us the earnest of the Holy Spirit as the guarantee (II Cor. 5:1-5).

Being glorified, we enter the presence of the Father in the image of the One in whom all the Father's delight and pleasure is found. We are forever with the Lord and like the Lord. We are the fruit of the Father's love and eternal purpose. He has made us His children and we are received as sons into the Father's house. This is our eternal state and joy. This is both the position and privilege of the church in Christ, resultant upon the rapture fulfilling her calling.[157]

In the dispensation of the fullness of the times (millennium) God will gather all things in heaven and earth into one Head – Jesus Christ (Eph. 1:10). The believer's portion in this gathering is to be in heavenly places in Christ Jesus (Eph. 2:6). Now our position is in spirit – sitting there *in Christ Jesus.* Later it becomes our place in glory – sitting there *with Christ Jesus.*

Jesus has entered into God's presence behind the veil. As the forerunner He has entered there for us (Heb. 6:19-20). All our Christian hope that serves as an anchor for our souls is that we will go in behind the veil where He already is – in the Presence. He did not go into an earthly tabernacle made with human hands. He went into heaven itself, now to appear in the presence of God for us (Heb. 9:24). If we ask where the veil is that our forerunner has entered in behind, it is in the heavens and in the presence of the invisible God. Our hope then, which is sure and steadfast, is that we will go in there as well.

We are blessed with every spiritual blessing in heavenly places in Christ (Eph. 1:3). We have this blessing now in spirit. Later we will physically be in heavenly places enjoying every spiritual blessing the Father has thought of – the exceeding riches of His grace in His kindness toward us in Christ (Eph. 2:7).

When the body of Christ is glorified we are taken to the heavens to be holy and blameless in God's sight (Eph. 1:4, Col. 1:21-22). That is our heavenly calling – *to be before Him in His love, holy, blameless, irreproachable, and as the image of His Son.* This is the moral nature of God. It also is our perfection as conformed into the Son's image. Jesus Christ, as the Son of Man glorified, is this now at the right hand of God. It is the only nature that God can delight in and that God allows in His very presence. Except for angels, everything else must stay at some measure of distance.[158] The Spirit through Peter tells us we have been made partakers of the divine nature (II Pet. 1:2-4). The believer has this now in soul and spirit, but the sinful flesh is still with us and we are still on this earth. When we are glorified into the image of His Son, the flesh will be changed – the corruptible will put on incorruption, and the mortal will put on immortality (Rom. 8:29-30, I Cor. 15:50-53). The true church will then leave this earth, and in the Father's house we will be perfect and complete in Christ. By this we will realize our true calling – the heavenly calling.

In the first chapter of Ephesians the believer/church is given two things as its portion through or in Jesus Christ – the calling of God (Eph. 1:4-5) and an inheritance from God (Eph. 1:11). We have our calling, but it is not completely fulfilled as yet. We have nothing of the inheritance at this time, although the believer in Christ is declared an heir of God and a co-heir with Christ. It is a truth and principle of Scripture that God will not give His inheritance until all the heirs are gathered and united together in one place. This place is the Father's house (John 14:1-3). The heirs of God are all the sons of God through faith in Christ Jesus (Gal. 3:26, 4:6-7, Rom. 8:15-17). Although the giving of the inheritance waits for this future gathering, we have received the earnest of the Spirit as its guarantee (Eph. 1:13-14).

The two aspects of our calling is given to us in Ephesians. The first is that we will be perfectly holy and blameless *before God* in His love (Eph. 1:4). The second aspect of our calling is in connection *with the Father* as sons (Eph. 1:5). Our portion is to be like Christ in glory and to be with Him forever. The results of our calling are to be in the heavens and enjoying all spiritual blessings in heavenly places (as Israel is destined to be on the earth with temporal and physical blessings – Eph. 1:3, 2:6). Therefore the Scriptures speak of our hope laid up for us in heaven (Col. 1:5). Also God's inheritance is reserved for us there, that is incorruptible, undefiled, and does not fade away (Eph. 1:11, I Pet. 1:4). So then it is said, *"...the eyes of your understanding being enlightened; that you may know what the hope of His calling, what the riches of the glory of His inheritance in the saints..."* (Eph. 1:18) It is the distinct testimony of Scripture that our hopes, our blessings, our place, our inheritance, and the glory Christ shares with us, is all celestial, not terrestrial.

I said earlier in the chapter that we can discover our purpose by knowing our calling. More so, it is the purpose of God for us, settled before the foundations of the world, which defines our calling (Eph. 1:4). He had these thoughts and intentions concerning us before time began. His calling of us is according to the good pleasure of His will (Eph. 1:5). He delights in doing so. Our calling serves to the praise of the glory of His grace (Eph. 1:6). It exalts God and glorifies

Him. God foreknew us and predestined us to be conformed to the image of His Son. This is the purpose of God towards the believer. These two words – *foreknew and predestined* – precede the word *'calling'* in the list in Romans (Rom. 8:29). The eternal purpose of God determined our calling. Of course we are not in the glory yet. However it is what we have been redeemed to, prepared for, and wait for. Our entrance into the glory of God is our heavenly calling (I Pet. 5:10).

Many sons into the Father's Presence

We should understand that the greatest part of God's purpose for the church is to be physically closest to Him and in His presence. His desire is for the church to be nearest to Him. This is His desire for Jesus Christ His Son and we are in Christ and united to Christ as His body. The church is bone of His bone and flesh of His flesh (Eph. 5:29-32). We are one with Christ, we are one spirit with Him (I Cor. 6:17).

Hebrews 2:10-11

"For it was fitting for Him, for whom are all things and by whom are all things, in bringing many sons to glory, to make the captain of their salvation perfect through sufferings. For both He who sanctifies and those who are being sanctified are all of one, for which reason He is not ashamed to call them brethren."

We are Christ's brethren. Jesus, the very Son of God, is the one who suffered and became the captain of our salvation. As a result, He is the one who brings the many sons to glory. This glory certainly includes the very presence of the Father. This is the church's ultimate privilege. God's calling and purpose for the body of Christ is to be His tabernacle containing His presence (Eph. 2:22). There is no reward, no honor, no power and dominion that will be given to us that can possibly compare in value to this privilege!

Can we imagine what it will be like to dwell in the Father's house for all eternity? This is the essence of this verse in Ephesians and the purpose for raising us up with Christ, *"...that in the ages to come He might show the exceeding riches of His grace in His kindness toward us in Christ Jesus."* (Eph. 2:6-7) It is the Father's love for His Son and His many sons.

The Church's part in the Government of God

Having said this, we should be able to understand another part of the purpose of God for the church. We replace the administration of the angels in the government of God in the heavens. It is there and then that we will be kings and priests to *His* God and Father (Rev. 1:6). We are seated in the heavens in Christ in the government of God over the millennial earth. God has not put the world to come in subjection to angels (Heb. 2:5). *"And do you not know that you will judge them?"* (I Cor. 6:3) Is this not the essence of these verses in Ephesians and the intended purpose of God in His government over the millennial earth, *"...to the intent that now the manifold wisdom of God might be made known by the church to the principalities and powers in heavenly places, according to the eternal purpose which He accomplished in Christ Jesus our Lord."* (Eph. 3:10-11) The church is a large part of the eternal plan of God. By placing the church in the heavens God will make known His multifaceted and manifold wisdom throughout the ages to come. These are the things angels desire to look into.

Having been glorified and conformed into the image of His Son, we will be holy and blameless in God's sight before Him in love. All the responsibilities given to us at that time, whether in the government of God or as sons in the Father's house, will be carried out in divine perfection according to the Son's nature we are conformed into. The government of God over all creation will be given to Jesus, the Son of Man. The true church is His body and His bride. As His help-meet we will reign with Him over all things visible and invisible. When the church is glorified the government of God on the earth is not over the sons of God. Through Jesus Christ and in Christ we are the instruments of God in His government. Both the corporate responsibilities of His body and the individual responsibility as sons will be accomplished in excellence to the glory of God. It will be an end to the failure of the church as well as to any individual failure of the believer.

A Walk worthy of our Calling

Therefore in view of our heavenly calling, we have a current walk on this earth in which we are pilgrims and strangers. This is individual. It is our responsibility before God to act and live according to our calling. We are to act and live as pilgrims and strangers to this world and on this earth. It is the responsibility of the ministry before God to always teach doctrine that shows the church how to maintain her separation from this world and earth. Our Lord said, *"They are not of the world, just as I am not of the world."* (John 17:14, 16) This speaks of our position in Christ and with Christ. Obviously our walk is a result of this position and relationship we have as sons of God and apart from the world.

"I, therefore…beseech you to have a walk worthy of the calling with which you are called." (Eph. 4:1) You get the sense that the calling is yet to be fulfilled while the walk is the present thing. Our calling is heavenly and future, while the walk is what we are engaged in now, on the earth and in the wilderness of the world. It is the current walk that should reflect upon the calling (I Thess. 2:12). Yet it is clear that the 'walk' is not the 'calling'. This must be seen and understood.

The Spirit instructs us as to having a worthy walk. *"…with all lowliness and gentleness, with longsuffering, bearing with one another in love, endeavoring to keep the unity of the Spirit in the bond of peace."* (Eph. 4:2-3) This is our corporate responsibility. Yet our walk, carried out in human responsibility, is not what determines our calling. It is only the purpose of God towards us, as He settled before time began, that fixes our calling and position.

2 Timothy 1:9

"…who has saved us and called us with a holy calling, not according to our works, but according to His own purpose and grace which was given to us in Christ Jesus before time began."

Our calling is according to God's eternal purpose. It is not determined by human works of responsibility (Eph. 1:3-9). This is the sovereign work of God. Nothing can hinder this in coming to its intended result.

Yet when the Spirit speaks of walk in Ephesians 4:1, we have that which is present on the earth. It is seen in Scripture as a unique mixture of human obedience through God's power and grace (Phil. 2:12-15, II Cor. 4:6-11). We are encouraged to walk in lowliness, gentleness, and longsuffering, bearing with one another in love. Only the life of Christ in us and the power of the indwelling Spirit enables the believer to do this (Gal. 2:20, Rom. 8:2-4).

Further in Ephesians the Spirit says (Eph. 5:1-2), *"Therefore be followers of God as dear children. And walk in love, as Christ also has loved us and given Himself for us..."* Here we see that the believer's walk in responsibility results from his position – as dear children of God. We follow God as Christ did, and love as He loved. We emulate His walk (I John 2:6). This is all human responsibility as a believer in our 'walk' in the wilderness of this world. It should be a walk worthy of our calling that is yet to be fulfilled. If we look closely we see that Ephesians 4, 5, and 6 is all instruction about the believer having a worthy walk while here in this world.

The Son of Man had nowhere in this world to lay His head, yet He said, *"Come, follow Me."* Jesus had a walk leading Him out of this world. As believers, we have the same thing in our calling. Even though we are presently in this world and on this earth walking, our calling leads us out of the world and into the heavens. If we are to follow Jesus, it is for the purpose of ending up where He is – seated in heavenly places in Christ Jesus (John 12:26, Eph. 2:6).

Of course we all know the believer has to tread through this world. Christ had to go through it, and He did so for us. Now we follow His example as our path through the wilderness. Our citizenship is in heaven and our passage through this world should reflect upon our heavenly conversation. The true believer does not have the spirit of the world, but the Spirit which is of God. We should be living in such a way to emulate where Christ sits, the One who has gone to prepare a place for us. We have to pass through this world. While we do, where are our hearts? Can we say that our associations of life are all up there in the heavens? Is that where our hearts are living? Does our worship and praise bear the mark of our conversation being in heaven? Does it bear the stamp of the happiness and blessedness which is the expression of our connection with Him there? *"The things which are seen are temporal; but the things which are not seen are eternal."* (II Cor. 4:18) Let us, then, remember that the Lord has given Himself for us that we might have the things that are unseen – the eternal things. Jesus has Himself entered there above as our forerunner.

The Corporate Responsibility of the Church

The purpose and counsels of God for the assembly are first mentioned at the end of Ephesians 1 (all that precedes this is the individual believer as seen in God's purposes). There the body is exalted in Christ to the right hand of God, far above all principalities and powers, and is the fullness of Him (Eph. 1:19-23). The sovereign work of God to establish the assembly as His house on earth is seen in Ephesians 2:11-22. Still speaking of God's sovereign purpose, the body of Christ is the mystery of God's will, which He kept hidden from the prophets and previous ages (Eph. 3:1-11) – the last two verses of this passage make the pairing of the church with and in God's eternal counsels quite straightforward. The remainder of Ephesians 3 speaks of our fellowship with the Father in view of this privileged position in Christ.

In Ephesians 4:8-16 it speaks of the body's corporate responsibility. This was God's intention for the body on the earth – *we all come in the unity of the faith and the knowledge of the Son of God, to a perfect man, to the measure of the stature of the fullness of Christ.* It goes on from here which you may read for yourself (vs. 14-16). The calling of the church is heavenly, but until then the church must walk on this earth with a walk that is worthy of its calling. The responsibility of the body was to be taught and to be edified, to grow up into a perfect man. The church was responsible to testify to the truth of God (I Tim. 3:15), and not to be tossed to and fro and carried about by every wind of doctrine. Yet we understand that what God starts in sovereign grace on the earth, with all gracious intentions from Him concerning it, must eventually be handed over to the responsibility of man. Therefore we have Paul laying a foundation in sovereign grace for the earthly building of God, a foundation no other man could lay (I Cor. 3:9-11). Then the Spirit says, *"...let each one take heed how he builds on it."*

The corporate 'walk' of Christendom on the earth has failed. As an external entity the professing church, having responsibility before God, has been proven corrupt and spiritually dead. This is a non-recoverable situation. To think otherwise is not hope or faith, but the greatest of pretentions and blindness. The individual believer has individual responsibility before God. This responsibility can be made good, or as good as we can make it, by walking as Jesus walked, with Him always as our example (I John 2:6). I have discussed this earlier in the book as well as earlier in this chapter, and so will not repeat it here. It is the individual walk that remains and is the emphasis, when the corporate entity is found corrupt. Again look at Philadelphia. It is a very individual message given to her from the Lord without the corporate entity of Christendom being addressed.

Colossians 3:1-3

"If then you were raised with Christ, seek those things which are above, where Christ is, sitting at the right hand of God. Set your mind on things above, not on things on the earth. For you died, and your life is hidden with Christ in God."

The things above are matters of hope that the believer is to be thoroughly acquainted with. If not, you will not be able to set your mind on them. Modern Christian teaching seldom teaches this. Contemporary teaching does not grasp the thoughts in the above passage. It doesn't comprehend the true calling of God for the church. The modern result is most often the church being taught in the light of the wrong calling — an earthly calling. And the church will be taught with the wrong instructions — earthly and Jewish. Modern teachings serve to pull the true church down to the earth and establish her life in the world. But the believer's life isn't in the world as you can see in the passage above. Our life is not on the earth. It is not about things on the earth (Phil. 3:18-21). Our life is Christ. Our life is about where He is right now in glory. Our life is only about Christ, and He apart from this world. A Christ in glory must be the object occupying the attention of our hearts (II Cor. 3:18, 4:4, 6). Our hopes? It is Christ in us, the hope of glory (Col. 1:27, Rom. 5:1-2).

Ephesians 4:1-4

"I, therefore, the prisoner of the Lord, beseech you to walk worthy of the calling with which you were called, (2) with all lowliness and gentleness, with longsuffering, bearing with one another in love, (3) endeavoring to keep the unity of the Spirit in the bond of peace. (4) There is one body and one Spirit, just as you were called in one hope of your calling."

The simple truth is that if you do not comprehend your calling, you cannot have a walk worthy of it. There is only one calling for the believer and church. There is no other. And this calling is in hope (Eph. 4:4). It is not on this earth, in this world, or of this present time. God's desire is for the church, and all individual members gathered by the Spirit forming her, to be conformed into the image of His Son, and to be with the Father and Son in His glory (John 17:22, 24). Our calling does not leave us short of the glory and presence of God (Rom. 3:23, I Pet. 5:10-11).

Chapter 20: Endnotes

[156] Many say that some Christians are so heavenly minded, they are no earthly good. There is not one portion of Scripture that supports this statement. Quite the contrary, the true believer is to be just this – 'so heavenly minded'. To set your mind on earthly things is to be equated by the Spirit of God as in the category of 'the enemies of the cross of Christ' (Phil. 3:18-19). Our citizenship is in heaven, and the spiritual believer is taught and trained to look only there (Phil. 3:20-21). Forgetting all things behind, Paul did only one thing – 'reaching forward to those things ahead'. And what are these things ahead? *"I press toward the goal for the prize of the upward call of God in Christ Jesus."* We are always looking at and pressing toward our calling, which remains before us, and is upward and heavenly. It will only be fulfilled by the rapture of the church – her resurrection and glorification (Phil. 3:10, 21).

In Colossians we get the spiritual reason for our heavenly gaze and the object of faith for our present walk on this earth – Christ is there, sitting at the right hand of God. Therefore we seek those things above and set our minds on things above, and *not* on things on the earth (Col. 3:1-3). Why? – Because you died. You died, and ended any relationship with the earth and world. *"For you died..."* Paul says, giving the Spirit's reason to not look at earthly things. Having died, the only reason the believer is alive is because he has been raised from death with Christ (Col. 3:1), and now possesses Christ's resurrected life (Eph. 1:1-6, Rom. 6:3-5, Gal. 2:20). If Christ is at the right hand of God and He is the believer's life, then our life is there as well, hidden in God as Christ is now hidden in God. So then the Spirit says, *"...Christ who is your life..."* This one who is our life is the Son of Man in glory. He is Christ in you, the hope of glory (Col. 1:27). Can there be any doubt why we are heavenly minded? God's purpose for our calling is to be in the glory of God with Christ and as made like Christ. His purpose in promising to conform us into the image of His Son will be so we can be near Him (the Father) in His presence and the objects of His delight (Rom. 8:28-30).

[157] The rapture and glorifying of the church into the heavens is written of extensively in the second book of 'the Son of Man Series'. Its title is 'The Blessed Hope of the Church'.

[158] The church will be found in the very presence of the invisible God. This is our privilege by virtue of our position as sons of God. Our position

matches that of Jesus, the Son of God (John 20:17). Those that are saved on the earth during the tribulation for the millennium, including the Jewish remnant and those born on the earth during the millennium, are at a distance from God. It is as far as the New Jerusalem is above the earth, with the Son of Man on the earth as their mediator. The wicked dead are destined to forever be separated from the presence of God and during the millennium are found in Hades. After the millennium is the great white throne judgment. This is when Hades gives up all the wicked dead to be judged by Christ. They are all cast into the lake of fire as the final destination of all wickedness. At that time Satan is cast in there as well. After this follows the eternal state in which the tabernacle of God will be with men on the earth as come down from heaven (Rev. 21:1-4). The tabernacle of God is the New Jerusalem, which is the church. At least it is the heavenly and eternal habitation of the church.

Chapter 21

The Mystery of the Kingdom of Heaven

The Jewish prophecies predicted that God would send a Messiah to Israel. He would be a natural descendent of Abraham and David. He would throw off the chains of bondage of the Gentiles ruling over them and establish the kingdom of God in Israel. All the Jews had this prophetic knowledge and eagerly anticipated the fulfillment of the promise of Messiah. This was Jesus as He came to Israel, according to the flesh (Rom. 9:5).[159]

It is important that we know the detail of prophecy, and we have Spirit-given understandings of Biblical principles. The first coming of Messiah to Israel has its basis in the principle of responsibility. Israel was being tested by God as representing all mankind. They had served as the test case for quite some time and the presentation of Messiah to them was their final exam. In all God's testing of Israel, as representing mankind, there was never any good fruit (Matt. 21:19). Finally they would not have Jesus as King. They cast Him out, and put Him to death (Matt. 21:37-39). There was nothing but failure by man.

Galatians 4:4

"But when the fullness of the time had come, God sent forth His Son, born of a woman, born under the law."

The Testing of Responsibility is Complete

This was Jesus as He came to Israel – born of a woman and born under Jewish law. Yet it was the fullness of time because it was man's final testing by God. It was the end of man morally and the fullness of time for testing responsibility. It was the end of the world (Heb. 9:26). This was Israel representing man, and these were the circumstances and principles existing when God sent forth His Son.

God has proven that man was utterly depraved. He has proven that man in the flesh could not have a relationship with Him. The kingdom of God could not be established in Israel under the principle of responsibility in man. What should have been a Messianic kingdom established as the kingdom of God in Israel, was rejected by the Jews when they killed the Son. Israel was man in Adam, man in the flesh, and sinners at best along with the rest of the world.

The kingdom of God was taken away from Israel. There would be no Messianic kingdom at this time (Matt. 21:43). The kingdom of God would have a different form and a new revelation. It could no longer be an attempt to establish a kingdom in Israel predicated on human responsibility. That had been thoroughly searched out and proven a failure. God would not attempt the same thing expecting a different outcome. We have the distinct understanding in John's gospel that from now on, a man must be 'born again' in order to see and enter into the kingdom of God. He would have to have a new nature – God's nature – in order to have a relationship with God and to be in His kingdom. Whatever new form God's kingdom came to (at the first a kingdom in mystery), the kingdom was taken from the Jews.

The New Creation – the Sovereign Work of God

Being 'born again' has no origin or foundation in the responsibility of man. These are those *"...who were born, not of blood, nor the will of the flesh, nor the will of man, but of God."* They were not born from human responsibility or by human decisions, but by the sovereign will and grace of God. These are born of God. The direct agent of God's work is the Holy Spirit. Therefore these are born of the Spirit.

John 3:6-8

"That which is born of the flesh is flesh, and that which is born of the Spirit is spirit. (7) Do not marvel that I said to you, 'You must be born again.' (8) The wind blows where it wishes, and you hear the sound of it, but cannot tell where it comes from and where it goes. So is everyone who is born of the Spirit."

Establishing the Kingdom of Heaven

Whenever John the Baptist preached, or Jesus and the disciples preached, they taught that the kingdom of heaven was at hand (Matt. 3:2, 4:17, 10:7). I have shown in this book, the kingdom of heaven was not established until Jesus Christ was glorified to the right hand of God. What we have before this time is the Jewish dispensation. Also what was taking place before this was the final testing of man in the principle of responsibility. These two things — the Jewish dispensation and the testing — are basically the same. In order for the kingdom of heaven to go from being 'at hand' to being 'established', at the very least in mystery, God had to finish the Jewish dispensation and the testing.[160]

1. The kingdom of heaven could not be established until God had set aside the Jewish dispensation. This involves setting aside the title of Messiah, the promises and prophecies to Israel connected with this title. Israel is set aside as a people and a nation — their earthly calling is set aside. Any thoughts of their land and their restoration in the land are all set aside. They are not considered by God at this time as His people and He is not their God (Hos. 1:9). God ends the practice of Judaism and destroys their temple. He allows their covenant to fade away into extinction (Heb. 8:13). Because the Jews are set aside, then prophecy and God's dealings with the

earth grind to a halt. Time counted in prophecy has stopped (Dan. 9:24-26).

2. The kingdom of heaven could not be established until God had finished the testing of man in responsibility. This testing was of man in Adam, man in the flesh, and it was by the law of Moses given to the Jews. Israel was the test case representing the human race. They failed to produce any fruit of obedience to God (Matt. 21:19). The last testing of man was the sending of Messiah to Israel (Matt. 21:37). The Jews failed in this by rejecting Him as King. God was finished testing man in Adam in the principle of responsibility. Now God could move on to something different.

The word mystery involves that which is secret or hidden. The kingdom of heaven (having been established by the glorifying of the Son of Man to the right hand of God and the sending down of the Holy Spirit) involves mystery at this present time.

The Mystery of the Kingdom of Heaven

1. It involves the revelation and spiritual understandings of its own mysteries (Matt. 13:11). The kingdom of heaven currently has secret and hidden things. These are mysteries that are unseen to the unbeliever and the world, but revealed to the eye of faith of the believer, who has the mind of Christ.

2. It involves Jesus, the Son of Man, going away to heaven, and presently being 'hidden' in God from the world in mystery (Col. 3:1-3). Again, He is hidden from the world, but not to the eye of faith. *"A little while longer and the world will see Me no more, but you will see Me."* (John 14:19)

3. The Son of Man at the right hand of God is the object of faith for the believer and the true church during the time of the kingdom of heaven in mystery. He is unseen at this time, and our faith is the evidence of things unseen, and in mystery. This is the character of true faith.

4. Our present walk of faith, which involves only the time the believer and true church are on the earth, makes up part of this present time of mystery of the kingdom of heaven. The faith by which we sojourn in the wilderness is all the evidence we need of the unseen things we hope for from God. Of course God has given us His Spirit, who is the guarantee of all our Christian hopes (Eph. 1:13-14, II Cor. 1:20-22, 5:4-7). The character of the true church is *'blessed are those who have not seen and yet have believed'*. (John 20:29)

5. In the kingdom of heaven the spoiled crop of wheat and tares all have a common profession of faith. This common confession, along with not being able to see the seal of the Spirit, makes it very difficult to tell the wheat from the tares. The common profession of faith, and water baptism as a Christian ordinance, are why the ten virgins look so much alike. The wheat has a true profession of faith from the heart (Rom. 10:9). The tares have no real faith and no seal of the Spirit (Eph. 1:13, Matt. 25:2-4).

6. The church is also the mystery of God hidden from the prophets and prophecy (Eph. 3:4-5, 9). Presently the kingdom of heaven involves the gathering of the true church on earth – this gathering of Christ's body is a hidden mystery from before time began (Rom. 16:25, Col. 1:26).

7. The Holy Spirit has been sent down to gather in the body. His work is unseen as He is unseen. He is like the wind blowing where it wishes (John 3:8). This is an unseen sovereign work of God.

8. The body of Christ is now hidden in the spoiled crop of Christendom and is also the treasure hidden in the field of the world (Matt. 13:44). This is a mystery as well.

9. The mystery of iniquity is presently at work in the professing church and the kingdom of heaven (II Thess. 2:7). Sin and leaven are secretly at work, spreading and growing (Matt. 13:33).

All these things are currently part of the kingdom of heaven in mystery. The entire time the true church is on the earth is this kingdom in mystery. It is not openly manifested to the world in power. Eventually the wheat in the crop will be separated from the tares, removed from out of the field, and placed in the barn (Matt 13:30). This is the true church being taken to the heavens in the rapture. This event ends the time of the church on earth and is a mystery as well. Paul says (I Cor. 15:51-53), *"Behold, I tell you a mystery: We shall not all sleep, but we shall all be changed – in a moment, in the twinkling of an eye...the dead will be raised incorruptible, and we shall be changed."*

The Kingdom in Patience

This kingdom is also currently called the kingdom of the Son of His love. It is the kingdom that every believer has been translated into (Col. 1:13). The kingdom of heaven currently involves all the time of the slain Lamb in the midst of the throne (Rev. 5:6). He is hidden there from the world and in mystery. This is all the time that Jesus Christ, the Son of Man, is sitting on His Father's throne, and not sitting on His own throne (Rev. 3:21). It is the same period of mystery that John, while on the isle of Patmos, identifies with the words, *"...companion in tribulation, and in the kingdom and patience of Jesus Christ..."* (Rev. 1:9). Christ's patience involves His sitting and waiting as hidden at the right hand of God (Heb. 10:12-13). We keep the word of His patience by waiting as He waits (Rev. 3:10). We are in the kingdom now, as John says he is with us, but during the time of its mystery we experience tribulation and waiting.

The Kingdom in Power

This time will not last forever. Soon this will all change. Soon it will be altered from the kingdom and patience to the kingdom and power (Rev. 11:15-17 and 12:10). Eventually, in His Father's timing, He will rise up from His Father's throne, and take up His power and reign on the earth, sitting as the Son of Man and King of kings on His own throne (Matt. 25:31), ruling over the earth (Psalm 8). *This is when the kingdom of heaven is no longer in 'mystery', but in 'open manifestation' to the world, and in power.* This will be when the kingdom of the Father is in the heavens and the church is His tabernacle there, while the Son of Man's kingdom will be reigning over man in Adam on the earth.

The Mediatorial Kingdom

The Son of Man's reign during the millennium will be a mediatorial work functioning between God and man on the earth (I Tim. 2:5). For Israel their two houses will be brought back together as one by a new covenant that Jehovah makes with them. It is a covenant mediated by Jesus Christ (Heb. 8:6-13). God will make a 'new covenant' with Israel based on the one who shed His blood and died for that nation (John 11:50-51). This is all done by God. The Israeli remnant saved and placed into the land at that future time is all the sovereign work of God.

Mediation is needed between two parties who make an agreement under certain conditions. In Scripture it is associated with covenants made between two, where both parties have responsibilities dictated by the agreement. Mediation is seen in general as between God and man in Adam, and specifically with Israel. Yet it is only seen in the two distinct covenants that are found in Scripture involving Israel.[161] Also we should remember that under both covenants Israel is man in Adam and in the flesh on the earth.

1. The first covenant was the law given to Israel at Mt. Sinai (Gal. 3:17-20, Heb. 8:7, 13). Blessings were promised to Israel if they could obey. Moses was the mediator between the two parties – Israel and Jehovah. Israel failed to obey and only found death, condemnation, and a curse. *"For if that first covenant had been faultless, then no place would have been sought for a second."* Even though Moses did a decent job in his mediation, God found fault with the first covenant because of man's failures in responsibility, and it had to pass away.

2. The second covenant between God and Israel has yet to be made. At the present time Israel is set aside by God and not

acknowledged by God as 'His people'. They have no covenant with God. Their first covenant has long ago vanished away (Heb. 8:13). The destruction of Jerusalem and the temple in 70 AD sealed the fate of the first covenant and stopped the practice of Judaism. Through the Spirit, Paul anticipated this event at the time he wrote the epistle to the Hebrews and said, the first covenant is *becoming obsolete and growing old, and is ready to vanish away.* Until 70 AD the sacrifices continued and the temple was still standing.

The new covenant will be for Israel on the earth during the coming millennium (Jer. 31:31-34, Heb. 8:7-13). This is established in Old Testament prophecy and spoken by Jeremiah directly to a rebellious Israel concerning a future remnant that God would return and establish in the land. This covenant is millennial. The details of the passages are very specific and obvious, and present the greatest of difficulties to spiritualize and apply to the believer/church. The epistle of Hebrews is written to Hebrews and was not written to the general Gentile church. Jesus Christ is the mediator of this future covenant (Heb. 8:6, 9:15). His blood, shed specifically for the nation (John 11:49-51), is that which establishes the covenant with them.[162]

These things are very clear from the Scriptures. They only become confusing when we bring our pre-conceived ideas and pre-suppositions to them. There is a new covenant for Israel that replaces the 'first covenant' (Heb. 8:8-9). It is for the physical and earthly blessing of Israel in their Promised Land (Ez. 36:23-38). It will be effective when they are with their Messiah. Israel will be blessed in Him because He died for the nation (John 11:49-53). His blood was shed for them so that the future Jewish remnant could have this new covenant – *not according to the covenant I made with their fathers in the day when I took them by the hand to lead them out of the land of Egypt.* Whose fathers? Is it not Israel's? How can the reuniting of the two kingdoms as one be something spiritualized to the church? It simply can't (Ez. 37:15-22). God keeps these two groups separate – Israel and the church.

The formal side (the letter) of all covenants is for man in Adam. Most of the covenants, in a sense, are with Israel, so that it may be said, "...

Israelites, to whom pertain...the covenants..." (Rom. 9:4) Even when you look at the specific promise made to Abraham and confirmed to His one Seed, it is intended for the blessing of the whole earth and all the nations on the earth (Gen. 12:3, 22:18, Gal. 3:16). When Isaac was offered up in type, representing the death and resurrection of Christ, God confirms the promise to Abraham by saying, *"In your Seed all the nations of the earth will be blessed."* By the sending down of the Holy Spirit, the double meaning of this promise has been revealed. In this present dispensation the Gentiles are blessed by the preaching of the gospel of Jesus Christ and the gathering of the church out of all nations (Gal. 3:7-9, 13-14). In the dispensation of the fullness of times all things on the earth will be gathered in Christ for blessing (Eph. 1:10). The language of all the covenants of Scripture is fairly simple and earthy. God will be faithful to fulfill every covenant He has made according to the direct and plain language of those agreements. Otherwise He will be found unfaithful and a liar, and no amount of spiritualizing the words of the covenants by theologians will save Him (Rom. 3:3-4, II Tim. 2:13).

[This might have given us opportunity to address the believer/church's connection with the 'new covenant', and what form that connection takes. However I realize that this would require a rather lengthy discussion and would better be saved for the next book in this series. It will concern the topic of redemption. The believer's place in the 'new covenant' would fit in better there. If I addressed it here, I could only do so in a cursory and limited fashion, which could not serve the true value and glory of the association.]

In the promises God made to Abraham you see Abraham being made a great nation and you see the blessing of the nations through him (Gen 12:2-3). The thought of nations or nationality is a relationship that belongs to the earth and the first creation. Nationality is at the core of Israel's on again, off again, relationship with their God Jehovah. When Jehovah says 'you are My people' it is the same as Him saying 'you are My chosen nation'.

There are some unique features in the covenants made with Abraham. They only consist of promises from God. These promises were unconditional. One unique feature is there was no need for a mediator. There was no responsibility on Abraham's part. The promises and their fulfillment do not depend on man, but rather, on the faithfulness of God. It is called the covenant of promise. The principle is that God made promises to Abraham and Abraham believed Him. The promises were confirmed to the one Seed of Abraham. This Seed is Christ, the resurrected Son of Man (Gal. 3:16-17, Heb. 11:17-19, Gen. 22:18). Confirming the covenant to Christ means that all the promises from God would be secured in the resurrected and glorified Son of Man. Confirmation is not mediation, and it was not confirmed with a Messiah come in the flesh to Israel (Acts 13:30-34).

The Mystery of Faith

Abraham is said to be the father of faith. It might benefit us to speak on the subject of faith, starting first with the example of Abraham. God made promises to Abraham concerning what He would do for him, and also concerning how He would use Abraham, especially in blessing all the nations of the world through him. Then Abraham took God at His word. He trusted God in spite of contrary circumstances in his life (Rom. 4:17-19). Sarah does the same in order to bear a son (Heb. 11:11). This was his faith, and in a sense it was fairly simple – God promises, Abraham trusted, and eventually God does the work exactly according to what He promised.

Romans 4:20-21

"He did not waver at the promise of God through unbelief, but was strengthened in faith, giving glory to God, and being fully convinced that what He had promised He was also able to perform."

God makes the promises – this is not His grace, but instead His word. When God does His work fulfilling the promise, it is then His grace. In between these two, Abraham and Sarah become fully convinced of the promise of a son. Of Sarah it was said, *"By faith Sarah...judged Him faithful who promised."* (Heb. 11:11) God promises first and on the other end He works in grace. In the middle we believe what God has promised, counting Him faithful. In this we can see the principle of sovereign grace through faith (Rom. 4:16). So then all believers are this (Gal. 3:7): *"Therefore know that only those who are of faith are sons of Abraham."*

Hebrews 11:1

"Now faith is the substance of things hoped for, the evidence of things not seen."

The Scriptures give us a definition of what faith is. This would be as applicable to Abraham's faith as it is to ours. What are the things the believer properly hopes for? This is a good question, for I'm sure we are not given license to hope for just anything that suits our pleasure. As with Abraham, the believer hopes for the things God has promised him. Do you know what God has promised the believer? The most detailed listing of these things is found in Revelation 2 and 3. After every one of the seven messages there are promises from God made to the true believer. These are the things hoped for. In making a list from the two chapters, I believe we find it to be quite comprehensive. All promises were spoken by Jesus Christ by the Spirit.

1. I will give you to eat from the tree of life, which is in the midst of the paradise of God.

2. You shall not be hurt by the second death.

3. I will give you some of the hidden manna to eat.

4. I will give you a white stone, and on the stone a new name written, which no one knows except him who receives it.

5. I will give you power over the nations, to rule them with a rod of iron; as a potter's vessels shall be broken to pieces' – as I also have received from My Father.

6. I will give you the morning star.

7. You shall be clothed in white garments, and I will not blot out your name from the Book of Life. I will confess your name before My Father and before His angels.

8. I will make you a pillar in the temple of My God, and you shall go out no more.

9. I will write on you the name of My God and the name of the city of My God, the New Jerusalem, which comes down out of heaven from My God.

10. I will write on you My new name.

11. I will grant you to sit with Me on My throne, as I also overcame and sat down with My Father on His throne.

Now the things we properly hope for as believers are things presently unseen. They are still just promises from God. But like Abraham, we take God at His word, and this regardless of what we see or circumstances around us in this world. We believe in what God has promised us, and wait. Wait? Yes, faith waits. For what? For God to do exactly as He has promised. While we wait, we do not see the things we properly hope for as Christians. They remain unseen all this time that we walk by faith. How long is that? All the time we are on this earth and in these bodies of flesh (II Cor. 4:17 – 5:7).

We might object by saying, "Abraham and Sarah received the son promised to them by God while they were still alive on this earth!" And God called Isaac the son of promise, as he was for Abraham the guarantee or confirmation of all the promises yet to come (Gal. 4:28). But I answer that God has done a similar yet better thing for us. We have already received *the promise of the Spirit through faith* (Gal. 3:14). For the believer, receiving the Spirit is the guarantee of our inheritance and all remaining promises to us from God. He has given us His Spirit as an assurance of all these things not seen – the promises yet to come (II Cor. 1:20-22).

- Because we are sons of God through faith in Jesus Christ, God gives us the seal of the Spirit (Gal. 3:26, Eph. 1:13). The Holy Spirit is the believer's seal of sonship (Gal. 4:5-6, Rom.

8:15-16). Because we are sons, we are children of promise just as Isaac was (Gal. 4:28). The indwelling Spirit is then the guarantee of the inheritance that God will give us (Eph. 1:13-14, Rom. 8:17, Gal. 4:7, 30).

- Being sealed by the Spirit is the guarantee to us that God will glorify our bodies (II Cor. 5:5, Rom. 8:11). When this transpires, God changes us into the image of His Son. God's ultimate purpose for our glorification is to bring us into His presence. Man in sin always falls short of the glory of God's presence. Man in the flesh avoids God's presence at all cost and every opportunity. He tries to avoid entertaining any thoughts of it. However for the sons of God, His presence becomes an ever increasing desire. This privilege becomes far more meaningful than any individual reward.

- Having received the Spirit through faith, He becomes to us the earnest of the hope of the glory of God that we will share with Christ (Rom. 5:2, 8:18, Col. 1:27, II Cor. 4:17, I Peter 4:14, John 17:22).

Obviously God had to give Abraham and Sarah a son while they were still living. There had to be a son before Abraham and Sarah died, or every promise God made to Abraham would, through time, be found false. God would be found a liar. According to the promise of having their own son, Isaac would be known as 'the child of promise'. He becomes for Abraham the assurance that God will eventually fulfill all the remaining promises He had spoken.

Romans 9:7-9

"...nor are they all children because they are the seed of Abraham; but, "In Isaac your seed shall be called." That is, those who are the children of the flesh, these are not the children of God; but the children of the promise are counted as the seed. For this is the word of promise: "At this time I will come and Sarah shall have a son."

Abraham receives a son through faith in God. But Abraham, in his lifetime, never receives any of the other things that God had promised him. He never possesses the land and never receives it as an inheritance. He is always a pilgrim and stranger in the land he was promised. *"By faith he sojourned in the land of promise as in a foreign country..."* (Heb. 11:9)

Hebrews 11:13

"These all died in faith, not having received the promises, but having seen them afar off were assured of them, embraced them and confessed that they were strangers and pilgrims on the earth."

This is the walk of faith of Abraham, Sarah, and all those who follow in their footsteps. They walked by faith in God, and then they all died in faith, *not having received the promises that God had made to them.* Oh, what a revelation of what true bible faith actually is! If only the 'faith' and 'grace' teachers had understood this and taught it! Here is the principle God is setting forth: In Abraham, the people of God are *characterized* as those possessing the promises while actually not possessing the things promised. This serves to draw out affections and hope in the people of God to that which is outside this world (Heb. 11:9-10, 14, 16). This character of faith made them pilgrims and strangers on the earth.[163]

We have a walk of faith like they did (II Cor. 5:7). And I will be so bold as to say that we will all die in faith, not having received the promises that God has made to the Christian. We are to see them as afar off. If we see them by faith, and we know the faithfulness of our God, then we also can be assured of them and embrace them. We follow their example of faith. *"And all these, having obtained a good testimony through faith, did not receive the promise."* (Heb. 11:39)

As the son of promise, Isaac was all that Abraham needed as a guarantee. He now knew that God would be faithful to him to eventually fulfill all He had promised, even though it would be after he died. In like manner, the Holy Spirit every believer has received from God is all we need as a guarantee (Gal. 3:14). Now we know, with all assurance of faith, that God will be pleased to someday glorify us, take us into His glory, and fulfill every promise He has ever made to His sons. We will abide eternally in the Father's house as sons and heirs of the living God.

This is the important point: All the promises God made to Abraham he never received in his lifetime. He believes the word of God and promises unseen, walking by faith as a stranger on the earth. The birth of Isaac is the guarantee and security to Abraham of the truthfulness of God and all He has promised to him. In the same way Abraham received a son by faith, the believer has received the promise of the Spirit through faith (Gal. 3:14). The seal of the Spirit becomes the believer's Isaac – the guarantee and security of all that God has promised us.

When the believer's time on this earth is over his walk of faith will end. In death, to be absent from the body is to be present with the Lord (II Cor. 5:8, Phil. 1:23). He will not need faith when he is present with Christ. But this is not the blessed hope of the church, nor do we realize our hope through death. Being absent from the body is not being in the glory. It remains for all of the true church to enter into God's rest. When we arrive in His rest after the rapture of the church, we will have been glorified in body and we will be in the glory. We will be complete, conformed to the image of God's Son, and not there as unclothed (II Cor. 5:1-4). We will see with our eyes the former promises that were unseen. We will be in possession of the things that we properly hoped for (Heb. 11:1). And so, faith as the substance of things hoped for, the evidence of things not seen, will come to an end.

The coming millennium on the earth, the dispensation of the fullness of times, will not be based on a walk of faith by Israel or the Gentile world. Rather the principle is that every eye will see. It will not be a dispensation based on the evidence of things unseen. The future Israeli remnant chosen by God, sealed and preserved by Him during the tribulation, will look on Him whom they have pierced (Zech. 12:10). They will receive their Messiah when they see Him. Thomas and the disciples are a type or figure of this, after the resurrection of Jesus (John 20:25). This isn't true bible faith or Christian faith. It is the lowest order of faith. Biblical faith is the evidence of things not seen. The Jews must see in order to know and are always requesting a sign (I Cor. 1:22). The law – their religion – is not of faith (Gal. 3:12). Judaism only produces a walk by sight, by the senses, and according to the flesh.

The mystery of faith is that it believes things that cannot be seen with the eye or perceived by the physical senses. The kingdom of heaven in mystery is partly so because the wheat and tares are gathered through the gospel and by a common profession of faith in Jesus Christ. God is unseen as the King in the kingdom of God in general, or as King over the kingdom of heaven in mystery. Jesus, the Son of Man, who planted the wheat, is also away and unseen at this time.

The Mystery of the Crop

The kingdom of heaven exists at this time as the spoiled crop in the field of the world (Matt. 13:24-26). One of the mysteries of the crop is the fact that it is indeed spoiled. The world does not see that it is. The mystery of the crop is that two separate works from two separate sources are mixed together – wheat and tares. The world doesn't see this nor think that it matters. The world doesn't see the evil, how it grows and ripens. This is part of the mystery of the kingdom. For that matter most Christians do not see the presence of evil.

The kingdom will experience a significant change and upheaval at the end of the age by the judgment of the tares and the removal of the wheat into the heavens (Matt. 13:30). The church is the body of Christ. It is the wheat in the spoiled crop. When the wheat is removed from the field and into the heavens, it will exist there throughout the millennium (Eph. 2:7, 3:10-11). The body of Christ never comes to an end, but will exist eternally as the habitation and tabernacle of God and the Lamb. During the millennium she is in the heavens. In the eternal state, the tabernacle of God will come down from heaven, dwelling with men (Rev. 21:1-3).

The transition of the kingdom of heaven from its current time in mystery is easily seen in Scripture. During the millennium there will be the kingdom of the Father in the heavens (Matt. 13:43) and the kingdom of the Son of Man and Messiah on earth.

Matthew 25:31

"When the Son of Man comes in His glory, and all the holy angels with Him, then He will sit on the throne of His glory."

Matthew 19:28

"So Jesus said to them, "Assuredly I say to you, that in the regeneration, when the Son of Man sits on the throne of His glory, you who have followed Me will also sit on twelve thrones, judging the twelve tribes of Israel."

Luke 22:28-30

"But you are those who have continued with Me in My trials. (29) And I bestow upon you a kingdom, just as My Father bestowed one upon Me, (30) that you may eat and drink at My table in My kingdom, and sit on thrones judging the twelve tribes of Israel."

Jesus has received a kingdom from His Father. He speaks of an earthly kingdom and reign. He is no longer sitting and waiting in heaven at the right hand of God. More specifically He speaks of the Messianic kingdom over the twelve tribes of Israel restored in the land. But we see Him and know Him in the broader title of the Son of Man, who will reign, not only over Israel, but over all the Gentile nations on the earth.

Matthew 8:10-12

"When Jesus heard it, He marveled, and said to those who followed, "Assuredly, I say to you, I have not found such great faith, not even in Israel! (11) And I say to you that many will come from east and west, and sit down with Abraham, Isaac, *and Jacob in the kingdom of heaven. (12) But the sons of the kingdom will be cast out into outer darkness. There will be weeping and gnashing of teeth."*

When the kingdom of heaven is manifest during the millennium, we see Abraham, Isaac, and Jacob, the forefathers of Israel, sitting down in the Messianic part of the kingdom on earth. Many coming from east and west to sit down in the kingdom of heaven imply they are on the earth, not in the heavens. This is the reign of the Son of Man over the earth as well as the Messiah over Israel. When Jesus speaks of the sons of the kingdom being cast out, He is speaking of the Jews (Luke 13:28-29). The whole passage is about Israel. It is about their lack of faith and their loss of the kingdom that was rightfully theirs by promise and prophecy.

The Kingdom Work – the Sovereign Work of God

We understand that the kingdom of heaven at this time is like a crop of wheat and tares mixed together in a field, and only the wheat is the workmanship of God. The wheat are the true sons of the kingdom, while the tares are the sons of the wicked one (Matt. 13:38). This means the tares are not actually in the kingdom of heaven, but simply appear to be in an outward way, fooling the world and sometimes even themselves. There is a common profession of faith, but the tares are not wheat. This is easily understood in other passages like this:

Matthew 7:21-23

"Not everyone who says to Me, 'Lord, Lord,' shall enter the kingdom of heaven, but he who does the will of My Father in heaven. Many will say to Me in that day, 'Lord, Lord, have we not prophesied in Your name, cast out demons in Your name, and done many wonders in Your name?' And then I will declare to them, 'I never knew you; depart from Me, you who practice lawlessness!'"

I believe this references the judgment of the tares at the end of the age (Matt. 13:40-42). The tares have great assumptions about God and His kingdom. But the works of man and the flesh do not count as God's work. God knows those who are His.

Israel assumes it will possess the kingdom by physical natural descent. This also is part of the evil leaven corrupting man. Thoughts of pedigree and natural lineage have always been a confidence of the flesh and a means by which man exalts himself (Phil. 3:4-5).

Matthew 3:9

"...and do not think to say to yourselves, 'We have Abraham as our father.' For I say to you that God is able to raise up children to Abraham from these stones."

John 8:33-47

"They answered Him, "We are Abraham's descendants, and have never been in bondage to anyone. How can You say, 'You will be made free'?"

(34) Jesus answered them, "Most assuredly, I say to you, whoever commits sin is a slave of sin. (35) And a slave does not abide in the house forever, but a son abides forever. (36) Therefore if the Son makes you free, you shall be free indeed.

(37) "I know that you are Abraham's descendants, but you seek to kill Me, because My word has no place in you. (38) I speak what I have seen with My Father, and you do what you have seen with your father."

(39) They answered and said to Him, "Abraham is our father."

Jesus said to them, "If you were Abraham's children, you would do the works of Abraham. (40) But now you seek to kill Me, a Man who has told you the truth which I heard from God. Abraham did not do this. (41) You do the deeds of your father."

Then they said to Him, "We were not born of fornication; we have one Father—God."

(42) Jesus said to them, "If God were your Father, you would love Me, for I proceeded forth and came from God; nor have I come of Myself, but He sent Me. (43) Why do you not understand My speech? Because you are not able to listen to My word. (44) You are of your father the devil, and the desires of your father you want to do. He was a murderer from the beginning, and does not stand in the truth, because there is no truth in him. When he speaks a lie, he speaks from his own resources, for he is a liar and the father of it. (45) But because I tell the truth, you do not believe Me. (46) Which of you convicts Me of sin? And if I tell the truth, why do you not believe Me? (47) He who is of God hears God's words; therefore you do not hear, because you are not of God."

What man does by physical birth and natural descent means nothing to God. It is truly a confidence or work of the flesh. Jesus says that He knows they are Abraham's descendants, but that they are not Abraham's children. In the last verse He explains that they are not God's people, even though they have natural descent. In reality their father is not Abraham and not God, but is the devil. Their continual accusations and blindness forced Jesus into being direct and blunt.

Natural descent and physical birth is not the sovereign workmanship of God. It is the work of man and the confidences of the flesh. The sovereign work of God would be God raising up His children from the stones, as in the first quoted verse (Matt. 3:9). After human responsibility was tested and man was found to be a failure, the only thing beyond this point is the sovereign work of God. God would raise up His own children. They would be born of God. That work looks like this:

Romans 8:28-33

"...those who are the called according to His purpose. (29) For whom He foreknew, He also predestined to be conformed to

the image of His Son, that He might be the firstborn among many brethren. (30) Moreover whom He predestined, these He also called; whom He called, these He also justified; and whom He justified, these He also glorified.

(31) What then shall we say to these things? If God is for us, who can be against us? (32) He who did not spare His own Son, but delivered Him up for us all, how shall He not with Him also freely give us all things? (33) Who shall bring a charge against God's elect?"

The believer and the true church are the elect of God, His workmanship, and those called according to His purpose. They are the wheat in the spoiled crop in the field in the present kingdom of heaven.

Chapter 21: Endnotes

[159] The title of Messiah is Jewish and according to Jewish promises and prophecies. It is distinct from the title of the Son of Man. Messiah always relates in promise to the son of David sitting on the throne of David as the King of Israel. It relates to Israel as the center of the government of God over the earth and from Jerusalem, the city of David the king. Jehovah has chosen Zion; He has desired it for His habitation; it is His resting place forever (Psalm 132). Accordingly, Matthew's gospel is the gospel of Messiah. One of the proofs of this characterization is the genealogy of Jesus presented by Matthew. It traces Jesus back to being the son of David and the son of Abraham (Matt. 1:1-17). These are the two great patriarchs of the Jews and the two who God made promises to that are distinctly Jewish promises.

The other genealogy of Jesus is found in Luke's gospel. There it is traced back to Adam. Luke's gospel is more characteristic of Jesus as the Son of Man.

[160] The completion of God's testing of man's responsibility in Adam proved man to be utterly depraved and lost. Man in the first Adam, in that state and position, could not have a relationship with God. Therefore a man must be born again or quickened (John 3:3). He will then come to knowledge of his position as a sinner before God, and will be drawn to faith in Christ. By faith in Christ the man is no longer in Adam, in the flesh, but now in a new state and position. He is in the second Adam and in Christ, and in the Spirit (Rom. 8:8-9, Gal. 3:26-27). This is an entirely new nature, and is one which can have a relationship with God (Eph. 4:23-24, Col. 3:10-11).

But being born of God by faith in Christ has no basis or root in human responsibility or human obedience. It doesn't even have any connection with human choice. It is God's choice of you. The believer is born of God (John 1:13). The believer as a new creation is the sovereign work of God, with the Spirit working as God's direct agent (Eph. 2:10, John 3:8). We are God's workmanship; we are God's new creation (I Cor. 5:17); we are created by God new, in Christ Jesus; *"Now all things are of God who has reconciled us to Himself through Jesus Christ..."* (I Cor. 5:18) We are not born of human responsibility, but all things are of God! We are not born by 'doing' anything, even our faith. That is given to us by God to complete His work of justification (Eph. 2:8). Actually, the seal of the Holy Spirit, which comes after faith, is the final step in God's work of justification (Eph. 1:13, Gal 4:6).

God has finished and completed His testing of human responsibility. God has proven man in Adam a sinner, utterly depraved and completely lost. This testing has already been done by God and is completed. It will not be repeated by Him and there is no reason to repeat it again. This Biblical understanding should end all Judaizing, all Arminian, and all Pelagiustic thoughts, doctrine, or influences. God proved the utter depravity of man. The entire Old Testament and most of the gospels is God doing exactly this. Yet we fail to see this testing and its Biblical importance. God doesn't just say man is utterly depraved. Certainly His word on the matter should be enough. But God goes much farther than this. He spends thousands of years testing man and proving his utter depravity. The giving of the law is the testing of man. Judaism, God's earthly religion, was the testing of man in the flesh. Man's final test was God sending Messiah to the Jews. When Jesus was rejected as King of Israel, the testing was completed and the unequivocal verdict was in. God Himself has proven man to be utterly depraved. Man is completely lost. Man is without hope. Man is without strength, without power, and without resources. Man cannot save himself. Man's 'will' is not free. Sin is its master. God has patiently proven this all to be true.

This is what I believe most theologians are missing in their systems. They do not acknowledge the principle of human responsibility and do not understand that God has thoroughly tested man. They look at Israel and wonder what if...and what could have been...and why was the outcome so disastrous? It results in pointing fingers at the Jews, often in a prejudicial way. What they fail to understand is that the results would have been exactly the same whether God chose Egyptians, Babylonians, or Canaanites to be His privileged people and His favored nation. The results of the testing would have been exactly the same and would have proven the exact same result – the utter depravity of all mankind in the first Adam.

The testing of Israel did more than just prove that the Jews were utterly depraved. God proved that all mankind is utterly depraved. There would not have been a different result if the test subjects would have been different. Israel was man in Adam, man in the flesh, and sinners just like the rest of the world. They were the people that God sovereignly chose and privileged above all other nations in order to serve as the test case for mankind. God proved the utter depravity of all mankind, not just the Jews (Rom. 3:19, Eph. 2:2-3). It is the Arminian leaven that blinds people to this Biblical truth. It is this evil Judaizing leaven that has you believing that the results could have been different. It is the Pelagiustic leaven that has you questioning why Israel was so thick-headed and spiritually blind.

When we take up Judaized, Arminian, or Pelagiustic doctrines and influences, we are denying all that God has meticulously proven through thousands of years of testing. These three are basically one and the same – man exalting himself by what he does. This is the insidiously evil and corrupting leaven that infests the whole of Christendom today (Matt. 13:33). You do not need to look at anything else. This is the evil. It was corrupting man in his thoughts when he was in innocence in the garden. What was it that the devil said? *"...you will be like God..."* Man exalts himself, and the root of this leaven has always been the lies of the devil.

If this evil leaven will not allow you to see the principle of human responsibility being tested by God, and the proving of the total depravity of man by this testing, the same leaven will blind you to the ruin and failure of the professing church on the earth. The leaven will water-down the interpretation of the seven messages of the Spirit to Christendom, in order to protect the works and doings of man. The same leaven will blind you to the failure of the dispensation, a pattern that was repeated in every dispensation previous to it. These thoughts are one and the same in principle. It is only the object being looked at that has changed. I speak here as a warning to all true believers, but specifically to Christian ministers and theologians – these are the ones who carry the greater responsibility as teachers (James 3:1).

[161] To say 'mediation' is necessary when there is to be an agreement or covenant between two distinct parties falls short of the full meaning of this term. Covenants and agreements by definition require two parties. If I said in earlier books that the Abrahamic covenant spoken of in the epistle of Galatians did not really have two parties, I believe now, after much consideration of the topic, I was misspeaking and off the true mark. The difficulty is with the meaning of this verse, *"Now a mediator does not mediate for one only, but God is one."* (Gal. 3:20) This is said by Paul in the midst of his comparison of the covenant of promise involving Abraham and the covenant of law made at Mt. Sinai involving Israel. What we know of truth is that Abraham's covenant had no mediator, while the covenant of law given at Mt. Sinai did. The question then becomes why? I previously taught that the reason the covenant of promise had no mediator was because there weren't really two parties. The more I think of this explanation the more it doesn't explain the difference. There were two parties in the covenant of promise – God and Abraham. I have to acknowledge the obvious truth that this covenant was made by God with Abraham, and that every covenant has two distinct parties. When

the quoted verse says, *"...but God is one,"* it doesn't mean that Abraham's covenant had one party instead of two. It means something different from this.

"Now a mediator does not mediate for one only..." simply means that mediation is always between two parties. When there is need for a mediator he represents and goes between both in the agreement. The mediator will never represent just one. The questions become: When is there need for a mediator? Why do the two covenants made with Israel have need of mediators – the first, Moses, the second, Jesus Christ? (Heb. 8:6, 9:15) Why didn't the Abrahamic covenant need a mediator?

I believe the answer to these questions is that there is need for a mediator only when responsibility is found on both sides of the agreement – where there are responsibilities with both parties. We realize that in every covenant God is a responsible party – He is responsible to do a certain work and to bring about a certain outcome or result. Regardless of which type of covenant it is, God always has responsibility. Now having said all the above, we may understand that in a general way there are only two types of covenants: ones with a mediator and ones without a mediator. We should notice where there is a mediator, there is human responsibility involved with the other party.

Many of the covenants simply depend on the faithfulness of God to do what He has promised to do, without man being responsible for doing anything. This is sovereign grace. These are unconditional covenants. This type of covenant has no need for a mediator. There is only one party with responsibility. When there is no mediator for a covenant, it is because God is the only responsible party. I believe this is what is meant by Paul saying, *"...but God is one."* In sighting two examples of this, it is the case in the covenant of promise with Abraham and the covenant concerning the throne of David. God will be faithful in these to fulfill what He has promised. It will be according to His own timing, and these things generally point to the dispensation of the fullness of times (Eph. 1:10).

The Scriptures speak of Israel's first covenant, given at Mt. Sinai, as having a mediator (Gal. 3:19). The first covenant has ended and prophecy speaks of a new covenant that God will eventually make with Israel. They will need a mediator with the new covenant (Jer. 31:31-34, Heb. 8:6-13, 9:15). Israel has responsibilities in the two covenants – the one past (the first) and the one yet future (the new). Under the first covenant Israel promised to be responsible for obeying all the commandments written in the tablets of stone (Ex. 19:8). It was proven that they could not accomplish it. The covenant became a ministration of death and condemnation (II Cor. 3:7, 9). Their failures only brought a curse from God to all those under Judaism (Gal. 3:10).

The Israelites broke the covenant at the foot of Mt. Sinai at its very beginning, but the mediation of Moses allowed for the survival of the nation. Under pure law Jehovah had the right to destroy the entire nation (Ex. 32:7-10). Moses appealed to the promises God made with the forefathers, and to what Jehovah's glory and reputation would be in the earth if He delivered a people out of Egypt only to destroy them in the wilderness (Ex. 32:11-13, Ez. 20:13-17). Jehovah relents and does not destroy the entire nation. He does not act according to the covenant by doing this. He falls back into His sovereignty and shows mercy to whomever He chooses (Ex. 33:19, Rom. 9:14-16). From this point, Israel is under a mixture of law and mercy (Ex. 34:5-9). The blessings they received in their history were not based on the nation successfully doing the law, but rather God acting in sovereign grace and mercy, apart from the covenant of law. The various judgments the nation encountered, beginning with three thousand destroyed because of the golden calf, were always based on breaking the law. This is how Israel survived, with occasional periods of blessings, because the nation and man in Adam could not exist under pure law.

This mixture of God's goodness and mercy with the law for Israel had its basis in the sovereign God and served to declare and display His glory (Ex. 33:16-34:7, 34:27-30, Rom. 9:15-18). *"So then it is not of him who wills, nor of him who runs, but of God who shows mercy...therefore He has mercy on whom He wills, and whom He wills He hardens."* It is the choice of God in Himself, and in His sovereignty that is spoken of. This gives us an understanding of Romans 3:25 – *"...whom God set forth to be a propitiation by His blood, to demonstrate His righteousness, because in His forbearance God had passed over the sins that were previously committed."* God passing over sins previously committed was during the time of Israel under the law. If there were to be Old Testament saints saved, and surely there were, it would not be by the law. It was by the choice of the sovereign God to show them mercy and to overlook their sins. God's previous action is now justified by the shed blood of Jesus Christ. God is justified in His previous actions. This entire scenario, culminating in the death and shed blood of Jesus Christ, declares God's righteousness in how He dealt with the previous sins. It shows how God remains just in light of His previous actions for Old Testament saints. And now after the cross and an accomplished redemption, He remained just during His justification of New Testament saints when they were still sinners (Rom. 3:26, 5:6-11). God's righteousness is declared and demonstrated by the death and shed blood of Jesus Christ. It is not declared by the sinless life of Christ in the flesh, but rather only by the death and blood of Christ. God's righteousness had to be exonerated by how He dealt with sins. God had to put Jesus to death because the wages of sin is death. Jesus had to die, His shed blood the proof of it, in order for God to remain just and righteous in His dealings with Old and New Testament saints alike. God's righteousness had to be maintained. The cross and Christ's death not only maintains God's righteousness, but glorifies it and glorifies God through it. Why did God raise Jesus from the dead? Because Jesus so glorified God. He established and exalted God's own righteousness by His death. So we see how God was able to choose and call Old Testament saints, even though they remained associated with Israel's first covenant.

After the removal of the church from the earth God will turn His attention back to Israel, His earthly calling. Everything God does for the Israeli remnant through the future tribulation to preserve them, defeat their enemies, and bring them into the land, is by sovereign power and grace. It isn't until they are 'saved' in this fashion that a new covenant will be made with them. This is similar to God's working on behalf of Israel before the first covenant at Mt. Sinai. He delivered the nation out of Egypt by sovereign power and grace, and brought them on eagles' wings to Himself (Ex. 19:3-4). This original deliverance of Israel was for the purpose of exalting His name in all the earth and bringing glory to Him (Rom. 9:17-23). Israel's future deliverance will be for the same purpose – to fill the earth with the glory of the name of their God, Jehovah (Ez. 36:22-28).

First God will deliver a Jewish remnant by sovereign grace and the right hand of His power. This will demonstrate to Israel and to the world His glory. Then He will make a new covenant with Israel with Jesus Christ is its Mediator. In establishing this covenant He writes His law in their minds and on their hearts (Jer. 31:33). It isn't a different law, but it is written by God in a different place. When Satan is bound for a thousand years and his instruments of evil are destroyed, Israel will live in peace in the land. It is then that they will diligently obey and observe carefully all His commandments (Jer. 32:37-42, Ez. 37:24-25). This will be their responsibility under the new covenant. In doing it they will be blessed by Jehovah according to Deuteronomy 28:1-14. The blessing of Israel and the setting them high above all nations on the earth is God's responsibility (Jer.

32:36-44). And Jesus, as a far superior Mediator than Moses, and by blood far superior than bulls and goats, will be the channel of all God's millennial blessings for Israel and the earth (Heb. 8:6, 9:14-15, Eph. 1:10).

The two covenants that have a mediator are the only two covenants that involve human responsibility. It is the reason for the presence of a mediator. The first covenant has passed away with the destruction of Jerusalem and the temple by the Roman army in 70 AD. By the new covenant, which is established by better blood and a more excellent Mediator, Israel will prosper and multiply in their land of inheritance (Jer. 32:43-44, 33:9, Ez. 34:25-31, 36:29-38). Jehovah will exalt them above all nations on the earth. It remains that during the millennium and under their 'new covenant' Israel will continually be offering sacrifices, burnt offerings, sin offerings, grain offerings and such in the millennial temple according to God's law (Jer. 33:18, Ez. 43, 44, 45, 46). For this they will need their Prince in the temple and their more excellent Mediator of their better covenant.

[162] The book of Hebrews was written to Hebrews. They were professing Christians who came out of Israel, but were living in the midst of the Jews in and around Judea. By their profession of Jesus Christ they had forsaken Judaism and were under great persecution and hardship in their circumstances. It wasn't easy for them. The persecution and suffering was so great that some of them were considering returning to Judaism and the temple worship and ceremonies. This sets the context for the writing of the epistle and helps explain many of the details of the letter, especially passages like Hebrews 6:1-12 and 10:29-39.

As I said previously, the main point of exposition in the letter is the fact of the change in priesthood (Heb. 8:1). It becomes the central point to Paul's arguments and proofs. Therefore we should realize that the Spirit brings the topic of the 'covenants' into the discussion *because of the change in priesthood.* This change necessitates the need for a change in the covenants – a new covenant. This should be the impression you get when these verses are put together (Heb. 8:1, 8:6-8, 9:11-15). Paul shows them that *'the days are coming'* when God will make a new covenant with Israel, predicated on the fact that the first covenant is actually passing into extinction. So why join back to something that is ready to disappear? Jesus became an infinitely better and higher High Priest, who has obtained a more excellent ministry. Therefore the feeble and earthly priesthood of Aaron is useless. Therefore the first covenant that is wrapped around and dependent on that earthly priesthood must fade away, and do so now. This is the context in which the new covenant with national Israel is brought in. It shows these Hebrews that the first covenant has now ended.

Let me see if I can make this point in another way. The nation of Israel is the people waiting outside the courtyard of the tabernacle on the day of atonement. This is where Israel waited. In actuality, it is where they are still waiting today. But what are they waiting for? They are waiting for the High Priest to appear to them, from out of the door of the tent. If and when the High Priest appears, Israel will know that the sacrifice has been accepted by Jehovah, the blood is in the Presence, and the High Priest is then free to bless them. The days are coming when Jesus will appear again to Israel, as it were, from the door of the tabernacle. They will see Him with their eyes and look on Him whom they pierced. Israel will then know that Jehovah has accepted the sacrifice – the very sacrifice the nation was responsible for offering up. That is when their Mediator will bless them with this 'new covenant'. Until then Israel waits, standing outside the gate of the courtyard.

Where in this scenario are the Hebrews that Paul is speaking to? They are not waiting outside the courtyard with Israel! Hopefully these do not turn back and do not fall away, but we can be confident of better things concerning them, things accompanying true faith and salvation (Heb. 6:4-9). It has been shown by Paul that these have a High Priest who is able to save to the uttermost those who come to God through Him (Heb. 7:25-26). *"For such a High Priest was fitting for us, who...has become higher than the heavens."* For them He is the great High Priest who has passed through the heavens (Heb. 4:14). Sitting down at the right hand of the throne of the Majesty in the heavens, Jesus has become a Minister of the sanctuary and the true tabernacle in the heavens (Heb. 8:1-5). Therefore, these Hebrews, if they have true faith in Jesus Christ, have become both brethren and partakers of the heavenly calling (Heb. 3:1). They would be among the many sons and brethren that Jesus, the author of their salvation, is bringing to glory (Heb. 2:9-11). They, with Paul, would be part of an elect remnant that has come out of Israel and entered the church, which we know is a heavenly body with a heavenly citizenship (Rom. 11:1, 5, Col. 3:20). If true in faith, these Hebrews have a great hope that is set before them by God, sure and steadfast. The forerunner for them had entered into the Presence behind the veil (Heb. 6:18-20). If He is a forerunner for them, then they will most assuredly enter into the heavens as well, and go behind the veil into the Presence. How different is all this, instead of waiting outside the gate in the courtyard on the earth?

The new covenant to be made with Israel, where it is said, *"Behold, the days are coming..."* is made with those standing and waiting outside the gate of the courtyard (on the earth - Jer. 31:31-34). Those that are inside the tabernacle are those who are in the heavens. They are not waiting for anything. Those inside are the ones who know the sacrifice has already been accepted and that the veil is gone. These are the ones who are 'in Christ' and are believers and Christians. They are in the High Priest who is presently seated at the right hand of the throne of the Majesty in the heavens. All believers are inside the tabernacle, inside the veil and in the Presence of God. They are not the ones waiting outside the courtyard on the earth for the blessing of a new covenant.

Many of the things spoken to these Hebrews are equally true for all believers. Together with them, we are all Christians and brethren, one and the same, especially of the same body. The differences however all stem from where we came from. This as seen as out of two distinct groups: we came out of the Gentiles, while they came out of Israel. The Gentiles are described as far off, while the Jews were near to God by privilege (Eph. 2:11-17) Gentiles didn't have to give up a failed ancient religion. We didn't have to go outside a camp that we were in. We didn't have to let go of worship in a beautiful temple. We didn't have to give up a covenant that was in existence for 1500 years.

The book of Hebrews is written by the Holy Spirit in such a way as to deal with the stumbling confession of this group (Heb. 10:23). The end result of the teaching and exhortations of the epistle is the hope that these Hebrews will unreservedly come outside the camp of Israel and Judaism. Jesus suffered outside the camp. They need to go there bearing His reproach (Heb. 13:10-14). From the beginning the Spirit does this by asking them to consider Jesus. He is the Apostle and High Priest of their confession (Heb. 3:1). There are many precious truths in the epistle that are applicable to any believer. Yet we should never put aside the context – of who it was written to and their circumstances – in which the entire letter is engaged in, and which is important for the proper understanding of its teachings.

[163] God called out a man – Abraham – to belong to Himself. This calling was outside the world (Gen. 12:1). Also God made Abraham the depository of His promises – the olive tree. Abraham became the source of a new race. Adam was the head of a fallen race of sinners. Abraham is the head of a new race, for even we ourselves, as believers, as being in Christ – Abraham's one Seed – are the seed of Abraham (Gal. 3:6-7, 3:16, 3:26-29).

One Final Thought

There is a human notion of divine love – that God being love, He will not judge or condemn. This notion denies the vindication of God's majesty and holiness against sin, and the eternal impossibility that light should have fellowship with darkness. This is an unscriptural and unholy notion.

God gives a testimony of Himself and man is obligated to believe it. If He does not believe it, he is guilty of despising the testimony of God. The day of judgment will show that it was not God who failed in giving a testimony, but that man's sinful heart has deceived him.

Romans 1:18-20

"For the wrath of God is revealed from heaven against all ungodliness and unrighteousness of men, who suppress the truth in unrighteousness, because what may be known of God is manifest in them, for God has shown it to them. For since the creation of the world His invisible attributes are clearly seen, being understood by the things that are made, even His eternal power and Godhead, so that they are without excuse."

Look at creation – it is a testimony God has given of Himself. Man is guilty if he does not see God in it. There are difficulties, many things he cannot explain, but the testimony is sufficient to condemn those who do not believe in God the Creator. He has manifested this testimony to all human beings and so, all are without excuse. You are at fault if you suppress the truth of God's testimony.

God has given another and final testimony of Himself. It is what we call the gospel of Jesus Christ. This is the testimony of all the realities and truths that met at the cross. There we find the love of God for the sinner. There we see the righteous judgment and wrath of God applied to sin. At the cross all man's hatred for God was demonstrated and all man's sins were brought there. We see the power of Satan was destroyed. The power and fear of death was defeated.

Romans 1:16-17

"For I am not ashamed of the gospel of Christ, for it is the power of God to salvation for everyone who believes, for the Jew first and also for the Greek. For in it the righteousness of God is revealed from faith to faith; as it is written, "The just shall live by faith."

Hebrews 1:1-3

"God, who at various times and in various ways spoke in time past to the fathers by the prophets, has in these last days spoken to us by His Son, whom He has appointed heir of all things, through whom also He made the worlds; who being the brightness of His glory and the express image of His person, and upholding all things by the word of His power, when He had by Himself purged our sins, sat down at the right hand of the Majesty on high."

God's final testimony is what He has spoken in the gospel of Christ and what He has done in the cross of Christ. His testimony to us in these last days is spoken to us by His Son. So John says, "He that believeth not God hath made Him a liar, because he has not believed the testimony concerning His Son." (I John 5:10)

Faith must be established on the testimony of God, otherwise it is not God who is believed. Further it must be founded on His testimony alone. I must believe because God Himself has spoken, or I do not believe God. Faith is the individual soul's reception, by divine power, of the testimony of God. He is known to the individual by this testimony. Believing when there is only God's authority and God's testimony, is believing God — nothing else is true faith.

Satan persuades men that God is too good to condemn us just because we are sinners. In spite of his sins and his conscience, man hopes and convinces himself that he will not be condemned. But God has proven that, even by the death of His Son, He will judge sin and He will not endure it.

One Final Thought

People believe they will be able to stand in the presence of God and the outcome will be favorable for them. I site here three examples of men suddenly found in the presence of God:

1. Isaiah and his vision of Jehovah's throne (Isaiah.6:1-5) – His response was, *"Woe is me, for I am undone! Because I am a man of unclean lips, and I dwell in the midst of a people of unclean lips."*

2. Peter and the net full of fish (Luke 5:4-8) – His response to Jesus was, *"Depart from me, for I am a sinful man, O Lord!"*

3. Jesus walks on the water to the boat (Matt. 14:33, 8:27, Mark 4:41, Luke 8:25) – The disciples response was that they were afraid and marveled, saying, *"Who can this be? For He commands even the winds and water, and they obey Him!"*

There is a practical discovery when man finds himself in the presence of God – a discovery of all the mischief and corruption of the human heart. Until the will has been examined, even laid bare, in the presence of the majesty of God, there cannot be a right state or condition of any man before God. A man never knows God until he gets to this question – "How can I stand approved and justified in the presence of the holy and righteous God?"

The Holy Spirit was sent to convict the world of sin (John 16:8). If the unbeliever doesn't know his guilt and sin before a holy and righteous God, and he doesn't have the realization that he cannot possibly stand before God, then he isn't being drawn by the Father to Christ (John 6:44). Those who become aware of their lost condition, that they are sinners who cannot stand before a holy God, are the ones that the Father is drawing to His Son. They are convicted of sin, their conscience having been awakened by God.

Without this true awakening of the unbeliever's conscience – like Isaiah, like Peter, and like the disciples in the boat – they are perfectly content with saying God is good, that He must overlook sin. Is God going to allow heaven to be like the world? Is He going to allow sin to enter heaven? Man's conscience also tells him that he cannot get rid of sin, not on his own, not by his own resources. And he knows that sin brings death.

The faith in our hearts to truly believe in the Son of God is the work in our hearts of the Holy Spirit, and a conscience quickened, which feels the need for grace and forgiveness. It will be a faith in our hearts bringing true repentance, godly sorrow, and a sense that we deserve to be condemned. This alone makes Christ and His work on the cross precious to us – His work of redemption meets the need of an awakened conscience.

One Final Thought for the Believer:

He that has an ear to hear what the Spirit is saying is compelled to listen to Christ's judgment of Christendom. We are called on to highly regard the word of God that judges the state of corporate Christianity.

The professing church is declared by God to be corrupt and in ruin. God also declares this state is irreconcilable. You may call out to it and pray for it with all your might and passion, but nothing will change its established course. Christendom is in ruin and judgment begins at the house of God. Our prayers should be a confession and acknowledgment of the sin of the professing church. The true believer must turn away from the corporate evil and corruption. The believer is left on individual ground. We are left to our understanding of the Scriptures to be faithful to Christ alone in the midst of the current evil circumstances. We should gather with the remnant in the way it may be accomplished through the light of His word. May God give you His wisdom, and may He guide you by His Spirit in His word.

The Son of Man Series

1. **'The Son of Man Glorified'** – this book is a broad work explaining biblical doctrine and understandings based on general biblical principles. It is by the knowledge of God's principles that the believer may understand the detail of Scripture. More specifically this book separates the two titles of Messiah and the Son of Man. It gives the believer a good understanding of how Scripture takes up both titles and therefore what God, in His counsels, associates with each. This book helps the believer to establish the important distinctions between Israel and the church, between Judaism and Christianity, and between the heavenly calling and the earthly calling.

2. **'The Blessed Hope of the Church'** – this book was written to prove from Scripture the doctrine of the rapture of the church, and this before the tribulation, which in turn precedes the dispensation of the fullness of times – the millennium. It particularly emphasizes the position of the believer 'in Christ' and the privilege of that relationship in view of the doctrine. The believer and church are wholly apart from this condemned world.

3. **'The Corruption and Death of Christendom'** – this book shows the ruin of the professing church in its testimony for God in the earth and world. Christendom has failed in its corporate responsibilities, and the truth of this reality is clearly taught by the Spirit of God in Scripture. This work puts the testimony of Scripture together for the believer to understand this important spiritual reality as it exists in the kingdom of heaven, and as we approach the end of the age.

4. **'The Redemptive Work of the Son of Man'** – this has not been written yet, but will be the next book of the series of seven. It will concentrate on explaining for the believer the full redemptive truth and realities of the Son of Man's work.

Correspondence with Jeff Reintgen may be directed to j.l.reintgen@gmail.com. Also there is an author web site with a blog at www.sonofmanseries.com